CONTENTS

BISHOP KELLY OF WESTERN NIGERIA

Michael O'Shea

Published by

**Society of African Missions,
Blackrock Road,
Cork,
Ireland**

Email: provincial@sma.ie

ISBN : 978-0-9553512-0-4
0-9553512-0-0

Copyright © Michael JB O'Shea 2006

FOREWORD

When we encounter special and extraordinary qualities in human beings, a force within us propels us to tell others about them. Biographies are the stories of cultures and people as much as they are the stories of individuals. The subjects represent qualities that far surpass the norm. Not to speak of them would be to deny history their relevance.

Recording the stories of its illustrious members has been a challenge for the SMA. In recent years this has been addressed through the publication of the writings of the founder, Bishop Melchior de Marion Brésillac, and other works on some of those who followed his vision. One such 'disciple' of Brésillac was Patrick Joseph Kelly.

When I was an SMA student in training for priesthood, Bishop Kelly had already retired from active ministry in Nigeria. He occasionally visited our seminary. We students rarely engaged him in conversation, but we noted that his day was dominated by time spent in the oratory. He was for us the quintessential *'holy man'*. To ask about him of any SMA priest who had served in Benin Diocese was, usually, to be met with an attitude of awe and reverence for *'a man out of the ordinary'*.

We are indebted to Fr Michael O'Shea for writing this account of the life of a truly extraordinary man. He has brought the character to life in a way that reveals, not just the essence of one man but of a whole era of mission and spirituality. From Bishop Kelly's home and school boy days in Co Galway, through his years as a young missionary, to his settling into the role of bishop, we have before us a record of maturing faith and missionary achievement. One senses from the book that Bishop Kelly would not want the glory that may attend the publication of his biography. However, he might be willing to accept this as the price to be paid for recounting a life that ought to be an encouragement, an inspiration, and a reproach.

I hope you enjoy reading this very fine book. May it touch all our hearts and minds so that we, not only come to know Bishop Kelly but, may also be imbued with something of his spirit of holiness to live whatever mission we have in life with greater commitment and integrity.

Fr Fachtna O'Driscoll SMA
Provincial Superior

INTRODUCTION

Patrick Joseph Kelly, Vicar Apostolic of Western Nigeria and first bishop of Benin City, died on the 18th of August 1991 just two weeks before his ninety-seventh birthday. He was, and still is, the longest-lived member of the Irish Province of the Society of African Missions and he is one of its most respected members. His work for the Church and for education in Western Nigeria was outstanding. He first arrived in Africa in 1921, and over the years came to be loved by the people he served and by the priests and sisters with whom he worked. After nearly half a century of dedicated labour he retired in 1973. In his lifetime, both in Ireland and in Nigeria, he gained a reputation for holiness.

The Vicariate of 'Western Nigeria' became the diocese of 'Benin City' in 1950. At the time of Nigeria's Independence from Britain in 1960 there were three regions in the country – Northern, Western, and Eastern. Benin City lay in the Western Region of which it was the administrative capital. In 1963, this region was divided into Western and 'Mid-West'; Benin was in the Mid-West part. In 1967, Nigeria was divided into twelve states, Benin City was then the capital of the 'Mid-West State'. In 1994 the diocese was raised to the status of an archdiocese with Archbishop Patrick Ekpu, Bishop Kelly's successor, as its first archbishop.

Bishop Kelly was baptised 'Patrick Joseph'. He was called 'Pat' by his mother, 'Africa man' by his brothers, and 'Pat Joe', or 'Pajo', by his fellow missionaries. He signed himself 'PJ Kelly' or 'PJK'. I have chosen to follow his mother in calling him 'Pat'. Not many people got to know him closely. My personal contacts with him were few – we participated in the same Society retreat on one occasion and, at another time, I interviewed him on the subject of missionary spirituality. Before I began that interview in Cork he asked me abruptly why I wasn't in Africa. For him every member of the Society, except Provincial Superiors, should be in Africa. When I told him that I had been given a study appointment, he apologised and bade me proceed.

For most of my missionary career I have worked in Zambia, which is still my mission but, from 1988 to 1992, I was appointed to the Republic of Benin, the western neighbouring country of Nigeria. While there I spent four months in Nigeria and visited Bishop Kelly's former diocese. In Zambia in 2003, Fr Fachtna O'Driscoll, the Irish Provincial Superior, asked me to write a biography of Bishop Kelly for the 150th anniversary of the foundation of the Society. Surprised, and flattered, I took on the task as a challenge.

Before long, I realized that a biography was one of the last things the Bishop would have wanted. He was not given to writing personal letters, memoirs, diaries, books or articles that might have facilitated the writing of his life story. However, he did write a large number of mission business letters. This correspondence and the interviews I made with those who knew him were my main sources of information.

Fr O'Driscoll suggested that the biography might treat of the Bishop's shortcomings as well as of his virtues and achievements. Knowing that most people would prefer to talk about his virtues, I pressed interviewees for a critical comment. Some readers may think that I have gone too far in depicting him as severe, ascetical and 'tightfisted'. But, as a 'young' missionary Bishop, he was undoubtedly 'tough'; he did not spare himself or his personnel. As time went on, Society authorities endeavoured to moderate his mode of leadership. And, rather than because of any 'mellowing' due to ageing, it was a combination of obedience, humility, and a sincere seeking of God's will that brought about change in him. Strangely, though strict, and tight with material resources, he won the enduring loyalty and deep affection of the vast majority of his personnel.

'Pajo', as well as being the diminutive of 'Patrick Joseph' captures something of the aura of the man and something of the filial, humorous, yet respectful, attitude of the missionaries towards him. A successful missionary like his patron, St Patrick, Bishop Kelly was, also, like St Joseph. He didn't draw attention to himself, always sought God's will, and was completely devoted to the divine Son and His blessed mother.

Born in the last decade of the 19th century, he provides a link with the early years of the African Missions in Ireland and with the origins of the Society itself. In Pat's boyhood, Augustin Planque, the very first member of the Society, was still its Superior General. Pat began his studies in the Society's college in Cork three years after the foundation of the Irish Province. His formation was directed by professors and superiors whose own training had taken place in the Society's seminary in Lyons, France. These men were well acquainted with Planque and with his successor, Mgr Paul Pellet. They were even better acquainted with Joseph Zimmermann, the Swiss superior in Ireland and founder of the Irish Province in 1912.

Bishop Kelly also provides a link with the past on the missions. When he arrived in Western Nigeria in 1921, many of the pioneer, continental missionaries were still there. One of them guided his first steps in mission ways. He saw the consolidation of the Vicariate of Western Nigeria under the Irish Province's first bishop, Thomas Broderick, and the transfer of the ecclesiastical capital from Asaba to Benin under Leo Taylor whom he succeeded as Bishop. Twenty years later he saw Nigeria change from being a crown colony to an independent nation. He was still in charge when the civil war broke out in 1967 and when the Government took over the mission schools in 1972. During all his time in Africa he worked tirelessly for the establishment of the local church. Before he retired, he had the joy of handing over his authority to Nigerian successors.

Nearing the end of my task of writing, pondering on the confidence people had in his prayers, it struck me that I had overlooked a strange coincidence in my own life. On the 21st of August 1991, in the course of trying to canoe around Ireland, I capsized in a rough sea off the coast of Co Louth. After an hour or so in the water, I was rescued by a fisherman who, after hauling me aboard his boat, said "Someone must have been praying for you". Later that evening I learned that Bishop Kelly was buried in Cork about the same time that I was sinking in Dundalk Bay.

Michael O'Shea sma,
African Missions, Blackrock Road, Cork, 19 March 2006.

Chapter 1

PAT KELLY of BALLINASLOE and TRISTAUN

The early 1840s were not the best of times for the poor in Ballinasloe. In winter they suffered greatly from the want of fuel. The price of turf was exceedingly high and any that came on the market was exceedingly wet. The Earl of Clancarty was lauded for selling timber and branches at low prices and Lady Clancarty was admired for distributing potatoes and meal to poor families. However, in February 1840 the establishment newspapers reported that fever was on the decline, the foundation of the Poor House had been laid, and the Asylum, which housed two hundred and twenty inmates, was undergoing repairs after storm damage. In fact, for the landed gentry and the not-so-poor, the town was quite prosperous; it had three tan yards, one flour and three oat mills, two breweries, factories for making felt hats, fine coaches, and for curing bacon. Outside the town there were quarries containing excellent limestone. Local farmers benefited from the town people's growing food requirements. Buyers and sellers from the length and breadth of the country flocked to Ballinasloe's October fair, recognised as the greatest horse, sheep and cattle fair in the whole of Ireland. But in the middle of the decade the Great Famine struck, bringing an end to progress and prosperity. Life for the poor in the town became even more wretched and in the hinterland the majority of small farmers faced penury, starvation and emigration. The population declined and did not begin to stabilize until near the end of the century, by which time the tan yards, mills, breweries and factories had closed; only the October fair survived.

Malachy Kelly, a carpenter of Clontuskert, and his wife were concerned for the future of their infant son, also called Malachy, who was born in the early years of the famine. He survived, but was marked by the penury of the times and the great fear of starvation. The family lived in Barnacragh, called 'Craugh' for short, a small townland three miles west of Ballinasloe on the road to Aughrim. According to a tithe book of the 1820s, a Thomas Kelly held nine acres there. Among Thomas's neigbours were the Goodes, Roman Catholics, who had four acres; and, with eleven acres, the Wakefields, a Church of Ireland family descended from an army doctor who had settled after the Battle of Aughrim. At the time of the Penal laws numerous hedge schools developed; as late as 1837 five of them still existed in Kilcloony parish, on the north side of Barnacragh and three in Clontuskert on the south side. Perhaps it was in one of these that young Malachy picked up a little education and learned to read and write. Later, when many of his friends took the boat to America and elsewhere, he decided to remain as he had found work herding sheep and cattle for the Cookes who had over a hundred and fifty acres in nearby Curragh and Urraghry.

In Malachy's youth, according to Griffith's Valuation, a 'Patrick Shea' farmed ten acres in Barnacragh, possibly the father of Catherine Shea, or 'Shiel', whom Malachy married. The names 'Shea' and 'Shiel' were not always distinct in these parts, some Sheas having changed their name to Shiel (or Sheil) when they moved from south Galway. Malachy was no youth when he married Catherine, usually called 'Kate', in St Michael's church, Ballinasloe, on 6 February 1892, he was nearly fifty, but that was not a very old age for grooms in those days. Both of their fathers were deceased at the time of Malachy's marriage, an indication that they too were advanced in years when they married. Kate, twenty-three years younger than Malachy, was entered as 'Catherine Shiel' in her marriage certificate, but grandchildren still refer to her as 'Shea' *or* 'Shiel'. After the Parnell and Kitty O'Shea affair, relatives teasingly called her "*our* Kitty O'Shea".

A quiet man, Malachy, called 'Lacky' for short, was noted for hard work, a wry sense of humour, good handwriting, and fidelity to religious duties. On his small farm of about six acres in Craugh he wasn't noted for excessive 'neatness'. It didn't bother him if his potato ridges weren't quite straight, "The spuds'll come out straight enough in the boiling water" he used to say. Like him, Kate was a hard worker and devout but, born almost a generation later, she hadn't suffered the same famine experience, and was more cheerful and out-going. A tidy woman in size and habits, she was noted for kind-heartedness and a fondness for cats! Joan Ward, the Post Master's daughter in Aughrim, remembered her for the beautiful Persian kittens she gave her when her own kittens died. The Quinns, Hurneys and many others remembered her for the ready welcome and cup of tea whenever they took a short cut through her farm on the way to Ballinasloe.

Malachy and Kate's first child, Ellen, born in 1893, was delicate; the next, born on the 31st of August 1894, was a sturdy boy, whom they christened Patrick Joseph. In neat two-yearly intervals, Mary, John and Malachy junior followed. At the age of five Patrick Joseph, called 'Pat', becoming a bit of a handful at home, was bundled off to the national school in Aughrim with Ellen, called 'Ellie'. Soon the younger children followed. When they complained about walking the two miles to school bare-footed, their father reminded them that he had walked all the way to Galway when he was called there to be a juror. Kate saw to it that the children took school work, catechism and prayers, very seriously.

Pat Keohane, the school master, was a 'blow-in' from West Cork. He had no time for slow learners, "a contrary, cross man with no patience, but a great teacher", was how a former pupil described him. Pat Kelly soon became the apple of his eye; quick-witted, well-behaved and keen to learn, he was amongst the brightest and most promising in the school. After he left, Mr Keohane used to hold him up as a model for others. Apart from book-learning, the master had quite an influence on Pat who, years later acknowledged, "I got my inspiration to become a priest from the good example of my primary school teacher".

The Kelly's lived in a two-roomed thatched cottage which had three windows facing the road to Aughrim. Behind the house were three sheds for animals, turf and hay. Their nearest neighbours in 1901 were Bernard and Michael Goode, who lived with their families in two bigger, slate-roofed houses. Malachy filled in the Census form of that year on 1st April, registering himself as "Lacky Kelly", farmer, fifty-six years of age, Kate, his wife, thirty-four and the children ('scholars'), Ellen, eight; Patrick Joseph, seven; and Mary, five. Ellie could read, but Pat could read *and write*. John, called 'Jack', three years old, and the seven-month baby, Malachy, kept Kate busy at home along with her many other household and farmyard tasks . The family were known as the "Lacky Kelly's" to distinguish them from the twenty-six other Kelly families, like the "Wren Kellys" or the "Chicken Kellys", in the neighbourhood.

By the next census, 1911, Malachy and Kate had three more children, one window less in the front of the house, and one more outhouse in the yard. The three latest arrivals were Kathleen, Michael and Gerald. Ellie, the eldest, was no longer at school. Pat, sixteen, was at the diocesan college of Clonfert called "The Pines", where he was obviously doing well, he was the only one of the family registered as being able to speak Irish and English, and read and write. Malachy must have been 'feeling his age' as he registered himself as 'sixty-eight', whereas he had registered 'fifty-six' ten years previously. Kate was 'forty-four'. A new column in the census form stated that they had completed twenty years of marriage. With one window less, the Kelly's house was demoted from "second class" to "third". The family of two adults and seven children, aged from eighteen to three years, did not have much space in two small rooms. With so many children to rear on a meagre income, Malachy and Kate wondered how they would manage and whether they were right to leave their eldest son at school instead of sending him out to work but, with high hopes that the Land Commission would come to their assistance, they let him continue for the time being. He had got a scholarship on completing primary school in 1909 and it was a matter of great pride for a labourer or small farmer to have a son in post-primary education.

"The Pines", so-called because it was situated among pine trees, was originally founded by Lord Clancarty as a school where Protestant teachers could learn Irish to help them convert Irish-speaking Catholics to Protestantism. Pat was happy to be there, but it was much farther from home than the primary school had been. Malachy got him an old 'push-bike'. His sister, Kathleen, recalled that it had a board for a saddle, spindles for pedals and no tyres or tubes. Half way through his classical studies, as secondary education was then called, family circumstances changed for the better but, ironically, led to his being taken out of school.

Tristaun

In 1912 the Irish Land Commission bought the Earl of Clancarty's Garbally Estate, which included the townlands of Barnacragh, Curragh and Tristaun. In the re-distribution of the land, Kate and Malachy received a good forty-acre farm at Tristaun just over two miles south-east of Aughrim in the parish of Clontuskert. They weren't the first Kelly's in Tristaun. Back in 1641, according to an old Survey Book, a Daniel O'Kelly was one of the proprietors of "510 profitable acres in Tristaan" of which a Peter Kelly rented 73 acres and a John McBrian Kelly, 16 acres. The 'Lacky' Kellys were very pleased with their good fortune and moved without delay to the new farm. Kate was delighted with the newly-built farm house. It had an 'upstairs' floor, a slated roof, and a well nearby. It was a dream come true, but the bigger farm required more labour than the small holding in Craugh and there was more rent to pay. Looking at her ageing husband, now nearly seventy, Kate knew he could not manage on his own, Pat would have to leave school to help him. She didn't make the decision lightly for she was aware that Pat wanted to be a priest. Though she suspected it all along, he had said so plainly to the neighbouring Woods family, one day when he was helping them with the hay. The Woods weren't very surprised and neither were they when their own daughter went on to be a nun. Though it would be a great honour to have a priest in the family, the road to priesthood was long and expensive; he might change his mind, or, be turned down. There were already many young Kellys to feed, and another was on the way. William, 'Bill', born in Tristaun, was the last of Kate's children.

In March, Pat said Goodbye to The Pines and, it seemed, to his vocation. However not long afterwards at a parish mission, when the preacher spoke passionately about West Africa where Irish missionaries were sacrificing themselves to spread the Gospel, he felt a very great desire to join them. But, for the eldest son, who had a keen sense of responsibility, family came first, he shelved his vocation and got down to farm work.

Other families that got farms around Tristaun were the Clarks, Larkins and Scotts. Sam Walshe, a member of the Church of Ireland, who farmed near the Kellys, became a firm friend of Malachy senior. Sam's sons Wesley, Herbie, and Sam junior were friends of Pat and his brothers. The Walshes impressed the Kelly children, not so much because they went to a different church, but because they didn't work on Sunday. The Sinclairs who lived in Glan were firm friends too, one of them, Jack, became a Catholic. Among Pat's Catholic friends were Pat Hurney of the Forge, Anthony Curley, Pat and Bob Larkin, and Joe Quinn. Joe, noted for dancing, music and story-telling, was a contrast to Pat who was quiet and serious.

Malachy Kelly and family lived in an historic area well-known for the Battle of Aughrim and for monastic foundations. It was called

Eachdhroim Ui Cheallaigh, "Kelly's Aughrim". The ruins of O'Kelly's castle stand in the centre of Aughrim village. A few miles away, St Baodán in 805 founded a monastery at a place called Cloontuskert Ui Maine. Ui Maine or 'Hy-Many' was the territory of Maine Mór, today East Galway and South Roscommon. The 'Cloontuskert', or 'Clontuskert', monastery near Tristaun, became a priory of the Augustinians in the twelfth century and, with Kellys as the principal patrons, the clan came to consider the position of Prior as theirs by right. Beside it was the inauguration site of the Hy-Manian kings. William Boy *(Buí)* O'Kelly, king of Hy-Many, founded an abbey for the Franciscans in 1353 at Kilconnell. Clonmacnoise, and Clonfert where St Brendan had three thousand monks in the sixth century, were not far away. The diocese of Clonfert corresponded with the territory of Hy-Many and several O'Kellys were its bishops.

Malachy's family may be described as a broken branch of the distinguished Aughrim Kellys. A story goes that in Cromwell's time some soldiers attacked the Abbey of Clontuskert and forced the monks to flee. Some of the Kelly clan members gave them shelter and in appreciation one of them prophesied, "Your family will never have a generation without a priest in it". Up to today, as far as Malachy's family are concerned the prophecy has turned out to be true.

The Battle of Aughrim, fought in 1691 between some 20,000 followers of the Catholic King James and about the same number on the side of the Protestant, King William, was the last great decisive battle to be fought on Irish soil and it was also one of the bloodiest. Some say a Kelly, whose sheep were taken by the Jacobite army, gave away military information to the Williamites before the battle. True or not, most of the great O'Kelly families of Hy-Many took part in the battle on the Jacobite side and about four hundred of them died, including seven Kelly brothers, six of whom were killed.

There were African drummers in the Williamite army and, no doubt, many of them fell too in the slaughter of Sunday 12 July 1691 when, following the decapitation by cannon ball of the Jacobite commander, St. Ruth, the Catholic side was thrown into disarray and some seven thousand of its men lost their lives. About two thousand Williamites also perished. One of the combatants, a historian, Colonel Charles O'Kelly, said his tears mingled with the ink on the page as he wrote about the slaughter. A depression in the battlefield near Lacky Kelly's farm in Tristaun filled with blood and to this day is known as Bloody Hollow.

~ ~ ~

Malachy and Kate's children inherited their parent's characteristics of hard work, piety, and wry humour in various combinations. All worked hard; young Malachy and Bill were noted for wit; Kathleen, Jack, and Mick for religion. Pat possessed the three traits in a unique blend which characterised him throughout life. With Malachy senior in declining health, Pat became more and more responsible for the farm. Of strong build, he was six feet tall, broad of shoulder, had penetrating blue eyes and a determined-looking jaw. He was mature and conscientious beyond his years and though he enjoyed a game of football and played cards, he was not very gregarious and, speaking with a slight stammer, he tended to remain quiet and could easily be overlooked in a crowd.

He passed a year of hard work on the farm and then a second year. In the third year, the priestly vocation, stowed in the back of his mind, re-emerged. Two incidents contributed to this. One of the Kelly farm horses had the habit of stealing chicken food near the house. If any of the family spotted him they would pick up a stone and throw it. The wily animal continued to steal but kept an eye out for stone-throwers. One day Pat harnessed this horse and another one to his father's new mower to bring it for hire to Loughbown. As he rattled along the Cill na hAbhann

Road the reins slipped from his hand onto the road. When he stooped down to pick them up, the food stealer, thinking he was about to be stoned, bolted. Pat was thrown on to the road. The horses panicking raced away. The expensive new mower began to come apart, bits and pieces flying into ditches and hedgerows along the way. Goaded on by the noise, the horses kept going until they were stopped by neighbours at Jenning's gate nearly half a mile from where they had started. The mower was wrecked.

The second incident took place one evening at the end of a day cutting turf on the bog. Throwing his *sleán*, a sharp spade, onto the seat of the cart, Pat jumped up after it. The horse took off rather fast, throwing him back onto the *sleán* which lacerated him badly.

While Pat was recovering from his injuries his brothers, Jack and Malachy, took over the farm work. Before long Pat realized that he was not indispensable. Jack was nearly as old as Pat was when he started farm work and Malachy was fourteen. Hesitantly, Pat broached the subject of priesthood again with his mother, telling her he'd like to continue studying. Glad that he had not abandoned his vocation altogether she encouraged him adding, with a smile, that if he didn't find a place in a college soon she'd ask him to join the Royal Irish Constabulary.

Since leaving primary school, farming had not been the only work he had undertaken. When the family was still in Barnacragh his uncle, a stone mason, took him on to help build an extension to the Protestant church at Glan. Pat's Church of Ireland friends later teased him, that the first church he built was a Protestant one! After the division of the land he dug ditches for the Land Commission at the rate of six pence a day; some of the ditches can still be seen. He also carted sand for a builder renovating the church in Aughrim. One morning Fr Dan Coughlan the parish priest, who knew the Kelly's well and had a lot of time for Pat, stopped for a chat. He ended the conversation saying, "Mark my words, young man, you'll be up there on that altar one day yet saying Mass".

For one reason or another Pat failed to get a place in the colleges he tried, including The Pines and the Jesuit College, Mungret, in Limerick. Then fate, or Providence, and the recently founded Province of the Society of African Missions in Ireland, stepped in. In the Summer of 1915, Fr Nicholas Heffernan, a newly ordained priest of the Province, visited his uncle, Nicholas O'Connor, who had a small printing press in Ballinasloe. While in Ballinasloe, Fr Nicholas said Mass in the Mercy convent. Over breakfast with the Reverend Mother he learned that the parish priest in Aughrim knew a young man who wanted to be a priest. Keen to find recruits for the little-known Society, Nicholas sought out Fr Coughlan who directed him to Tristaun. At the farm he was impressed by the hardy young man who was called in from the fields, though quiet, he appeared intelligent, mature and highly motivated. Pat himself warmed more and more to what Fr Heffernan was saying about the missionary Society and its work in Africa. Kate raised the question of fees. Heffernan set her mind at rest, assuring her that the Society would look after such matters. He departed, leaving them to make their own decisions. Pat was clear, he wanted to go to the Society's college in Cork; Kate and Malachy consented.

Paddy Hurney's cottage near the Forge.

The Church of Ireland chapel at Glan, showing the vestry Pat helped to build.

The Kelly's house, Tristaun.

St Catherine's Aughrim.

Chapter 2

STUDIES in CORK, 1915-1921

Pat was one of thirty-six young men from all over the country who arrived at St Joseph's college, Wilton, Cork, in October 1915. The look of the place pleased him and he quickly felt at home in the big house situated on a large farm about two miles west of the city centre. 'Classical studies' normally took five years, Pat, with a bare two and a half years in The Pines, expected he would have to spend another two or three years in Wilton. As he got down to work, he couldn't help sensing some of the zest and enthusiasm that pervaded the college and the young Province, in whose foundation, just three years previously, the former superior of Wilton, Joseph Zimmermann had played a major part.

On the world scene the Great War was raging and Irishmen were divided on the issue of fighting on the side of Britain or of opposing her in support of an independent Ireland. Already many Irish men were in the trenches in France and, by the end of the War, some fifty thousand of them would have lost their lives fighting "for the freedom of small nations". The Great War made 'heroism' and 'dying for a cause' commonplace. After the 1916 Rising in Dublin the spirit of Irish nationalism ignited; independence from Britain became more and more hotly debated throughout the country – not least in St Joseph's, Wilton.

In 1915, the Wilton staff was composed of Michael Rowan, superior, three newly ordained priests, Patrick Harmon, John Lupton and John Levins, and two men with missionary experience, Patrick Moylan and Joseph Butler. Both of the latter, aged thirty-six, had been ordained at the Society's headquarters in Lyons, France, in 1902, after completing philosophy and theology there. On the missions Moylan had worked in Egypt and Butler in Nigeria and Liberia. The three newly ordained men were among the first to complete their seminary studies in Ireland. Rowan, thirty-eight, had also studied in the Society's seminary in Lyons but, due to illness, had returned to Ireland to complete his theology under Zimmermann in Wilton. While there he taught English to the students and to some French confreres (members of the Society) residing there. Ordained in Cork in 1901, his first appointment was to continue teaching in St Joseph's.

Rowan played a significant role in the early development of the Province, especially in the training of students. Extremely ascetical, hard on himself and on the students, his aim was to produce modern Patricks and Colmcilles for Africa. He outdid the French in their "Salesian methods", which included constant "protective accompaniment" of the students. His intention was not 'to police', but to show interest, which the Irish in Lyons had felt to be lacking. But, overdoing the surveillance, he earned himself the name "Nix" Rowan. Other sides of his character were, a genuine concern for his students, especially needy ones on whom he often spent his personal allocation, and an unwavering fidelity to prayer.

In Pat's time in Wilton, Rowan, as well as being superior, was house bursar and a Provincial Councillor. He demanded high standards and brooked no slighting of the Rule. Sparing no one – lazy student or tardy member of staff – he would personally rouse them from bed if they were late for morning prayer. He also tangled with the local gentry. The president of the Bride Hare Hounds wrote to St Joseph's college from "The Wigwam" in Ballincollig, complaining about Rev Fr Rowan, who "stopped them while hunting through one of Wilton's outlying farms and, in an aggressively offensive manner, ordered them off". Imitating his former professors in Lyons, he wore a French cape and sported a beard – until he heard a 'Shawlie woman' in Cork's Coal Quay remark, "Looka de Proddy minister, de fella wit de berd!"

Wilton house and farm had been bought by Zimmermann in 1888 and opened as a college the following year. The early superiors and many of the staff were French men who felt that house rules, programmes, and ways of doing things should replicate those of the Society's houses in France. So 'frenchified' did the college become that a young student, Simon from Alsace, was sent there "to improve his French"! An earthy history of the college, 1888 to 1917, was penned by a Brother Denis McCarthy, who was Wilton's long-time farm manager and general-factotum since the early days "when the cook was a saucy old dame fond of the bottle". Self-styled "Domestic Architect", Brother McCarthy didn't like the staff, the curriculum, the horseplay, or the 'Frog-leap' of the students. He praised the farm highly, which, due to his efforts, was "a model, famous for its barley and mangles" and he liked Fr Rowan whom he thought was "a jewel". "Mr Kelly", the quiet student from Galway, also liked him.

St Joseph's church, Wilton, built by Joseph Zimmermann, 1897.

Older and more serious than the majority of the students, Pat was not put off by the Superior's watchfulness, asceticism or strictness regarding rules and was much impressed by the long hours he spent in chapel. No doubt Fr Rowan in turn was impressed by Mr Kelly and, taking into consideration the Galway man's intellectual ability and his age, already twenty-one, hurried him through 'classical studies'. Much to Pat's satisfaction, after only a few months, he was promoted from third year classics to fifth year, thus enabling him to complete his college studies in one year and graduate from Wilton in June 1916.

Blackrock Road Seminary

In September, after the summer holidays which he spent at home, Pat presented himself at the Society's major seminary, also called St Joseph's, situated on Blackrock Road on the east side of the city. He found he was one of eleven first-year 'philosophers'. Ahead of them were seven second year 'philosophers' and nineteen 'theologians'. The beginners faced two years of philosophy and three of theology.

In 1909, in a bid towards the establishment of an independent Irish Province of the Society, Joseph Zimmermann, then Society superior in Ireland, had sought and received, permission from the Congregation for the Propagation of the Faith ("Propaganda Fide") to set up an Irish seminary for one year. The Blackrock Road seminary, the first in Ireland exclusively devoted to the training of students for the 'foreign missions', opened in September that year. But, to the consternation of the Irish members, it was closed the following year by the Society's Superiors at Lyons and its four theology students were told to report to the seminary at Lyons. Outraged, three of them left and continued their priestly studies elsewhere. Following intense negotiating, in which Zimmermann enlisted the help of Irish bishops, the Seminary re-opened. Zimmermann, continuing his struggle for an independent Province, was frequently absent. Fotunately, he had on his staff an excellent young priest, Thomas Broderick a Kerry man who, as well as teaching philosophy, acted as Superior and as Spiritual Director when required. In fact most of the work of organizing the seminary, including writing its Rule and daily timetable, had fallen to him. Just three years ordained, he was only twenty-six when he took up the seminary appointment.

Among the other staff members in the five years Pat Kelly was there were, James McGettigan, Patrick Moylan, Michael McCaffrey, Peter Harrington, Michael Collins, and Stephen Kyne. McGettigan, the bursar, taught scripture, and succeeded Broderick as Superior in 1917. Moylan and McCaffrey joined the staff in 1917 and taught theology. Peter Harrington, whose younger brother Stephen was in Pat's class, was professor of canon law and liturgy 1919-1920. During the War, he had been an army chaplain in the Middle East. Michael Collins was Superior from 1920 and lectured on moral theology, liturgy, and homiletics. Stephen Kyne, the first Provincial Superior, was Spiritual Director. There were other professors who spent a year or two in the seminary, among them the newly ordained Claude Taylor who taught church music and was editor of the Province's new monthly magazine, the *African Missionary*. The Provincial Superior, Maurice Slattery, also resided in Blackrock Road and, following the first Provincial Assembly in 1918, William Butler; both of them, occasionally, gave talks to the students.

Some building work was still going on in and around the seminary, but much had been completed: new dormitories, students' rooms, lecture halls, refectory and library; new boundary walls and gates; new walks and a small football field. The Sisters of Our Lady of Apostles (OLA) were in charge of domestic affairs and, with their new kitchen range, they could cater for ninety students though, with less than forty students and six staff members, the seminary already seemed somewhat overcrowded. Lack of space in house and grounds was advanced by Broderick as a reason for the generous amount of free time he had put on the timetable. The seminary had a gas lighting system, but electric lighting had been installed in the seminary church which, built in 1881, was open to the public. The church was popular with the neighbours who, for want of wit or because of it, referred to the seminary as "The Zulu Mission"; the Zulu War in South Africa having made headlines shortly before the church was opened.

The Superior, Fr Broderick, was a very different man from Michael Rowan. Urbane, articulate and refined, his motto was *Mens sana in corpore sano* – a sound mind in a healthy body. A first class academic and teacher, he aimed at making his lectures "interesting and instructive" and endeavoured to have the best modern books available for the students. As a seminarian in Ireland and in France he had been an inspiring influence amongst his fellow students. As superior his "sweet reasonableness", exceptional ability, and kind and dignified manner won the loyalty and affection of all. His seminary Rule was more relaxed than that of the Lyons seminary which had rising at 5 a.m., studies throughout the day, manual work after dinner, and only one hour of recreation. Broderick believed in free time, relaxation and healthy exercise, not only manual work, but long walks, hurling, football and tennis.

The seminary opened for the "eighth year" of its existence on the 12th of September 1916. The following day "Mr Kelly" took his seat as a "First Philosopher". Apart from Philosophy, Scripture, Ecclesiastical History, Liturgy and English, Broderick insisted that the students receive extra classes in the evenings on the Society's *Constitutions* and *Directory*. He was convinced that they should have a sound knowledge of the Society's laws and customs.

Things went rather smoothly until 9 December when, quite suddenly, six students were struck down with influenza. The next day the number rose to ten plus one Father. Four more were down the following day and the next day the number reached twenty. Doctor Coughlan was called in. With the help of his pills, injections, and bed-rest, the numbers began to diminish. By December 16 all were fit enough to go home for Christmas holidays!

1917

On Whit Sunday, Solemn High Mass was sung for "the souls of those who fell for Ireland in Easter Week 1916". This became an annual commemoration with, after a few years, the addition of "and for those who fell for Erin's sake since 1916". Meanwhile, far away in the Society's mission in Western Nigeria, an unexpected death occurred on the 30th of January 1917, that of the Prefect Apostolic, Mgr Carlo Zappa, an Italian. To the surprise of the Irish confreres, Rome nominated Thomas Broderick, as his successor. Broderick had had only two years experience in the Gold Coast, and had never been to Nigeria. James McGettigan, much to his own dismay, was appointed Seminary Superior.

With food being rationed due to the war, the students were beginning to feel the pinch. Fr McGettigan, trying by all means to get more for them, fell foul of the local RIC sergeant for requesting an extra 224 lbs of sugar from the Royal Commission on the Sugar Supply, "to preserve 5 cwts of apples". Having failed in that, he acceded to the students' petition (inspired by the example of the diocesan students at Maynooth) that they be allowed to smoke tobacco. He even gave them a cigar each on feast days. While not addicted, Pat enjoyed the odd cigarette.

On the daily timetable, "Lunch", was at the unusual time of 5.30 p.m., while dinner was at 1 p.m. Rising was at 6 a.m. and *Couvre-Feu* (curfew or Lights out) at 10 p.m. 'Unusual' student responsibilities were "Lampist", "Prefect of Walk", and "Prefect of Cleanliness". The Lampist tended the gas lamps; the Prefect of Walk organized the walks, and the Prefect of Cleanliness, an office Pat got twice, saw to house cleaning and manual work. The Superior, a keen walker, usually accompanied the students, taking them to places like Rochestown Monastery, Glanmire, Ballincollig or Blarney. Dinner on Wednesdays was half an hour early to facilitate the long walk. They walked farther on free days, even as far as Crosshaven, though usually some would have to take the train back. Annual excursions, after the "May devotions", took in places like Youghal, Ballycotton, "Queenstown", and Kinsale. A popular Free Day idea was the "five shilling excursion" when the students were given five shillings each and allowed to go where they pleased.

The seminary had an accomplished hurling team which included at least one inter-provincial player, Mr Conway. The seminarians played frequently against Wilton college, but the classical scholars were no match for them, much to the irritation of Fr Rowan who used to get quite 'ratty' at the repeated defeats of his side. Once he abruptly withdrew his team after only twenty-five minutes of play and, while marching his men home, threatened fire and brimstone on the Blackrock side. The seminarians also played against the University in the Mardyke, beating them by seven goals on one occasion, and against the Christian Brothers' school "the North Mon". The Gaelic Athletic Association allowed them to use the nearby Athletic Grounds for important matches. Pat enjoyed the games, but preferred football to hurling. Indoors, he liked playing billiards.

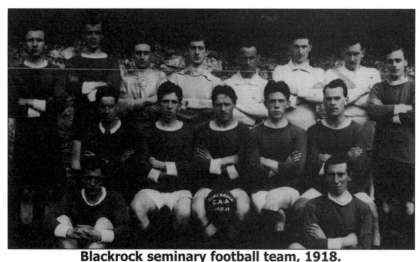

Blackrock seminary football team, 1918.
In front P. Christal, and Pat Kelly; *seated on left,* Stephen Harrington and Francis McGovern; *standing on left,* John Cadogan.

Blackrock seminary hurling team, 1918.
In front Pat Kelly and Denis O'Hara.

1918

Towards the end of the Great War, the British government, planning to extend conscription to Ireland, stirred up intense opposition in the country. African Missions students attended an Anti-Conscription meeting in Cork on 15 April and took the Anti-Conscription pledge in Blackrock parish church the following week. Nevertheless, fearing the Conscription Bill would be passed, they requested and received, permission to go home, where they would be less 'conspicuous'. With only two of their end of term examinations written, they began to leave the seminary on 24 April. However, a hugely supported General Strike on the 23rd persuaded the government to drop the Bill.

During the summer holidays the first Irish Provincial Assembly was held in Blackrock. The Fathers unanimously approved a motion that the students' food be improved; and, no doubt recalling their French roots, approved (with one vote against and one abstention) a motion that "A moderate use of wine, such as half a pint of light wine, as a daily drink at dinner after the War" be provided for the Fathers. An additional suggestion that, "a modicum of whiskey should be allowed on First Class feast days", was passed unopposed. Plain chant, hymn-singing and church music were recommended for the seminarians.

For some unfathomed reason, singing of the ecclesiastical type never quite flourished in the Irish seminaries as it did in France. Stephen Kyne, who had been Spiritual Director in Lyons in 1918, insisted on the "vital importance" of having a competent music teacher in Cork and tried to enlist a French Father for the role. But the idea did not germinate and the "musical lacuna", as he termed it, continued. There were, however, weekly classes of music and plain chant conducted by the seminarians themselves and the more gifted ones were encouraged to play the harmonium. Non-singers were taught the bare essentials: how to attempt a sung Mass and Benediction.

That year, the seminary became the reserve of 'theologians only' as it had been decided to send the philosophers to Cloughballymore in County Galway. The big house there, with its large demesne, was one of the gifts of the Province's great benefactor, Llewellyn Count Blake, who had died on 8 September 1916, just a few days before Pat and his fellow students arrived in Blackrock Road. Their first walk that year was to St Joseph's, Wilton, to lay a wreath on the Count's grave near the church.

As a first year theologian in September 1918, Pat and his class were nearly half way through their preparation for priesthood. In October, the names of those selected to take the Oath of membership of the Society, tonsure and Minor Orders were announced; Pat's name was among the twelve called out. Now was the time for them to decide whether or not they really wanted to become members of the Society and missionaries in

Africa. They were given a week-long retreat to help them make up their minds.

Pat's vocation, born in the deep faith of his own people, had begun as a desire to be a secular priest in an Irish church which was then fully occupied with its own rehabilitation after centuries of persecution. He had not, at first, thought of being a missionary. Being a "Foreign missionary" in his time meant going to England, America, Australia, or South Africa and serving the Catholic populations there, many of whom were Irish. A great number of the clergy and hierarchy were also Irish and, while Ireland had no overseas colonies, her 'spiritual empire' was vast. Pat had no desire to be a priest of these 'foreign missions', and neither had he any thoughts of evangelising the native peoples of Africa until that parish mission in Aughrim when the missioner drew attention to West Africa. The seed that was planted in him then was nourished in Wilton and in Blackrock. His idea of being a priest in Ireland receded as his missionary vocation grew. Though in Wilton and Blackrock he had sometimes been discouraged, especially by the departure of fellow-students, he had never seriously considered leaving. He had come to accept the Society and its mission as the place where God was calling him. With humility and conviction he went forward to take the Society Oath along with his classmates on 1 November 1918, each with hand on the Gospels, reciting the formula of the Oath in Latin before the Provincial Superior and the house staff. That day, and on many days subsequently, he thanked God for the straitened family circumstances that led him to the Society of African Missions.

On 11 November 1918 the armistice was signed and the Great War came to an end. Demobilised soldiers returned home and, experienced in the art of war, some of them joined the Irish Republican Army. The first General Election in Britain in eight years was held on 14 December and the African Missions students were among the voters. The nationalist party, Sinn Féin, gained a huge majority. The elected members, refusing to sit in the British Parliament, formed *Dáil Eireann* and declared an independent Irish Republic.

Meanwhile Thomas Broderick had been consecrated Vicar Apostolic of Western Nigeria in Killarney Cathedral on 8 December. He was the youngest bishop in the universal church at the time, only thirty-six. Ten days later, he visited the seminary and received a "hearty clap" and "three cheers" from the students. They put on a concert for him and he got them a free day. With only theologians in the seminary, major changes were made in the Rule; one of them being the cancellation of Christmas holidays at home. Following McGettigan's example, the new bursar produced cigars after a late Christmas dinner and a great time was had by all in the "Smoke room".

Pat missed Tristaun and the family that Christmas, but took advantage of the light holiday rule to spend some extra time in the Library. Though not a totally committed book-worm, he didn't like to miss anything and had a good eye for the "right book for the right subject at the right time". Many of the books in the library reflected the French origins of the Society: *L'unique Chose Nécessaire, ou réflexions, pensées et prières pour Mourir Saintement* (The One Thing Necessary, or reflections, thoughts and prayers for a Holy Death) by a Trappist. Along with it were several other tomes by the same author with equally morbid titles, *Au Tombeau de mon Sauveur* (At my Saviour's Tomb); *Litanies pour une bonne mort* (Litanies for a good death); and *A Jésus Crucifié* (To Jesus Crucified). Encouraging reading for future missionaries in 'The Whiteman's Grave' thought Pat, as he put them back on the shelves.

The library had been improved year by year and, by the time of Broderick's departure in 1917, it contained a good selection of more recent works on scripture, philosophy, theology, liturgy and missions. Many books, even whole libraries, had been donated by generous confreres and friends. Auctions were attended and books bought. An interesting aspect of the Library was that the students themselves made monthly contributions for spiritual books and the "Spiritual Library" was entirely under their management and control. By 1917, the spiritual books were "almost entirely in English"! Broderick often told the students that in it they would find "the best spiritual pabulum (nourishment), second only to the Holy Scriptures", and that spiritual reading was "one of the missionary's greatest helps and safeguards in the mission field".

1919

In January, Mr Kelly was appointed to the prestigious office of "Prefect of Cleanliness", a job which had more to do with manual work than personal grooming or hygiene. The Rule said, "By manual work is meant whatever the College authorities or the Prefect of Cleanliness consider proper for the decent upkeep of the house and its surroundings". He was not relieved of the job the following year as would have been normal and he was also the only one of his class to get a room to himself.

On 5 February, Pat and classmates received tonsure and Minor Orders from Bishop Broderick. Things were going nicely until the seminary received word in April that the Holy See, following the new code of Canon Law, required four years of theology instead of three before ordination. This worried the seniors as they had already completed their theological courses. In May they breathed a sigh of relief on hearing they had received a dispensation. The succeeding theologians hoped they also might be dispensed, but before any news of this arrived, Pat was informed that his father had passed away. On 3 June, regretting that he hadn't seen him at Christmas, he began the sad journey home on the early morning train to Dublin in the company of the Provincial Superior, William Butler, who was going as far as Dublin. Pat travelled on to Galway alone. Alighting at Ballinasloe he recalled the many times he had attended the

October fair with his father, admiring his skill at bargaining. After selling a beast, they went shopping for necessities in the town and then returned to Tristaun where they paid Pat Hurney what they owed at the forge. Malachy was buried in Clontuskert cemetery near the church where he had often prayed and attended Mass.

Near the end of the year, much to the relief of the younger 'theologians', the Holy See agreed to dispense all in the house from the necessity of doing a fourth year of theology.

1920

In response to increasing IRA activity, a reign of terror was unleashed in the country by the British forces, especially by the reinforcements brought in from England, the "Black and Tans" and the Auxiliaries. One of the first victims was the nationalist Lord Mayor of Cork, Tomás MacCurtain, who was brutally murdered by masked men on 15 March. On the 20th, the day nine SMA students were ordained to the deaconate in Faranferris chapel, MacCurtain's remains were transferred to the City Hall. Among the huge crowds that attended the transferral, and the funeral two days later, were the African Missions students.

On 20 September 1920, on their usual Wednesday walk, Pat and company were held up at Tivoli by a lorry load of armed soldiers. A few students in the front ranks were searched. When no arms or military equipment was found, the soldiers ordered the group to "retrace their march and return to barracks immediately". From then on the students went on their walks in separate groups of three.

Some of Pat's fellow seminarians, and professors, were passionate nationalists (and one or two were actively involved in the struggle for independence). Pat, while proud of Ireland's culture, language and religion, was not very strident in political discussions. He admired leaders like Pearse and De Valera, but said they had no influence on him. Nevertheless he was happy to say that he had been of service to Terence MacSwiney, MacCurtain's successor as Lord Mayor. MacSwiney died in Wormwood Scrubs prison, London, in October 1920, after a seventy-three day hunger strike. While seeking to evade arrest in Cork, he had occasionally taken refuge in the African Missions seminary where there was a secret 'hiding room'. Pat was the custodian of the room.

On the 29th of October a novena to the Irish Saints began in the seminary to pray for peace and liberty for "holy Ireland". MacSwiney's body was brought back from England and on the 31st, the students joined in the funeral procession which became a huge demonstration of support for the national cause. A Solemn High Mass was celebrated in St Joseph's the following month for the deceased Lord Mayor. With the national spirit rising in Ireland, the students decided to give a half-hour on Monday and Wednesday evenings to the study of gaelic. Pat, a fluent Irish speaker, was very keen on its revival and fully supported the movement.

In December, congregations at evening Benediction, at choir practices, and at the Departure Ceremony of the new missionaries bound for Africa, were reduced in number for fear of the "Tans". That month the centre of the city was torched by Auxiliaries on a rampage after eleven of their men were killed in an ambush. From the upper windows of the seminary the flames of the burning city were clearly visible.

1921

In January a curfew was imposed; all had to be indoors by 5 p.m. The usual Patrick's Day procession in the city on the 17th of March was cancelled; in St Josephs the rosary was said in Irish.

Having returned from Africa for Leave and for Society meetings in Lyons, Bishop Broderick conferred the order of sub-deacon on eleven candidates including Mr Kelly in February. In May the diaconate was conferred, again by Dr Broderick. In honour of the new deacons, the students of Blackrock staged the popular play, *The West's Awake*, in Wilton. The following day, a much travelled confrere, DJ O'Sullivan, presented a "magic lantern" slide show for students, Fathers and invited quests, illustrating "the heroic works of self-sacrifice and zeal performed by the pioneer missionaries of the Society in Egypt and in Equatorial West Africa". In June, Dr Broderick gave a memorable lecture entitled, "Prospects of missionary enterprise in Nigeria intermingled with a brief account of the habits and customs of the natives". These, and other talks by visiting missionaries, served to whet the appetites of the would-be apostles.

On 15 June, Pat and the other 'ordinandi' had their "canonical examinations" conducted by Dr Broderick. In his five years in Blackrock, exams had never been a problem for Pat. A well-above average student, he was usually among the top three or four in his class. In his first exams in Blackrock, February 1917, he received one "honour" (which meant 66% of the marks or above). His one 'honour', in Scripture at which he was consistently good, was actually more than most of his class got. Students took time to settle down. In June 1917, he got three honours, adding Church History and English to his list. In February 1918, he again got three honours and a 9 out of 10 in an oral exam. Due to the Conscription scare in April 1918, only Dogma and Moral Theology exams were written; Pat got honours in both. From then on he was consistently "tip top", as Broderick liked to say, gaining five or six honours in seven subjects in each of his biennial exams. He did exceptionally well in Church History, gaining 90% on two occasions, and in Moral Theology he was in the high 80s. Marks for "Sacred Eloquence" were not recorded and only once were they recorded for "Music". Then he got 6 out of 10 (which was not bad considering the young prodigy of the class, Stephen Harrington, got only 3). His canonical examination with Dr Broderick gave him no difficulties; examiner and examinee both enjoyed legal teasers and were quite enthusiastic about the new Code of Canon Law. Bishop and missionary-to-be, hoped they would meet again soon in Western Nigeria.

Three of the seminary staff who impressed Pat very much were: Michael Collins ("he inspired me most, a very spiritual man"); James McGettigan ("a great man for the Rule"); and Thomas Broderick ("a very good man"). Pat first encountered Collins in Wilton where he was a teacher and later in Blackrock where he was Superior in 1920. Michael, from West Cork, did his seminary studies in Lyons, taught English to French students and priests in Egypt, and spent many years in Lyons as a General Councillor. Inevitably, he became fond of France and the French, but he never lost his love for Ireland. Pat said, "He made the Irish saints, and the story of Ireland's conversion and early missionary activity known in the French houses, and succeeded in getting Patrick, Colmcille, and Columbanus included in the Society's "Morning and Evening Prayers". Having chosen him as his spiritual director, Pat, years later, said he knows me "nearly as well as I do myself".

Pat also admired James McGettigan, a Donegal man, ordained in Lyons in 1911 and appointed to the training of students in Ireland. Teacher, bursar, and Superior in the seminary, he was elected Vice Provincial in 1918. After he succeeded Broderick as Superior in 1917, he was no longer at ease, believing that he was not capable of raising students "to spiritual heights" and form "stern manly characters". After two years of personally unsatisfying efforts he asked to be relieved of the office and given a chance to go to the missions. His wish was partially granted, he was appointed to take over Michael Collins's vacant post of General Councillor in Lyons and to teach in the Seminary there.

The third member of staff, Pat greatly admired, was Thomas Broderick. Apart from the Superior's qualities and talents already mentioned, Pat was impressed and influenced by his great love for the Eucharist. Broderick's spirituality was Eucharist-centred. In his youth he had seriously thought of joining the Fathers of the Blessed Sacrament. As superior in Blackrock he stressed that "the Tabernacle should be the heart of the Seminary" and in his Vicariate in Nigeria he established a Confraternity of the Blessed Sacrament in every mission. Pat was devoted to the Mass from boyhood, but from seminary days he developed a concern, like Broderick's, for absolute correctness in its liturgical performance. He also developed a great love for eucharistic devotions and prayer before the Blessed Sacrament.

Near the climax of Ireland's war of Independence, Reverend Kelly and nine classmates were privileged to have Bishop Broderick again for their priestly ordination in Blackrock Road on 29 June 1921. Stephen Harrington, too young to be ordained, had to wait until the following year; even then he was eighteen months below the canonical age and required a dispensation. From (later) correspondence it would seem that Pat and Stephen got on well together but, in general, Pat did not appear to cultivate personal friendships.

The class of 1921 with Mgr Thomas Broderick. *Standing:* Nicholas Clery, John Cadogan, Pat Christal, Tim Cadogan, R.B.O'Sullivan, Francis McGovern, Stephen Harrington. *Seated:* Jerry Sheehan, Michael O'Donohue, Bishop Broderick, Pat McCarthy, Pat Kelly.

On the missions the class of '21 must rank among the highest for the level of sacrifices they made for Africa and the Gospel in terms of health and mortality. The first to die was Francis McGovern, only five months after arrival in Liberia, probably of blackwater fever in 1922. Michael O'Donohue, who travelled with Pat on his first voyage to Africa, had to be invalided home in 1924 and died in 1935. Tim Cadogan, after two years in Liberia was invalided home and, though he lived until 1984, never recovered his health. Nicholas Clery, sent to Western Nigeria in 1931, was invalided home in 1937 and died in 1939. Ironically, Patrick Christal, who suffered from tuberculosis during his seminary years and was thought to be too delicate for Africa, taught for thirteen years in the home houses before being appointed to Egypt where he continued to work for thirty years!

The day after the ordinations the new priests departed for home holidays, but Kelly, O'Donohue, John Cadogan, Tim Cadogan, McGovern and Baker returned to the seminary for the Departure Ceremony on 12 November. At 7 p.m., after a short concert put on for them by the theology students, they went to the public church where friends and local people had gathered. The five processed to the altar where they led the congregation in the recitation of the Rosary in Irish. Then Fr Joe Crawford, an accomplished orator, preached about the Province's difficult mission in Liberia where he had been for six years. Following this, everyone in the church went forward to kneel and kiss the feet of the departing missionaries. The ceremony concluded with the emotionally charged singing of Charles Gounod's farewell hymn written for the Paris Foreign Missions Society of which Marion Brésillac, the Founder of the Society of African Missions, was a member:

> Go forth, farewell for life, O dearest brothers;
> Proclaim afar the sweetest Name of God.
> We'll meet again one day in Heaven's land of blessings.
> Farewell, brothers, farewell.

Standing in the sanctuary, the young priests raised their hands in unison and imparted their solemn blessing.

The following day the students went to the Glanmire railway station to give a last "God Speed" to John Cadogan, Michael O'Donohue, and Pat Kelly who were starting off on the first leg of their journey to Nigeria.

Departing for Africa, 1921.
Front, Pat Kelly (Western Nigeria), Henry Baker (Liberia). *Standing,* Michael O'Donohue (W. Nigeria), John Cadogan (W. Nigeria), Tim Cadogan (Liberia), and Francis McGovern (Liberia).

Chapter 3

NIGERIA, 1921-1926

In November 1921, after a good holiday, Pat bade farewell to his mother and family at Tristaun and made his way to Dublin and then Liverpool. With him were classmates John Cadogan, Cork, and Michael O'Donohue, Laois; both were two years younger than Pat who was twenty-seven. In Liverpool they spent a few days at the African Missions transit house on Ulett Road, while waiting on the departure of the Elder Dempster liner bound for West Africa. In the city they bought suitable clothing and footwear for the tropics, a pith helmet for protection against the sun, and quinine for malaria. On boarding ship, the purser directed them to first class cabins; the 1918 Provincial Assembly had decided that the confreres should travel first class. The trio appreciated the comfort, but were a bit ill-at-ease at the thought of rubbing shoulders with colonial nobs in the first class dining hall. As the ship got under way, the new sailors in the Roman collars clutched the rail and spoke quietly as they watched the land recede.

A few days later, the ship's radio picked up the news that the Anglo-Irish Treaty had been signed in London on 6 December. Recalling it, Pat said, "We heard that the Free State was established and we were glad". As he was not given to talking about himself or his activities, we are fortunate to have an account by him of his first missionary journey:

> A fortnight after leaving the port of Liverpool we began to feel the heat and we knew that we were nearing Africa. The temperature increased daily and we perspired from

morning to night. Early one morning, an indescribable sight lay before us. The ship lay off the mouth of a big river called "Rokell". On either side hills, decked with stately palms, rose majestically to the sky. Fog on the water was already being burned off by the sun as it rose like a golden ball above the hilltops. Shops and the fine houses of white people stood near the river, behind them the dwellings of the Africans. Freetown lay before us! A ferry came out to take the passengers ashore; lots of canoes with two or three natives in each followed. The canoe men easily climbed the sides of the ship; port holes and windows were closed for fear of pilfering. One of the sailors saw a black man near an open window and, having nothing else at hand, threw his pipe at him. Catching it deftly, the canoe man made off delighted with the pipe.

They did not go ashore to visit the tomb of the Founder of the Society, Marion Brésillac, who with four companions had died here of yellow fever in 1859, the year of the Society's first mission, Brésillac himself dying within forty-one days of arrival. Visiting the tomb had not yet become a custom among the Irish confreres, nor did Pat, in his narrative, mention the Founder or the tragedy of that first year. Pat, John and Michael had arrived on the west coast of Africa which, for good reason, had earned itself the title 'the White Man's Grave". A fellow passenger beside them on the deck recited for their benefit an old sailors' rhyme, "Beware!

Beware! The Bight of Benin where few come out, though many go in". At nightfall the ship weighed anchor and steamed out of the bay.

Freetown, the tomb of the Founder and his first companions, RIP 1859.

Five days out of Freetown, Lagos appeared before us – the capital of Nigeria. We spent a few days there and received a great welcome from the priests. About 100,000 people, black, white and brown live in the city. Lagos has shops, stores, houses of every kind, and fine, wide streets as good as any in Ireland. Every type of faith is represented, Catholic and Protestant, but the Christians are few ·in comparison to the Muslims. Catholics number only about 10,000.

Since Lagos was the liner's final destination, the three missionaries transferred to a smaller boat bound for the ports in the estuary of the mighty river Niger to the southeast. After a couple of days they reached Warri in Bishop Broderick's vicariate of Western Nigeria. "The priest there gave us a *Céad míle fáilte*, even if he wasn't Irish", said Pat. It was probably Luigi Cavagnera, an Italian confrere, who was the first resident missionary in Warri. His mission embraced swamps, creeks and islands in the low-lying Niger delta. Forcados, established in 1912, had been the first Catholic mission in the area in the modern era, but before long Warri, called 'Sacred Heart' mission, outgrew it and Luigi took up residence there in 1917. After welcoming them, he explained that they hadn't yet reached their destination – O'Donohue would have to go to Onitsha-Olona quite far away and Cadogan and Kelly to Aragba, forty miles from Warri. Pat continued his account:

John and myself bought bicycles and, after breakfast the following day, we set off on our first African journey. A black man on another bike was our guide and interpreter. We carried only a change of shirts while our guide carried a bag of food. Our loads, in two boxes, were to follow us, carried on the heads of two men from the missions to which we were going. However a row broke out between them over the weight of each box and was only settled after a fight. When we got our boxes, we found that much of

34

John's luggage was in my box and some of mine in his!

On the road we met people going to the market. They seemed strange to us. Everyone was walking with a load on their heads, a few were on bicycles. Bicycles have a hard life, you find two men on a bicycle and a lot of baggage as well. You also see three on a bike, one in front of the rider and another behind. It would be the same if the people had horses or donkeys, but these animals don't survive here because of some kind of insect. We saw young people and old, fat and thin; women with children on their backs; one man with a live goat on his head and another with just an empty bottle. There were more women than men and all were talking at the top of their voices, sometimes a conversation was going on between the first and last person in a line a hundred yards long!

After an hour we reached a big river. The guide 'halooed' loudly and an answering call came from somewhere in the forest. A boatman appeared and invited us into his canoe, our bicycles were lifted in, then the locals piled in until the boat was nearly sinking. The two of us sat very still until we reached the other side, where we had to pay before leaving the boat: sixpence for a white man and sixpence for each bike; it was only three pence for a black man!

We cycled on, exhausted from the heat of the midday sun. We passed three or four towns with about three or four thousand people in each. The people do not live in the "bush" for fear of robbers who prowl at night. The towns all looked the same, rows of houses with thatched roofs, no chimneys, and low brown walls, the streets meandered, seemingly going nowhere in particular. Usually each town has a central market place, where old people like to sit and talk beneath the shade of a big tree. The houses had one door and one window, but the door is only five feet by two in size.

We were tired and thirsty when our guide eventually stopped at a head catechist's house. As soon as we sat down old people and children flocked around us. They were very surprised when the guide told them we were missionaries. The man of the house wanted to prepare a proper meal for us, but we still had fifteen miles to go, so we ate the food the guide had brought and got on our way.

En route they encountered a group of men working beside the road. Greeting them, the travellers asked for a drink; one of the men climbed a tall tree as if he were a squirrel and threw down a few coco-nuts. While they drank the delicious juice, a woman, complaining loudly that a man had run off with her daughter without paying the brideprice, approached. The guide told her that the two white men were missionaries not administrators so she went away.

The sun was setting when we reached the mission and the parish priest's house. What joy and welcome he and the people had for us. We were lonely no doubt after leaving our own country, but who could remain lonely with such kind and joyful people around us. Yes, we were happy and light-hearted that night as we sat with the priest in the gentle light of the moon. The dream I had as a student in The Pines had materialised. The harvest was ripe and I was in the middle of it, reaping hook in hand, to do a little for the glory of God and the honour of Ireland.

Pat wrote this article at the request of the editor of *The Pines*, the magazine of his old school (now St Joseph's, Garbally). He wrote it in Irish with the title *"Turas Misinéara"* (The journey of a Missionary), and signed himself *Pádraic Ó Ceallaigh, A.M.* (African Missions). First appearing in 1929, "The Journey" was published again in 1940. Introducing it the second time, the editor paid tribute to Pat's fluency in Irish.

~ ~ ~

Pat and John had arrived at Aragba, where Georges Krauth was parish priest. A friendly, bearded man from Alsace, he was delighted to welcome them and set a good meal before them, nearly all of which came from his own vegetable garden and chicken run. While they ate he talked enthusiastically about the mission. The Vicariate of Western Nigeria, with headquarters at Asaba on the west bank of the Niger, extended some 600 miles from Zaria in the north to the Bight of Benin in the south. Though boundaries were not well defined, it was nearly 200 miles in width from the Niger river westwards to Ondo-Ekiti. The Catholic population of about 10,000 was served by twenty priests among whom was Paul Emecete, the first African priest in British West Africa. He had been ordained by Bishop Broderick in 1920.

Georges Krauth

Paul Emecete

Early history of the mission

In the sixteenth century Portuguese missionaries tried to introduce Christianity in the Niger area and had some success around Warri and Benin, but their efforts did not take root and no further efforts were made until 1841 when two Anglican missionaries participated in the British Government's 'Niger Mission'. Composed of a hundred and forty five white men and a hundred and fifty eight Africans, this expedition proved to be a disaster, at least for the whites – a hundred and thirty of them died of fever, none of the Africans died. This convinced the Church Mission Society (CMS), a missionary 'wing' of the Anglican Church, that "Africa must be converted by Africans". Another expedition was organized in 1854, this time with fifty-four Africans and twelve Europeans. It succeeded without fatalities, thanks to the use of quinine, to sail beyond the confluence of the Niger and Benue rivers. A remarkable Yoruba man, Samuel Crowther, was a member of both expeditions. Having been captured by slavers as a boy in his home country, he was rescued by the Royal Navy and put ashore at Freetown, Sierra Leone. After studies in the Anglican college there and in England he was ordained a priest. In 1864 he was consecrated Anglican bishop of the Niger Mission. Though his residence was in Badagry near Lagos, his main station was Onitsha which lay on the other side of the Niger from Asaba. The Church Mission Society had considerable success in the Niger Delta, Crowther's own son being a pastor there from 1871 to 1937. In 1884, Bishop Crowther welcomed the Fathers of the African Missions Society to Lokoja, a town built at the confluence of the Niger and Benue rivers, and the following year he welcomed the Holy Ghost Fathers to Onitsha. Unfortunately the cordial relations between the Protestants and Catholics did not last.

Different tribes lived west of the Niger but, as the predominant language was Ibo, the vast area was called "Western Iboland". East of the river was called "Eastern Iboland". Traditional religion held sway on both sides of the river, idolatry and human sacrifice were commonplace. On the west bank of the Niger, Catholic missionary efforts began in the modern era in 1884, when the Society of African Mission's Jules Poirier and Pierre Piolat, both French, and Filippo Fiorintini from Italy, set up a station at Lokoja. After a year Fiorintini died of fever. The following year, Piolat, run down in health, took ship for home but died at sea. Reinforcements came but some of them died too, including a young Belfast man, Andrew Dornan, who died of fever in 1886 shortly after arrival. The first Sisters, Emile, Cornelie, and Paul, members of the congregation of Our Lady of Apostles, arrived in September 1886. These young women, who had no previous mission experience, faced extremely difficult conditions and suffered especially from fevers. Emile died at Lokoja in February 1889 aged twenty-nine. One of the other Sisters died not long after her.

Asaba

At Lokoja, the African Missions made little progress because of a strong Moslem presence, the people's attachment to traditional ways and their fear of defying rulers and fetish priests who were hostile to the missionaries. Slave raiding was widespread and the location would have been dangerous for the missionaries, had it not been for the presence of the National African Company, which had its headquarters at Lokoja and provided some protection. The only adult converts the mission made were 'redeemed' slaves who had been purchased by Poirier at the market in Bida. In 1886 the company, on being granted a Royal Charter, moved its headquarters to Asaba, 140 miles downstream, and changed its name to the Royal Niger Company. Requested by a Catholic judge at Asaba, James Marshall, to start a mission there, Poirier and an Italian confrere, Carlo Zappa, went to investigate in 1888. Asaba, an Ibo town of some 12,000 people living in peace seemed to offer an attractive field of labour. Zappa remained and established a mission station. In 1891, with little happening in Lokoja, the community of two Fathers, two Sisters, and twelve redeemed slaves abandoned Lokoja and went to Asaba. The following year the first indigenous convert was baptised, Thomas Okolo.

Poirier, the first Prefect Apostolic of the "Upper Niger", as the jurisdiction was then called, went to Lyons in 1893 to attend the first General Assembly of the Society. After it, he was detained in administrative posts at home. To replace him in 'Upper Niger', Rome appointed Carlo Zappa *superior ad interim* and, in 1896,

Prefect Apostolic. By 1894 he had already opened residential stations at Issele-Uku and Illah, and outstations like Okpanam, Ibusa, Ogwashi-Uku, and Ubuluku. Progress in terms of conversions remained painfully slow. The indigenous people despised the missionaries for their relationship with the hated Niger Company and for their dealings with slaves and tribal outcasts. Decades later, "Slave" was a taunt still used against mission boys and girls. Once when Zappa tried to save the life of a young slave about to be sacrificed, he came close to being killed himself.

More devastating to the missionaries than the disfavour of the people, was their high mortality rate due to fever. Between 1884 and 1898, twenty-four Fathers arrived from Europe, five died after one or two years, two died as they were returning to Europe, and seven were invalided home. Fourteen Sisters arrived, four died and three had to return to Europe for good. During the "Ekumeku Wars" against Niger Company rule in 1898 and 1904, mission stations and churches were attacked and burned down. At Illah the Fathers and Sisters fled after receiving a warning in the dead of night, from a man they had once helped, that some five thousand Ekumeku were on their way to kill them. The community got away just fifteen minutes before the warriors arrived and torched the mission. In his station in Issele-Uku, Adolphe Rousselet refused to flee and the Ekumeku, suspecting he had powerful juju, left him alone.

Aided by a trickle of new men from Lyons, Zappa opened new stations at Illah, Agenebode, and Ibusa. Lokoja was re-opened in 1906 and from it outstations to the west and north were opened: Kabba, Okene, Oka and Zaria. Between 1908 and 1917 more residential stations were established: Ubiaja, Ukoni, Ogwashi-Uku, Forcados and Warri.

Zappa believed strongly in the value of catechists and trained many in Asaba. Preparing for an indigenous clergy, he opened a minor seminary at Iviankpodi near Agenebode in 1908 which, while preparing a few young men for priesthood, trained many more to function as catechists. He promoted a direct apostolate – visitation of the villages and catechetical instruction for any who were willing to listen. The Sisters visited, nursed the sick, and cared for the old, abandoned, and orphan girls; their charitable work won good will and prepared the way for conversions. Zappa, preferring to count success in terms of numbers of Christian families rather than numbers of children in school, believed that a Western education would alienate the people from their roots and turn them into minions of the colonists but, after seeing Mgr Joseph Shanahan's "school miracle" in eastern Iboland, he relented somewhat; at least Catholic schools, he thought, would be better than Government or Protestant schools. Mgr Shanahan CSSp, Prefect Apostolic of 'Lower Niger', and a friend of Zappa, had made spectacular progress with schools among the Ibos of Eastern Nigeria. His headquarters at Onitsha were quite near Zappa's at Asaba but on the other side of the Niger.

In 1911, Rome more clearly identified the boundaries of Zappa's Prefecture and changed its name from "Upper Niger" to "Western Nigeria". The following year sixteen of Zappa's confreres petitioned Rome to raise the Prefecture to the status of a Vicariate with Zappa as the first Bishop. When he discovered this, he asked Rome not to comply with the request – at least not with the last part. Rome didn't.

~ ~ ~

Returning to Pat and John on their first evening at Aragba, their host, Fr Georges, noticed that the two new missionaries had long finished their meal and were beginning to fidget. Calling the cook to clear the table, he suggested they continue their conversation outside on the verandah. A beautiful African moon had risen, bathing the compound in yellow light. When they were all seated comfortably on wicker chairs, Georges, prompted by a question from John, spoke about Zappa, whom he knew very well. Describing him as short in stature, grey-bearded and very energetic, he said he was one of the best known personalities of the Niger. Called "the eternal traveller" by the people, he was not only a highly successful missionary but a scholar and geographer. An accomplished linguist, he wrote an Ibo catechism and a prayer book with the help of his catechist, Jacob Nwakobia, also a French-Ibo dictionary, and *Statuta et Notae* for the missionaries, all of which remained in use long after his death. At Christmas 1916, Zappa spent some time with Georges in his mission station at Ibusa and, for the first time ever, Georges heard him complain of "feeling tired". About the middle of January, Zappa crossed the river to the hospital at Onitsha where he was detained. Suffering from a liver complaint which was not getting better and, sensing that his end was near, he asked to be taken back to Asaba. He died there, 30 January 1917 and was buried the following day by Mgr Shanahan. Though only fifty-six, his thirty years' labour in the Niger region was quite phenomenal when compared with the short lifespan of so many of his confreres.

In 1900 the British Government, having withdrawn its Royal Charter from the Niger Company, formed the Protectorates of "Southern" and "Northern Nigeria", using the name "Nigeria" for the first time. As the British consolidated their hold on the country, the English language became more important, and English-speaking missionaries, especially British subjects (like the Irish), were preferred. Zappa, apparently, favoured the presence of Irish missionaries and an Irish successor for himself. As mentioned already, after Zappa's death Rome appointed Thomas Broderick, Prefect, and the following year Vicar Apostolic.

In 1917 the Prefecture recorded that it had eighteen priests, all 'Continentals' except for two Irish confreres; eleven residential stations Asaba, Issele-Uku, Illah, Agenebode, Ubiaja, Ukoni, Ibusa, Lokoja, Ogwashi-Uku, Forcados and Warri; over eighty churches and chapels and about 8,000 Catholics. In November 1918 the Great War came to an end, Germany lost her colonies in Africa and German missionaries were expelled. Parts of Togo were allocated to the SMA and many of the Society's francophone missionaries in Western Nigeria were transferred there and replaced in Nigeria by the Irish.

Aragba

Georges went on to speak a bit about himself and Aragba. Born in Ohlungen near Strasbourg in 1886, he was ordained in 1910 and appointed to 'Upper Niger' where he arrived at the end of the year. At Asaba, he learned Ibo and English and travelled a lot on foot and by bicycle in the district, and farther afield into the land of the Etsakos with the seminarian Paul Emecete as his assistant and interpreter. Happy in the mission, he had asked to be allowed to remain when others were being transferred to Togo. However, he wasn't long in Aragba; in fact, he had just opened the parish and he hadn't yet finished building the Fathers' house, which was one reason, he explained, why he would be sending them off soon to two of his outstations.

Georges asked Pat and John about themselves. Cadogan, he noticed, seemed knowledgeable, self-assured and spoke freely, while Kelly was quiet, and appeared to be struggling to come to grips with his new environment. Many years later in Ireland, when Pat was asked by a nephew, going to Africa for the first time, "What's it really like out there?" Pat pointed to the moon and said, "That's about the only thing you'll find the same!" Georges wasn't the first Alsatian Pat and John encountered. There were three in the senior class in Blackrock when Pat and John arrived in 1916. Hard-working, cheerful and studious, these three took most of the first places in the theology exams and were ordained with their Irish classmates in 1917. Like most of the Alsatians, Georges appeared to be a kindly, robust, practical man, of a simple, spiritual, and somewhat ascetical nature. The Alsatians were good at adapting both to the people and to the terrain; speaking the local languages well, they were familiar with the native customs and culture and took pride in living off the land, keeping vegetable gardens and fowl. Attached to their missions, they remained without home holidays for much longer than the Rule required. (Now on his second tour, Georges would remain for nine years before going home in 1929 because of illness.)

Pat felt he would get on all right with this man. "It wasn't difficult", he said later with a touch of humour, "he lived in the main station and I lived sixteen miles away, but we visited one another once a week!" Georges referred to Pat as "my dear old friend Pat Joe" and, when he was convalescing in Alsace, he invited Pat, more than once, to visit him, but Pat never managed such a visit. In Africa, Georges preferred the bush to town life and was constantly on the move visiting out-lying villages. On one occasion in 1922, he and Pat cycled from Aragba to Ashaka, a distance of 30 miles, to give a court clerk the opportunity of "making his Easter duty" (going to Confession). When they arrived the man was not to be found; neither were any refreshments. Georges searched the bush and found a wild pineapple. After devouring it, they turned their bicycles round and rode home. Such was Pat's introduction to 'Alsatian missiology'.

Of all the dioceses in France, Strasbourg, the 'capital' of Alsace, gave twice as many vocations to the SMA as the next highest diocese. The Irish regarded the Alsatians as 'French' because they spoke French, but they also spoke German and were from the east side of the Rhine which, from 1871 to 1919, was under German rule. After the War, Alsace was restored to France, but the Alsatians remained 'different' and in 1927 the Alsatian members of the SMA formed their own independent province. On being transferred from Western Nigeria the Alsatians, and other Continental confreres, faced the painful task of uprooting themselves and starting all over again elsewhere. A number of them remained to help the Irish get started or, because of age, they would have found change too difficult.

It wasn't the tradition in the Vicariate to have two or three men living together in one house and so Krauth, even if his house was finished, would have dispersed the parish team anyway. He gave them a short introduction to mission life and work, and then sent Cadogan to Oria and Pat to Eku. In these outstations, their first task was to learn the local language, often called "Sobo", but more correctly called "Urhobo", and to get to know the people and their customs. The Urhobos numbered about 130,000 and inhabited an area roughly the size of County Cork in what was then Warri Province. It was a low-lying swampy area, devoid of roads or decent bridges, interspersed with creeks, and banked by stretches of dense rain forest. Unpromising as it seemed, Bishop Broderick thought it "the most interesting and progressive of his Mission districts". Krauth had opened the two stations only a few months before Pat and John's arrival and there were only about a dozen Christians in each of them.

First impressions about the new missionaries were favourable. Bishop Broderick wrote to William Butler, the Irish Provincial, in June 1922, saying, "Frs Cadogan and Kelly are getting on right well at Oria and Eku under Fr Krauth who is stationed at Aragba. Oria is but a short distance from Eku – a cycle run of twenty minutes. Both are learning Sobo and quite settled down to their work. Fr Krauth is an indefatigable worker and gets on tip top with his two curates. The houses and churches at Oria and Eku were built by the natives. The house at Eku is a neat mission house with two bedrooms and a dining room. It has shutters, doors and woodwork, is quite solid and very neatly finished off. The all-important thing, they are both enjoying excellent health, thank God".

In the same letter Broderick requested more missionaries for Western Nigeria and, while acknowledging that the Province in

Ireland was still getting off the ground, said that some men in important positions at home should be sacrificed for the missions. He believed in hard work and sacrifice on the mission, but also at home. The French-speaking missionaries, *les confrères* as he sometimes called them, included Italians as well as Alsatians and 'pure' French. Pioneers of the mission, their achievement had been outstanding, setting high standards for the new Irish. Inevitably there was some condescension towards the newcomers and Broderick was hopeful that his compatriots would prove that they were as good as any. Writing to Butler he said, "Fr Krauth wrote in glowing terms to Fr Frigerio, of Frs Kelly and Cadogan. Fr Frigerio seemed quite surprised that Irish confreres could come up to that standard. That is why, when occasions offer, I tell our young men we have got to show that Irishmen can be missionaries, sober, zealous, attached to this country and the natives". In most things Cadogan and Kelly appeared to be developing as desired. Krauth wasn't condescending and, after recovering his health in Alsace in 1929, wrote to Butler saying, "I have always liked to work with Irish confreres and it is my most anxious desire to return to Dr Broderick's Vicariate".

In the outlying villages of Eku and Oria, Krauth had begun to organize centres for teaching catechism: seven in the Eku area and three in Oria. Pat visited his centres frequently but, without the vernacular language, or a catechist, it was difficult to make headway. Picking out the better-instructed Christians, he relied on them to instruct the others, and sat in on their classes, learning by heart the catechism answers along with the catechumens, listening carefully to their pronunciation and trying to repeat the sounds as best he could – to the great amusement of his 'classmates'. Back in the mission station he studied both questions and answers in Zappa's catechism and prayer book, working late into the night with the aid of a bush lamp.

Like Zappa, Bishop Broderick esteemed catechists highly and promoted their training. Pat quickly saw how indispensable they were. Usually a catechist looked after half a dozen outstations, not only instructing, organizing, and leading prayers but, when occasion demanded, defending 'his flock' against chiefs who wished to punish converts for not taking part in fetish worship or other practices forbidden to Christians. Most of the catechists were men of integrity and gave very good example. At times their lot was difficult; often they had to bear the brunt of the hostility and resentment of chiefs, fetish priests, or Protestant Church leaders. The catechists' perseverance was all the more commendable as, having some training, most of them could have got better salaries by working for colonial employers. Usually each parish priest had at least one good catechist to help him, and often there would be a catechist in each village of importance but not all Fathers, especially new ones, could afford them. Pat's lack of a catechist throughout his first tour meant he had to communicate with the people unaided. Frustrating as this was, it accelerated his progress in the vernacular and also helped him to get to know the people. Through sheer hard work and application, he had the whole of Zappa's catechism off by heart in a relatively short time. In the different centres, after catechism classes he joined the people in the recitation of the prayers which he soon knew by heart. Mass, of course, was in Latin but Pat encouraged the people to pray and sing in the vernacular especially before and after Mass.

For those who lived alone, as Pat and Cadogan did, Society rule obliged them to make weekly visits to one another to make up for the lack of community in their lives and to make possible weekly Confession as the *Directory* required. As classmates, alone in their first mission, they had plenty to talk about: work, the people, customs and language difficulties, but they were quite different in personality. Cadogan, well-organized, neat and self-confident was quite impressive. Pat, lacking Cadogan's savoir-faire, did not seem to be coping quite as well. While they both appreciated their weekly meetings, both were glad to get back to their own stations and carry on with their own business. Apart from his many dealings with the people, Pat was raising a few chickens in his backyard and he sometimes used this as an excuse to be off, "Well now, I shouldn't be keeping the fowl waiting for their supper".

Chickens abounded in the villages, scrawny creatures, most of them, left to forage for themselves. Pat fed his, but before long he realized that the hawks ate more of them than he did, so he dropped the project. For his first year, not only did he not have a catechist, he didn't have a cook either. He 'made-do', with boiling "fowl" in a big tin can. He usually had an egg or two for breakfast, chicken for lunch and chicken left-overs for supper. No wonder he took to calling chickens, the "missionary's best friend" and, on home leave, would eat anything *except* chicken. As the missionaries didn't have 'fridges, meat had to be consumed the day the animal or bird was killed, hence the inevitable chicken supper. There was plenty of plantain, yams, and rice. He didn't have much tea or coffee, but developed a taste for cocoa. Later he planted a few coffee trees and started grinding his own coffee beans. Butter was a rarity, on the odd occasion he got some, he had to spoon it on to the bread, as it liquefied in the heat. He discovered that the flesh of avocado pears made a wonderful substitute for butter. He loved fresh bread lathered with avocado or, even better, with Golden Syrup out of a green tin which reminded him of home. Whenever he was in Sapele, a big town with a bakery and a few big stores, he would bring home bread and syrup. Like many men in their first mission, he foolishly drank 'uncooked' water from the river – boiling took time and tepid water didn't taste good. But, after getting dysentery in his third year, he became very careful, from then on he always filtered and boiled water. Dysentery plagued him for the rest of his mission career. He escaped malaria his first year, but got a bad attack in the second. In his first tour he relied on three safeguards: a pith helmet for the sun, quinine for malaria, and prayer for everything. All three worked in their own fashion. There was nothing for yellow fever. He got inoculated against it in Warri, but the following year the doctor told him there had been nothing in the syringe except *"acqua pura"* (pure water).

After a few months in Oria, John Cadogan, having won Bishop Broderick's approval, was transferred to Warri, a big port town, to take charge of the district. Pat took over Oria and its outstations and began weekly visitation with Krauth.

Though Broderick thought the bungalow with the thatched roof in Eku quite a neat affair, Pat had other ideas. He drew a rough sketch of a rectangular two-storey, mud-walled house with an external stairway, wide balconies and a pan roof. Wasting no time, he began to build. Leading the work himself, he got the people to help; even women and children joined in, clearing the site, digging foundations, carrying and fetching timber, sand, water and refreshments. The atmosphere was like a day on the bog or making hay, "but you have to watch them closely or they wouldn't do a tap". Once the building was going up he was everywhere, checking levels with a bottle of water and verticals with a weight on the end of a string, nothing escaped his eye. He tried to follow the conversation of the workers, at first without success but, having passed a certain stage of frustration, he found that he was beginning to understand a word here and a phrase there. The people were delighted when he began responding to them in Urhobo and they egged him on to greater efforts. Working hard, helped by the people, and never wasting materials or money on style or non-essentials, he built the house for a fraction of the cost of other mission houses. Early in the work, Phil Cassidy, who was ordained a year before Pat but arrived in the mission a year later, came from Warri to see how Pat was doing. Impressed, he wrote to the Provincial, "he has already got the natives to make the bricks. All the help he will need will be about £200 from the bishop and he may be able to pay it back in a short time. You will see how much he has saved when I tell you that the Warri bungalow is to cost £900". Evidently Pat would not be outdone by *Les confréres* when it came to thrift.

Eku, the house that Pat built.

Krauth completed the Fathers' house at Aragba. It was well done and comfortable. Pat commented, "you wouldn't think you were in Africa at all when inside it". No fear of such illusions in the house that he built, even Irish confreres thought it "quaint", "economical", and "Pajoesque". But half a century later, he was able to say, "Well, it's still standing!"

Eku had a reasonably big mud-walled church, but no bell – *a sine qua non* in any self-respecting mission. Pat got a fine one sent out from O'Byrne's of Dublin. It cost over £9, no small sum in those days when the missionary's allocation from the Bishop was only £5 a month, and that only *if* "the cow wasn't dry" (as the Bishop was wont to say). Pat's first letter to Provincial Butler, in September 1922, was about payment for this bell, but contained a few other items as well, "So far thank God I'm in good health here in Eku, nothing to complain about, save my great difficulty in getting my tongue around Sobo. I know no Father or white man

50

that can speak it yet, and so I must pick it up bit by bit from the natives". He grumbled that he wasn't making more progress in evangelizing, "I'm not making good headway in the line of conversions. The Urhobos have greater zeal to learn secular knowledge than catechism. However, we must not forget that it's God who has to do all".

Pat did not find visiting Georges Krauth onerous, because Georges, though well-experienced in the mission and eight years his senior, was not at all patronising and was a mine of information and practical know-how. On one visit Pat raised the matter of community life in the Vicariate, which, as far as he could see, wasn't being practised much, despite what was said in the *Constitutions* and *Directory*. Georges explained that most of the stations in the district had been opened by Alsatians nearly all of whom were in favour of one-man missions. Without beating around the bush he said, "We have no community life here, because the Fathers don't want it". Pat felt somewhat ill-at-ease at not living within the letter of the law, but had enough 'savvy' to keep his mouth shut and his ears open. Krauth liked the way he was developing and wasn't at all deceived by his reticence. Cassidy observed, "Whenever Fr Georges is in difficulty he consults Pat, and he says Fr Pat's opinion is always right".

While still in his first year, Pat thought he'd save a bit of time and materials in the morning by growing a beard like Krauth. Cassidy reported, "Pat Kelly is growing a whisker. The natives think it makes white man look like Our Lord. But Pat looks more like Judas". Cadogan was more charitable, "Fr Pat is now a typical missionary with a fine flowing patriarchal beard". Cassidy went on to compare the two classmates, "Cadogan can get through an enormous amount of work, but he lacks a great deal of Kelly's initiative. Pat is really one in a hundred".

Like many newcomers, Pat paid little attention to the limitations of his own flesh and bones. Revelling in his strength and in getting things done, he didn't like to take a break, not even, it seemed, for Society Retreats and meetings. A rare critical comment he made in his first tour did not give the impression of great enthusiasm for Society retreats, "The authorities deemed it more prudent for our spiritual existence to have the Fathers make Retreat in three or four different centres before proceeding to the Conference at Asaba. Well, I experienced a retreat in Asaba only once and I did not feel like getting into an ecstasy either during it or soon afterwards". The Annual four-day Retreat in Asaba had been instituted by Zappa; Broderick authorised retreats in different centres, but required the missionaries to come together annually at Asaba for four days or more of instructions in Canon Law, Statutes, liturgy and 'business'. These events gave newcomers the opportunity of meeting old friends and making the acquaintance of old-timers like the Alsatians Eugene Strub and Charles Burr, and the Italian, Berengario Cermenati.

Replying to an early letter from the Provincial, Pat didn't say much about himself or the mission, but enquired about things in Ireland: political developments, the Seminary and changes in its staff. News of the outbreak of the Irish Civil War saddened him, "There is nothing to do now but pray for the old land, and may God and Mary and Patrick save a nation from ruin that was so faithful to the Holy Catholic Church in the past". Responding to the Provincial's remarks on the deaths of a number of the Province's missionaries he said, "We must be perfectly resigned to God's holy will for He knows what's best". Refusing to let the burden or the heat of the day get him down, he said, "Out here you are inclined to blame the climate for everything, not only as regards physical inertness, but also intellectual and moral. Well, whether the climate is the cause or not, it's a good job it's there to throw the blame on".

Keen to increase the number of outstations, he cycled throughout the district looking for suitable places to start new centres. Taking with him a boiled chicken in a banana leaf for his lunch, he drank water wherever he was offered hospitality. At a village called Aghalokpe, about 12 miles from Eku, he asked the chief for a plot of land on which to build a church and a school. The chief asked him, "How many wives can a man have in your church?" "One", said Pat. "That's enough", said the chief, "you can go ahead". Small churches were easy to build and schools were easy to open, "All you needed for a school was a blackboard and a piece of chalk", he said. Teachers were paid very little, not much more than seven shillings and sixpence a month. Before long, Aghalokpe became one of the busiest outstations in the whole district.

As yet there was no Government educational policy worth talking of, but most District Officers appreciated what the missionaries were doing. Some of the officers were Irish, especially from 'the North'. Pat didn't court their company unless he wanted something from them, then he found most of them "alright". A rare one was hostile; one told Pat, "You gave us a stab in the back in 1916". In general, Pat thought the officials treated the people fairly; the only time real friction arose was when the Government introduced poll tax.

Before long Pat was busy enough to need, and 'wealthy' enough to afford, a cook. This important member of staff, apart from cooking, accompanied him to the outstations along with a mission boy who carried his Mass box, camp-bed, and the chicken wrapped in the banana leaf. But it was rarely a picnic – especially in the wet season when one had to dodge the rains. Once when Pat's bed got soaked, he was given one of the Christian's beds to sleep in. The following morning he was told he had slept in a leper's bed.

A little literary work

The nights are long in the tropics, but they afforded time to study the language, do a Holy Hour or two, and still have time to write something for the *African Missionary,* the Province's monthly magazine. Stephen Harrington, Pat's classmate, was the editor and had appealed for articles. Pat, writing in Irish, sent him a few. Four of his first tour contributions (a letter and three articles), were published. In the letter, he expressed satisfaction that the attempt to introduce Irish in the seminary, begun in his time, had grown. Speaking of the missionary spirit, which was beginning to glow in Ireland, he hoped it would fan into a great flame.

Two of his articles had to do with women! Certainly he was not a "lady's man" but, despite his gruff, shy manner he was very compassionate, especially towards suffering African women. "Marriage among the black people" and "Women's life in Africa", could be classified as early (unconscious) examples of the 'feminist' genre! He considered marriage to be the biggest source of 'palaver' (trouble) among the people. In many marriages women were condemned to a life of work and drudgery for non-appreciative husbands. A man selected a bride, spoke to her father, and a bride-price, usually about £20, was agreed on. Though the woman had no say in any of this, after the customary marriage, she had to live under her husband's roof and obey him. If she showed signs of running away she would be 'guarded' until she settled down. If the man was dissatisfied with her he might send her packing at any time and claim his money back from her father. However, if the husband blamed her unfairly (and this would be judged in a court), he would get nothing. On a few occasions, married Catholic men came to Pat looking for a suitable concubine from among his parishioners, "They retreat as fast as their legs can carry them when I find out what they're up to", he said.

The second 'feminist' article, though signed only *"Misiunéir"*

(Missioner), was surely Pat's. It has all the hall marks of his style and there was no one else writing in Irish for the *African Missionary* at that time. In it the missionary tells the pathetic story of Obo, an orphan girl, who was helped by a priest. Though the priest was un-named and the story told in the third person, it was surely Pat himself. Not only has it the ring of personal experience but, in a couple of places, the personal pronoun"I" intrudes – apparently inadvertently. The priest first encountered Obo when she was fifteen years of age. Her mother had died giving birth to her; her father, a much-married chief, had no interest in looking after her, so she was raised by her grandmother. Obo was a Catholic and always attended Mass whenever the priest visited her village, which was about twenty miles from the central station. Life was fine until her seventeenth birthday, when an old pagan with two wives, wanted her and paid the bride-price to her father. Obo fled into the forest and walked all night until she reached the priest's house. He took pity on her, got a Catholic family to look after her and, later, arranged a suitable marriage for her. The conclusion of the article was, "Faith is a beautiful gift for women out here – taking them out of slavery and giving them the right to live as God created them to".

The third article, "A journey in the night", written in 1924, was also signed "Missioner", but not for the same reasons. When writing about Obo, Pat probably desired anonymity because he didn't wish to be associated too closely with any young woman. In "A journey in the night" he probably didn't want his family at home to worry about the dangers he might face in his work. The priest in the story, "Fr Seán", could have been himself, but more likely, was John Cadogan who, apart from having the name 'John' (Seán in Irish), was stationed in the port town of Warri and would have been obliged to travel frequently by canoe. The story began, "Fr Seán lay back comfortably in his big chair. It had been a hard day teaching the villagers about the Gospel as he had done for the past three years since leaving Ireland ..." After nightfall a young man came with an urgent message: Fr James, who lived ten miles away near the sea, was seriously ill with fever and wanted Seán to come immediately. The priest and the young man roused three paddlers and set off in their canoe. About midnight a storm blew up and the boat capsized. Seán thought his last hour had come but, before losing consciousness, he felt someone catch and pull him towards the shore. At sunrise he awoke on the beach. Sprawled nearby was the young man who had summoned him. Though he was dying, the young man begged Fr Seán not to delay, Fr James needed him. Seán blessed him and departed realizing then that he was the one who had saved him, but at the cost of his own life. On reaching the mission he found Fr James out of danger. The moral of the story was, that if the people of Ireland knew what good effects the Gospel was having in Africa, there would be no shortage of missionaries.

Pat's ingenuous articles succeeded in painting a simple picture of life on the missions. He wrote with something of the traditional Irish story-teller's turn of phrase: "Poor Obo was in a proper fix"; "The sea was calm as well water"; He didn't feel the night falling, but it was dark when he heard a knock on the door". Despite his reluctance for self-exposure, some of his personal traits and values emerge – dutifulness, prayerfulness, loyalty to the Church. Though revealing satisfaction with his work and relations with the people, his pen inevitably indicated that he still had a little of the contemporary European (often unconscious) patronising attitude towards Africans – with the help of his equally-superior Irish readers' prayers, he would do his best "to save the benighted Africans' souls from Hell". One can see too that his thoughts frequently drifted homewards. Did he give away something about his own childhood when, in one of the articles, he contrasted the joy and happiness of African children with "poor, sad" Irish youngsters? In these few, brief, literary sallies, Pat couldn't help revealing that he was a serious fellow, even when he was joking! Surely not all women in Western Nigeria would agree with him that "marriage is the day of misfortune" – and he wasn't joking when he said that.

While Pat was reticent about mentioning names or talking about others, his former superior and now his bishop, Thomas Broderick, was not. Of course it was his duty to keep the Provincial, who was also a personal friend, well informed: "Phil Cassidy is a hot-headed S.F. [Sinn Féiner]" (he's up against the arrogant Captain Archer the pro-Moslem District Officer resident in Agenebode); "Fr Cermenati has a volatile temperament" (he's at loggerheads with the Moslem paramount chief of Okene); "Fr X is disgruntled, his Carmelite novice master told him, 'You were born awkward, you will live awkward and die awkward', a prophetic utterance that has already been verified over and over"; "O'Hea is *sui generis*"; "Flynn is abnormally hot-headed, dictatorial and off-handed with chiefs"; "Fr G is lonely, does nothing, and is a problem"; "Fr O'Herlihy is too severe"; "Cullen shows a Bolshevist mind" and "Cavagnera has Bolshevist views"; "in general the Irish are anti law and order".

At first Pat escaped such scathing remarks, only giving the Bishop cause for concern about his health, "All the Fathers are quite well, Fr Kelly however complains of piles". And, "Quite recently Frs Kelly and Heffernan [who recruited Pat] were in hospital – the former run down owing, I believe, to inattention to kitchen and house cleanliness. Then he has such mixtures – coconut water onto which he pours raw cocoa. He suffered from ingrowing toenails, possibly due to too thick socks, too small boots, or inattention to both. I have not heard what Nicholas Heffernan was suffering from – very probably stomach trouble or fever".

In the Seminary, Broderick had been a stickler on matters of hygiene, table manners, tidiness and cleanliness. Lack of attention to these on the missions infuriated him. Writing to the new Provincial, Maurice Slattery, a fellow Kerry man, he said, "Some of our men keep their houses in a wretched way, no order, no neatness – soiled linen that even the people comment on. As for the latrines ------- (sic). The Irish hovel seems to pursue some of our men – no matter how often they are spoken to. Cleanliness, I repeat, should be <u>pounded</u> into their heads, their hands, their whole person, their linen, their rooms, their beds".

In 1925 Broderick visited Eku and found Pat on top of a ladder, "Fr Kelly looks quite well. He's building a new house. It should be completed in May". Perhaps the Bishop didn't appreciate the finer points of Pat's architecture, or thought the existing bungalow had been quite all right, whatever was bothering him, he continued with some very unflattering observations on Pat, "Poor man – he speaks English as a native – 'Make Mass' et cetera, even in his church announcements. And such a stutter – repeating words four and five times in the presence of clever natives! White men must think his upbringing sadly neglected".

Illnesses and deaths
It wasn't the spirit of the times to wear one's heart on one's sleeve, nevertheless Pat was more reserved than most in keeping his feelings to himself. He hadn't mentioned the Founder's grave at Freetown, nor did he mention the near tragic end of the Society there in 1859 when all the pioneer missionaries had been wiped out. During his first tour, death still struck quickly and arbitrarily in the West Coast. Scarcely had he arrived when, George Lacey, just a year ahead of him in the seminary, died of malaria in Lokoja. George, a hardy young man from the island of Inishboffin off the Galway coast, was only twenty-nine. Pat's comment was, "It's God's holy will, we must be perfectly resigned, for He knows what's best".

Another premature death was that of one of his own classmates, Francis McGovern from Leitrim. Ordained with Pat in 1921, he participated in the same Departure Ceremony and departed for Africa two days after Pat. Appointed to Liberia – the Irish Province's first mission, and arguably the Society's most difficult and unhealthy one – he died suddenly of fever in the mission of Betu on the Kru coast in 1922 at the age of twenty-three. Six months before him Denis O'Hara, only nine months in the country, had died in the same mission aged twenty-nine. Speaking of McGovern's death, Pat said, "The news brought me great sadness. But when I realized that it did not discourage John [Cadogan], it lessened my grief and I understood that the best thing for us to do is to unite our wills with God's holy will. We have great confidence in the Sacred Heart that He will give his special blessing to the work we are doing because of all who died for his sake". When Bishop Broderick heard the news, he wrote to the Provincial, "Is it God's way of blessing the Province – trying it as he tried the Society from the very start? *Sanguis martyrum ...* [The blood of martyrs ... is the seed of Christians]. It brings home to all that the conversion of West Africa is not to be considered a human work, or to be judged by human standards". Not long afterwards, the Kru coast claimed another young life: John Barry from Kerry, only two months in the country, died 6 January 1925, aged twenty-four.

Western Nigeria witnessed other tragic deaths, apart from George Lacey's, during Pat's first tour. A French confrere Pierre Piotin, "apostle of the Etsakos", called "the good white man" by the people, died in 1924. In 1926, two young men of the Irish Province, Phil Cassidy (whose letters we have quoted), and William Bond died within two months of one another. Bond had worked for a short time with Pat in Eku before being appointed to Sapele. He died in one of Sapele's outstations – Benin City. Sixty years later, Pat, in retirement said, "In my last year in Eku, Fr Bond an Englishman, was appointed 'second man' to me, but then they decided to make Sapele a residential station and after a month or two he went to take charge there and died shortly afterwards". Unsentimentally, Pat continued, "There was another Father called Cassidy who got blackwater fever after a long journey on a bicycle and died". Cassidy, ordained the year before Pat, like him, loved the Irish language and delighted in local customs and stories both Irish and African. Not long before Phil's death, Pat spoke of "anticipating a hearty shake hands from Phil" and of "showing him a kind *céad míle fáilte* when he comes to Eku". A number of men after experiencing 'close calls' with death in Western Nigeria had to be invalided home. One of them was Michael O'Donohue, who was with Pat on the voyage to Africa. He became very ill in Onitsha-Olona and had to be sent home in August 1922. Pat, who had not seen him since their ways parted in Warri, believed that "the climate did not agree with him at all". (O'Donohue never fully recovered and died in New York in 1935). Phil Cassidy, a late vocation, was thirty-seven when he died. Bond was twenty-nine and Pierre Piotin was an 'old man' of fifty-seven.

The attitude of resignation towards premature death expressed by Pat was not unusual. Deaths did not discourage the missionaries; if anything, they stimulated them. The missionaries believed that their deceased brothers interceded for them in Heaven and that their deaths were sacrifices somehow desired, or even demanded, by the "good God", who had asked no less from His own Son. The Founder of the Society often quoted John 12, 24, "The seed must die if it is to bear fruit". Val Barnicle, who was with Phil Cassidy when he died, said "He died for Africa. He had no regrets in giving his life – it was the one thing he desired". Missionaries of Pat's time, and even later, went to Africa with little expectation of return. The French Revolution had given rise to theories about the necessity of 'blood sacrifice'; later, the Great War, and in Ireland, the Easter Rebellion, re-evoked thoughts about the worthiness of dying for a cause. Missionaries considered the 'salvation of souls' to be the greatest of causes and dying for this cause was identified with the death of the Saviour himself.

Whatever personal sense of loss or sadness Pat suffered interiorly on hearing of the deaths of confreres, externally he did not give the impression of being unduly disturbed or upset; if anything, he pressed on with his work even more energetically, mindful that no one's time was unlimited.

At the end of June 1926, he and John Cadogan, their first five-year tour in Africa completed, took ship for home. Pat was quite run-down. When his superiors in Cork saw him they became concerned for his health and, being also concerned to staff their new seminary in the North of Ireland, they appointed him Professor of Moral Theology.

'Dromantine castle'

Chapter 4

DROMANTINE, 1926-1929

The African Missions major seminary on Blackrock Road, even from its early years, was felt to be too small. As years went by, the number of students increased and the site, situated in a residential area, did not allow for expansion. The Province also wished to have a presence outside of Cork and the West of Ireland. The Provincial Assembly of 1925 gave Fr Maurice Slattery, Provincial Superior, the task of finding a suitable place in which to re-locate the seminary. An astute man of action, by May 1926 he had found a magnificent house and property in County Down, seven miles north of Newry. "Dromantine Castle", the ancient seat of the Magennises, had been taken over by the Innes family and one of them, Arthur Innes, built a fine Georgian mansion on an elevated part of the land in 1806. His son Charles Arthur, fifty years later, re-built the house in Italian-Renaissance style. This impressive mansion of cut sandstone stood on 300 acres of arable land, pasture and woodland. Some of the demesne near the house was given over to an exotic-sounding "Pleasure Garden" and, in front, at a lower level, was an extensive artificially dammed lake, home to ducks, swans and fish. From the house there was a magnificent view of lake and rolling drumlin hills. The Mountains of Mourne could be seen to the east, and the craggy head of Slieve Gullion to the south. Slattery thought it eminently suitable and wasted no time in buying it.

The transition from Blackrock Road to Dromantine took place in September 1926 under the care of William Butler, Vice Provincial and Superior of the new seminary. The vice superior was Martin Lavelle from Inishboffin who, since ordination in 1918, had been teaching in the Society's seminaries of Cloughballymore and

Blackrock. In Dromantine he taught dogmatic theology and sacred scripture. The Spiritual Director was Henry Baker, who, ordained in 1915, spent eight years on Liberia's Kru Coast and in Monrovia before being invalided home. He had taught in Blackrock until the move to Dromantine, where he lectured on pastoral theology and liturgy. The professor of canon law, church history and music was "Red Paddy" McKenna. Ordained the year before Pat, he had been spiritual director and teacher in Wilton. He shared Pat's great love of the Irish language. The bursar was John Prendergast who had spent many years in Egypt, and since 1921 had been procurator of the Province's house in Liverpool. Pat, with five years in Western Nigeria, completed the staff's wide range of home and mission experience.

Dromantine 1926
Staff and students with Dr Mulhern, Bishop of Dromore
Left to right seated: Paddy McKenna, John Prendergast, Henry Baker, William Butler (superior), Bishop Mulhern of Dromore, Maurice Slattery (Provincial Superior), Martin Lavelle, Pat Kelly.

"Dromantine Castle", opened its doors to students for the first time on 21 September 1926. There were forty-seven, theologians only, in four classes from first to fourth year theology. Much of the first term was devoted to settling in. A hydro-electric system powered by a turbine at the outflow of the lake was supposed to light the college and pump water, but it almost emptied the lake after two or three nights in use. An oil-powered generator was procured and it proved more satisfactory for lighting; the turbine continued to be used for pumping water. The first week in 1926 was devoted to preparations for the college's official opening on 29 September. The bishop of Dromore, Dr Edward Mulhern, who had welcomed the Society to his diocese, presided over the ceremonies, which were attended by a host of well-wishers. Pat was deacon at the solemn High Mass. The student choir, ably conducted by Fr McKenna, performed superbly. The Provincial led the after-dinner speeches, toasting the Pope and expressing the Society's gratitude to Dr Mulhern who, in turn, proposed a toast to Fr Slattery, the College and the students. He then spoke energetically on "Catholic Rights, Ireland and the Gospel Message". A few days later, Newry's *Frontier Sentinel* published a full-page account of the "Inspiring Scenes" at Dromantine in an article entitled "Dromantine Castle's new Career", which was accompanied by photographs of the house, staff, students, Dr Mulhern and Fr Slattery.

Not as well off as the professors for panoramic views, the students were, nevertheless, comfortably accommodated. A second year student, James Ward, who kept a diary since his childhood in Belfast wrote:

> September 1926: I am very well lodged here in a big attic with two skylights and one companion, John O'Flaherty. John was far-seeing and supplied himself with some pretty prints and colours, these we now have around our walls and things look homely and neat, and we are exerting every effort to make things look even more so. [Later with snow

visible on the Mournes, James recorded] The turf-fire is in now; but the electric light is not very good so far, there are no accumulators [batteries] at all.

Perhaps the 'grandeur' of his new surroundings, influenced the morale of the young diarist, he found it hard to re-capture the spiritual fervour of his Blackrock seminary days chiefly due, he thought, to "timidity regarding fasting and abstinence since the Superior pulled me up over it". He intended seeking spiritual advice on the point, "I have chosen Fr Lavelle as my Director, or at least as Confessor this year. My discipline is also lying idle – more shame to me". The discipline was a whip or scourge, part of the ascetical equipment of the era. Self-administered, even "to the drawing of blood", it was recommended for keeping sensual passions in check. Reeds grew on the banks of Dromantine lake and the students harvested them to make scourges, which they called 'whangs'. Quite a market for these developed among the stricter religious orders around the country. John Cadogan, who joined the staff temporarily in October, told the students that a dose of prickly heat in West Africa would render the whangs unnecessary.

For the new location, some changes were made in the seminary rule of Blackrock. Smoking was permitted, but only out-of-doors; in wet weather, the recreation hall could be used. Card games were allowed but, "stakes in games are strictly limited". Young Ward, as zealous for smoking and card playing as he was for using his 'discipline', won nine shillings at Solo in his first term. Student walks were changed from Wednesday to Sunday, and were made "in one body" as before the "troubled times" in Cork. Newry was out of bounds and, to avoid numerous trips to town, a doctor, a dentist and a tailor visited regularly.

Without the benefit of any extra courses in moral theology, Professor Kelly relied heavily on the three-volume *Summa Theologiae Moralis* of Hieronymous Noldin, the contemporary luminary on the subject. A Jesuit, Noldin had spent nineteen years teaching before publishing his great work, which treated of fundamental problems relating to the commandments and the sacraments and was replete with appendices on the thorny questions of the sixth commandment, marriage, and ecclesiastical penalties. Pat prepared his lectures with painstaking diligence and attention to detail. One of his students, Martin Bane (a future missionary in Western Nigeria), noted in his book *Heroes of the Hinterland* that Professor Kelly had "a mania for the small print and the footnotes". However, Pat was able to bring an African flavour to his marriage cases and, in response to rascally student queries, could elaborate a little more on the life of Obo and the heroic Fr Séan. Ironically, Bishop Broderick had advised the Provincial in 1925 that the Professor of Moral Theology in the home seminary should be in touch with the Missions so that he could give examples of real African cases. The Administration took his point, but went a step further appointing to the post a man from his own mission.

In October, after attending his brother's funeral, Paddy McKenna went down with a heavy cold which turned into pneumonia. As it became serious, John Cadogan, on home leave (then one year's duration), was called in to take Paddy's canon law classes while Fr Butler took church history. McKenna's music classes were ably led by the more musically-talented students: Johannes O'Shea on harmonium, James Ward on violin, John Kilbey on clarinet, and Tommy Greene on flute. Cadogan concluded his classes in December. Bidding him farewell, Pat felt a little envious, as John was returning to Nigeria. Meanwhile two Alexian brothers had come from Warrenpoint to look after McKenna. After consultation with two doctors, it was decided to operate to remove an abscess from his lungs. The operation was successfully carried out in Dromantine by a Belfast surgeon.

Before the Christmas break, examinations were held. Pat's were the longest – three hours. A conscientious marker, he didn't believe in being generous with his marks; more students appeared to fail Moral than any other subject. Those who failed exams had to remain for two weeks during holidays to catch up, and those who repeatedly failed moral or dogma would either be dismissed or have their promotion to Clerical Orders postponed. Other causes of dismissal included, visiting another student's room, consorting with the girls in the kitchen, or writing "love letters".

At the end of January '27, Dr Mulhern ordained nine deacons and two sub-deacons from Dromantine in Newry cathedral. Among them were men who, after priestly ordination in June, would be sailing for Western Nigeria: Tommy Greene, Walter Keary and Danny O'Connell. Dr Mulhern was a frequent visitor to Dromantine, sometimes bringing other dignitaries with him, like Mgr McCaffrey, the President of Maynooth. Word spread about the beauty of the new seminary and its surroundings, and it received many visitors, especially missionaries on leave. Leo Taylor called in January the same year, before departing for the 'Vicariate of the Bight of Benin' as the jurisdiction of Lagos was then called. In October '28, the Superior General, Jean-Marie Chabert, and his Vicar, Edouard Laqueyrie, escorted by Fr Slattery, made an official visitation. Before their arrival, a thorough clean-up took place. Classes were suspended for three days so that the students could get the Pleasure Grounds into shape. Mgr Joseph Shanahan CSSp, Vicar Apostolic of 'Southern Nigeria' and his Coadjutor Dr Heerey visited, as also did Frs Blowick, O'Boyle and Tierney of the "Chinese Mission". Their visits reminded Pat of his own mission and, wondering if he would ever see Nigeria again, let his superiors know that he wanted to return.

For exercise, he liked walking the fields, and hunting rabbits, which were so numerous that they were a pest in farm and garden. He may well have had some skill in this, because, when John Creaven, a future Provincial Superior, was doing research in

67

the National Library, Dublin, the head librarian told him of a wonderful holiday he had spent in Dromantine, the highlight of which was a rabbit shooting expedition with Fr Kelly. Pat showed him how to creep up close, to get within range before firing. However, Pat's hunting sprees were insufficient to keep the rabbit population down and a professional trapper had to be brought in.

Confined indoors on wet days, Pat browsed in the Library. Many of the books there, like those in Blackrock, reflected the spirituality of the times. They were grim and dolorous with titles like, *The Sufferings of Our Lord Jesus Christ*, (with contemplations on His 'forty-nine sufferings'); *The Via Dolorosa*, which, Pat saw in the register, had been borrowed by James Ward; and books in French like, *Le Bréviaire des Vies Souffrances*, and heavy tomes of moral theology in Latin like *Casus Conscientiae*, which Pat felt he ought to read, sometime.

In October '28, Paddy McKenna, fully recovered in health, departed from Dromantine to take up a new appointment in Liberia. The students knew of Pat's desire to return to Africa and were sympathetic. Ward noted in his diary, "Fr McKenna is going out. Poor Fr Kelly is disgruntled at being turned down again". McKenna was replaced by Joseph Donaghy, who had been invalided home from Liberia.

Paying heed to a pre-Christmas vacation warning that "unreasonable late-coming" in the New Year would result in the loss of a week's holiday in summer, the students all returned promptly on 22 January '29. By the end of the month most of them were sick with influenza. Staff members, Pat, Henry Baker and Joseph Donaghy were also smitten. Early retiring and "late" rising (6.30 a.m.) were prescribed for all. However by 6 February the students were well enough to attend a matinee performance of *Iolanthe* in Newry town hall, performed by St Patrick's Operatic Company. Pat's thoughts, while he was recovering from the 'flu, turned more and more to Africa. Though he liked Dromantine, appreciated the opportunity of visiting his family in Tristaun, and of spending holidays in Connemara improving his Irish, he did not feel that professing moral theology was what he wanted to do for the rest of his life. His heart was in Africa and, fearing that if he didn't get away soon he might never get the chance, he wrote to the Provincial requesting re-appointment to Nigeria. This time his wish was granted and, even though he had only three-quarters of his Noldin course completed, he sailed for Africa in October 1929 with the young men ordained that year.

Chapter 5

NIGERIA, 1929-1934

For his second voyage to Nigeria, Pat embarked on the m.v. *Adda*, sailing from Liverpool on 12 October, 1929. On board were his former students of the class of '29, James Ward and Paddy Hughes, both of whom had been appointed to the Vicariate of the Bight of Benin, and Tom Duffy, Bill Fegan, John Lynott and George McCormack who, like himself, were going to Western Nigeria. Pat didn't write about this journey but Ward, ever the keen diarist, recorded events like landing at Freetown, stopping at Takoradi, and encounters and conversations with passengers and crew members. He didn't mention "PJ Kelly" until after disembarking at Lagos on 23 October when he and Pat went to stay with Fr Georges Laugel at Laviagi, as the main mission, Holy Cross, could not accommodate all of the arrivals. Ward remained there when Pat and the others departed a few days later by lorry for Asaba.

At Asaba, Bishop Broderick warmly welcomed them all. After entertaining the newcomers, he called Pat aside and told him that, for the time being, he was appointing him to Sapele, whose parish priest, Pat Shine, had just gone on home leave. During most of Pat's first tour, Sapele had been a non-residential outstation cared for by John Cadogan based in Warri thirty miles away. A large port town on one of the Niger river creeks, Sapele was a busy place due to its timber industry. The huge forests of the hinterland contained some of the world's most valuable timber, 'Sapele mahogany', 'Bini wood', 'Obeche', iroko, cedar and other types. The first sawmill in Nigeria was built in Koko, an outstation of Sapele, in 1912 by Miller Brothers of Liverpool.

Sapele's 'Africa Timber and Plywood Company' was already on its way to becoming the second largest timber company in the world. The port town also had rubber factories, flour mills, grain stores and a navy depot. The timber industry, factories and mills attracted thousands of workers, many of whom were Catholic Ibos from eastern Nigeria. The port was 80 miles from the sea, but large ships could sail right up to it and it was connected by a rough road to Benin City, 30 miles away. Road users began their journey by crossing the Ethiope river on a precarious 'car ferry' which consisted of a timber platform resting on two large canoes.

The first baptisms recorded in Sapele took place on 22 October 1922, when an infant was baptised by John Cadogan and an adult by Bishop Broderick. The first resident priest was the short-lived William Bond who, after an initiation period in Warri, lived briefly with Pat at Eku, before taking up residence on his own in Sapele. Three months later, while returning to his base from Ibadan on a motor cycle, he began to feel ill and stopped at Benin City, one of his outstations. His condition rapidly deteriorated and he died of yellow fever within a few days. Aged twenty-nine, he was less than one year in Africa. After his death, Pat Shine, who had also been with Pat for a while, was appointed to Sapele. He remained there a long time, becoming known as "Oga Shine" because he addressed everyone as "Oga", a title of respect. Illness finally forced him to leave Sapele, and Africa, for good in 1942.

Labour camps of different tribesmen, Urhobos, Itsekiris, Ijaws, Ibos and others had developed around the town and farther afield where the tree-felling and rubber-tapping took place. Cadogan had begun regular visitation of the camps, many of which were difficult of access and required the use of canoes. On arrival at a camp or outstation, the missionaries erected their own tents and remained for a week or two. When Pat arrived, Sapele had nearly 900 Catholics and 12 outstations. The parish extended about twenty miles westwards along the Benin river to Koko, and about the same distance southwards towards Warri. His former mission, Eku, twenty-eight miles to the south east, had no resident priest, so it also fell under his care. He was happy to be back in Africa and, now in his mid-thirties, he felt more self-confident than he had in his first tour.

He wrote an occasional letter for the *African Missionary*, telling a bit about his parish and appealing for prayers and funds. On the days he visited the Catholics in the timber concessions and rubber plantations to say Mass, he had to start off very early in the morning as the men began work at 5.30 a.m. In one camp he found himself saying Mass in "the smallest church in the world". "I was head and shoulders over the eaves, but the Christians in these isolated places are often an example to those more fortunately situated". He gave a humorous, but telling example of their simple faith, "A man came to me a few days ago with an offering for Mass, 'that God would take out of the minds of thieves the thought of stealing my clothes again'. The poor man had already been relieved of £6 or £7 worth – his entire possessions".

A new-fangled machine becoming popular at the time was the motor cycle. Pat quickly learned to use Shine's, finding it was much like a bicycle but faster, noisier, and more expensive to run. A disadvantage, he thought, was that once travelling at speed you didn't feel like stopping to greet people along the way. Of course it was less fatiguing than the 'push bike' and was a great boon for visiting distant outstations.

Personally devoted to Our Lady and the rosary, one of the first things he did at Sapele was to found a Holy Rosary Society. A photo in the *African Missionary* of January 1931 shows him seated in the midst of twenty men all dressed in white, rosary beads about their necks or in their hands. Likely he also formed a female branch, but no photograph appeared!

Pat Kelly with members of the Holy Rosary Society,
Sapele, 1930.

His mud church at Sapele, too small for the congregation, was in poor condition; one of its walls had collapsed during the previous year's rains. He began to build a large church that could double as a school. In the first few months, with the aid of a good brick layer, rapid progress was made. But when his stock of cement, which had become increasingly scarce and expensive due to the World recession, ran out he lacked money to buy more. Regretfully, he dismissed the bricklayer, leaving the partially-built church exposed to the elements and in danger of being washed away. With the onset of the rainy season, he felt like the man in the Gospel who began to build but could not finish. The thought of failure, both worried and galvanized him into action. Quickly writing an appeal, in English, for publication in the *African Missionary*, he endeavoured to loosen his readers' purse strings by contrasting his situation with that of nearby Protestant missionaries, "How the heretics with their Cathedral-like places of worship not more than a few hundred yards away will point their fingers in derision! There is yet time to come to the rescue. A gift of £200 would save Sapele's future new church from its inevitable fate and, besides laying up treasure in Heaven, some generous benefactors would earn the lasting gratitude of one poor missionary".

Though busy with building, Pat did not neglect pastoral visitation. "Trekking in the bush is the only work that counts out here, the oftener you see the people the better", he told the Provincial, and, referring to a new man, said "He's showing what a missionary can do. Six long weeks in Ijaw country and no sooner back than he's off to the Bush again". Pat, of course, was doing the same, but didn't mention it. More at ease in his contact with the people, he was approaching fluency in the major languages. While engaged in church matters, visiting the sick, catechizing, or "sending souls to Heaven", he was never in a rush, exhibiting more of an African sense of time than European. Mass, or the administration of other sacraments, especially in outstations, could take place at any time, even after nightfall! But delays were always "in favour of the faith", never for his personal convenience. His only hurry was to spread the Gospel as far as possible and to save as many souls as fast as possible. Thus motivated, he rode his motor cycle and drove his car, when eventually he got one, at too great a speed, sometimes with near-tragic results for the human race and, quite often, with tragic results for fowl and livestock. But, whenever bird or beast fell victim to his driving, he always returned to make restitution to the owner, if not on the day of the incident, shortly afterwards. Then, after haggling over the value of the deceased animal, he always paid up.

Despite his desire to go fast, he never lost his love for the humble bicycle, and always used it around town and on shorter trips. Once on a very hot day when cycling to an outstation, with five or six miles to go he stopped and asked someone for water. He was given palm wine, a very fine non-intoxicating drink when fresh, but potent alcohol when fermented. "I drank it and continued on my bicycle as if I had no legs, as if my feet were not on the pedals at all", he said. Though abstemious, he usually kept a bottle of beer or two in the house for visitors.

In 1931, Georges Krauth, at home in Alsace, was preparing to return to Africa. On hearing that Pat was back in Western Nigeria, he wrote to Fr Slattery, "I wish to thank you in particular for having sent Fr Pat Kelly once more to the missions. You know that we worked together for four or five years and I have always looked on him as a holy priest who needs must draw down on his work the blessings of God. I shall be immensely glad to meet him in spring somewhere in Eku or Sapele".

1931, Society 'Visitor'

Bishop Broderick had a number of commitments to look forward to during his Leave 1931-1932: the Silver Jubilee of his priesthood in July '31; the Provincial and General Assemblies the same year, and the Eucharistic Congress in Dublin the following year. During his previous leave in 1925, he had visited his brother in America, but this time he would confine himself to the Assemblies and the Congress. He worried about the running of the Vicariate in his absence. Fr Eugene Strub, an Alsatian, was Pro-Vicar since Broderick had become bishop in 1918. An outstanding missionary, Strub had arrived in 'Upper Niger' in 1898. In addition to his pastoral work, he was writing a history of the Vicariate and had contributed a number of articles on African art and culture to scientific magazines in Europe. Musically talented, he played the harmonium and conducted a three-part choir in Asaba. He had also been Society 'Visitor' or 'religious superior' up to 1925 but, with the increasing numbers of Irish missionaries in the Vicariate, it became more appropriate to have an Irish confrere in that role and William Porter was appointed. In 1930, Porter was transferred to Northern Nigeria as Prefect Apostolic, and John Cadogan became the Visitor. However, Cadogan, as Visitor, would also be attending the

Assemblies, so someone else was needed to look after the Vicariate.

The office of Visitor, a Provincial appointment, had been established to see to the confreres' spiritual and temporal needs on the missions. The Visitor was rather like a Society superior, responsible to the Provincial. His role included keeping the Provincial informed as to how men and mission were faring and how the Society's rule was being observed. Having only consultative voice in his appointment, the missionaries were inclined to regard him as a spy and, as he acted for the Society and the superiors based at home, the Bishop, concerned for the local church and responsible to Rome, was inclined to see him as a rival or as an obstacle to local progress. Often, the Visitor's lot was not a happy one. While Society authorities tried to articulate his precise role, most of those appointed to it tried to have themselves replaced as quickly as possible, and most of the confreres prayed that the office would be abolished.

Broderick wondered whether Strub could be Pro-Vicar *and* act as Visitor at the same time, but quickly dismissed the idea. Strub was getting on in years, and while still a wonderful missionary, he was, in the Bishop's opinion, too soft, especially on the Irish, who were much more demanding than the Continentals and needed firm handling, "It costs me twice as much to maintain an Irish missionary as a Continental", he grumbled. It also irritated him that his compatriots didn't volunteer to overstay their five-year tour as the Alsatians did. In fact, the Irish were even clamouring to have it reduced! Strub, who already had nine years done in his present tour, had told him that he would stay on for another year in view of the impending absence of the Bishop. Nevertheless it would be decidedly better to have an Irish confrere acting as Visitor. Broderick wanted someone with a sense of dignity and decorum as well as having a sense of responsibility and ability to lead, someone who presented himself well and, for instance, followed the Bishop's instructions about wearing the white soutane and cape. Pat Kelly came to mind, but not for his dress-sense. He *did* wear a cassock, but it was usually far from white. He lacked 'sparkle' in other ways too but, these the Bishop knew, weighed far less in the balance than his undoubted zeal, progress in the vernacular languages, and prayerfulness. Though not a great socialiser, "Pajo" as he was known, was popular with his Irish confreres and with the Alsatians. Broderick made up his mind; it would have to be Kelly and he informed Cork of his choice. Pat was duly confirmed as Acting Visitor by the Provincial. Hence, scarcely a year and a half in Sapele, he moved to Warri when Cadogan left. He didn't at all desire this appointment, and even less wanted to keep it. But, after the Provincial Assembly, Cadogan was appointed to Dromantine and Pat was left as Society Visitor. The same Assembly returned Stephen Harrington as Provincial and Maurice Slattery as Provincial Bursar.

"Sacred Heart" mission, Warri, had grown in the ten years since Pat had disembarked there in 1921. It now had forty-five outstations, nearly 2000 Catholics and eleven schools. Its founder, Luigi Cavagnera, had built an impressive mission house in Italian style which could comfortably accommodate four Fathers. When he went on leave in 1923, he had been replaced by John Cadogan who, among other activities, had begun the building of the large church which was eventually completed by Danny O'Connell and Bill Fegan in 1930. There were four main tribes in the area: Urhobo (the largest), Ijaw, Isoko and Okwani and some smaller tribes like the Itsekiri inhabiting the swampy territory of the Niger delta. Each tribe had its own language, though Urhobo and Isoko were similar, and Ibo was widely spoken. At Sunday Masses, sermons, given in English, were normally translated by interpreters into Ibo and Urhobo which, of course, lengthened the already very long ceremonies. With mosquitos reported to be "as big as elephants", average temperatures at 86 degrees Fahrenheit, high humidity, and hardly any place more than 5 feet above sea-level, the parish of Warri was a difficult place in which to work.

As Visitor, Pat had more than pastoral duties to perform. An important one was distributing and accounting for Mass intentions for all the priests of the Vicariate. Stipends for Masses offered by members of the Society do not go to the individual priest, but to the Society. Mass intentions and stipends were sent to the missions by the bursar in Cork, the Visitor endeavouring to ensure that there were enough intentions for all the priests of the mission, in Pat's case, twenty-three. As well, he had to keep an accurate account of stipends received and Masses discharged. Keeping the account was not easy, as not all Fathers were prompt in sending in their monthly 'returns' of Masses said to the Visitor. Donors' requests for different kinds of Masses also complicated the task, for there were not only 'single' Masses, but also 'novenas' (nine consecutive Masses to be said by the same priest), and 'Gregorians' (thirty consecutive Masses). Pat asked Maurice Slattery about the possibility of allowing the interruption of novenas, "The reason I ask is that most of our men are a great part of the time alone and are liable to be down with fever any day". Men who resided far from the nearest mission station did not find it easy to get another priest to fulfil the obligation to say a Mass if they were ill or called away. Another query he had was about the exact day the missionaries' obligation to say Mass for "Superior's intentions" began – on arrival in the mission (which was what they were doing), or when they boarded ship at Liverpool, which was what the Rule seemed to say, "but only Fr McGettigan observed it that way". He decided not to stir things up just then, unless Cork insisted.

In 1931, in his first letter as Visitor, he asked Fr Slattery for 480 masses per fortnight for the following two months. Later, he thanked him for a thousand masses, saying he now had 4,000 in reserve. At the end of September he had 6,000 Masses to discharge, but had sent 250 'Dollar Mass intentions' to the Visitor in Lagos, who was in short supply. Stipend money was banked by Eugene Strub in Asaba (and he didn't approve of Pat's largesse in giving away dollar intentions to Lagos; the usual Mass stipend from Ireland was four shillings). Pat didn't know how much Strub had in the bank and the Pro-Vicar wasn't in a hurry to tell him. Mass stipends were a major part of the Vicariate's income, and Pat, with his scrupulous disposition, took this part of his office very seriously both financially and spiritually.

Recession, following the Wall Street crash in 1929, brought hardship and poverty to many people worldwide and resulted in diminishing financial support for missionary work. Straitened circumstances in Ireland were exacerbated by the "Tariff War" of the early Thirties when England ceased buying Irish beef. In 1933, the number of Mass intentions Pat received was well down on previous years, and he feared the number would drop to half, or even lower, the following year, "Cash will be a greater difficulty than low numbers of men in the future", he said. In September he begged Slattery, "for a cheque for Asaba as a 'Christmas box' so as to enable us to carry on until March without going into debt". In 1934 he pleaded for an extra hundred Masses a month, cutely 'bribing' the bursar with gifts of Nigerian birds' eggs and Bini bronzes. As well as numbers, the value of Mass stipends also dropped, from a pre-Recession average of four shillings to two shillings and six pence in 1935. Though worried, externally Pat retained his unflappable manner and exhibited a great ability to make-do. In 1934 he was able to state, "despite the slackness of the past year or two, I hope to be able to hand over as good a banking account as there was when Mgr Broderick went home".

Another task of the Visitor was the sorting out of problems between confreres, and between them and the people or government officials. Such problems in Nigeria came under the general name of 'palaver' and there was no end to the number and kind of palavers. Pat proved to be very good at solving them, so good that the Bishop began to hand over more and more of them to him, sometimes even transferring a difficult missionary to Warri to live for a while in the remedial presence of the Visitor. This demanded a lot of patience and good humour on Pat's part – qualities he had, "You see now Father, I'm a rascal too, but I'm a more likeable one than you!" was how he began to disarm one contentious confrere.

While Broderick was in Ireland, Pat handled all the palavers, telling the Provincial not to bother the Bishop if he wasn't already aware of the case. After returning from the Eucharistic Congress however, the Bishop was suddenly faced with a 'big palaver'. A deputation of all the elders of a sizeable village came, alleging that one of his priests had burned a house, killed a goat, broken calabashes, and beaten women! The Bishop was taken aback; but much farther aback when the accused admitted guilt on all counts! On investigating, the Bishop discovered, to his horror, that not only were the charges true, but that the Father had also dismissed Catholic teachers on unproven charges, falsified annual returns of the mission, and was frequently absent from his station without permission. "Briefly", said Broderick, "I found it imperative to relieve him of his charge and I appointed him to teach in a Training College". "But", the Bishop explained with irritation, "the Father refused to comply, hence I had to uphold authority by suspending him and hand him over to the Visitor".

Pat welcomed the delinquent to Warri and, after a short time, reported to the Provincial with a masterpiece of understatement, "Father O and Bishop had small palaver which they settled up". Later he confirmed, "Yes that matter was settled up all right between His Lordship and Fr O. He is here in Warri at the moment and will probably continue here to the end of his tour. I find him all right, save that he does not yet fully understand that we cannot afford liquor every day, but I will try my best in that respect". Before long a "Detailed Statement" from *G.B. Ollivant and Co. Ltd.*, a general provision store in Warri, addressed to Fr O for goods bought between 22 November and 29 December, arrived on Pat's desk. The bill was for the purchase of whiskey and soda (seven bottles of White Horse and six packs of soda). The only other 'groceries' bought were, two tins of Prize Cup Cigarettes, one tin of pure butter and two jars of chicken soup. The bill for the whole lot came to £4.14. 3. A bottle of White Horse in those days cost 9s and 9d and butter 1s and 3d. No doubt Pat appreciated how much Fr O was saving on foodstuff!

It should not be thought that Pat was soft on rogues or lacked gumption to deal with them. "More than one developed a taste for intoxicants", he said, writing to the Provincial about another man, who had to be invalided home, adding, "Under no consideration should he return here or to any other Mission".

A different type of problem, and a more painful one for the Visitor, was dealing with cases of sudden death. Ten months after Pat's return to Nigeria (when Cadogan was Visitor), twenty-nine year old Walter Keary from Bohola, Co Mayo, died in Kabba. Pat knew him well, as he was in the senior class in Dromantine in 1926 and was one of the first group of African missionaries to be ordained in Newry, 16 June 1927. He was appointed to Western Nigeria where, in August 1930, he contracted blackwater fever and died within four days. Writing to his parents Bishop Broderick said, "Blackwater fever, still largely a mystery to medical men, is fatal in the majority of cases. God in His inscrutable designs demanded the supreme sacrifice – the death of Fr Walter for the conversion of the pagans".

Pat wasn't long in office, when one of the men he greatly admired since seminary days, James McGettigan, died in Asaba. After a long time at home, McGettigan finally received a mission appointment, Western Nigeria. When he arrived in Asaba in October 1931, Bishop Broderick put him on the staff of his small seminary and made him Procurator of the Vicariate. Sadly, eleven months later, he died of malaria. Remembered by small children for the sweets he gave them, he was remembered by adults for his kindness, holiness, and for baptising Patrick Ugboko, who became the first Asaban to be ordained a priest.

Pat wrote to William Butler, Vice Provincial and Superior in Blackrock, "It is very sad news and God willing there will not be such a sad story from the missions again". As Visitor he had to administer McGettigan's temporal affairs and, as it was his first time being involved in such a task, he didn't realize the importance of keeping letters and receipts relating to the deceased's belongings. An officious Chief Registrar worried him about a few personal effects Pat had sent to McGettigan's brother in Donegal: "a fountain pen, pocket watch; a picture worth 1 shilling; a small case worth about 3 shillings; and a pocket book worth 3 shillings". The brother sent a letter of acknowledgement, but Pat mislaid it. The Registrar refused to cooperate until Pat got another letter from Ireland. Small as the incident was, it upset Pat and showed his great need to get things right 'according to the letter of the law'.

The unexpected death of McGettigan sorely grieved the Bishop, "I thought him the strongest Father in Nigeria, his death was one of the many sacrifices demanded by God in his inscrutable designs for the conversion of Nigeria's millions". At this stage one might be forgiven for querying these "inscrutable designs", and asking *why* God required so many sacrifices, or any sacrifices. But the missionaries weren't asking such questions. Unknown to Broderick, more "supreme sacrifices" were soon to follow and the next "victim" would be himself. His personal 'way of the cross' had already begun but, mindful that he had often preached to others about willingness to suffer, he had kept to himself the increasingly severe stomach pains he was experiencing. In December he admitted that he had "excruciating pain". Doctors in Lagos diagnosed severe kidney disease and told him it was imperative that he go home for an operation. Having decided to go, he again worried about the administration of the Vicariate in his absence, "I only wish I had a more suitable man for the job than Fr Strub. He has no memory and he is hopeless as far as discipline is concerned. I shall try to get Kelly or Fr Krauth to assist him". Bishop O'Rourke of Lagos appreciated the seriousness of Broderick's condition and his difficulty in choosing a Pro-Vicar. Writing to the Provincial he said, "Broderick is in a very bad state of health ... the doctors give him six months ... Fr Strub does not seem to have any control over the Fathers and Fr Kelly is scrupulous and cannot come to any decision on important matters".

On 15 December 1932, Broderick wrote a Circular to the missionaries announcing his departure and the appointment of PJ Kelly as Pro-Vicar and Fr Strub as Vicar Delegate. This brief one-page typed circular, not as impressive as his copperplate handwritten letters, was mainly about the impecunious state of the Vicariate. He begged the missionaries to cooperate with the new Pro-Vicar: not to incur extraordinary expenses or demand money from Asaba; not to contract debts – a subject that caused him "much anxiety and pain"; to spare every penny, especially to avoid spending money on drink; to be careful and prompt in accounting for church monies and accurate in 'returns' of statistical information. He even went as far as suggesting that the missionaries might try to live without their monthly allocation or, at least, to live on a diminished one. He counselled them to avoid 'palavers'; to see to their own spiritual lives and to give good example. Finally he asked for prayers for a successful outcome of the operation he would have to undergo, and a speedy return to Nigeria. In private, he exacted a promise from Pat that he would not run down the Vicariate's bank balance.

After his departure, he wrote to Pat, indicating that he was hopeful of recovery and glad that Rome was "in no hurry with his resignation". But, after many examinations, no kidney-specialist in Ireland or England would hold out any prospect of a successful operation. In much distress, in January 1933, he wrote to William Butler, "I may never again return to Nigeria. I have cried and sobbed and sighed ... You may consider me as resigned from Western Nigeria". The doctors ruled out return to Nigeria, but advised him to go to the south of France for rest. He went to San Remo on the Italian side of the French border, but his condition continued to deteriorate. On 22 March he sent his formal resignation to Propaganda Fide. In San Remo in August, he heard of a pilgrimage from Genoa to Lourdes. Always regretting that he had not known his own mother – she died when he was an infant – the Mother of God had a special place in his life. In pain and discomfort he joined the pilgrimage. At Lourdes he met the Cardinal Archbishop of Genoa, who introduced him to Professor Durand, chief surgeon of San Martino hospital in Genoa. Professor Durand took a professional interest in him and thought that the removal of one kidney might offer a chance of recovery. A week after surgery, Thomas Broderick, aged fifty-one, passed away, 13 October 1933. He was buried in the Capuchin plot in Genoa's municipal cemetery.

Bishop Broderick, the first bishop of the Irish Province, was described by Tommy Greene, who had been his secretary for six months in Asaba, as "the perfect bishop", and by Michael Collins, his biographer, as "probably the best member of the Irish Province and possibly of the Society in general". The Archbishop of Genoa presided over his Requiem Mass and spoke of Broderick's sufferings borne with fortitude. News of his death was received with great sadness in Western Nigeria. Pat wrote to Maurice Slattery, "Sad news that Dr Broderick passed away so

Bishop Broderick

suddenly after all. Imagine I am just in receipt of a letter from him and a long one at that". Later, he wrote again, "I am very grateful to the Province and the Society for all they have done with regard to the obsequies of our beloved bishop. You have aptly described the winding up of the career of a great Church man and missionary when you said, 'His grave points to Sacrifice'. We never missed our father until he was gone; but I hope that his Vicariate will reap the benefit of his sufferings and that like the Little Flower he will spend his Heaven in doing good upon earth for his spiritual children whom he loved so well. More than once he told me he was offering up all his sufferings for us. Yes, we all pray that God may grant him a worthy successor".

The Bishop had made a will in Asaba in 1928, in which he bequeathed his ecclesiastical outfit to his successor; his library to candidates for the priesthood; personal money for "Four shilling Masses" for the repose of his soul and his intentions; his watches to his brother Daniel; and his episcopal rings to his sister-in-law Gertrude. His pectoral cross, a cheap French one worth about £3, was given to the Capuchin guardian of San Remo who had requested it for the friary's new Marian shrine.

1933, Asaba
Pat moved from Warri to Asaba early in January 1933, and from there carried out his double role of Pro-Vicar Apostolic and Society Visitor. He feared that his tightness with money, accentuated by the Vicariate's penury and his promise to the Bishop not to run down the bank account, would make him unpopular with the men but, with little funds available, he was not in a position to be generous, and he had to make cut-backs on grants that would have been given in better times.

Since Bishop Broderick's death, speculation as to who his successor would be, was rife. John Cadogan, now Superior in Dromantine, appeared to be Pat's choice and the choice of the men in Western Nigeria, though he strongly opposed the idea himself. Pat, aware of Cadogan's disinclination, instructed the missionaries in a circular letter: "In the event of Fr Cadogan's declining the dignity of Vicar Apostolic of this Vicariate, kindly forward by next mail direct to the Very Rev. Provincial, Cork, three names in a sealed envelope". Apart from Cadogan, Pat thought it might be William Porter, seeing his promotion to Prefect Apostolic of Northern Nigeria as a stepping stone to episcopacy in Asaba. The members of the deceased bishop's council – Pat himself, Strub, Krauth and Tom Bartley – were all 'possibles', as was one of the Provincial Councillors, Pat's former colleague in Dromantine, Henry Baker. Pat, already Pro-Vicar and Society Visitor couldn't help worrying that his name might appear. Aghast at the thought, he wrote to Michael Collins, then a General Councillor in Lyons, stating his reasons against being nominated and, he was confidant that Collins, "would never consent to my name going forward". He also wrote a number of times to the Provincial, requesting him "to leave me out of these appointments". In January 1934, on sending some more African artefacts to Slattery for the Dublin Missionary Exhibition he said, "We are all guessing who the new Bishop will be, but I suppose our guesses are only wild ones. Anyway, speed him up so that I may have the pleasure of handing over this responsible position [Pro-Vicar] as soon as possible". Later in the same month writing about finding a Doctor for a leper settlement, he said, with a rising note of alarm, "Regarding the Appointment here, I suspect that some of the men have sent home my name, in which case you will not take it into account. I'm a bit on the scrupulous side for such a job ... anyway there is not the slightest need for me to worry".

A statistical picture of the Vicariate

Annually every Bishop, or 'Ordinary', prepares a detailed *Prospectus Status Missionis* (for the year preceding the 30th of June) for Propaganda Fide in Rome. The task of compiling the 1933 statistical report for Western Nigeria fell to Pat. Some figures from it give a bird's eye view of the Vicariate as it was then.

Personnel consisted of 33 priests (but at least six or seven would always be away on home leave, ill, or convalescing at home); 12 European and 2 Indigenous Sisters; 140 paid catechists (including 2 women); 437 male and 126 female 'Baptisers' (persons commissioned to baptise). While most of the figures showed a small increase on the previous year, the figures for male 'Baptisers' showed a big increase – from 276 to 437. Could this have been due to Pat? Baptising, especially persons in danger of death, was something he was particularly zealous about. However the number of female baptisers went down from 147 to 126!

The Vicariate had 18 mission stations where a priest, or priests, resided (an increase of 1 station on the previous year's report), and 263 non-residential stations. There were 20 churches capable of holding more than 400 people, and 251 smaller ones, (an increase of 2 large churches in the year). The Catholic population was 22,244 and there were over 10,000 catechumens (an increase of over 400 Catholics and over 1,600 catechumens). The figure given for the number of Protestants was 61,500; for Moslems 200,000; and for traditional religionists 717,000. The Catholics then were quite a small minority, only about one-fiftieth of the total population.

The Vicariate had 131 Schools (a big increase on the 79 of 1932 – largely due to the assistance of new Government grants). It employed 296 teachers, 11 of whom were women; the school population was 6,051 boys and 755 girls. The Teacher Training College, which Bishop Broderick had opened at Ibusa in 1928, had 58 students. The Vicariate also had 8 medical clinics; 3 orphanages with 73 girls and 6 boys in residence; 4 'refuges' for old people with 38 residents; and 4 leper settlements with 230 residents. The seminary in Asaba had 10 students.

The total expenditure of the Vicariate for the year was over £13,000 and the income about £12,300. The bank balance in Asaba was £1,750. In a concluding remark Pat said, "We take out an average of £400 per month and for the next five months we have nothing to hope for save a small donation of about £20".

Despite Bishop Broderick's absence from the Vicariate, for most of the period 1931 to his death in October '33, and despite the World recession, the statistics indicate that steady progress had been maintained. While not attributing all this to Pat, he was a major link in the running of things; and for most of the time in question had been the one responsible for maintaining progress and anticipating future needs. Unintentionally slipping into a proprietary role, he wrote to the Provincial in February 1934 saying, "*I* would require – I mean the *Vicariate* would require – if possible five new Fathers". He also knew what kind of men he wanted, "If Fr Cadogan is the Ordinary I know he will pick them himself, if not tell him – he must know – to divide virtue, zeal, and intelligence equally all round".

For some time, the Government had been setting up a leper settlement at Ossiomo about thirty miles from Benin City. Before he left, Mgr Broderick appeared to be close to clinching negotiations with the Government to make it a Catholic mission institution, provided he got a Doctor for it. A German doctor was interested but, in May '33, he began to insist on a salary of £700 a year, which neither the Government nor the Catholic mission could afford. In the 'battle for Ossiomo', which involved the Government, Catholics, and Protestants, Pat's sharp business sense and bargaining skills came to the fore. He felt the Government, in general, favoured Protestant missionaries, and this raised his hackles. With the German doctor ruled out, he stormed Heaven and the Province for another doctor, preferably an Irish Catholic. He promised a Government salary of £350 (which he thought he could raise "to at least £400") which, in turn, would be supplemented by £100 from the Vicariate or (more likely) from Cork. Most instruments, medicine and drugs would be provided by the Government and the doctor's length of 'tour' would only be eighteen months with six months paid leave.

In Ossiomo a European 'Sanitary official' was busy laying out the site and building native houses. Many lepers were already in residence and the sanitary official was giving an occasional hypodermic injection when required. "A great pity we could not have a couple of priest doctors like the Church Mission Society", said Pat. He heard that the sanitary man had a salary of £400 and that his position was not permanent. After travelling over 80 miles to Benin City to speak to the chief colonial officer, 'the Resident', Pat was told that the Government was also badly hit by the Recession and that the Native Authorities had collected less than half their taxes that year, hence money would only be granted for essential services. Despite this unpromising note, Pat hung on, telling the Resident that the majority of the Christians in Ossiomo were Catholics, and that a Father who visited them from time to time could not hold a Service, as there was no church there. The Resident promised that he would try to have one erected as soon as possible. Pat guessed then that the authorities had decided in favour of the Catholics, "I have no fear now that they are calling in any other missionary body", he said. Terms and conditions had still to be worked out. In January 1934, the Resident offered a Government grant of £500 per year for the Doctor's salary provided that the Catholic mission would take care of all other expenses. Pat wrote to Cork in haste, urging the Provincial to accept the terms, "It's just what you wanted. Do not delay, the CMS or others will only be too glad to take it. If the salary is too low Cork must come to our aid by adding something. A little private practice at Ossiomo could augment the Doctor's salary (tell him, but don't tell the Government); the Elder Dempster Line will surely offer the same fare concessions for him and his wife as for missionaries and Government officials. The Government will not expect us to employ another doctor during the six-month leave; a Father skilled in giving injections could hold the fortress".

Pat was concerned for the welfare of the lepers and for the administration of the sacraments, but he was also determined to prevent the settlement going to the Protestants, to get the best possible deal from the Government and from the Irish Province (and he wasn't above a little bit of 'sharp practice' – "Don't tell the Government"). He had almost achieved his aims when a serious threat arose from, of all places, within the leadership of the Vicariate. The new Bishop Elect (whose name will be withheld for the moment), "did not seem keen on embarking on any enterprise unless it was financially sound", reported Pat. "He told us he did not believe in buying what he could not pay for". Exasperated, Pat declaimed, "If he does not accept the Leper Settlement he will be handing over the greatest charitable work of the Vicariate to the Protestants and I believe the Government will be glad of the refusal". It was at this time, 1934, that his prayers appeared to be answered; a Catholic doctor arrived, but not from Ireland or Germany. Dr Louba Lengauer was a Russian, who had been working in a mission hospital in Eastern Nigeria since 1931. With the help of some Belgian nurses she established a leprosarium on the east side of the Ossiomo river. She was the settlement's first doctor. With her in the camp, it was only a matter of time before Pat changed the Bishop-Elect's attitude to taking on the settlement, and the Government agreed to entrust it to the Catholics.

Ossiomo leper settlement

Travel occupied Pat quite a bit. As Visitor, he had to see men who were sick, or who had palavers, often in far-away stations; travel to Benin City for business with Government officials; welcome new men, and attend meetings in different places with his councillors, school boards and others. A task he looked forward to was escorting his classmate, the Provincial, Stephen Harrington, on his first tour of the Vicariate in 1933. Pat did the driving and, as usual, drove as fast as he could. The corrugated laterite roads were hard on vehicles and, in the middle of nowhere, the car broke a spring. Provincial and Visitor had to sit by the roadside for a day while a local blacksmith tried to fix it.

With frequent comings and goings due to leave and illnesses, Pat had to see to numerous changes of personnel. In July, John Murphy, who was with Tommy Greene at Agenebode, suddenly became ill with cerebral malaria and was only saved from death by the good fortune that Tommy was able to call "on the wire" Dr Hunter in Benin City. Unconscious for fifty hours, Murphy's life hung in the balance for four or five days. When he regained sufficient strength, Pat decided that he would have to be sent home. Also invalided home that year were 'Oga' Shine and Bill Fegan. Pat himself was ill in February '34 and spent a few days in hospital. Shortly afterwards, in the midst of other business, he negotiated a new contract with the Sisters involved in school work. When finished, he acknowledged uncomplainingly, "I'm a bit of a busy fellow".

He did not turn out to be unpopular as he had thought he would be. On the contrary "Kelly rule" was going down very well: "We are okay with Fr Kelly, and have no objection to his reign for a year or so" was a general opinion. Tom Duffy spoke of Warri district "where Fr Kelly is so popular"; Joe Dervin in Ogwashi-Uku said, "Things are going on very nicely under him. He is a great man and an ideal confrere". The men were even sending in their annual Accounts promptly, which surprised Pat, "I only asked once", he said. Even if he didn't want it, his star was rising.

While the pundits were still guessing who the new bishop would be, Rome appointed a total outsider, Leo H. Taylor!

Leo was born in Duluth, U.S.A. His father was an English travelling photographer and his mother was from the North of Ireland. At an early age he began his secondary education in St Joseph's Wilton. One of the first group of seminarians at the Society's new seminary in Blackrock, he was ordained in 1914. He remained in the seminary for another year, teaching Canon Law, after which he was transferred to Wilton as tutor to the students (one of whom was Pat Kelly). The same year, 1914, he became founder and

Bishop Taylor

first editor of the *African Missionary*, the first missionary magazine in Ireland. Extremely sensitive about his 'English' background, he became an ardent Irish nationalist! In 1920 he was appointed to the Vicariate of the Bight of Benin, where Mgr Terrien assigned him to Holy Cross parish, Lagos, the oldest Catholic station in Nigeria, founded by the SMA in 1868. Taylor learned the Yoruba language to the point where he could correct an interpreter (and often did). He was noted for his pioneering work and tireless trekking to outstations usually on a bicycle. He distinguished himself in the educational apostolate and, in 1928, founded the first Catholic secondary college in Nigeria, St Gregory's Lagos, where he remained as Principal until his appointment to Asaba.

Everyone was surprised at Taylor's nomination, not least himself. Writing to the Provincial from St Gregory's he said, "It must be a mistake, I haven't the minimum of sanctity required for a bishop. I know nothing of the people and the country, I am a 'foreigner' (however 'pro Dev' and Sinn Féin)". He begged Harrington to help him in his rapport with his Irish confreres. Writing to Maurice Slattery he said he didn't want to be Bishop and explained that even in St Gregory's his relationship with the Irish was very difficult, "I have three or four of the finest men here but I can't make friends with them. I shall never be able to make friends with an Irish confrere – I got such a scare, such a scorching from H., M., and S. that no leaf can grow from that side again". He felt like an "intruder" in Western Nigeria, "among strange people and strange confreres". He also believed that Asaba had for long been "a dumping ground for difficult cases". Perhaps he had a point there, for even Pat said, "no wonder Cadogan refused the nomination, he knew the kind of men he'd have to deal with". Taylor, hoping for Slattery's support, concluded his letter, "Pray for me, I feel awfully small". The bishop-to-be thought that his nomination had not been well-received by the missionaries in the Vicariate, and he feared especially some "troublesome confreres". Pat thought his fears were "groundless".

In May '34, Pat and Eugene Strub drove to Lagos to meet the bishop-elect. "We nearly paid for it with our lives", said Pat. They had a motor accident on the return journey in which Pat sustained a broken collar bone and was laid up in Benin City hospital for five weeks. He didn't say who was driving but, in the Visitor's account for 1933, there was an entry stating that he had just bought an old Ford from the Bishop for £40! Taylor returned the visit, but spent only one night in Asaba, to make arrangements for his episcopal consecration.

The Bishop-Elect wrote to Cork, asking for Bishop Broderick's episcopal outfit (willed to his successor) and, being smaller in size than Broderick, joked that he'd have to find some nuns to tighten the mitre for him! Like his predecessor he believed in thrift, "It seems absurd for a man in a poor mission field to spend pounds on a geegaw [the ring]". When Slattery sent him an old one, probably Broderick's, Taylor commented, "it is a very tight fit for two fingers together, but hangs very loosely on one".

On 24 June 1934, in Asaba, Taylor was ordained bishop by Francis O'Rourke (Mgr Terrien's successor in Lagos), assisted by three bishops and a prefect apostolic, including William Porter, then bishop of Cape Coast, and Mgr Charles Heerey CSSp of Onitsha. Pat was assistant priest. About fifty priests from all over Nigeria attended and, discounting Taylor's fears of being unwanted, *all* the Irish confreres of the Vicariate, except two, one of whom was sick, were present. A dozen lay Europeans and a huge congregation of Nigerians participated. "Everything went well", reported Pat, "He should have a successful career here and I am sure he will have the whole-hearted cooperation of all his confreres". Pat, also attentive to the cost of things, added, "The expenses of the consecration were high, but the Asaba Christians collected sufficient to cover all – £110".

Whatever about his fear of some Irish confreres, Taylor quickly learned to appreciate PJ Kelly. Asking the Provincial whether he should re-appoint him as Pro-Vicar, he added, "He is Visitor and I should think a good one". In September, with a better knowledge of how things had gone since Broderick's departure, he said, "Fr Kelly seems to have done extraordinarily well, he was told to save money – and he never forgot he was *locum tenens*" (keeping a place for someone else). Following Pat's advice, Taylor set about transferring 50,000 francs from the Vicariate's account in Lyons to Cork, saying, "I suppose Kelly knows best". After consultation with Bishop O'Rourke, he raised the sum to 75,000, "Kelly left the amount to me". In 1934, the franc was not worth a great deal, "but", said Pat, "it was becoming of greater value every day – only seventy-seven of them now to make a pound". Taylor re-appointed Pat as Pro-Vicar and chose Strub, Krauth, Pat O'Connell, and John Mahon as his four councillors. Pat continued as Society Visitor.

Despite the Recession and the Tariff War, another 'war' was going on in the Society – the "length of tour War", which then, officially, was of five years duration. Most of the Irish, including Pat, were in favour of a four-year tour. Taylor was of the opinion that a four-year tour should be followed "once the rule was laid down", but it had not been. He further argued that the Vicariate didn't have money to pay for extra passages home, and he said that about seven men would be due leave in 1934 if the four-year tour became the rule. With another seven due to return from leave and the homeward and outward boat fare costing about £184 for each confrere, he asked where the money was supposed to come from. Pat, who had arrived in 1929, was overdue leave, but he was the first one Taylor asked to stay on a bit longer, "to guide my infant steps". Pat agreed. Five days after his consecration Taylor, overcoming his 'fear' of the troublesome Irish, "read the Riot Act to them about Leave Taking". (Relevant to Taylor's mood at the time was the news he had received from home a month before his consecration that his mother was dying. He was upset and also worried about the cost of "providing her with a decent Christian funeral", but he did not seek to go home. As it transpired his mother did not die then.)

After a quick tour of the Vicariate, Taylor listed his priorities: Community life – in every station he wanted to see at least two men living together; spiritual exercises – "I expect every man to make his morning prayer, meditation, night prayer, visit the Blessed Sacrament, say the rosary regularly and when possible pray in common ... all the Fathers do it, at least when I am with them!" Mindful that Protestant missionaries had hospitals and doctors of their own, he thought of establishing a Catholic mission hospital. Furthermore, he wanted a church built at Ubiaja, and a sanctuary built onto a school at Benin City so that it could accommodate the large number of people who wished to attend Mass there on Sundays. Perhaps the most consequential of his ideas was that of moving the Vicariate's headquarters, **"I'm going, I think, to push out of Asaba, Benin City is the capital for everything"**, 15 October '34.

Observing the Bishop settle in, Pat commented, "I believe he likes us and we like him". Having successfully guided the new bishop's "infant steps", Pat left for home leave in September 1934. Tom Bartley, one of his Councillors, took over as 'Acting Visitor'.

Chapter 6

NIGERIA, 1935-1940

The second half of the 1930s saw change and the beginnings of 'modernization' in Western Nigeria – the possibilities of air travel, motor cars, typewriters, refrigeration, and air mail. At the same time the superiors of the Society of African Missions at home became more concerned that missionary life-style correspond with the rules and ideals laid down in the *Constitutions* and *Directory*, particularly regarding community life, and they empowered Society Visitors to check on divergent life-styles. Bishops on the missions began to worry; the Visitor now appeared to have more control of the men and the money than they had, "I don't seem to have any business except to save my soul", said Bishop Taylor. Efforts to implement community life caused quite an upheaval in Western Nigeria where most of the stations were 'single' ones. The length of tour had been finally fixed at four years; the length of leave remained the same – one year. Standards of living began to improve, and hopes were high that serious illnesses would be cured by improved medical facilities and that premature deaths would be a thing of the past. Unfortunately this optimism was not warranted. On the negative side income, depressed since the World recession, had not picked up; Government grants were minimal, and Mass stipends, if they could be got, remained at two shillings and sixpence. With capital deposits being eaten into, Bishop Taylor feared the Vicariate would soon be bankrupt. Talk of the likelihood of another world war did not help.

Precise on the length of his one-year leave, Pat Kelly embarked on the Elder Dempster liner at Liverpool on the 18th of September 1935. Travelling with him was another returning confrere, Bill Fegan. Pat had spent most of his holiday at Tristaun, delighting in the fresh air, the good food, and the work in the fields with his brothers Jack and Bill. Both of the latter were still single, while Malachy, Mick and Gerald had married and settled in New York. Kathleen, his sister, now 'Mrs Tommy Cunnane', lived near Ballinasloe. May had joined a religious order in Dublin, and Ellie remained at home with Kate. During the leave, Pat, with the Provincial, Stephen Harrington, had travelled to America, where they helped to raise awareness of the needs of West Africa, and visited Pat's three brothers and other relatives living in the Bronx, New York. (One reputed distant relative, gaining fame at the time, was Gene Kelly singer, dancer and movie star. If Pat attended any of his performances, he didn't mention it!) Pat's companion on his first voyage to Nigeria, Michael O'Donohue, was working in New York, raising funds for the Province. He showed Pat some of the sights, but he was not in good health. He died the following November of tuberculosis.

At Asaba, Bishop Taylor welcomed Pat back and, for the second time, Pat was appointed "temporarily" to Sapele, "between Shine's coming and Murray's going". Tom Murray, a Belfast man, was due to depart for leave in the first week of November, Pat Shine was expected back from Leave in a "month or so". The Bishop thought Sapele should be self-supporting, but currently had to be helped with £50 a year from the Vicariate. He hoped that Pat, with his thrifty ways, would make it financially independent. Pat knew the parish well, but it had become much busier since he was there. The fine new church, which he had helped to build, now accommodated a large congregation, and newcomers were joining all the time.

Pat's work as Visitor frequently took him out of Sapele. Shortly after arrival there, his fellow county man, Joe Dervin, fell ill with "gastric malaria" and was hospitalised in Warri. After visiting him, Pat was relieved to find that his case was not too serious. Later, John Murphy in Ubiaja, became seriously ill with cerebral malaria. He had not enjoyed good health since he arrived in 1929, and already had a very close call with death. Following medical advice, Pat sent him home. Similarly, Jerry Sheehan, repeatedly ill with malaria in the Training College in Ibusa, was sent home. When visiting sick confreres, Pat, forgetting his own younger days, sometimes was shocked by what he saw, "I remember going to one Father and the water filter he was using was a broken bottle turned upside down; even in Asaba mission, for a long time, only a piece of porous rock was used".

Pat, also very busy at Sapele with parish work and supervising the building of a new mission house, was over-working and, little inclined to look after himself, he fell ill with his old complaint, dysentery, in the New Year of '36. By March he was over it, and the following month went on visitation of the North. As time went on, and Shine hadn't returned, he requested the Bishop to give him an assistant, not only because of the work load, but because of the Society rule that men should live in community. Taylor was sympathetic, but didn't have anyone to spare. Pat wrote to the Provincial, requesting more men for the Vicariate, and tried to persuade the Bishop to ask for more. But Taylor, judging that the Vicariate could not afford them, was loath to do so. Pat remained alone, until George McCormack returned from Leave and was appointed to Sapele. But George was also required at Ozoro, where a new mission house had just been opened and, after a short time at Sapele, he transferred there. Eventually, Shine returned and in June was re-appointed to Sapele as Pat's assistant.

Not long after Pat's own return, Bishop Taylor, a careful man but given to worrying, especially over money, decided to check the Visitor's Mass books. In Pat's absence, Tom Bartley, Acting Visitor, had kept the accounts. Taylor thought the figures were in a tangle and feared that Masses were being said twice for the same intentions. He asked Pat to check the books and George McCormack to do an audit. Pat's review and Tom's accounting were not found wanting, but the Bishop maintained a critical stance, saying he would have to check the books himself from time to time in future. If Pat felt offended, he kept his feelings to himself.

The two men had great respect for one another. Taylor, a warmer and more extrovert person, admired Pat for being "tolerant, pious and clever", but he admitted that "there was not much love lost between them". He didn't mean they were quarrelling, in fact he didn't like 'yes-men', he meant that they met for business and there the contact ended. Apart from doubts about Mass accounting, Taylor was irritated by Pat's 'God-will-provide' attitude and by his over-optimistic reports to Rome. The 1933 Statistical Report, which Pat had compiled, had been well received by the Cardinal Prefect of Propaganda Fide, who expressed great satisfaction at the increase in the numbers of Catholics (to which Pat had drawn attention). The following year when the same Cardinal acknowledged Taylor's report, he said he "was struck with grief" because of the "tardy increase"! Pat had a cute way of putting things, which Taylor, according to himself "a stupid idealist who maintained that truth-telling is best", lacked.

Refusing to be upset by episcopal innuendos about statistics or Mass accounting, Pat thanked the Provincial Bursar for new intentions received, remarking that these ones were easier to discharge and record as they were all 'single' ones, "like a lot of the young men in Ireland". After further requests for intentions, he had more than enough and, returning some to Cork in July '36, said henceforward "480 every six weeks" would be sufficient. For 1935-'36 he reported that £1,222 was received in Mass stipends.

Many of the confreres took a break in July 1936 to celebrate with Georges Krauth the Silver Jubilee of his ordination. In fact it was twenty-six years, rather than 'twenty-five', since he had been ordained. Almost continually in Western Nigeria since his arrival, he had taken very little home leave. After recovering his health at home in 1931, he was appointed Spiritual Director in the Society's 'noviciate' in Chanly, Belgium but, after a short time, he asked to be allowed back to Nigeria. His Provincial agreed and Bishop Broderick was glad to have him back. In charge of Aragba mission since he founded it in 1921, and Dean of the Delta area, he had won the esteem of the people and the missionaries for his dedication and hard work. Many confreres, including Pat, were grateful to Georges for guiding their first steps in the mission. One of the things for which he was popular among the people was his "rheumatism medicine". One new missionary on being asked if he had any of "Fr Georges' medicine", discovered to his embarrassment that "rheumatism" was the people's word for gonorrhoea. Georges, having learned from an Alsatian doctor that crystals of permanganate in water cured the disease, imported sacks of it from London. It proved effective, and his medicine was widely sought.

Joining him that day, in the singing of his jubilee Mass, were his fellow Alsatians, Charles Burr and Eugene Strub. These three were now the only continental confreres remaining in the Vicariate. Burr, thirty years in Nigeria, was alone in Issele-Uku. Strub, sixty-two years of age, the oldest missionary in the Vicariate, and thirty-eight years in Nigeria, was currently residing in Asaba. Pat described them as "exemplary Fathers in every way, and though advanced in years, very active and successful missionaries". The Jubilee was a fitting tribute to Georges' great contribution to the mission in Western Nigeria; the following year he was transferred to Togo.

When the Alsatian Province ("Alsace-Lorraine", now called the Province of Strasbourg) was established in 1927, the General Council agreed that the various missions, where Alsatian confreres were working, would help the new Province financially.

Alsace-Lorraine, relatively small in area, had suffered grievously in numerous wars and political disputes. The young Province had little financial resources and needed assistance to pay for its students in the Society's formation houses at Chanly and Lyons. Called the "Alsatian tax", the amount due from the various missions where Alsatians worked, accumulated over the years. In 1936, Bishop Taylor was quite put out to receive a stiff bill from Strasbourg for 21,000 francs. Bishop Broderick had faced the same difficulty and, the year before he died, had requested Pat, as Society Visitor, to try to persuade the Alsatian Provincial to "remit at least half of the tax, or better still the whole amount". The Provincial declined to do so as his Province needed the money and was acting in accordance with agreements already made and ratified in the Directory. When Pat was responsible for the Vicariate in 1933, he tried again to get the tax reduced, pointing out to the Provincial that the confreres in Western Nigeria were now saying Mass for little or no stipends, and that aid from Rome had been drastically reduced. "Soon", he said, "the Vicariate will be struggling to provide its missionaries with the bare necessities of life". Following this, the Provincial, while maintaining the status quo, said he would try to procure good Mass stipends for Western Nigeria missionaries. The "Alsatian tax" highlighted both the contribution the members of the Province were making in Western Nigeria, and the straitened financial circumstances of the Vicariate in the 1930s – the decade in which PJ Kelly took his 'first steps' in Society and ecclesiastical leadership.

One-man stations and community life

In 1935, the majority of mission stations in the Vicariate were "one-man stations". Over the years the Vicariate had expanded, new stations were opened, and the numbers of staff in the seminary and in the teacher training college in Ibusa had increased. The supply of new missionaries had not kept pace, hence single-man stations became the norm rather than the exception.

Community life today is accepted by most as the norm, but it was not always so. The Founder in his sketchy Fundamental Articles of 1856 and of 1858, did not specifically legislate for community life, but did appear to envisage it as 'normal'. In the 1858 Articles he said, "One can join the Society at any age ... [and enjoy] the advantages of community life with the confreres". Dying the following year (in community in Sierra Leone), he did not have the opportunity to elaborate on his rules. His successor, Augustin Planque, was adamant that the Founder had envisaged community life as the norm and he, Planque, made it obligatory in his 1864 Constitutions. However, the long-lived Planque was not as popular as the short-lived Founder, and Planque's Constitutions proved to be very unpopular. At the request of the General Assembly of 1907, Mgr Paul Pellet, who would before long succeed Planque as Superior General, wrote a Society *Directory* to interpret and explain the Society's Constitutions of 1900. These, in fact, were the Society's first definitively approved Constitutions. Pellet's *Directory* which, after some modifications, received the unanimous approval of Society superiors, clearly endorsed community life but, while useful and appreciated, it did not have the force of law. The latest approved Constitutions, 1990, would appear to reflect the Founder's liberal view of living in community, as they state that, "The Society will provide the members ... with the opportunity of belonging to apostolic communities".

When Pat, in his first appointment, had been living alone at Eku, he maintained weekly contact with John Cadogan in Oria and, after he departed, with Georges Krauth in Aragba. Such contact was thought to make up for the absence of full community life, and it provided the opportunity for regular Confession. Though in the Society's official prayers, the missionaries prayed daily to be spared from "sudden and unprepared death", they didn't like to go too long without absolution, just in case. Pat, John, and Georges, lived within cycling distance of one another, so the weekly short visit was thought to be sufficient. When distances separating confreres were greater, or other circumstances obtained, a solitary confrere was required to spend a week or, ideally, ten days, each month residing with another or with a community. When Krauth left Aragba in 1937, Shine went there, but spent a week every month with Pat who was alone at Sapele. Charles Burr was content to live alone at Issele-Uku, but was visited regularly by Fr Paul Emecete. Bill Fegan was alone at Ashaka, but he and Tom Murray, who replaced Shine at Aragba, visited one another. Others were living alone too and, in all stations, community might be disrupted at any time by men going on leave or, being hospitalized.

Now with the new emphasis on community, Bishop Taylor found he was being forced to appoint a man to a station, not for the sake of the work, but "to make up community", even if there wasn't enough work in the mission, or space in the house for him. It also happened that a relatively happy individual, or community, was saddled with a difficult man who, because of the Rule, could no longer be left on his own. One confrere, suffering in such a community, said, "only my mother's prayers kept me sane". The Bishop knew that community living didn't always succeed in solving or containing problems, sometimes it spread them. It pained him to contemplate closing stations and 'abandoning' Christians and catechumens because of a rule. "I honestly don't believe in [two-man stations]", he wrote to Harrington, arguing that individual catastrophes and 'falls from grace' were not caused by living alone but by character flaws and by putting inexperienced men in difficult situations. He said the fault, if it was a fault, was the opening of so many one-man stations in the first place, but they existed and he shuddered at the thought of closing them. He believed that there was a good spirit of independence and self-reliance among the confreres and he hoped that they would continue to be able to stand on their own feet, "Personally I have no use for the meek and mild obedient invertebrate because I've seen so few who were any use to anyone ... surely a priest should be a man not merely a male".

In his time, Bishop Broderick was well aware that the mission would need far more men if the regulations on community were to be fulfilled. In 1938 Taylor complained, "In the last ten to twelve years the number of Fathers has scarcely increased ... Since I took over, four years ago eight new men have come to the Vicariate and eight have been withdrawn. The only addition is Fr Erameh [a Nigerian priest ordained by Taylor in 1936]". For Taylor the problem was compounded by lack of finance, "We could take more new Fathers *if* we could pay for them, but that is impossible". A year after the 1937 Assembly, which had emphasised the necessity of conforming to the community rule, Taylor said, "I'm finding the carrying out of the Assembly's ideas not only very difficult but impossible". He asked the Provincial to send "at least three new men" adding, "It's up to you to pay for them". He insisted, "I haven't changed my own ideas, I could run the Vicariate, and well, with fewer men and less financial worry, but *if* I must follow the rules it should be done properly, not meanly or evasively". He asked how he could provide community life in eighteen stations with only twenty-six missionaries and one Nigerian priest. Making matters more difficult, new men were not supposed to be given a work appointment for the first six months to give them time to learn the language and the customs. Taylor said he would need ten more Fathers "just to hold down what we have – and there is no prospect of getting them". The only way to satisfy the community rule would be to close stations, "not one or two, but five or six". The idea appalled him, "The thought of Christians without Mass and the sacraments either in life or at death, children of Christian parents without instruction ... is a fear-inspiring thought". Endeavouring to spread the responsibility, he appealed to the Provincial to make the decision and command him to obey. If he, the Provincial, insisted on community life, he should telegram just one word, "Fathers", which would mean, "Close stations in favour of community life". If he didn't want that radical step, he should cable the word "Christians" which would mean, "Maintain services for the Christians and see to community life as best you can". Understandably, the Provincial did not send any such message.

Pat was more of a rule man than Taylor. He approved of community life and, as Visitor, did his best to promote it according to the letter and the spirit of the *Constitutions* and *Directory*. He maintained that confreres in community were always mutually helpful even if they disagreed from time to time. However, even more than the Bishop, he disapproved of leaving Christians without the sacraments, and such situations would influence him to bend rules for "the good of souls". Later, he quite coolly went to reside on his own in the officially 'closed' station of Ubiaja so that the Christians there would at least have Sunday Mass and not be without a priest in an emergency. He also thought of an argument against closing stations, which had not struck the Bishop ("Kelly has twice my brains", said Taylor), namely, that Christians of closed stations might complain to Rome, and Rome might divide the Vicariate or bring in another congregation, as the SMA were not able to look after their flock. Missionary congregations were quite territorially-minded in the Thirties and the prospect of another congregation taking over part of one's jurisdiction was not a welcome idea. Apart from such considerations, Pat believed that the Society had serious obligations towards those it had evangelised and could not just close stations and walk away.

Though in favour of community life, Pat was not the quintessential community man. His 'work-aholism', abstemiousness, and reticence in personal, and many other, matters did not make him everyone's idea of the perfect live-in companion. Though respected and popular as the Society Visitor, he was not the kind of confrere with whom everyone wanted to live. Neither did he socialize with neighbouring confreres or with the 'whites'. If he visited government officials, it was to seek something for the church or the people, never for a chat or a gin and tonic. Among the confreres he didn't mind the occasional round of beer, but he disapproved of the habitual "Tonickers" (as he called them), heavy smokers and big entertainers. The very practical, down-to-earth and popular confrere, John Mahon, probably expressed the feelings of many, despite the obvious exaggeration, when he said, "I look forward to [Pat's] visit with fear and trembling. If he were a man who would take a little drink of gin or something!! but no [he doesn't]". A contrast to Pat in this matter, Bishop Taylor, an affable mixer with all, Catholic and non-Catholic, Christian and Moslem, African and expatriate, described himself (also with exaggeration) as a "Boozer".

Taylor and Pat had many "friendly quarrels" about community life. In 1936, for instance, Taylor appointed a new missionary, Pat Fleming, to Kabba mission which was neglected and had no resident priest. The young man refused to go there, saying it was against the community rule to live alone. The nearest confrere Val Barnicle, a friend of his, was alone at the station of Oka, 50 miles away. With *Pat's* consent, Fleming went to reside at Oka. Taylor was annoyed, but admitted that the young man was within his rights, adding, "Fr Kelly is delighted!" "However", continued Taylor, "in spite of his being within his rights, I must condemn his conduct, so unlike the general spirit of the Vicariate". In fact, Barnicle had already confided to Taylor that he did not want a second confrere at Oka as the house was not finished, and there wasn't enough work for two. Describing Barnicle as a kind of Vicar Forain for the district, Taylor also said that it was Barnicle who had first suggested that Fleming go to Kabba. Fleming remained for some time at Oka, before being appointed to the Teacher Training College at Ibusa. Nicholas Clery was then appointed to Kabba on his own, but, due to ill-health, he was invalided home the same year. Despite his pro-community stance, Pat, according to Taylor, was the first to protest at the closing of stations, "He has a *horror* of letting anyone die without the last sacraments".

Pat, aware that some men needed community more than others,

asked the Provincial to let him know in advance about individuals who definitely should not be put on their own. He feared that men living outside community would grow indifferent to Society Rule, especially regarding spiritual exercises. Of one of the mission 'builders', who for a year and a half was alone while supervising the construction of the new seminary at Benin City, Pat said, "I have some doubts as to whether he used to make his meditation and I believe no man wants community life more than a man that is in charge of building and nothing more". Pat did not believe that young men should be put in authority too quickly – as happened when they were appointed to a one-man station in their first tour. Lacking the guidance of seniors, some new Fathers tended to be self-willed and ill-mannered towards the people, and some wished to be on their own just to avoid being subordinate to older men. However, he felt that the new regulations (*three* in a community, and a ten-day sojourn in community once a month for men on their own) were too idealistic, "It would have been more practical at least in this Vicariate had they insisted on two living together and not mind about three, or the ten days in the month". In 1939, when universal community living was almost achieved in the Vicariate, Bill Fegan, one of the last to be living alone, was visited by Pat and John Mahon from Ubiaja, the two taking turns at spending "ten days" a month with him in Uromi.

~~~

Meanwhile Bishop Taylor in Asaba, where he 'enjoyed' community life with two Fathers, was working on his idea of moving the seat of the Vicariate to Benin City, where the colonial authorities had their headquarters. For long, Benin City was an outstation of Sapele, and only became a residential station in 1928. Moving the centre from Asaba, did not at all please the older missionaries. Eugene Strub, pointing out that Asaba had been the headquarters for half a century, stated categorically that Bishop Broderick had intended that it should remain so, and

Broderick had set up a fund to build a new cathedral there, which already had over £1,500 in it. Ironically, it was Taylor who laid the foundation stone for this cathedral in August '36 but, even as he did so, he felt a cathedral and episcopal residence in Benin City would be far more practical. He realized that moving would greatly dismay, and even enrage, the Asaba Christians, but he felt he had to risk this. In an effort to placate them, he promised to name the Vicariate, "Asaba-Benin".

He built a new Rest House in Benin City, and commissioned Bill Fegan to build the new inter-vicarial seminary there which would replace St Paul's in Asaba. The rest house was completed by September '36, and Taylor hoped to move to the new headquarters after his Leave in '37. The new seminary was completed in 1938 and, after Easter, fourteen seminarians with John O'Shea, Superior and lecturer in philosophy, and Maurice Walsh, bursar and professor of moral theology, moved to the new St Paul's in Benin City. Catering for students from all the SMA jurisdictions in Nigeria, the seminary already had classical studies, philosophy and theology on its curriculum. Located beside the Bishop's residence, it facilitated contact between bishop and seminarians. The Staff, soon to be joined by Dr Alfie Glynn, also acted as chaplains for the OLA Sisters whose convent was two miles away.

Bishop Taylor had a number of important things to do, or to undergo, during his Leave: first, he had to have a hernia operation in Port Harcourt; then attend the Provincial Assembly of 1937; raise funds for the Vicariate in America and meet his brother Claude, one of the pioneers of the SMA mission in Illinois. Following his operation and a brief period of recuperation, he took ship for home with Tom Bartley in December, leaving PJ Kelly, Pro-Vicar and Visitor, once more in charge of the Vicariate.

Pat moved to the Bishop's residence in Asaba, took advantage of Taylor's new headed stationery and, using two fingers, tapped out a few letters on the new mechanical writing machine. With his large hands, Pat found the 'typewriter' a bit cumbersome and continued most of his correspondence in 'long hand'. His handwriting was good – large, clear and firm; his letters were brief and to the point, wasting neither time, paper nor ink (but, unfortunately for the biographer, hardly ever saying anything about himself).

Christmas passed as usual. Pat took advantage of feasts to preach long catechetical type of sermons. Most of the people didn't mind the length, though some did. In January, the annual priests' retreat took place at Asaba. Preached by Fr Mellet CSSp, Pat and most of the older men attended it. Mellet preached another one in July, which most of the younger men attended. In return, Pat preached a retreat for the Holy Ghost men in Onitsha in August – "tit for tat", he said. After his own retreat in January, he went north where he gave two retreats, which took him nearly a month. In February, he went south on visitation in Warri and around the Niger delta. In May he was in Ubiaja. The parish priest there, John Mahon, having completed the building of a fine new church, had gone on leave and the station was 'closed', but Pat took up residence there for a while, afterwards going to Agenebode whose parish priest, Tommy Greene, had also gone on leave.

Visit of Apostolic Delegate
Antonio Riberi, an Italian, was a member of staff of the Nunciature in Dublin for five years, before he succeeded Archbishop Hinsley as Apostolic Delegate of East and West Africa in 1934. In May 1937, Riberi was scheduled to make an official visitation of Western Nigeria. He was not over-popular with the Irish, partly because of general distaste for Italy's 'Abyssinian War' and Mussolini's foreign policies, but also for other reasons. James Ward, the Education Supervisor in Lagos, for instance, had 'palaver' with him the previous year after Riberi instructed him to promote an Austrian catechism. Ward, already

working on a Yoruba catechism, told him that an Austrian catechism was "the maddest possible thing for this country". In high dudgeon, the Delegate complained about him to Bishop O'Rourke.

Pat became very nervous about the imminent visit, and wished that Bishop Taylor was present to show His Excellency around. At ease in relating with ordinary people, Pat dreaded high-ranking visitations, especially this one, and requested prayers from all and sundry that everything would go all right. On the 20th of May, the Delegate met the Ordinaries in Lagos. They discussed the organization of the apostolate, the role of catechists and preaching. After it, Pat drove him to Asaba. Quite likely this was when Pat started praying while driving; even more likely, it was when the Delegate started! Pat need not have feared; the visit went well, and, though it was not his intention, he made a very favourable personal impression on the Delegate, which would affect his future in no small way. Pat didn't comment on the visit but, later, he remarked that English Delegates, like Hinsley, got on much better with the colonial Government than the Italians. Riberi departed at the end of June. Perhaps Pat's 'pray-as-you-drive' way was somehow efficacious for, two years later, Riberi, travelling with Mgr James Moynagh SPS in Onitsha, was involved in a car accident, which obliged him to do the rest of his visitation with his arm in a sling.

The General Assembly at Lyons in the summer of 1937 saw the election of the first non-French confrere as Superior General, Maurice Slattery. At the Provincial Assembly, Stephen Harrington was re-elected Irish Provincial. Pat sent congratulations to him by the new Air Mail service explaining, "it's faster than ordinary mail and less expensive than a cable". Pat's next letter to the Provincial contained a query about new General Assembly regulations on "Masses for deceased confreres". According to these regulations it seemed that after death ordinary confreres would have only one Mass offered for them by each member of the Province, while members of the Generalate would have one Mass offered by every member of the Society. "Whoever thought of that", said Pat, "does not deserve to get out of Purgatory in a hurry". He also raised the question of a new Visitor for Western Nigeria, expressing the hope that he himself would not be re-appointed, "After seven years a change would probably be good for both the confreres and myself". He recommended John Mahon or Nicholas Clery for the post.

Sad news reached Asaba in October '37; two young men, John Marren and Tony O'Dwyer had died of yellow fever in the neighbouring Prefecture of Jos and a third, Pat McAnally, was lucky to have survived. The deaths were a great shock to Mgr William Lumley and his small team of about ten young Irish confreres. Lumley was well known to Pat and the confreres in Western Nigeria, as he had worked there from 1926 until his nomination as the first Prefect Apostolic of Jos in 1934. Marren, from Sligo, was twenty-nine years of age, O'Dwyer, from Galway, twenty-seven. O'Dwyer, stationed in Shendam, on hearing that Marren and McAnally were seriously ill in Kwande had gone to their assistance. Shortly after arrival, he also became ill and died within a week. McAnally recovered and was invalided home. Two years previously, the Society Visitor of Jos, Florrie O'Driscoll, a student of Pat's in Dromantine, had died of typhoid fever, at the age of thirty. In Bishop O'Rourke's Vicariate of Lagos another young man, Eddie Murphy, twenty-seven years of age, died of fever in Ibadan in December '37. On board ship en route to Nigeria, Murphy had heard of the Jos deaths. At Freetown, after visiting the Founder's and Pioneers' tomb, he wrote to a friend, "I have visited the graves of those who found and cleared the way, and I asked God that I too may have the privilege of dying in the black Continent without seeing again my homeland if my death might serve the cause. It is my will to die here as did Frs O'Dwyer and Marren. May it please God to hear my prayer". Some prayers are answered, Murphy died thirty-seven days after arrival in Lagos, four days less than it took Marion Brésillac to die in Sierra Leone! Pat visited the graves of the young men in Jos; and, in a letter, referred briefly to Murphy's death, "Another young man went down in Ibadan, may he rest in peace".

With a drastic increase in the number of deaths from fever at this time, the Director of Medical Services advised all Europeans, especially missionaries, to get inoculated against yellow fever. People coming from Britain were advised to have it done in London, otherwise they would have to be inoculated in Lagos and remain ten days in quarantine. Pat urged the Provincial to see that outward-bound missionaries got their injections in London, to avoid delay *and* the pound-a-day fee in the mosquito-proof clinic in Lagos. He also recommended inoculation against typhus – of which Florrie O'Driscoll had died.

After the Provincial Assembly, Patrick O' Herlihy was appointed Bursar. Though a very exact man, who had worked in Western Nigeria, he left Pat short of Mass intentions. Protesting that he was "high and dry", Pat motivated the new bursar to expedite a double amount. A basic 480 intentions a month was agreed, "but", Pat added, "sometimes twice a month". At this time, the bursar began to charge a tax of three pence, four pence, and even six pence, on each stipend sent to Western Nigeria to defray the cost of missionaries' accommodation in Blackrock Road during leave. As the stipends on average were only two shillings and sixpence, this tax was considerable. Pat, complaining that the loss of income meant "a loss of souls and Protestant gains", got the Provincial on his side and before long 'the tax war' was won, and money already deducted was restored. Pat was also concerned about 'November Masses' for deceased confreres, "practically all Fathers have omitted to say them". It wasn't so much that the Masses had not been said as that there was no record of them in the books of 1934-35 (when he was on leave). He sought, and got replies from most of the Fathers except eight who were on leave, one of them being Fr O of earlier mention. Despite a number of requests, he did not reply, but while at home, Fr O had requested the Provincial to help pay his debts (which had reached three figures). Pat suggested that Fr O's £7 station allocation per month be doubled so that he might pay off his debts in instalments. Hoping that the popular man's entertainment bills would diminish if confreres abided by the Bishop's instructions on not visiting him, Pat concluded, "economy never found a place in his manner of living".

Bishop Taylor returned from leave in November '37 and took up residence in Asaba, but intended to move to Benin City as soon as possible. He got new "Benin City" stationery printed with his episcopal crest and motto, *Viriliter age* (Act manfully), on it. Using it now he added "Or Asaba" by hand to the address. After leave he had many things to attend to. Precise contracts between the SMA and OLA were required. Stephen Harrington thought it would be better if both congregations were independent of one another, but this was a matter for their Generalates. Meanwhile the local Ordinary would have to continue dealing with "Sisters' palaver" as best he could. On the SMA front, Taylor was occupied with re-arranging personnel so that no one lived alone. Already a number of stations had been closed, or made non-residential: Ogwashi-Uku, Onitsha-Olona, and Illah. These had been residential stations when Broderick took over in 1918. Afashio was closed later and not re-opened in Taylor's time; Ubiaja faced closure. Taylor believed that Rome would make new ecclesiastical divisions in the territory soon. Probably much of the northern part of the Vicariate, Kabba district where, Taylor admitted, the Christians were neglected due to the shortage of priests, and also Oka, would be removed from his jurisdiction. This would reduce the size of his territory, but not release men, as those working in separated parts normally remained there. He might even lose men, if one or two currently working in other parts of the Vicariate, were nominated to lead the new divisions.

Despite the difficulties, Taylor succeeded in moving the Vicariate towards community life – at least two men in a station – as norm rather than as exception. In his report of September 1938, Pat said, "the present Ordinary has done his utmost to comply with this point of the *Directory* ... It is his intention to bring his Vicariate further into line in this respect so that in the course of another year or two there will be no exception to the Rule". Taylor then had eighteen occupied stations including the Seminary and the Training College. Seminary and College were separate from the parishes of Benin City and Ibusa. Of the confreres resident in these stations and colleges at the time of the Report, twenty men, including the Bishop, Visitor, and Fr Erameh, lived in community and eight lived alone. Of the latter, five lived in one-man stations (four Irish and one Alsatian); two were in two-man stations but their confreres were on leave, and the eighth, George McCormack, was 'alone' at Ibusa, but his house was adjacent to the Training College. The situation varied as men went on, or returned from leave, were hospitalized, or invalided home. The single stations were: Issele-Uku (Eugene Strub); Okene (Willie Keenan); Kabba (Nicholas Clery); Aragba (Tom Murray); and Uromi (John Lynott). Full community living for everybody would require more confreres or more closures.

The Bishop moved to Benin City in February 1938, taking up residence in the Education Supervisor's House. To date he had spent about £8,000 on improving mission houses and by now all the stations had fairly decent accommodation except the one he occupied himself which, with the Supervisor and another Father in residence, was overcrowded. He intended building a new house or, at least enlarging the existing one.

In Lagos for a Board of Education meeting, Taylor took time off to buy a car for PJ Kelly. An enthusiastic salesman pointed out a highly-polished two-seater Chevrolet – a showroom model, old stock but never used and going at the bargain price of £95. Taylor bought it, Kelly definitely needed a car, but others disappointed him by fund-raising at home and providing themselves with cars without his permission. He admired Bishop O'Rourke's policy of prohibiting his men from doing this. Ruefully, Taylor observed, "Two cars in the Vicariate outshine mine". Murray had brought back a new Chev after leave, and Clery had bought a new one in Nigeria. Less dazzling was the second-hand 'Baby Ford', known as "the bread van", which Sexton Cahill had bought and sold to Pat Braniff the builder.

As yet there was no policy on cars in the Vicariate or in the Society, though there were Guidelines agreed at the SMA Ordinaries' meeting in Cork in 1937. The Provincial advised Taylor "to take a stand against cars, or better still to form men's minds to accept the idea that transport is a Mission matter and men should not be making collections at home unless they got permission". Taylor doubted that cars were a real help to missionary work, "It wants a very steady Father to confine the use of a car to what *is* necessary and useful, and cars are a big expense". He feared costly repairs, and thought that Fathers tinkering with defective machines would only make them worse, "*None* of us really knows a hang thing about cars". Running costs were expensive: the license alone cost £6 a year for a small car and £9 for 'an ordinary car'. "Some Fathers won't pay", he predicted, "resulting in a bad name for us all, and difficulties later when trying to sell a car". He did recognize their usefulness for travelling to outstations but argued, "Two miles are done in joy rides for every mile done for outstation work".

Regarding the training of new men on the mission, Stephen Harrington, the Provincial, proposed a scheme whereby Visitors would have a large house where new men would spend their first six months in a training programme. He called the training idea, a *tyrocinium* – the word used in the Roman imperial army for the first period of training of new recruits. Harrington suggested that the old seminary property in Asaba, which

S. Harrington

belonged to the Society, could be used. Taylor agreed, adding, he'd be happy if his Vicariate took a lead. But in 1937, the conference of Ordinaries rejected the idea. Harrington, "bowing to greater experience", told Taylor he could use the old seminary for the maternity centre he had planned. Actually the vacated seminary was small, with room for only two in the Fathers' house, and the students' block was in "a ruinous" state. After Taylor restored it, OLA Sisters took it over as a care centre for infants.

1938

In the New Year, Bishop Taylor was still wondering who the re-elected Provincial was going to appoint as Visitor for Western Nigeria. Though he was sure that PJ Kelly would get 90% of the votes of the confreres, and agreed that he was the best man for the job, he hoped he wouldn't get it because he wanted him to continue as Pro-Vicar. The 1937 General Assembly had decreed that the two offices, Visitor and Pro-Vicar, could not be held by the same man. Taylor, understanding Kelly's desire to be free of administrative responsibilities to devote himself to pastoral work, "for which he aches", suggested Val Barnicle or Pat O'Connell as alternatives. Some of the confreres also felt Pat deserved a break. The gregarious Fr O, with his ear to the ground, said, "PJ is tired and doesn't want to be Visitor so we're not going to stick him". However, despite all, it was PJ Kelly who was again appointed. Pat accepted the decision as God's will. Brushing off Stephen Harrington's praise as "Blarney", he said there were several others in the Vicariate who would have been just as good.

In 1938 quite a large number of the missionaries fell seriously ill and had to be sent home. When Pat visited Joe Barrett, hospitalized in Onitsha, he was told by the doctors that the patient was not likely to recover in Nigeria. Overlooking the fact that he hadn't finished his four-year tour, Pat and the Bishop agreed that he should be sent home. It was a similar story with Nicholas Clery, Tom Barron and Eugene McSweeney, all had to be invalided home. Unfortunately Clery and McSweeney did not recover sufficiently to return to the mission. Tom Duffy, suffering from rheumatism, requested and was granted permission to go on leave six weeks before the end of his tour. Departures meant vacancies in the stations and disruption of community life. Adding to the problem, a number of men were late in returning from leave. "JJ" Healy was involved in a drawn-out family, legal 'palaver'; Alfie Glynn hadn't yet finished his doctorate in Rome, and others were late due to personal problems.

In a bad storm in Sapele in May, Pat Shine's new church, hardly two years old, the one Pat had helped build, was hit by lightning and burned to the ground. Everything in it was destroyed (including Pat's spare copies of the *Constitutions* and *Directory*). Shine, preparing to start *ex nihilo* again, asked the Provincial for £1000. Pat, cautious in expending Society money, and thinking of the danger of precedents, didn't support the request, but suggested that Shine be allowed to keep any Mass stipends he received. The Bishop, for his part, suggested to the Provincial that he give Shine at least £600.

At this time, 1938, Bishop Taylor was peeved that over the years, the balance of power between himself and the Visitor had tipped in favour of the Visitor, "All the time that I was in Lagos I never heard, or almost never, of a Visitor. All orders came from the Bishop who was regarded as the only boss. We sent our Mass accounts to the Visitor and he used to talk to us sometimes about morning meditation. I carried that on when I became Bishop here. True, Fr Kelly sometimes pointed out, very gently and tactfully, that I was poaching on his grounds and of course I apologised and withdrew. But actually, as the Book goes, *everything* is in the hands of the Visitor". Taylor rejected the idea that there was a "dual authority" on the missions, with bishop and visitor independent of one another, "I couldn't carry on for three months without the Visitor's money – a gift from the Society. The Bishop is dependent on the Visitor, if he reduces the surplus I'm sunk. My position is a cod and so is the idea of the two authorities on the mission".

Nevertheless, he believed there was a good spirit in the Vicariate. Believing the same, Pat sympathised with the Bishop on his financial worries and agreed with him on the need for economy. There was no mistrust between them about getting the Provincial Bursar to open a joint bank account in Cork in the Bishop's name. In fact Pat told the Bursar to close the bank account he had already opened for him in Cork. At the end of the year the Visitor's credit balance in the joint account would go, as a gift from the Society, to the Bishop. All Pat wanted was a statement every six months of the amount he had in the account. However, he kept an accurate estimate in his own head of how much should be there.

In September, the Vicariate received the sad news of Georges Krauth's death by accident in Togo. Transferred from Western Nigeria at the end of '37, he took up his appointment to the mission of Mango in the New Year. On 29 August 1938, after a long hot morning exposed to the sun while repairing the roof of the mission house, he was overcome by the heat and fell to his death. Pat, presuming the Provincial's permission, instructed all the Fathers to say Mass for him even though he was not a member of the Irish Province. Regarded as one of the "old-timers" in Western Nigeria, he was, in fact, only fifty-two when he died. In his passing, Pat lost his first mentor and confidant on mission. Though little given to expressing personal sorrow, Pat often spoke about Georges Krauth to younger men and, later, he named a new Grammar school at Obinomba, a station Krauth had opened, "St George's" in his honour.

News of Georges' death was quickly followed by that of Bishop Francis O'Rourke in Lagos, 28 October. This distinguished classmate of Bishop Broderick had first arrived in the 'Bight of Benin' in 1906. Appointed to Holy Cross cathedral in Lagos, he had worked especially in education until 1911 when he was sent to England and America to raise funds for the soon-to-be-erected Irish Province. He remained in America until 1925 when he was chosen by the confreres there as Delegate for the Provincial Assembly. At the Assembly he was elected Provincial councillor and appointed to the Province's transit house in Liverpool. In May 1929 he was nominated Prefect Apostolic of Northern Nigeria but, when Mgr Ferdinand Terrien, the Vicar Apostolic of the Bight of Benin, died at sea in August the same year, O'Rourke was appointed to succeed him. He continued the work of developing the Vicariate and began building the new Holy Cross cathedral in Lagos. After the Assembly of 1937, he was detained at home for medical reasons. Though not in good health he returned to Nigeria in September '38, and died the following month. Like Broderick, and Terrien who died aged fifty-two, O'Rourke was comparatively young, fifty-six. Now, rumours, which seemed to be supported by a letter from the Generalate in Rome, gave rise to speculation that O'Rourke's successor would be Leo Taylor and that Taylor would be replaced in Asaba-Benin by William Lumley of Jos.

At the end of 1938, Taylor thanked God that there had been no deaths among his personnel, but there had been serious illnesses, "1938 was a dark year in my life, 'fittingly' ended with the loss of Fr Clery [kept at home for health reasons], which I feel very much, and the illness of the Catholic doctor and assistants at the Ossiomo Leper Settlement, which may lead to its passing out of our hands". He was also very worried about the Vicariate's financial situation and he prayed God that 1939 would bring some relief. On the other hand, he found that "the spirit of fraternal harmony among the Fathers continued unbroken. I thank God for the fine team of men; I suppose I must pay in some way for the help and consolation they give" (27 December '38).

1939 opened with the death of James McNicholas. The same age as Pat, he had been invalided home from Liberia in 1926, in his first year of mission. He died in Cork on 1 January. The following month, the mission-minded Pope, Pius XI died. Pat remarked, "I hope we will get as good a Pope for the Missions as the last one". Cardinal Eugenio Pacelli was elected in March, and took the name Pius XII.

In June, Bishop Taylor, still sharing quarters with the Education Supervisor in Benin City, began crossing out "Asaba" from his old headed note paper and typing in "Box 35, Benin City". With Pat, he worked on his plan to hold a Synod of priests in July after the annual retreat. It would be the Vicariate's first Synod. The Provincial, Stephen Harrington, supported the idea and sent a number of suggestions and proposals for the agenda, especially points about his 'tyrocinium' idea. The consensus of the confreres' thinking on the tyrocinium, according to Pat, was that such a six-month training period should be done, not on the missions but at home! However, he admitted, "There is no doubt that the present system [new men being trained by different Fathers in different stations for six months] is not attended with good results". Taylor was even more negative about it, "It's not working ... it's a cod ... Instead of fitting the man for his job, it knocks the enthusiasm out of him". But more urgent than the initial training of new missionaries, was the financial situation of the Vicariate, Taylor wanted to put the reality of the situation before his personnel, and introduce drastic measures to avoid bankruptcy.

Unfortunately the Synod had to be cancelled. In June, Rome, proving that rumours can be half right, nominated Leo Taylor to succeed Francis O'Rourke, but didn't name anyone for Western Nigeria. Taylor's nomination coincided with the Silver Jubilee of his priesthood. He fielded the double congratulations modestly, ruefully pointing out that, "to exchange this nice Vicariate of Western Nigeria for the palavers of Lagos is rather a matter of commiseration". Memories of former unpleasantness from confreres in Lagos returned, "I was a pariah, it's not too strong a word". He planned to take up his new responsibility before 14

September, the feast of the "Holy Cross" – the name of the cathedral of Lagos. John Mahon, appointed Pro-Vicar on 17 March, would take over in Benin as soon as Taylor departed. Pat would remain in office as Visitor and be "a general stiffener" in the Vicariate, said Taylor. Wondering who his own successor would be in Asaba-Benin, Taylor hoped it would be PJ Kelly.

Though the Synod had to be abandoned, the Vicariate's financial crisis was too urgent to leave entirely to the new bishop. In the past year, expenditure, without any exceptional disbursements, had exceeded income by £800; capital continued to decline and income to diminish. After meeting with his councillors and the Visitor, Taylor sent a circular to all the confreres announcing strict new measures to keep the Vicariate solvent. Aimed at orienting mission stations towards self-sufficiency, the measures included severe reductions in allocations. Men would have to live more economically; building would have to cease; no new Fathers would be sought for the time being; the faithful would have to increase their support; and more overseas funding would have to be sought. He concluded by thanking the men for their loyalty, kindness and forbearance which, along with the friendliness of the Africans, made his five years in Western Nigeria very happy and increased his grief in departing.

To his surprise, the circular was well received and this helped to cheer him up. But, writing to the Provincial at the end of July, he admitted he was tired and had been suffering from low fever for two months. He hoped to take a week's rest in Okene, a pleasant mission in the north of the Vicariate, before going to Lagos, but the fever got the better of him and, instead, he had to spend the week in Warri hospital.

Meanwhile, Pat was thinking of his own home leave. He had left Liverpool on 18 September 1935 and, wondering whether the four-year tour began at Liverpool or on arrival at Lagos, he thought he might be able to get away 'a little bit early' so as to meet his brother who was home from America, but would return there by 19 September at the latest. The confreres argued that the tour began when they arrived at Liverpool, because that was when the Visitor expected them to begin offering Mass for "Superior's intentions". He put his request "to go a little bit early" to the Provincial. Independently, Bishop Taylor backed it up, saying he suspected Pat was suffering from appendicitis. But, when Pat heard that Taylor was nominated to be Bishop of Lagos, he dropped the idea saying, he "wasn't too pushed about going home anyway". Already, Val Barnicle had gone on leave, "a little bit early" and, at heart, Pat was not in favour of cutting tours short. Having delayed his own departure, he thought he would, henceforward, be "in a better position to stand out against those 'little bits early'." There was a more compelling reason for him to wait on. Maurice Slattery, the Superior General, had intimated that he, Pat, was in fact the one Rome was going to nominate as Taylor's successor and he should wait at least until the nomination was made public. Pat was shocked, "I went as far as I reasonably could in asking Fr Slattery to pass me over. I believe it would have been far better for myself not to get it, and even yet I have last moment hopes that the Holy Ghost will know better than all the Superiors".

~~~

Early on Sunday, 3 September 1939, in response to Hitler's invasion of Poland, war was declared on Germany by France and England. That morning most Irish minds were focused, not so much on the ominous events in Europe, but on the All-Ireland hurling final to be played that afternoon between Kilkenny and Cork in Croke Park. In a tight game, Kilkenny just beat Cork, 2 goals and 7 points to 3 goals and 3 points. As the crowds left the Park, thunder and lightning broke out, and news of the beginning of the Second World War passed from one to another.

With the War, prices rose, goods became scarce and, in many

places, rationing was introduced. Thinking ahead, Pat requested the Provincial bursar for "guaranteed flour" in sealed tins so that they could make their own altar breads if supplies were cut off. Elder Dempster's weekly shipping schedule between Liverpool and Lagos was disrupted and the voyage was no longer safe. Missionaries were instructed to travel in pairs – so that they could absolve one another if their ship came under attack. Thinking of his own leave Pat said, "We must trust in Providence".

The Sacred Congregation for the Propagation of the Faith, having chosen the man to be Vicar Apostolic of Western Nigeria, formally communicated his name to the Superior General in December. Around the time the decision was being made, the bishop-to-be was playing football with the school boys in Ubiaja. In a crucial tussle for possession, he received a kick on a varicose vein and had to remain in bed for a week. The General wrote informing him of the nomination:

> I'm delighted Pat beyond words. Never a missionary more deserved the honour. Never was a mission of ours put into safer and holier hands. God bless you and spare you. I hope your great admirer Mgr Riberi will consecrate you in Asaba. Again greetings, congratulations and God's choicest blessings.
>
> M. Slattery, Rome, 13 December 1939.

A week later Slattery wrote to the Pro-Vicar, John Mahon, in Asaba, "I'm sure you'll be pleased with your new Bishop. He is a perfect man, one of the best of priests and the greatest of missionaries. Of course he'll find it hard to accept the office, but that is only part of his worth, of his humility". John Mahon breathed a sigh of relief for, privately, he had feared that he might be nominated himself. He replied to the General, "Yes, we are really delighted, we could scarcely have got a better man" and to his confreres said, "the best thing Riberi ever did in Nigeria was to make Pat Kelly bishop".

When Pat got the news, he wrote to Stephen Harrington, expressing his trepidation and disinclination for the high office, "The nomination so long threatening has come at last and the Superior General seemingly did not take my request into account. Anyway it must be himself or Archbishop Riberi, or both, that had the final say, so I had only to agree and take it as God's will when the news came. So I replied to both saying I accepted to be Vicar Apostolic of Western Nigeria". He asked for prayers "that I may be able for it and carry out the designs of Almighty God in my regard".

In view of Slattery's hope that the consecration be in Asaba, Pat requested Stephen Harrington's support that it be in Ireland. He was due leave and, fearing for the health of his seventy-five year old mother, said he "hoped to see her alive once more". While waiting for a reply he appointed Sexton Cahill, already a Visitor's councillor and superior of the Benin City mission, to act as Visitor from 1 January 1940.

One of Pat's last official functions as Visitor was seeing to the obsequies of the longest-serving missionary in the Vicariate, Eugene Strub. Since his arrival in 1898, Strub had served not only as pastor, especially among the Etsako people, but as Visitor and Pro-Vicar at Asaba. His final tour, which had begun in 1919, continued without a break until his death. He became ill at Asaba before Christmas and died on 28 December '39 at Enugu while on the way to hospital in Port Harcourt. He was sixty-five. Writing his obituary Pat said, he died "in the odour of sanctity, for he was not only our oldest missionary but also our most saintly one". Solemn Requiem Mass was sung for him by his compatriot, Charles Burr, now the only Alsatian left in the Vicariate, assisted by Bishop Heerey CSSp of Onitsha and a great congregation of laity and religious. Pat instructed all the priests to offer Mass for him. Two years later, Pat wrote a tribute about Strub which was published in the *African Missionary*. Clearly admiring him and, seemingly unaware of the numerous similarities between himself and Strub, Pat praised his knowledge of the people's languages and customs, his dedication, and good counsel. "By nature he was most retiring, yet when the need arose, he readily opened a profound store of learning, yes, and of wit and humour also". Though not sharing in "dear old Father Strub's" musical talents, Pat was impressed by his school-boy choir "famous for its rendering of Plain Chant". He was even more impressed by the veteran's spiritual qualities, "I will personally testify to his holiness and perfection. Rarely did he miss his daily Holy Hour before the Blessed Sacrament and then only by necessity. Even travelling, he was quietly saying his Rosary; but the one virtue, all had to note, was his Patience ... even the most headstrong melted before his placidly forbearing reception of their wrongs. The needy, the poor, the distressed, all sought his door as by right". Admirable too was Strub's relationship with his long-time catechist, who though not formally professed, was known to everyone as "Brother Ignatius". Pat concluded his tribute, asking for a prayer for "the Beloved Pastor of Asaba" and "for those of us who are striving to follow in his footsteps".

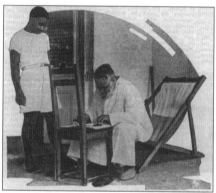
Eugene Strub and Brother Ignatius

In the first week of January 1940, after preaching a retreat for Sisters, Pat received word from the Superior General agreeing that he be consecrated at home. He booked his passage and sailed at the end of the month with Willie Keenan and Bill Fegan.

Chapter 7

VICAR APOSTOLIC

From many points of view Pat was an excellent choice for leadership of the Vicariate. With fifteen years experience in Western Nigeria, including almost a decade as Visitor and Pro-Vicar, he was well-acquainted with the people, languages, customs, missionary personnel and the terrain. A man of deep prayer and faith, he had won the respect of all for his hard work, simple life-style, and ability to deal with problems quickly, sensibly, and compassionately. Mentally razor sharp, physically he was as tough as nails.

Kate Kelly, Pat's mother, knew almost as soon as he did of his definitive nomination as Vicar Apostolic. On receiving the news from the Provincial in Cork she replied immediately:

Tristaun, 13 December 1939
Dear Rev Father,
Your wire of the 13 inst. informing me my son Pat is appointed Bishop came as a great surprise. I never thought he would be found worthy for such a high calling. I thank you most sincerely for your kind regards and trouble. Enclosed find a few shillings for the Mission.
I just had a letter from him saying he would come home in January with some other priests. I wonder will he come at all now?
Yours most sincerely, Mrs Mal. Kelly.

It was cold when Pat arrived home in the New Year of 1940, but the welcome was warmer than usual. His mother and family struggled a bit with the idea that their "Africa man", as his brothers called him, was going to be a bishop. But they quickly sensed that essentially he was still the same humble man. The first day home he walked to the stream at the end of the farm, surveyed the fields and the cattle and, on returning to the house, said he'd be saying Mass as usual and, "Yes, he'd have an egg for his breakfast afterwards". The neighbours came to see him; they too were surprised that 'episcopacy' didn't seem to be showing on him. In winter, there wasn't a great deal to do on the farm, he spent more time than ever praying.

Fr Spelman, the parish priest of Aughrim, brought him to Loughrea to see the Bishop, Mgr John Dignan, to talk about the consecration. Mgr Dignan was helpful and spoke about his own consecration, "It cost me £1,500, I only paid off the loan from the bank the other day ... Avoid a banquet, it cost over £300". Pat felt that while Mgr Dignan was willing to give way to others, he would like to do the consecration himself. When Pat asked him, he readily agreed. Leaving the choice of date, place and co-consecrators to Pat, he loaned him a book by 'Martinucci', an authority on ceremonies and rubrics. Pat studied it by the turf fire at home. He chose Sunday, 2 June, as the day of consecration – it was in the octave of the feast of the Sacred Heart – and St Michael's, Ballinasloe, as the venue. Dr Mulhern of Dromore, who had ordained so many Dromantine men, and Mgr Neville CSSp of Eastern Nigeria, agreed to be co-consecrators. A boyhood friend, Fr Antonine Kelly OFM, Dublin, would preach, and a priest from Ballinasloe would be master of ceremonies. For his episcopal motto Pat chose, *Turris fortis mihi Deus*, "God to me is a tower of strength" – the motto of the Kelly clan. His coat of arms portrayed on one half, an Irish round tower and on the other, an African palm tree.

His old school master, Pat Keohane, called at Tristaun to present him with the poem he'd written specially for the occasion and to discuss what his former pupil would like as a gift. A verse of the poem read:

A scion of a noble clan
– Hy-Many's chieftains bold –
His Lordship will enhance the name,
And win to the True Fold
Nigeria's sons and daughters,
Who still in Darkness stray,
With Jesus' help and Mary's
To aid him thro' each day.

After discussing a gift, they agreed on an episcopal ring. However, the ring Pat wore on the day of the consecration was the gift of the Reardons who lived near the seminary in Blackrock Road, Cork. Thanking them he said, "The ring got a great blessing and a great kissing after the ceremony and I swanked the very nice alb presented by Mrs Reardon and comrades". He wrote to the Provincial about a mitre, joking, "Taylor's will have to be widened for me".

Pomp and ceremony was not at all to his liking. Writing to Alfie Glynn in Nigeria to thank him for the Masses he and the confreres had offered for his intentions and their gift of a silver chalice, he said he hated the fuss and wished it was all over. The missionaries in Western Nigeria were pleased at his nomination, but some wondered how he would turn out. Tommy Greene in Agenebode, writing to the Provincial said, "How is dear old PJ? He is a grand old man and we are glad to have him as Bishop, though we guess he'll be a bit of a Hitler when he get's going".

The sun shone brightly over Ballinasloe on Sunday the 2nd of June 1940. The streets were colourfully decorated with flags, bunting and streamers. Townspeople, mingling with farmers and their families from Tristaun, Craugh, Clontuskert, Aughrim and farther afield, dressed in their Sunday best, headed towards St Michael's church at the end of the town square. Children on the look-out, cried shrilly that "Two Popes have just gone into the church". The imposing limestone church, suitably decorated, quickly filled up. Pat's mother Kate, brothers Jack and Bill, sisters Ellie, May and Kathleen, spruced up and nervous, sat in the front pew. Among the special guests were: Dr Walsh, archbishop of Tuam; Mgr Hynes, president of the University in Galway; Stephen Harrington, SMA Provincial Superior; Rev J. Cogavin, President St Joseph's College, Garbally; Parish Priests, including J.F. Fallon of Clontuskert and Spelman of Aughrim. Outside the altar rails on a special chair, sat Mr W.T. Cosgrave T.D. A large contingent of missionaries on leave from Western Nigeria and former members of the Vicariate were also present. Among them: Val Barnicle, who was Pat's assistant at the ceremony, Tom Bartley, Willie Keenan, Pat Fleming, Jerry Sheehan, George McCormack, Harry Kenny, Bill Fegan, and John Cadogan. Holy Ghost missionaries Frs Ryan, Murphy and Mangan, along with Bishop Neville, represented Eastern Nigeria.

The sun shone brightly through the church's many stained glass windows, one of them, appropriately, depicted a mitred missionary under an African palm tree. The bishop elect, impressive in his Celtic vestments, looked pale but composed. The measured tones of Bishop Dignan's sonorous Latin hushed the congregation. For most, it was the first time to witness the ordination of a bishop: the taking of the oath, the interrogations and profession of faith, the acceptance of the signs and functions of office, the awesome prostration, the long litany, the touching of the open book of the Gospels on the shoulders of the bishop elect, the binding and anointing of his hands *What you bless may it be blest, what you hallow may it be hallowed,* the bestowal of pastoral staff, ring, and Gospels.

Fr Antonine ascended the steps of the stone pulpit and began his sermon, "Another successor has been added to the long line stretching back to the Apostles..." He went on to speak of the War, "When dictators of our day are laid low in their elemental dust, and the power of arms has blasted itself to silence in a maelstrom of misery ... the Divine Promise will continue to find fulfilment, 'All days even to the consummation of the world'." He held the congregation spellbound and, coming to an end, paid tribute to the work of missionaries, mentioning that the African Church was one of the most promising in the world.

The Mass continued with Consecrator and Elect sharing in the enunciation of the eucharistic prayer. Finally, wearing a golden mitre and bearing an episcopal staff, the new "Vicar Apostolic of Western Nigeria and titular bishop of Tignica", emerged to give his episcopal blessing, first to his mother and family and then to the whole congregation.

Blessings imparted, the new Bishop, dignitaries, family and friends repaired to the Mercy Convent where the sisters had prepared a very fine lunch. After dessert, Pat Keohane delivered his poem in praise of the bishop. Somewhat embarrassed, Pat proposed a toast to the Pope and thanked Bishop Dignan and his co-consecrators. Archbishop Walsh of Tuam, replying to a toast, said that Ireland had taken the foreign missions to heart, in no other country in the world was such enthusiasm found. He added proudly that no other diocese in the universal church had given as many priests to the Society of African Missions as the archdiocese of Tuam!

Episcopal ordination,
2 June 1940
Kathleen (sister),
Kate (mother),
May (sister),
Ellie (sister); Back,
Jack (brother),
Bill (brother).

When everything was over, Pat borrowed Fr Spelman's Morris Minor and, helping his mother, three sisters and a small niece to squeeze in, drove off carefully, mindful that the ladies were unused to cars and it was the little girl's first time in one. Near Walshe's, his Church of Ireland neighbours, the car broke down! The Walshes, in high good form, turned out in strength and, anticipating an ecumenical movement, put their weight behind the Minor and got the new Monseigneur going again.

It had been a great day, but there had been so much hand-shaking, ring-kissing, congratulating and advising on how to be a bishop that Pat felt more exhausted than if he'd spent a month in the Bini bush. He was glad to get home, put the ring back in his pocket, and pray in peace for a while. Among other odd 'highlights' of the day, the words of Fr Spelman rang in his mind, "Don't ever suspend a priest!". After a cup of tea in the kitchen, he took his breviary and ambulated up and down the avenue saying Evening Prayer as the sun slowly set at the end of a long June day.

Vicar Apostolic of Western Nigeria

One week after his consecration, Pat ordained three young men for the diocese of Clonfert at Bishop Dignan's request: Tom Keys, Peter Dunne and John Higgins. Also in June, he ordained nineteen Dromantine students to sub-deaconate. Apart from these ceremonies, the new bishop did not have a great deal of 'episcopal' work to do. Though keen to get back to his mission, he was unable to do so, as passenger ships were prohibited from sailing to Africa because of the risk of attack from German submarines and planes.

With time on his hands he joined the African Missions students' Thirty Days Retreat in Cloughballymore in August. The retreat master, at first taken aback at the idea of a bishop joining in the novices' retreat, was put at ease by Pat's simplicity once he arrived. The young students, uncertain whether it was normal or not to have a bishop amongst them, were greatly impressed by the amount of praying he did. The retreat master, Tom Counihan, a very ascetical Jesuit, prayed much, fasted often, and used his 'discipline' three times a week. Not everyone in the African Missions liked his methods or his severity, but Pat was not put off. In fact one of the retreatants, Vincent Boyle (later a missionary in Western Nigeria), observed that "the Bishop and Counihan were up the one street in spirituality". Vincent's cherished memory of the Retreat, was "the sight of the Bishop going around the walks in his scarlet soutane with the turkeys following him and he trying to shoo them away". After the retreat, Pat, when sending £1 to the Provincial "for cigarettes for the Brothers", took the opportunity to advise him to do the long retreat too. He did.

The long retreat, Cloughballymore, 1940.

On Bishop Kelly's right is Tom Counihan sj, next to Counihan is Fr Dinny Slattery sma. Four students of this class would be appointed to Benin: **1.** Jim Flanagan, **2.** Mick Grace, **3.** Vincent Boyle, **4.** Mick Cavanagh.

Before the end of the retreat Pat wrote his Resolutions. These, and many subsequent ones, written on odd scraps of paper and the backs of envelopes, were among the very few personal items that he preserved. The oldest surviving ones are of his 1940 long retreat. No doubt he followed the recommendation of his Jesuit retreat master when he began by writing "A.M.D.G." at the top of the page. A.M.D.G., the initial letters of Ad maiorem Dei gloriam (For the greater glory of God) was the motto of Ignatius of Loyola and his Society of Jesus – the Jesuits.

Pat's first resolution was "To keep the Rule punctually", especially in the areas in which he felt he was negligent: "Particular Examen [a daily 15 minute examination of conscience, usually performed before lunch], Visit to the Blessed Sacrament and Monthly Retreat; and to say the Office [Breviary] and do Spiritual Reading as far as possible at a regular hour.

2. "Not to complain about food", to which he added, in parenthesis, something that would surprise those who lived with him, "[this resolution] does not prevent me from remedying things quietly".

3. "For at least one month to follow the preacher's method of writing out points of meditation and marking Particular Examen".

4. "Until I leave for Africa and perhaps afterwards I will mortify myself at each of my meals in some little thing and abstain from taking sugar in my tea.

5. "To give up smoking cigarettes".

6. "Not to take intoxicating drink as people commonly understand it – out of a glass in liquid form".

7. "Not to play cards until I leave for Africa and then only when I see it may be for the good of others".

8. "To cut out the cinema, unless the film is purely religious or educational".

9. "Not to go out shooting alone and, to go with others only when they suggest it".

He concluded, "Trusting in the Sacred Heart through the intercession of the most Pure Heart of Mary and of the Angels and Saints, especially the Angels and Saints I have devotion to, to keep these [resolutions] for the Love of my Saviour and to make myself more and more like Him".

PJK   29 August 1940

As often happened with Pat, no sooner had he finished a letter or a document than he thought of something else. This time he added at the bottom of the page, "And to avoid as far as possible playing billiards".

Clearly, Pat intended to make spiritual progress. Now in his mid forties, strong and energetic, he had firmly decided to leave behind the things of youth and middle age, cigarettes, alcohol, card-playing, cinema, shooting, and billiards but also, it would seem, some of the normal socialising and healthy recreating that went with them. Already possessed of a rather demanding spirituality, he now appeared to be intent on honing it in a search for "spiritual perfection" by means of an exacting fidelity to Rule. Evidently a man given to exercising his 'conscience' and scrutinising it regularly and systematically, he had determined to strive even more towards a higher state of spiritual perfection, hoping that in the end he would "make himself more like Him". No doubt he would make great demands on himself.

He departed from Cloughballymore and returned to Tristaun where he remained for a short time before travelling on to Newry, Co Down, where, in the cathedral on 13 September, he was to confer the order of deaconate on the nineteen Dromantine sub-deacons and one student of Dromore diocese. He also conferred Minor Orders on other SMA students. A week later, he spoke to the students in Dromantine on "Initial difficulties encountered by young missionaries in Africa". He emphasized the importance, and the difficulty, of learning the vernacular language. Having spent most of September in the College, he departed on the 27th, which was proclaimed 'a free day' in his honour. He returned to Dromantine in December, to ordain the deacons. Seven of the nineteen would serve later as missionaries in Benin: Jim Byrne, Joe Donnelly, Jim Healy, Michael McFadden, Maurice Maguire, Ben Nolan, and Joe Stephens. A few days before the ordination, Belfast suffered an aerial bombardment. The noise of the explosions and gunfire could be heard in Dromantine and brought home to the students the reality of the War.

In January '41, following a request of the President of the diocesan college at Garbally (formerly The Pines), Pat gave a talk to the students about his work in Africa. As the New Year passed, there was no sign of an end to the War or of a passage to West Africa. Elder Dempster's waiting list of passengers, already long, continued to grow. Unexpectedly, early in May, passengers were told that a ship would sail from Liverpool within a few days. Pat and some twenty SMA confreres, including the Class of 1939, on their first voyage to Africa, packed in haste and rushed to Dublin's Northwall from where they crossed the Channel at night with all lights extinguished because of the 'black out'. On the ferry to Liverpool, Pat remembered that he'd left behind a box of altar stones, which he'd wrapped in new-mown hay for taking to Nigeria. Someone else would have to bring them later. Liverpool at dawn looked grotesque: half-sunk, bomb-damaged ships littered the harbour and much of the city was devastated after thirteen consecutive nights of bombing by the Luftwaffe. The confreres disembarked and made their way to the African Missions house on Ullet road where they were welcomed by Fr Eugene McSweeney. They retired to bed early, but their sleep was disturbed by the drone of German bombers overhead, fortunately for them, the planes' targets lay elsewhere.

Next day they boarded the s.s. *Abossa* bound for Lagos. Once out of the harbour, she steamed north to join a large convoy anchored off Glasgow which, under navy escort, hoped to be protected on the Atlantic voyage against enemy attack. Huge numbers of allied ships had already been sunk in the Atlantic and rumours abounded that the route to Africa was infested with U-Boats.

Among the Class of '39 was Dinny Slattery, who gave an exciting account of the voyage in his book, *My Life Story*. As luck would have it, he shared a cabin with "a Catholic missionary Bishop!" After a few days at Glasgow, the convoy of fifty ships sailed out of the harbour in single file, while a sepulchral voice on a loud hailer wished them, "Good luck and God bless you". The passengers were called on deck, given lifeboat drill and instructed what to do in the event of an attack – basically, go below if attacked from above and go above if attacked from below. They were also assigned to night watch, three hours at a stretch, alone, scanning the dark seas for any sight or sound of the enemy. After a few days they heard that Dublin had been bombed by the Germans. An argument started among the confreres whether it was really the Germans, or the British attempting to influence neutral Ireland to join the Allies. Called the 'North Strand bombing', 31 May 1941, thirty-eight people were killed and 141 were injured. (Recent research revealed that Hitler himself ordered the bombing.)

The *Abossa* ploughed on at a steady 18 knots, zig-zagging in the hope of evading submarines lurking below them. But the attack came from above! A solitary low-flying plane suddenly emerged from the direction of the rising sun, singled out the *Abossa*, bombed and machine-gunned it. Pandemonium broke out, as bombs exploded and bullets ricocheted off the iron superstructure. Below decks, passengers and furniture were tossed about. Adding to the noise, the *Abossa's* anti-aircraft gun began firing. Some of the priests, including Dinny, were saying Mass. Ordered back to their cabins, they divested quickly and hurried to their quarters. Reaching his cabin, Dinny found one of his confreres in the corridor giving general absolution to the whole ship, another was calmly shaving. His cabin mate, the bishop, was pulling on his trousers over his pyjamas. Just as the bishop was fastening his belt, there was a loud explosion and the ship's engines went dead.

Eventually, the 'All clear' sounded and the passengers gingerly emerged on deck. Thankfully there were no casualties, most of the crew and passengers were below deck when the attack occurred, but the engines were damaged. The convoy was scattered across the horizon and the *Abossa* lay far behind. Over the radio the Captain was told that he had forty-eight hours to repair the engines and rejoin the fleet, failing this the *Abossa* would be left behind. After some hours of serious mechanical activity, and even more serious intercessory prayer "led by that saintly Bishop Kelly", said Dinny, the engines came to life and the ship raced to catch up with the others.

Freetown, the first port of call on the West African coast, afforded the passengers a few days on terra firma. (It seems Pat and the new men didn't visit the Founder's grave this time either.) Ignoring a warning about U-Boats, the convoy sailed on. Near Monrovia, the terrifying sound of the alarm went off again. Pat, saying Mass, was told to hurry up and return to his cabin. After a period of nervous waiting in eerie silence, the 'All clear' was sounded. Without further excitement, they rounded Cape Palmas, sailed due east in the Gulf of Guinea and at last hove to off Lagos. To their disappointment, the *Abossa* could not enter the harbour, as a ship sunk by the Germans blocked the channel. Compelled to go on to Port Harcourt farther east, they arrived offshore after midnight, but here the tide was out and the ship couldn't cross the bar. Anchored offshore in the bright moonlight, she was 'a sitting duck' for enemy plane or submarine. Finally, with the near full-tide at dawn, on the 13th of June, they entered the harbour and docked. The weary passengers gladly disembarked, their voyage had taken thirty days – more than twice the usual time. Port Harcourt, in the Niger delta, suited those like Pat going to Asaba–Benin, but not those like Dinny going to Lagos, they had to make a long detour of 1,500 miles by train to Kaduna in the north and then south west to Lagos.

From Port Harcourt, Pat telegrammed Stephen Harrington, "All safe thank God – wire mother, Kelly", and he posted a letter he'd written him at Freetown saying, "We had a narrow escape". Not having had the privilege of reading Dinny's book (published many years later), he said, "*Your* prayers and the prayers of so many good people at home must have been in our favour".

He travelled on to Benin City by road where he was welcomed by **John Mahon**, the Pro-Vicar and superior of the Benin City mission. Mahon, a Kilkenny man, ordained in 1926, was one of the last class ordained in St Joseph's seminary in Cork. Arriving in Western Nigeria the same year, he quickly became one of the pillars of the Vicariate, serving as superior of St Paul's seminary at Asaba for three years, then as superior in Ubiaja until 1939 when he moved to Benin City. Nine years younger than Pat, he was a quiet, determined, practical man, particularly competent in financial affairs. While Pat was away, he had further reduced the allocations to some mission stations in an effort to stem the Vicariate's deteriorating financial situation. Exhorting the missionaries to be self-supporting, he had insisted that they "observe the strictest economy in the use of non-essentials". With the War, grants from Europe had virtually dried up and the price of goods had rocketed. Petrol was expensive and difficult to get, the price of meat had doubled in the space of a year, even the price of altar wine had doubled.

Mahon gave Pat the latest news, especially about the death of Pat Bermingham who had died while the Bishop was away. Bermingham, an Offaly man, had fallen ill with yellow fever on the last day of the priests' retreat in Benin City and, though rushed to Warri hospital, he died within a week, 18 July 1940. Despite the advances in medicine, premature deaths still occurred, Bermingham was only forty-four. Known as 'Brum', he had first arrived in Nigeria in 1925, worked with Cadogan in

Warri and with Krauth in Aragba. Superior of Aragba district at the time of his death, much of his early mission work had involved visitation by canoe in the Warri creeks. He nearly lost his life one night when, responding to a sick call, the canoe, in which he was travelling, capsized, but he managed to swim ashore.

The Bishop in residence
In Benin City, availing of Bishop Taylor's headed note paper with *Viriliter Age* on it, Pat got down to responding to an accumulated pile of letters. When his predecessor's stationery ran out, he used sheets of plain paper, quickly writing "Box 35, Benin City" at the top. Taylor hadn't been long enough in Benin City to begin building a better episcopal residence for himself, and Pat didn't think it necessary. He moved into a small, 1933-built, three-roomed, mud block bungalow, without water or electricity, and whitewashed it. This small house remained his episcopal palace until he retired over thirty years later. Roofed with corrugated iron, it had a verandah in front and steps down to ground level; on the right hand side was the Bishop's office, on the left an oratory where, if he wasn't in his office, he was usually to be found. When Mattie Walsh, as Visitor, began to install running water and indoor bathroom facilities in all mission houses, the bishop's was one of the last to be worked on, as Pat was keener

on saving money than on indoor plumbing. Never a paragon of tidiness, he didn't appreciate well-meaning Sisters, or others, tidying up, "You see now I can't find anything". The best room in the palace, swept and cleaned by Pat himself, was the oratory. Containing no more than an altar, tabernacle and a few chairs, it was the centre of his home in which, daily, he spent hours on his knees before the Blessed Sacrament.

The bishop's compound, on what became the Airport road out of Benin City, was about thirty acres in size, mainly of bush and tall grass. It contained a primary school, a maternity centre, and an annex near the 'palace' which became his secretary's office and living quarters. Next door was the inter-vicarial major seminary, St Paul's, and its church. The bishop enjoyed interacting with the seminarians and created a pleasant rapport with them, especially with those of his own Vicariate. He missed them when the seminary moved to Ibadan and worried that life in the big city would spoil them. To be in touch, at least with the younger ones, he opened a minor seminary, also called St Paul's, in the vacated buildings next door.

His daily routine was regulated by the Society *Directory*. Rising at 5.30, he shaved quickly – using an old paint brush for the lather! After meditating in his oratory, he joined the two Seminary priests in their chapel for morning prayer and Mass, assisting at their Masses before saying his own. After thanksgiving, he returned to his house to breakfast on porridge, bread with syrup or avocado, and a boiled egg on those occasions when one of the Seminary hens laid on his side of the fence. The rector often accused him of stealing eggs, but the Bishop always retorted, "They're stealing my grass, you should feed 'em on your side".

Cooking was done behind the Bishop's house. Each day, Pat would go to the back, count out pennies into the cook's hand and haggle with him for fifteen minutes over the price of vegetables to be bought at the "green market". Loud were the cook's complaints, "All the Fadda's cooks get more than the Bishop's!" More expensive shopping Pat would do himself on bicycle, first tucking the hem of his 'off-white' soutane into the belt of his shorts. He had made the belt himself out of packing case elastic. Parking the bike outside a big economy store like Kingsway, he'd enter and search for 'special offers'. When finished selecting his 'choice items', the shop assistants, who knew him well, would call him to the head of the queue, past the well-heeled ladies and gentlemen with their laden baskets, to pay for his purchases – which might be no more than one small can of beans or a doubtful-looking tin of old butter. Michael Boyle, a secretary, one morning at breakfast complained, "There are black spots in the butter". "They're in my egg too", agreed the bishop. "At least you know where the egg came from", complained the secretary.

Doing a great deal of his own office work he didn't believe in *full-time* secretaries. Having had about a dozen secretaries altogether over the years, he expected each of them to do a lot more than secretarial work. Tasks such as training catechists, helping in the seminary, hearing confessions, saying Mass in out-stations and in the central parish, sick calls and hospital visitation all fell to them. They didn't complain, as he was doing as much, and more, himself. With a prodigious knowledge of the Vicariate at his fingertips, he was always ready to help a secretary, but he was never 'bossy', or given to looking over their shoulders. If ever he wanted one to do something out of the ordinary, he was most humble and apologetic in his way of asking. Working for him was all right, but sharing his table, especially when he was the main 'shopper' was, hopefully, meritorious in the next world, for it was not very satisfying in this one. Extremely frugal himself, his secretaries felt starved. Some of them survived by making visits to other mission houses around 'chop' time. It was noted, however, that the Bishop had quite an appetite when eating out. Saving money by all means, one of his habits was turning down the wick of the kerosene fridge, a consequence of this was that his secretary's bottle of water, or 'cool' beer, remained at a steady tropical temperature. To distinguish his own bottle of water from his secretary's, he hung a label around his own inscribed, "I am Kelly's".

In the morning, he would spend an hour or two teaching the trainee catechists on the verandah before going to his office, where he would remain until it was time to visit the Blessed Sacrament before lunch. His favourite food was *eba* (fried cassava), but what he usually got was yam, or boiled rice, and 'fowl'. With a liking for chickens' legs, he often asked the cook, "Was that bird lame, had he only one leg?" If a visitor arrived, Pat might ask him if he'd like an egg on his yam, or a sausage (out of a tin), or beans. If beans were the preference, the Bishop would extract a small tin from a dusty cupboard, open it and plonk it down cold before the guest. On better days there was 'palm-oil chop' and groundnut stew; on Fridays fish. After lunch, he took siesta of about an hour, and then had some bread and tea. If there was a visitor, he made a show of driving the flies off the bread with the bread knife and, then holding the loaf firmly 'under his oxter' (elbow), he sawed off thick chunks, working the knife towards his chest.

The few bottles of beer and minerals stowed in a corner of the dining room were not for himself, but for visitors. If Sisters called, he entertained them on the verandah, but not for too long – following his own recommendation that his men observe 'a ten minute rule' when visiting convents. A half-wild tom cat was a regular visitor and Pat, perhaps influenced by his mother's love of cats, encouraged it by dropping thick globs of Peak's condensed milk on its head. Pat appeared to enjoy watching the creature's frantic efforts to lick it off. When Sister Norbert OLA called to see him on her first visit, she noticed that he didn't seem to mind the antics of a couple of small kittens who were playing with his hands which he had clasped behind his chair. Another caller was a simple youth whom the Bishop used to help. Called

Alexander, he had the knack of appearing at the wrong time, rolling on the ground and throwing off all his clothes when the Reverend Mother was there. After such a scene, Pat would comment to his secretary, "Sister was shocked!"

Pat had a red episcopal soutane, but wore it only on special occasions. His normal dress was the simple white one like all the priests wore, except his was no longer white. He liked the priests to wear soutanes, and didn't mind what condition they were in, he disapproved of shorts and shirt. To a new man, red and raw from insect bites on exposed arms and legs, he'd say "You see Father, if you wore your soutane the sandflies wouldn't get at you". One newly-arrived Father was taken aback when the Bishop, on turning to lead the newcomers into the house, revealed that his soutane was rent from waist to hem like the veil of the Temple. Pat disliked anything fancy in the line of clothes – like shirts with long-sleeves. Using only his hands he would tear the offending sleeves off at the shoulder. Wearing these improved models gave him "a Robinson Crusoe look", said Vincent Boyle (the former 'fellow Retreatant' in Clough, who became his secretary in Benin). Once, nearing St Patrick's Day, OLA Sisters made a fine white shirt for the Bishop and sent it to the palace. On the feast, Sr Mary Maddock and a companion went to greet him. Drawing near they noticed workers building a mud house. From behind it, the Bishop emerged, resplendent in his new shirt, but carrying two wet mud blocks up against it! Adding to the 'Robinson Crusoe look' was the ancient brown scapular that he always wore around his neck; Boyle called it "the original teabag". On one level Pat's unconcern for smart dressing imparted a message about simple living, on another it gave advance warning to those thinking of 'worrying' him for money. The "dishevelled look" had long been his style but, no matter what he wore, he was always 'himself', and radiated a strong sense of 'presence'.

In something of the same spirit, if invited to official functions by 'Residents' or District Officers, he would go in an old banger of a car that needed to be push-started. At the end of the function, it pleased him to get some senior colonial officers to give him a push. After Independence, he did the same with ministers and chiefs, many of whom had been his former pupils. No one took offence and 'the old boys', enjoying their special rapport with the Bishop, recalled school days and the pranks they played on him.

He liked the trainee catechists and devoted a lot of his time to teaching them. Holding up very high ideals, he gave them spiritual retreats, lecturing them especially on the serious topics of "the World, the Flesh, and the Devil". On one occasion when he was called away during class, he gave them some questions to learn until he got back. On his return, he found them playing football. Striding to the goal post, he broke the crossbar with one strong pull. Study continued without another word. Usually, after seeing the catechists in the afternoon, he went on local visitation, going on foot or on bicycle when possible. This was about the only exercise he got except when, occasionally, he slashed grass, or joined the seminarians doing manual work. One task he helped them with was filling in a huge pit some thirty feet deep where, in olden days, human sacrifice had taken place. On Saturdays, he helped at Holy Cross cathedral, hearing confessions and, on Sundays, celebrating Mass. If he wasn't busy in the cathedral he would climb the stairs to the gallery where he had a favourite quiet place for prayer. After Vatican II, a Saturday evening Mass began and this became his Mass. Normally he drove to the cathedral, but occasionally went by bike, cycling as before with his soutane tucked inside his shorts. By this, he probably hoped to inspire his men to use bicycles more, as he thought they were becoming too attached to their cars, "the more wheels, the less spirituality" he grumbled.

Well-versed in the affairs of the diocese, he didn't occupy himself much with the news of the world. He didn't have a radio, but kept abreast of major affairs by taking a break on a Sunday evening – the only break he took in the week – to read the

Southern Herald, a Catholic paper, which a well-wisher sent him regularly from South Africa. Having ordered the *Irish Ecclesiastical Record* for the seminary, he glanced through it himself first. The only other periodicals he looked at were the *African Missionary* and the *Nigerian Catholic Herald.* The editors of the last two frequently asked him for articles, but he didn't have time for writing and didn't want to encourage his missionaries to do so either in case they became distracted from more important school or pastoral work. As Visitor he had started a small library for the confreres but, as Bishop, he left the palace library rather empty.

He was far from being a house-bound, bureaucratic bishop. A great deal of his time was spent away from home, especially on Confirmation tours. Reporting to the Provincial in 1942, Sexton Cahill, the Visitor, said, "The Bishop, when in residence, which is pretty seldom, stays in Benin. He is in good form, thank God, and the pace he sets for the rest of us is pretty fast. Like myself he has some silver threads among the black – but it all tends to make one 'venerable'!"

The Bishop with John Mahon, Andy O'Rourke, catechists and parishioners.

Confirmation tours were the most distinctive part of his ministry. Taking place throughout the year, each one lasted two or three weeks depending on the size of the parish and the number of outstations. Frequently, as many as 1,000 candidates, sometimes even more, were waiting to be examined. He regarded catechizing as one of the priest's most important tasks and these tours helped him find out how his men were doing. Normally he gave notice of his forthcoming visit but, on arrival, would still give the priest every chance to be 'prepared'. Parking his car in a prominent place in full view of the mission house, he walked to the church and, after praying at length, went to sit on the verandah, where he'd cough and clear his throat until the Reverend Father emerged, properly attired and prepared, to welcome him. However, he was capable of surprising men when he wanted to, as Vincent Boyle found out one evening when he was enjoying a cold beer in a government rest house. Out of nowhere the Bishop appeared, "Fr Boyle, I see you're doing your missionary work in the rest house!"

On confirmation examination days he seated himself about 9 a.m. on a hard chair under a tree with a table before him and a large round stone or piece of wood, a cloth, and a basin of water beside him. Immediately, scores of youngsters would crowd around, planting their baptismal cards on the table shouting, "Me Lord, me Lord". In feigned anger, he would sweep the cards off the table and make the petitioners begin all over again with a little more order. But confusion didn't bother him; in fact he often stirred it up. He soothed one exasperated priest, "Father, the more confusion the better!" Pat didn't believe in spoiling confirmation day with efficiency.

Calling a candidate forward, the Bishop asked what language he spoke, and then conduct the examination in that tongue. He didn't use English and, while good in about seven indigenous languages, he knew enough of the dozen or so other languages in the Vicariate to be able to ask questions, and to understand the responses, in all of them, following the numbered questions in the catechism. If a candidate failed some questions, he wrote the numbers of those questions on the candidate's baptism card and told him to go home and learn them again. Nearly all failed on the first attempt. He demanded near-perfect answers, and believed a little suffering and further study, improved the quality of one's Faith. Regularly he asked, "What are the chief mysteries?" and, "What is perfect contrition?" But the most important question was, "How do you baptise a dying pagan?". Anyone who failed this would not be confirmed. The examinee had to demonstrate his proficiency in administering the sacrament by whispering into the Bishop's ear the questions he would ask a dying person and then 'baptise' the stone or piece of wood by the bishop's side, first wiping it carefully "on the forehead" before pouring the water and saying, "I baptise you in the name of the Father, Son and Holy Ghost". If he did it satisfactorily, the Bishop would write "Pass" on his Baptism card and sign it "PJK".

Examining continued from morning to, sometimes, late at night with the aid of a bush lamp. Short breaks were taken for meals. Noisy youngsters milling about the Bishop's room during siesta, on at least one occasion, had a basin of water thrown over them. It was an exhausting time for everyone, especially the parish priest, and it could be an embarrassing time for him too. If a candidate gave poor answers, the Bishop enquired, "Who instructed you?" Normally he wouldn't criticise a priest but, believing that rewards were for the next world, he wouldn't praise him either. He often dropped cute comments like, "This is the best parish I've been in this year", especially when it was his first tour of the year! Even if he said nothing, priests knew when he was pleased, and when he was not.

No matter how late he finished in the evening or night, he never failed to do a Holy Hour, before retiring to bed. Kneeling, often on the rough cement floor of a classroom, he never cut short the hour, but timed it with an alarm clock that he carried especially for this purpose. The priests were thankful that he didn't expect them to accompany him in this. Although he cared little about lack of comfort, he could be disturbed by a loudly ticking clock or by snoring. He moved such a clock and, if disturbed by a snorer, he moved himself.

When candidates passed the examination on second or third attempts, he crossed out the numbers written earlier on their cards and wrote "Pass". Eventually every genuine candidate passed. 'Special cases', like the elderly or handicapped, he sent to the parish priest, knowing he would probably be less scrupulous about passing them than himself. Finally, all examining over, he put on his red soutane, red sash and red cap in preparation for the Mass and confirmations. It was then that someone was likely to ask for Confession. There was no point in the parish priest protesting that it was getting dark, or that there had been ample opportunity for confession for the past two weeks. "Father, it's a great opportunity for grace" was Pat's cold comfort, and confessions would go on as long as the people kept coming. The open-air scene became highly charged as darkness fell and the moon and stars came out; men, women and children milled around with candles and rosary beads, kneeling, standing, talking, walking, praying and singing. On one such occasion in Ubiaja, Tommy Greene turned to Jim Higgins, a young Father who was teaching in the school, and said, "Bishop is an extraordinary man, Père. He has arranged all this deliberately so that the people will never forget the night they were confirmed: he's trying to make it as memorable as their tribal initiation". Eventually the liturgy got under way. Candidates with cards marked "Pass" came forward, including an odd tricky fellow with his thumb covering the place where "Pass" and "PJK" should have been, but weren't. Ever alert, the Bishop, who even in old age didn't need spectacles, would push the concealing thumb aside and banish the deceiver. Candidates who wrote "Pass" and forged his signature were likewise detected and dismissed. For the many who were confirmed, their proud boast in later life was "Bishop Kelly confirmed me!"

Baptising the dying

Believing that baptism was absolutely necessary for salvation, Pat was most concerned that no one should die without receiving it. He went to great lengths to seek out the dying and appeared to have a special gift of knowing where they were. Many people tell of incidents apparently manifesting his prescience. Driving to Uzairue one day with Jim Healy, his car broke down. While Pat was looking under the bonnet, a woman passed apparently unseen by the Bishop but, when Pat straightened up, he told Jim, "Follow that woman and attend to the sick person in her house". On another occasion with Jim, his car bogged down in sand. A man passed, "Follow him" said Pat, "someone is dying". In fact the local chief was dying and wanted baptism. Passing through another village in the wet season on a very bad road, Pat ordered Vincent Boyle, who was driving, to stop. Vincent protested that if he stopped he might not be able to start again on the muddy road. Pat insisted. When they stopped, people told them that an infant nearby was at the point of death. In another case, Anthony Okuduwa, a teacher in Uromi, accompanied Pat on one of his confirmation tours. Passing a village, the Bishop said, "I must stop here". They went into the village where they found an old lady dying. She begged the Bishop to baptise her; after receiving the sacrament she died.

After a visit to Uromi, where three new missionaries were undergoing their 'tyrocinium', the Bishop drove off in the direction of Agbor. On the way he passed an old woman on the side of the road who didn't look well, but he kept going. Arriving at his destination, he sent a note back to the tyrocinium saying, "Go to Mile 18 on the Agbor Road, find the sick old woman, instruct and baptise". Three eager young missionaries, Sexton Doran, Gerry Sweeney and Jim Tobin, set out to do the Bishop's bidding. At Mile 18 they halted, searched and found, not one but, six sick old ladies. Keen to have a positive report for the Bishop, they baptised all of them.

In Benin City, Sister Magdalene, a non-professed Nigerian Church worker of high-repute, ran an orphanage which the Bishop had started. One evening she refused to admit three motherless children because their fathers, who had brought them, would not contribute towards their upkeep. She informed the Bishop who, later, became worried lest the children might die without being baptized. After praying, he roused his sleeping secretary. Apologising for the late hour he said, "We must look for those children". With the secretary driving and Pat giving directions, they located the first two children who, however, were not in danger of dying. While searching for the third child, they were stopped by a man with a cutlass who demanded to know their business. He turned out to be the father of the third child, and she was in danger of death. Pat asked his secretary to baptise her. This concern of his to baptise the dying was well known and even long after he departed from Nigeria, people still requested priests to "Do for me what Bishop Kelly did for my father before he died".

Chapter 8

MISSION BEFORE MAN

The early Forties

"A new broom sweeps clean", though in Pat's case, as he'd been Visitor and Pro-Vicar, he was not so much a new broom as an old one with a new handle. While developing the work of his predecessors, he also responded energetically to new situations and needs – especially the school apostolate which, in his time, included a huge expansion in the number of primary schools, the initiation of secondary education, and the recruitment of teachers with university degrees. Bishop Taylor, in the Thirties, had been cautious about asking the Province for more men, saying he couldn't afford them. In every letter, but one, Bishop Kelly begged for more. In the one exception he said he couldn't afford *pastoral* men, but wanted men with a university degree who, as recipients of Government salaries, would not be a financial burden and would attract grants for the schools they taught in. They, of course, would also be engaged in pastoral work, especially on week-ends and during school holidays. But even Pat's 'go slow' on pastoral men was temporary and, in fact, he rescinded it after only one year. He needed priests – he would find the money to support them somewhere (but they wouldn't want to expect very much). He stressed the Vicariate's need of finance, but he didn't let penury stop development – he grasped every possible way to collect and save; and he succeeded.

Realizing that the numbers of academically qualified SMA priests would be insufficient to cope with the expanding school apostolate in Asaba-Benin, he looked for Orders of teaching Brothers and Sisters, recruited lay graduates (mainly from Ireland), and sponsored Nigerian men and women for University degrees abroad. Convinced that schools were, not only instruments of education and national development but, a primary means of evangelization, he spared neither himself nor his personnel in developing the school apostolate. Also convinced of the unique position of the Catholic Church and its responsibility to teach the 'truth', the progress of the Church Mission Society (CMS), Baptist, and Government schools spurred him on to greater efforts.

While the school apostolate advanced, traditional pastoral work continued apace, as also did his promotion of trained catechists, indigenous priests, and the medical apostolate. Regretting that SMA priests were not trained as doctors like the CMS, he wished to have medical missionaries and offered to pay the expenses of any OLA Sister who would undertake university studies in medicine. He wanted to build a Catholic general hospital, a leper settlement (apart from Ossiomo), and wished to staff with lay Catholics as well as religious personnel a new Government leprosarium in Warri. He also wanted more maternity centres and homes for the elderly. None of his aims were pie-in-the-sky but practical and down-to-earth, most of which in time he did achieve, but not without a lot of help from others. Inevitably he also met with difficulties and resistance. A believer in self-sacrifice he expected and, sometimes, demanded too much from others. Society Visitors were the first in the chain of command to have to deal with him. The first Visitor in Bishop Kelly's reign enjoyed a good rapport with him but, sadly, he died young.

Sexton Cahill from Co Down arrived in Western Nigeria the month Bishop Broderick died in Genoa, October 1933. Pat, then Pro-Vicar, appointed him to Warri for his six-month induction period, after another six months there he was appointed to Benin City. In 1936 he became a member of the Visitor's Council, and in

'38 superior of Benin City mission. After returning from his first home leave, in January '39 he was given another heavy responsibility, Supervisor of Schools, which involved travelling, visiting mission schools, solving problems and corresponding with the Government.

Sexton Cahill (centre) with Pat Braniff and Tom Murray.

As Bishop Taylor had done, Pat, early in his episcopacy, checked the Visitor's books. Satisfied in general, he advised Cahill against accepting Mass stipends lower than the Vicariate's norm of four shillings. Cahill held Bishop Kelly in great respect, but wasn't overawed by him as is indicated by his light-hearted references: "All eyes are on the Bishop" (referring to a problem in Kabba, where there was trouble between CMS adherents and Catholics), "His Lordship has no time to say his extra Aves"; "Between Dr Glynn (in the Seminary) and the Bishop, woe betide the unfortunate individual who makes a liturgical or theological *faux pas*". Cahill's more serious priorities and attitudes were similar to Pat's, notably, the importance of keeping the Rule and the Constitutions, and the need to pursue personal sanctification by regular prayer and visits to the Blessed Sacrament. Regarding these visits, he pointed out that "men had no excuse for omitting them, as every mission house, except Benin City, was within thirty yards of the church". He thought a daily hour of contemplation would be of great benefit to all missionaries, and advised the Provincial that "a deep study of the Breviary should be hammered into the students in Dromantine". Like the Bishop, he believed in self-supporting missions and in keeping travelling expenses down. As supervisor of schools he supported wholeheartedly the Bishop's emphasis on education and begged the Provincial to send more men with university degrees. He believed in close contact with the people and in learning the local languages. Though not as accomplished a linguist as Pat, he had progressed sufficiently in '42 to be able to take over the examination of new Fathers for faculties to hear Confessions.

Cahill's reports to the Provincial gave a bird's eye view of developments in the Vicariate. In Ubiaja in April 1942 while on tour in the North, he wrote a short report and elaborated on it later in a longer report from Benin City. The first, seven pages long, and the second, fourteen pages (much longer than Pat's when he was Visitor), recorded that Tommy Greene, parish priest of Ubiaja, had the "best school in the Vicariate"; had established a miniature rope factory; and wanted to found a secondary school for the Ishan people. Joe Barrett had just opened St John Bosco's Elementary Training College in Ubiaja with twenty-five students on a two-year course of teaching and catechizing (the Bishop wanted every teacher to be a catechizer as well as a teacher). The number of students in the ETC was expected to double or treble within a year, provided professors could be found. Pat O'Connell was building a new school and house at Owo. Dr PM Kelly DD, Principal of the Teacher Training College in Ibusa, and his staff members, Joe Conboy and Ned Coleman, were pleased with their results that year – eleven had graduated. Tom Murray, rector of the Seminary in Benin City and Dr Glynn, professor, had two students ready to be ordained sub-deacons in June. On other fronts: Joe Hilliard had gone to Lagos as army chaplain; Martin

Bane and Harry Begley were keen to go, but it was Pat Braniff who was the next to be selected by the military authorities. Dan O'Connell, well again after an appendix operation, was back in his station in Ibusa where, along with pastoral work, he was teaching the people the use of corn mills and spinning wheels. Joe Styles was in Warri hospital recovering from an operation.

A not too serious point of variance between the Bishop and the Visitor was the latter's encouragement of the missionaries to write articles for the *Nigerian Catholic Herald* and the *African Missionary*. Cahill was proud of the fact that most of the articles in *The Herald* were written by Western Nigeria confreres and he was pleased that some Fathers wanted to initiate the publication of Nigerian folklore. Pat thought that such writing efforts might distract men from pastoral work and achieve little. Overall, Cahill reported that the confreres were in good health, but some of the new ones, who had attended medical courses at home, distrusting the medical 'savvy' of their seniors, felt they had to go for medical attention every time they got a scratch. Three newly arrived Fathers, Jim Healy, Michael McFadden and Maurice Maguire, whom Pat had ordained in 1940, were working well under their superiors in Benin City, Asaba, and Okene respectively. They had received a clear daily timetable and a comprehensive list of subjects to be studied and other things to do, which Cahill hoped would give them "a correct view of mission work and the religious exercises". He felt that, in general, the *Constitutions* were held in honour and that infringements were not tolerated; many stations were self-supporting and, "Times demand that those which were receiving some allocation to date will be deprived of it within the near future".

Sexton Cahill wrote his 'long' report on 17 August '42. By the time the Provincial received it, the Visitor had died of yellow fever. Pat rushed to Warri hospital when he heard that Cahill was there in a critical condition, but there was nothing he, nor anyone else, could do. He spent the night, along with some others, at the dying man's bedside (and was the only one to refuse a cup of tea during the long vigil). Aged thirty-five Cahill died, 4 September 1942. Writing to the Provincial, Pat said, "You have already got the sad news of Fr Cahill's death, he was sick only four or five days and died in Warri hospital R.I.P. He seems to have got it out in the Sobo bush, Sapele district ... He died a very happy death having got the Last Sacraments beforehand. May God rest his soul and accept the sacrifice of his life for the conversion of the Africans". Naming Willie Keenan Acting Visitor, Pat asked the Provincial to pray "that God may spare us to do good work in His vineyard and in His great mercy save us from all danger and sin of soul and body". In his will Cahill, leaving all his property to the Bishop, asked that Masses be said for him with the £26 he had in the SMA account. He was buried in Asaba next to Pat Bermingham. The Acting Visitor suggested that two small marble stones be sent out from Ireland and, eventually, Celtic crosses were erected over their graves. Cahill's premature death shocked everyone. Pat, who held him in high regard, was reported to be 'feverish' for a couple of days after it. Dr Alfie Glynn, said, "Fr Cahill was a little Saint in a big way. Thank God we have such priests to send to make eternal intercession for us before God!" Joe Hilliard, one of the historians of the mission, commented, "The loss of Fr Cahill is, I think, the greatest sacrifice Bishop Kelly's Vicariate has been asked to make for a long time". [Two nephews of Fr Cahill, both named after him, Sexton Doran and Sexton Cahill, joined the SMA and arrived in Benin diocese in 1964 and 1966 respectively.]

The graves of
Sexton Cahill
(1942),
Pat Bermingham
(1940), and
James McGettigan
(1932),
St Joseph's
cemetery, Asaba.

Willie Keenan, from Longford, was forty-five when he took over Cahill's responsibilities as Visitor and Supervisor of Schools. A classmate of the Pro-Vicar, John Mahon, he had been ordained in 1926 and, after a home appointment, arrived in Western Nigeria in 1930. His first steps on mission were taken at Asaba with Eugene Strub and Paul Emecete. Bursar of the Vicariate for a time, he later worked in Benin City, Warri and Okene before going on his first home leave in 1934. Returning the following year he was made superior of Okene, where he remained until he took leave in 1940. He attended Pat's consecration in Ballinasloe and returned with him to Nigeria on the *Abossa* in 1941. Shortly after arrival, he was appointed one of the Visitor's councillors. At the time of Cahill's death, he was stationed at Ogwashi-Uku near Asaba.

Willie Keenan

A kind and generous confrere, he didn't think he had "either the knowledge or the grit" to be a Visitor or a Supervisor of Schools. To be an ordinary missionary in a "middling" parish was all he wanted, and he admitted that he found "picking up the thread of things after Fr Cahill's death" very difficult. Occasionally, he had disagreements with Pat, who thought he was too 'flaithool' (over-generous with money) – a characteristic that wasn't likely to be indulged by a tight-fisted bishop in a near-bankrupt Vicariate in war time. Writing to Harrington in 1942 about the rising cost of living Keenan joked, "The Bishop may have a false bottom in the safe ... where else does he get the ha'pence of which he is mighty careful!"

Keenan became Acting Visitor when Pat, starting to get into his episcopal stride, was concentrating on getting the most out of his personnel and stretching his meagre resources to the limit. The new Acting Visitor, ten years older than his predecessor and only three years younger than the Bishop, despite his modest self-view, was quite capable of taking a stance and of being outspoken when roused. In his first report to Cork, while stressing the Vicariate's need for missionaries with relevant training, he complained that little or nothing was being done in this regard on the home-front, "Our Society, it seems, will always be fifty years behind the times".

Many of Keenan's priorities, like Cahill's, harmonised with those of the Bishop – education, indigenous vocations, community life and self-supporting mission stations. "Education Fever has taken hold of the country", he said, "we are very short of teachers and Fathers, who are qualified and competent to take charge of secondary schools and are able to fit in with Government ideas on African education". In particular, he lamented the lack of a science graduate for the Training College in Ibusa which, in 1943, had eighty students (including those from Lagos and other SMA jurisdictions in Nigeria) and was expanding to take in an extra sixty students the following year. He praised the work of the Principal, Dr PM Kelly, who was striving to make the college self-supporting by introducing farming, and had installed a hydraulic ram for pumping water and a turbine on the Oboshi stream to generate electricity.

Also in 1943, Keenan reported that Joe Barrett had fifty students in his ETC at Ubiaja, twenty-five of whom would graduate that year and, a significant development, that Tom Duffy was clearing land for a *secondary school* at Asaba. Keenan affirmed that there was, "A good spirit in the Vicariate, not much money is wasted, and there is not much indifference ... All the Fathers are working well and the Bishop has reason to understand that all are zealous from the interest taken in the Conference which followed the annual Retreat". Agreeing with the Bishop, he said that a problem would arise when the war ended, as many missionaries would want to go on leave at the same time. And, like Pat, he had not been happy about the dismissal of one of the three candidates for subdiaconate in '42, "Fr Murray (the rector) may be a bit 'nettly'," he said.

Keenan noted an improvement in the Christians' support of the missionaries, "The people have made great efforts to make us self-supporting ... but more is required. Our little schools can't do much if we just give a, not very competent, teacher a blackboard, register and a bit of chalk". He appreciated the Bishop's concern for community life, "If anyone would be scrupulous about leaving a man alone it would be the Bishop. He does all he can for the good of the Fathers and the good of the people". But he feared that his tightness with money might result in losses later, "I hope the Bishop won't carry too far the cutting down of Fathers' living allowances when they should be going up. There are very few luxuries nowadays. The cost of living in the Seminary is high and the Fathers there have asked for extra money, as they have no chance of getting a 'dash' from the people".

In May '43, as Keenan was still only *acting* Visitor, Pat wrote to the Provincial, "I can't see any better man for Visitor than Fr Keenan, except perhaps Fr John Mahon, but he is Pro-Vicar". While judging that Keenan was too generous with money, Pat admitted, "perhaps I'm the other way". A few days later, Keenan wrote to Harrington, on behalf of the Seminary staff, "Fr Murray asked for an increase in the allocation of £1 each for himself and Fr Maguire. I thought I had authority to give it but I find that I have not. The Bishop put it to Fr Murray that another Father could be got who would be glad to live on £7 a month". At the time the allocation for a station was £7, while a confrere's *personal* allocation was 30 shillings. Keenan espoused the cause of Murray and Maguire, emphasizing that they were 'teetotallers' and that their circumstances were difficult. Another man, John Duffy in Kabba, "who is very economical", also found it hard to manage on his £8-10 shillings a month for two. In his time as bishop of

Western Nigeria, Leo Taylor had felt upstaged by Kelly the Visitor; now Keenan, as Acting Visitor, felt upstaged by Kelly the Bishop. "I want to know", Keenan asked, "does the Visitor have any authority in financial matters and what money has he control of?" To add to his worries, some of the Fathers were reluctant to hand in their quarterly accounts to him, saying that it was the Bishop who gave them their allocations.

Tension over money increased as Pat maintained tight control over finances. Drawing a hard line with Sisters too, he gave them even less than he gave the Fathers, only £5 per month, but he noted with satisfaction, "the Sisters stay longer than the Fathers". However, there was at least one missionary who didn't blame the Bishop for the small allocation he received and, at the same time paid him a great compliment, "Bishop Kelly's *Sensus Christi* is penetrating things like the leaven it is ... As the Principal of the first proper Catechetical College we've had, I don't hesitate to ask you [the Provincial] for at least £100 – through the Bishop if you like, but make sure it comes here as an extra to the meagre allowance he can afford", so wrote Joe Barrett from the Elementary Training College in Ubiaja.

In 1943, the official title of the Vicariate of Western Nigeria was changed to that of **"Asaba-Benin"**. The same year Willie Keenan gave up his role as Supervisor of Schools and was confirmed in office as Society Visitor. In November, the Provincial sent him a six-page typed letter, answering some queries of Willie's and airing many ideas of his own, especially on "Our Missions"– the title of a paper he was preparing for circulation. Harrington said, "I believe bolder schemes for education, for social service, for native cooperation, for organising Christian and pagan alike are needed. Our tendency is to be too small and parochial and conservative. It is not the need of money [which hinders us] – but we are rather obsessed by money. Time will pay off the cost of any scheme and we have God with us".

On the question of the Seminary allocation, the Provincial said, "It is the Visitor's duty to see that the Fathers have an adequate allowance to live on and where he is satisfied that it is not sufficient, he should get the Bishop to increase it". He recommended an annual or quarterly budget for the Seminary and the Training College. The Fathers' personal allowance should be treated likewise, "the Bishop is entirely responsible for it and the amount is fixed in agreement with the Visitor. Of course it is the Visitor's business to see that the Fathers get reasonable treatment, as it is also his business to see that the Fathers make every effort to make their stations self-supporting for that is an obligation of our *Directory* ... In general it would not be right that the Visitor gives supplementary grants to stations".

Acknowledging his confirmation as Visitor, Willie Keenan joked, "It will be with difficulty that I shall take the cross from the Bishop, for he has been Acting Visitor all along in his own nice way carrying my cross". Keenan also inferred that Pat might be "saving money, but losing souls". The joint bank account of Visitor and Bishop in Asaba worked to the satisfaction of both when Taylor was bishop, but now with Pat as bishop, the Visitor felt very restricted, "the Bishop has absolute control of cash ... I cannot get my hands on much".

Keenan, who had moved to Sapele in April '44, sent the Provincial the results of votes for Visitor's councillors, remarking that he hadn't asked the Bishop to vote. Subsequently Pat asked him if he still regarded him as a member of the Society! "I'll have to remind him", said Keenan, "that *Constitutions* and *Directory* must be observed in high as well as in low places. Many points seem to have dissolved in favour of the Ordinary". Keenan asked the Provincial, "Has the Visitor power, with the deliberative voice of his councillors, to transfer a Father to another station for the advancement of the work? The *Directory* is vague; nearly everything in it is 'without prejudice to the right of the Ordinary'." Hopefully he asked, "what about two coffers on the Mission?"

adding, "This time (1944) Visitor and Council will draw up the Budget for the new financial year. I guess the Procurator at home might send me cash if I asked".

In June 1944, Pat spent three weeks in Warri hospital with dysentery. Tom Bartley, the administrator of the cathedral, advised the Provincial, "When you come out, you must tell him to take proper care of himself". Illness did not soften Pat's attitudes, writing to Harrington he said, "The Visitor is pushing me to increase the allocation of the Fathers teaching in the colleges. I don't say that they don't need a little war bonus of a pound a month, but I have not got it to give them". He admitted that there was money in the Asaba account, but it was designated for special works such as building, education of native priests and the care of lepers. He pointed out that many of the stations were self-supporting, "chiefly by contributions from teachers and school boys ... the Training College and the Seminary Fathers have their own resources". He reminded the Provincial that he, Pat, had agreed to increase some allocations as soon as the Province honoured some promised donations, "but I see no sign of these on the Provincial Procurator's accounts up to November last. So, up to you". Two years before this in May '42, he explained that he was drawing on the building fund in the Asaba account to the tune of £500 or £600 a year just to keep going, "I suppose in war time there is an excuse for drawing on reserve funds ... The only income from outside the Vicariate is what comes from the Propagation of the Faith in Eire – £1,200, and £150 for the Seminary, and the Stipends from you". Though many of the stations were self-supporting Pat still had to cover the cost of missionaries' travel home, holiday expenses and support, not only the seminary Fathers but, 'non-earning' personnel like himself, the Visitor, some six or seven needy Fathers, two nursing Sisters, and provide all the Fathers' personal allocations, which came to nearly £600 a year.

In June '44, commenting on Harrington's rather idealistic paper on "Missionary Organization", Pat said, "All agree it is the right thing, but to reduce it to practice is another matter. The weak link in the chain will be the superiors. Most of those here now are getting on in years and have got into a groove, out of which circular letters won't lever them". On Harrington's cherished hopes for a grand tyrocinium building and a whole year's 'tyro' Kelly said, "No tyrocinium will, or can, make up for a year's noviciate in the early years of the home training". Regarding catechists, he strongly endorsed Harrington's insistence that they be properly trained and given full-time employment.

The same month, Keenan met his recently appointed councillors, J.J. Healy, Tom Murray and Maurice Walsh, in Asaba. After it, he put the idea of a Visitor's Budget to Pat but, as he reported to the Provincial, "The Bishop is not prepared just now to hand over an amount to cover the allocations of the Fathers for the coming financial year, but he might at the beginning of the next". The Visitor and councillors also proposed that the monthly allocation for the Fathers in the Seminary and in the Training College, should be raised to £18 for two Fathers and to £24 for three, "His Lordship said that he would not give this, saying at first that the Visitor himself would have to find the money, then he said he would not increase the allocations until the Provincial gave a grant. If the Provincial did so, then he would agree to give the sums quoted". Softening a little after this, the Bishop said he regretted "the wrong impression he had about 'unnecessary' spending in the Seminary". Keenan, also softening, deferred to Pat as "His Lordship" and supported his plea for more personnel, "His Lordship needs to be free from worry about schools, teachers, salaries, transfers et cetera. Indeed he would need a Secretary who would deal with most of the office work, or a General Manager of schools".

But far from becoming 'a Bishop's man', Keenan, before the end of November, was pointing out to Harrington some serious weaknesses in the running of the Vicariate: no overall plan and no visitation by the Bishop, who seemed to be avoiding Sapele in particular, which he hadn't visited since he, Keenan, had taken up residence there! The visitation part of Keenan's criticism was hardly fair as the Bishop had been hospitalized in May-June and, everyone, including the Visitor himself, was complaining about the difficulties of travelling in war time because of the strict rationing of petrol, the necessity of travel permits, and the difficulty of finding spare parts for cars. Criticism of Pat's reluctance to spend money sounds more realistic. For example, he refused to give more than £10 for an extension to Phil Mahon's house. Phil, a brother of John, lived alone in an isolated mission in Ashaka. Keenan wanted to extend the second bedroom of the house, which was only 10 ft by 6 ft, so that another confrere could be appointed there. The Bishop's £10 was not enough.

By the end of '44, Keenan, tired and overworked, had moved again, this time to Asaba where he was looking after the Procure, acting curate for Tom Duffy, and answering sick calls from the Sisters' new maternity centres. All the men, many of them overdue leave, were feeling the strain of the war years and their over-long tours. To mention just one situation, the Training College at Ibusa, which had increased its student population to 114, was understaffed and low in food supplies. In January '45, it had only five days supply of yams left and the staff lacked transport to look for more. Keenan concluded a brief report to the Provincial, "I have to repeat that we are understaffed and the men are feeling the strain of coping with difficulties".

Demanding more

The Bishop pushed ahead with plans for higher standard schools, demanding more qualified men from the Province and expecting more work from the personnel he had. He too was under strain and had suffered a number of disappointments, especially over losses of personnel. Paul Emecete was seriously ill and unable to work; only two (Anselm Ojefua and Stephen Umurie), instead of three of his major seminarians had been ordained; three missionaries had departed as army chaplains; John Mahon, the Pro-Vicar, had been co-opted on to the Provincial Council in Cork; and Dr Alfie Glynn had been appointed to Dromantine. Making matters worse, the Provincial informed him that he would be keeping Dr PM Kelly (the Principal of Ibusa Teacher Training College), at home after his next leave. Shocked and outraged, Pat begged for replacements, mentioning specifically a canon lawyer for the seminary and a graduate for Ubiaja ETC as Fr Barrett, run down in health, had gone home on leave. He also needed graduate teachers for the secondary school he was planning for Asaba or Benin, which would be the Vicariate's first secondary school.

Due to the drain of personnel, community life was becoming impossible to maintain. Kabba, where John Duffy was alone and Agbor, where Pat Fleming was alone, might have to be closed. In 1944 hopes were high that the War might end soon, if it did many would want to go on leave, about ten already had nearly seven years done without going home. The Bishop said he'd "need ten new men, not the four he had been appointed". His hopes that committed and trained laymen would replace priests in the schools as catechizers had not materialized as the teachers graduating from the Training College, "so far have shown a marked indifference to religion and the teaching of catechism". Another disappointment was the lack of financial support for a leper settlement he wished to establish, despite many appeals, including a radio appeal he had made in Ireland.

In 1945 he suffered a grievous personal loss – his mother passed away. Having received news only in February that she was ill, he cabled Harrington for details, but Kate, aged eighty, had died on 29 January and been buried beside Malachy Kelly in Clontuskert cemetery. Pat was on tour in Ogwashi-Uku when he got word of her death. Thanking Stephen Harrington for his condolences, he said simply, "I hope she has attained the eternal reward R.I.P".

Despite many anxieties in the war years, one development must have given him a lot of satisfaction. In November 1943, the Vicariate's credit balance in Asaba showed a slight increase! Not wishing to take credit, or give the impression that the Vicariate was prospering, he said it was due to the cessation of building caused by lack of materials during the War. Meanwhile he continued to demand much of his missionaries in both the spiritual domain as well as the temporal. Writing to the Provincial in May '42 he said, "Yes this Vicariate has room for improvement. No matter how much perfection there is in the young men coming out, the tradition tells. You would achieve not a little if you got the average African Missionary to take five minutes longer saying Mass". Imbued with the spirituality of the SMA *Directory,* he believed that imperfections in one's personal spiritual life diminished missionary effectiveness. In May '43, he wrote again to Harrington, "The whole thing is to make the Fathers faithful to their spiritual exercises and put their own personal sanctification first as the chief means of winning souls for the Love of Christ. There is a tendency for each to turn aside in his own path – not much *esprit de suite* [a readiness to follow] about them and they are not so pliable to direction either, not so much through slighting authority as through lack of reflection and a *laissez faire* attitude". His fellow bishops, Taylor of Lagos and Hughes of Ondo-llorin, appeared to agree with him for, in '44, the three of them brought out a joint circular on the necessity of fidelity to the 'Daily Exercises' according to Canon Law. Willie Keenan, however, thought the men were doing all right but agreed, "Reminders are good of course". In a postscript to the

Provincial in October '44, Pat said, "I don't think the Tyrocinium will work wonders either. Men of prayer and self denial are what we need".

Pat's most serious criticism of the missionaries came in his response to Harrington, who had asked him if he would attend the 1946 Provincial Assembly. Pat replied that, even though he was due leave, circumstances demanded that he remain in Benin. Though Pat didn't refer to it, not only was he due leave, he would also be celebrating the Silver Jubilee of his ordination to priesthood that summer. But Harrington hadn't forgotten it and, with his congratulations, sent him a gift of £50 which, he insisted, Pat was free to use in whatever way he wanted. In his reply to the Provincial, Pat said he didn't have points for the Assembly's Agenda, but did have some observations to make:

> Fathers in general are not equal to the sacrifices that real missionary life out here entails and the first sacrifice they should be prepared for is to do what they are told wholeheartedly even though they can't see the good of it. Ye should not be too soft with them in their demands for higher allocations, shorter tours et cetera. The more they spend on themselves the less remains for mission works. Of course it is their spiritual life that is lacking and the higher motive of pleasing God and not themselves in the daily round of duties. I was half-thinking of suggesting a month's retreat for all after first home leave.

> Being too lazy to visit outstations is another fault and finding a hundred and one things of little or no importance to keep them busy at home instead of going out ... Lack of method and regularity is a defect, but not as much as lack of sticking power in keeping to what does not appeal to them. The young priests are well enough trained when they come out, except in the spiritual life where there is always room for improvement and which is so necessary

for success as missionaries. When a young man rattles off his Mass in 17 minutes his spiritual thermometer must be low. Lastly our weakest link is the superiors (10 February 1946).

Closer to the time of the Assembly, he wrote again, even more critically, of those who sought shorter tours and of those who lacked a true apostolic spirit, "Seeking after material comforts and expensive living is not exactly what one would expect from a man with the true missionary spirit". But being a realist he acknowledged, "On the whole we must not be too pessimistic about ourselves and our methods", and being a man of God, he recalled that "God can make up for the defects of the instruments He uses".

His critical views should not be considered as mere abstract thoughts for an Assembly. On the mission he wanted his men to strive towards the highest of spiritual standards as expressed in the *Directory,* and he could be quite abrasive in dealing with men whom he thought were not sufficiently zealous. To one of his missionaries whose parishioners were complaining of neglect, he wrote, "Dear Father ... If these people are any good at all as Christians, I think it is in spite of the parish priest. You might be a good parish priest in Ireland, but you have no missionary zeal". The Father in question rejected the complaints, accused the Bishop of being unfair and, appealing directly to the Provincial, said, "I am asking you to tell Bishop Kelly to be just a bit more careful in his statements and to try to appreciate the little that is done by the Fathers". Returning to Ireland ill, this Father, on being declared unfit for work in Africa, joined the American Province, and continued working for many years in the Society's ministry to Afro-Americans. Another Father, disgruntled in Asaba-Benin, got himself transferred to the Prefecture of Kaduna, where he continued working for seventeen years. A number of other men, including Tommy Greene, seriously considered leaving the Vicariate and going to America; three did, Tommy remained.

Hard on himself, the Bishop could be quite severe on those whom he perceived to be 'good-timers', 'short-tourers' or 'gin and tonickers'. A teetotaller, he maintained the view of alcohol he had had when Visitor, "Though I am all in favour of a man having a little liquor now and then ... I shall do everything possible to discourage the methodical whiskey and soda". In the early years of his episcopacy Pat had very high expectations of his personnel and, apparently, was disappointed. His style of being Visitor, noted for tolerance and defence of men, gave way, in his first decade as Bishop, to a tougher style, in which he pursued, with growing insistence, a policy of "mission before man".

He spoke sharply to the home administration too. Astutely monitoring bursars' statements, he pointed out with alacrity any short-fall in what he thought was due to Asaba. Like many missionary bishops of the epoch, Pat's view of the home administration was that it and the Province existed mainly to supply men and money to the missions. In conversation, he once said, "the *only* confrere at home should be the Provincial; all the others should be in Africa". On reading the Psalms one morning, he said, he couldn't help changing the line, "The Lord stripping the oak trees bare" to "The *Provincial* stripping the *missions* bare". At this time, letters to his classmate, the Provincial Stephen Harrington, with whom, hitherto, he had an affable relationship, became noticeably shorter and more demanding, even accusatory when men were withdrawn, or when his expectations were not met: "You have taken our best men"; "It would be much better for the Mission if we had our experienced men back"; "I remind you of my former request for a BSc, your silence on this point makes me wonder"; "I must tell you that if a station is closed down it takes years to bring it back to what it was"; "Many are overdue leave and clamouring to go, but there is no one to relieve them". When he got an allocation of new men, he usually wasn't satisfied, "We asked for four, we got one"; "We need ten, not four";

"I wish to thank you for Fr Nolan, but you must get us two more BA's and ... there must be no 'perhaps' about that BSc coming here"; "I received your letter announcing five new men, but I hope that BSc is among them ... we need him immediately ... I am only speaking for the good of souls and I trust you for fair treatment"; "I regret very much you keeping Fr Mahon... You are free to do so but the Mission suffers. He is one more gone from our weakest line of defence – namely reliable and experienced superiors".

Though later he gained a reputation for giving men a chance, in November '44 he told Harrington to tell the missionary who sought to return to the Vicariate that the Bishop was sorry to have to say "No". He was not impressed with Harrington's circular 'Our Missions', but avoided saying so, "we'll discuss all those other matters when you come". The Provincial had informed him that he would visit Nigeria in '45 and, never one to miss an opportunity, Pat requested, "Please bring out olive oil and balsam". These were for liturgical use and were expensive and difficult to get in Africa.

In 1945 the War came to an end in Europe. Stephen Harrington surprised everyone by arriving early for his Nigerian visit. He wrote to Pat from Lagos in March, saying he would tour the other jurisdictions first and then Asaba-Benin. Willie Keenan, who would have to escort him around the Vicariate, hadn't used his car for some time. After checking it, he wrote to Harrington, "I searched in Onitsha last week and think I have almost everything for the car, apart from tyres, tubes, and a pinion ball race. You might pick up in your travels a rear pinion ball race for a Chevrolet Saloon 1937 and two parking brake extension springs. I'll apply for tubes and tyres"! The Bishop's request for olive oil and balsam wasn't so bad after all. Parts from his car, Willie claimed, were 'borrowed' by confreres who thought their need greater than his.

~~~

After an abnormally long nine-year mandate due to the War, the Superior General announced that the Provincial Assemblies would take place in the summer of 1946 and the General Assembly some time later. In Asaba-Benin, Keenan organized the voting for delegates. Dr PM Kelly, who had greatly impressed the missionaries by his educational and development work in Ibusa, easily headed the vote for delegate for the Provincial Assembly, and tied with J.J. Healy for the General Assembly. Healy, the senior by ordination, was declared elected. As both men were already on home leave, their election saved further disruption in the mission. It was a time of change but, whatever plans Stephen Harrington had had for Dr Kelly, they hardly included Dr Kelly's replacing him as Provincial Superior. Dr PM Kelly was elected Provincial, and Harrington, who had served in that capacity since 1931 was elected Vice Provincial. At the General Assembly the following year, Harrington was elected Superior General and, at home, John Cadogan was elected to replace him as Vice Provincial.

Bishop Kelly should have been pleased: a classmate was Superior General; a member of his Vicariate was Irish Provincial and his early companion on mission, was Vice Provincial.

Chapter 9

TWO KELLYS and a SCHEME

In 1946 the British Government, aiming at the creation of a Nigerian elite that would be favourable to British interests after independence, brought out a "Ten-year plan for development and welfare in Nigeria". Education was to play a large part in this but, as yet, education, mainly in the hands of missionary bodies, was in its infant stages. Even by 1951, halfway through the time-frame of the plan, there were not many more than a million children in Government primary schools in the whole country, but the desire for education was growing like a bush fire, school certificates were the way to employment and prosperity. On the political front, though radical changes were made in the Constitution of Nigeria in 1947, a new one was written in 1951 and another in 1954. The last one ushered in the Federation of Nigeria and, in 1960, the country gained full Independence.

In 1946 Dr Patrick Martin Kelly began his mandate as Irish Provincial Superior. Ten years younger than Bishop Kelly, he was born into a very religious family of Ballinakill, Co Offaly, on 7 November 1904. Three of his sisters joined religious orders and a brother became a Christian Brother. His formation was different from most members of the SMA as, after secondary schooling with the Christian Brothers, he joined the Order. After studies, from 1919 to 1924, in the Congregation's preparatory college in

Dr PM Kelly

174

Marino, Dublin, he took temporary religious vows and was sent to teach in Drogheda and in Sullivan's Quay School, Cork, where he became Principal. Desiring missionary life, he was released from his vows in 1929, in order to join the African Missions. In Cloughballymore, 1930-1932, some of the Cork 'novices' were astonished to find 'Brother Kelly', their erstwhile Principal, amongst them. His outstanding intellectual ability was recognised and, after 'Clough', he was sent to Rome to study theology at the Lateran University. Ordained there in 1935, his first appointment was to continue studying for a licentiate in theology which he gained in 1936 and a doctorate in 1938 – the first member of the Irish Province to be a 'doctor of divinity'; henceforward, he was called "Doc" in the Society. Appointed to the Bight of Benin in '38, he began his mission career teaching in St Gregory's College, Lagos. As manager of the Holy Cross schools, he introduced a post-Primary course of commercial and technical subjects and, having studied the 'theology of adaptation' in Rome, announced his interest in starting an experimental college adapted to Nigerian needs and culture.

Early in 1942, Bishop Kelly, hearing of PM Kelly's talents, sought him for the Training College in Ibusa and, in February, he was appointed Principal of that College. Once there, with the Bishop's blessing, he worked at making the college self-sufficient. With the help of the students, he started raising sheep and goats, planting rice, soya beans, corn, citrus trees, sisal plants, Cape gooseberries and custard apples. As mentioned already, he harnessed the Oboshi stream to generate electricity for the college, and he got the people in Ibusa and neighbouring villages to start weaving and spinning. With a flair for writing, he produced two modern guides for the teaching of Christian Doctrine. Both entitled *My Faith*, they were published in 1944 by Longmans and Green in English and in Swahili. Two years later a Yoruba translation appeared. Bishop Kelly, however, preferring the more traditional *Graded Catechism* from Ebutte Meta, instructed his personnel to continue using it. Ideally, Dr Kelly's

'Ibusa scheme' was intended to be the nucleus of a multi-facetted, self-supporting Christian village. At a time when Pádraic Pearse's critical thesis on the British educational policy in Ireland, "The Murder Machine", was much discussed, PM Kelly was developing his own philosophy of education which, moving away from 'foreign' book-learning, stressed the advancement of indigenous local development and the promotion of native arts and crafts. He published his ideas in a booklet entitled *Lead Kindly Light, Being Educational Hopes of the SMA in Africa*, in 1947.

His predecessor as Provincial, Stephen Harrington, met with the SMA Ordinaries of Nigeria in Lagos in 1945 and discussed with them the promotion of a uniform missionary life style as laid down in the *Constitutions* and *Directory*. It was agreed that, "the many exceptions arising out of the exigencies of the apostolic work would not render impossible this attempt at uniformity". No doubt the Provincial and the Ordinaries would have regarded the life style emanating from Dr Kelly's 'Ibusa scheme' as exceptional, and while his scheme was admired, not many felt capable of establishing or promoting such schemes themselves. Early in his mandate, the new Provincial clearly stated that he did not wish to break entirely from traditional methods, "Reverence for the Rule and union with Christ must still be our greatest weapons", but he hoped that new methods would be attempted and that the Ibusa scheme would become a model for imitation elsewhere.

Despite Dr Kelly's absence, the Ibusa Native Authority remained enthusiastic about the scheme and, following his instructions, cleared land around the College in preparation for further developments. Keen to continue the work, they begged him to return. Bishop Kelly informed him that the Education Department was holding up the scheme until he returned and wished to know what the mission's plans were in its regard. Requesting the Provincial to find an order of Brothers to take over the College and the scheme, Pat said it was probable that the

Government would fund it. Dr Kelly, not keen on giving the scheme to another congregation, asked Pat, rather belligerently, to let the Province run it, "If you are willing to hand it over to another Society why not give the first offer to your own? Why ask Brothers to do something that they can't do and we can? It seems to me that we ourselves are our own greatest enemies, standing in our own way". Pat replied that he would leave him entirely free to do whatever he wished as regards the "water, lighting, and technical school", but he would like to maintain some control over the teacher training side and the "religious side" – meaning the sacraments, worship, and catechizing. The following year in May, Pat told the Provincial to feel free to choose any one of the sites he had surveyed, Ekpoma, Ogwashi, or Ekiti, in which to establish a scheme, advising him to start with one first and see how it developed before embarking on others, "the Government would not be likely to fund more than one". He further advised that an engineering expert be called in to assess the resources and, probably remembering the rapid depletion of water in the Dromantine hydro-electric system, questioned the reliability of the flow of water in the Oboshi stream. Knowing that the Ordinaries planned to transfer the intervicarial seminary from Benin City and establish a technical college in its place, he suggested that Ibusa could be an alternative site for the technical college, "you may make it a work of the Society on the mission if you like". Meanwhile Ben Nolan, an Offaly man with a BA in philosophy and a higher diploma in education, had replaced Dr Kelly as Principal of the College. Having arrived in Nigeria in 1943, he had been teaching in the College since January '44.

Tom Murray, Belfast, in the mission since 1931, secretary to both Bishops Broderick and Taylor, and currently rector of the seminary, was Acting Visitor while Willie Keenan was on leave. Like most of the missionaries he admired "Doc" and his schemes, but he agreed with Pat that expertise, which they didn't have, was required, "If I remember from our talk", he said to the Provincial, "your scheme embraces something like they have in South Africa (at Mariannhill): a Training College, Agricultural and Technical works – all different departments, but the one establishment. We are a little late on the Technical side. The Government has already stepped ahead in Yaba, Lagos, where the buildings and the staff are ready and can cater for 2000 students". He encouraged the Provincial to visit the mission soon and assured him that "the men are eager and willing to cooperate and help in the policy. You have an excellent team behind you and we have supreme confidence in you".

"Chappie", Michael Convey, a colleague of Dr Kelly on the Ibusa College staff, when congratulating him on his election as Provincial, seemed to think, with regret, that the scheme would not survive without him, "it would have put us on our feet and show that Catholicism and Progress can go hand in hand". Johannes O'Shea, who had worked in Ibusa in the early days, congratulated the new Provincial and joked, "You can threaten Bishop Kelly with instant removal if he doesn't put that scheme through immediately!!" Obviously the scheme had potential but, with Dr Kelly based in Cork, its future looked uncertain.

Tommy Greene, transferred from Ubiaja to nearby Uromi in 1947, was one of the many who admired Doc and his work and wanted a 'scheme' in his own area. In March, having spent a week in Ekpoma country surveying and discussing the feasibility of a development project with the local Chiefs, who "offered him as much land as he wanted", he sent the Provincial a detailed hand-drawn map with notes about water resources, minerals, and agriculture. Already involved in a number of

Tommy Greene

simple development projects with the people, Greene believed in helping them advance on the road of education and self-reliance. Though very different in personality and lifestyle from Pat, the Bishop regarded him highly. In fact Tommy had been instrumental in getting him to establish St John Bosco's Elementary Training College, Ubiaja, in 1942 and two years later Sacred Heart Training College for girls run by the OLA Sisters, also in Ubiaja. It was quite a coup to get *two* training colleges in the same mission area at that time. Generally called *'Père'* because, tending to forget confreres' names, Tommy called everyone, except the Bishop, *'Père'*. The Bishop was one of the few who didn't call him *Père* and, though normally Pat addressed everyone as "Father" without the surname, he addressed Tommy as "Father Greene". Not only was Tommy one of the most popular men among the confreres, he was also very popular with the people. Extremely kind and sociable, he had a great way of empathizing with, and of trying to understand, people at a deep level. A great one for conversation and camaraderie, he also had a nice way of making a serious point. To a new missionary he'd say something like, "By George, *Père*, you're a very intelligent young man. What you should do now is read all about the culture of the people". For many, *Père* was "the uncrowned king of Ishan", but at one stage, Pat, thinking he was going too far in trying to Christianise the Etsako customs, moved him out of the area.

Though Tommy was keen to have a scheme, he felt he didn't have enough skills to start one and see it through. Furthermore, he didn't want to give the Chiefs the impression that preliminary investigations guaranteed a project. But after Pat visited the Ekpoma site, Tommy informed the Provincial that the Bishop was not opposed to a scheme, in fact he had said, "Let Dr Kelly run the show as he wants to run it. Let him present the man he chooses to act as parish priest and I will give the necessary faculties".

Other parish men enthusiastic for the Provincial's schemes were: the multi-talented, if somewhat eccentric, Dan O'Connell from Kerry who was stationed in Ibusa, and Ned Coleman from Cork who was in Asaba. However without the presence of 'Doc' to show the way, it was difficult to get "schemes" up and running.

While schemes for Nigeria held centre stage for the Provincial (even when he was in Cork), the Bishop in Asaba-Benin was caught up with other matters: scarcity of personnel and finance, building projects, Government and Ministry of Education palaver, and confreres begging for greater allocations and shorter tours. A number of men were overdue returning to the mission after leave and, Pat was aware, a number of them would probably not come back at all. He was overdue leave himself and hoped to go in June. Among other things, he wished to go to America to raise funds for the Vicariate and to see his brothers – one of whom, Mick, had been conscripted into the army.

While Dr Kelly's popularity was ascending, Pat felt his own was declining, but that didn't bother him. He saw with satisfaction that the various works of the Vicariate *were* making progress, especially the schools and, despite continuing shortages of building materials, new schools were being built. He was fortunate to have Bill Fegan among his personnel. A late vocation, Bill had been a carpenter in Co Down before joining the SMA. He became the main builder in the Vicariate and was much in demand. Currently, he was building a school in Asaba, but Pat wanted him to start one in Agbor for girls as soon as possible. Pat liked to locate schools in rural areas so that the people there would have the benefit of a priest, at least for Mass on Sundays and for the administration of the sacraments in emergencies. Other works were progressing satisfactorily: two new catechetical training centres, one in Benin City and one in Ashaka, had been opened; a girls' school had been founded at Sapele by the OLA Sisters and it already had 400 pupils; a maternity centre, the eighth run by the same Sisters, with the help of Nigerian lay staff and two Belgian nurses, had also been opened. Almost everywhere in the Vicariate the numbers of Christians were increasing.

The problems Pat faced were the kind of ones associated with progress. Urhobos, who had been promised a priest if they raised a certain sum of money, were angry because, having raised the sum, they still didn't get a priest. They expressed their feelings by refusing "to make Harvest" (a large collection for the Church at harvest time). Similarly Ase people were complaining that they had no priest, though they had a mission long before Warri. With eighteen towns in their district, they said they could easily support a priest, and they had already built a solid two-storey house for a Father and cleared a large area of land around it. They protested that priests were sent to the Moslems in Yorubaland, who didn't want them, while they, who wanted them, had none. Agbor, where Visitors and Acting Visitors resided from time to time, badly needed a permanent priest. The new school to be built there would not get a Government grant unless there was a qualified person to run it. American Baptists were making great strides there, and in Eku where they had built an Elementary Training College. The Ekpoma people were also crying out for a priest, and so were the northern Afenmai.

On the medical side, the Acting Visitor, Tom Murray, feared that the Vicariate would lose its influence in Ossiomo leper settlement if they could not maintain a priest and some medical personnel there. Involved in a growing number of schools and clinics, the OLA Sisters were finding it difficult to provide staff for their own works. Pat wanted them to provide a Sister who would supervise all the girls schools of the Vicariate, but the Education Department would only recognise such a supervisor if the Vicariate had at least fifty girls schools. A bungalow was being built for a nurse-supervisor who would take responsibility for all the maternity centres. Murray was keen to put a lay nurse in charge. The Bishop was too but, as Murray said, "The Lord is keen on the idea, except for dishing out the salary". Murray wondered if the Province would advance loans to get transport for the nurse and for some mission stations – because the Bishop wouldn't.

~~~

After sending many letters to Pat about the Ibusa Scheme in his first year in office, Dr Kelly's mail to Benin dried up. His next letter, dated November '47, found Pat in New York. It was not about the scheme, but about late changes in the courses of one of Pat's Nigerian priests in University College Cork. Enclosed was a letter of protest from the University's President, Dr O'Rahilly. Dr Kelly complained, "We really cannot expect that the authorities will tolerate being treated in this inconsiderate manner ... we all mean well, but that does not sometimes prevent us from making a mess of things". Pat replied that he didn't mind what courses the Father followed, but the original arrangements, made between himself and Dr O'Rahilly, *had* been completed in good time and had been in order; subsequent changes must have been made by the priest himself. Reading between the lines, one suspects that the Provincial was irritated with the Bishop, not over changes in university courses, but over lack of enthusiasm for the development schemes.

Dr Kelly hadn't easily got over the apparent disinterest in his schemes shown by the Nigerian Ordinaries and by Bishop Kelly in particular. When he was in Nigeria in March '47, he had discussed the setting up of a scheme with Pat. Afterwards writing to Stephen Harrington, his Vice Provincial in Cork, he said, "I had a bit of a struggle in Asaba, but won out I think ... Bishop Kelly caved in after wasting nine or ten days ... We had some very straight talk. He got hot a few times and said he would resign if he were considered an opponent of the Scheme – he fears for his jurisdiction!" Eventually, only Bishop Thomas Hughes of Ondo facilitated the establishment of a major scheme, the "Oye-Ekiti scheme". This large-scale scheme was organised and run, mainly by two artistic and enthusiastic young men, Frs Kevin Carroll and Séan O'Mahony. In fairness to the Ordinaries, it must be said that even one of the most progressive and open-minded of them, Bishop Taylor, had difficulty in comprehending the Provincial's plans. In response to two letters from PM Kelly in August '46, Taylor said that he was vague about the Ibusa scheme, but he knew that Bishop Kelly was very short of men, and even if he had more, they probably would not be qualified to take charge of technical type of schools. Reacting sharply to PM Kelly's idea that he, the Provincial, would take charge of the Ibusa scheme, Taylor said, "I don't understand just what you'd propose to do when you say you couldn't hand it over to anyone else. YOU can't run it and be Provincial at the same time" and, he affirmed, "Any Ordinary would be hopeless".

Like Pat, Taylor initially thought that the Government would support such schemes, but few people at the time knew just how much finance would be required. F.X. Velarde, B.Arch., F.R.I.B.A. of Liverpool, Dr Kelly's architect, drew up a detailed plan for a scheme and estimated that the cost, "based on present day English prices under austerity conditions" would be £1,293,000! Though Velarde admitted that "African costs" would be less – just over three quarters of a million – either sum was astronomical in terms of non-Governmental projects in post-War Nigeria. Velarde's scheme included: a church estimated at £70,000; a cinema, £40,000; boys and girls colleges, £100,000 each; a fire station, £10,000; and a road network, £300,000! Admittedly his scheme was idealistic, but even so, the plans and the figures were out of all proportion to the pastoral and developmental realities with which the missionaries were familiar.

Though the Nigerian Ordinaries were less than enthusiastic, Dr Kelly's ideas were not without support in high places. After discussions with the Apostolic Delegate, Archbishop Riberi, in Nigeria in March '47, the Provincial reported, "The Delegate declares the scheme excellent, new and necessary and will give it every support he can". Pius XI and the Sacred Congregation of Propaganda Fide were very keen that missionaries would take more interest in indigenous culture and art. In 1937, the Pope had decreed the creation of an Exhibition of Missionary Art in the Vatican and, in 1940, Cardinal Constantini, the Prefect of Propaganda, had written, *L'art Chrétien dans les Mission*, a book which had inspired many, not least Kevin Carroll. Stephen

Harrington, who became Superior General in 1947, was also a firm advocate of missionary adaptation and he was hopeful that Dr Kelly's schemes would succeed and prove to be a new way of evangelising. He wrote to PM Kelly, "I hope Velarde is coming on well with his plans, and that the whole scheme will be getting under way in the coming year (1948). It will be splendid to have a special plan for presentation to the Pope; but have one for Propaganda too". Perhaps, after scanning Velarde's estimate of costs, he changed his mind.

Fr Kevin Carroll, who later became an internationally acclaimed expert in Yoruba art and architecture, travelled with Dr Kelly in Nigeria in 1947 in search of a suitable site for a scheme. At first, Dr Kelly wished to establish his scheme near Ibusa Training College. On their way to Benin from Lagos, the two men stayed with Bishop Hughes at Akure. Hughes suggested that they consider locating a scheme in his Vicariate and advised them to look around Ekiti country. They did so

Kevin Carroll

and were fascinated by what they saw – a profusion of Yoruba art displayed in everyday situations: carved doors, pillars, thatched palaces, shrines, and beautiful hand-woven cotton cloth worn by the people. When, eventually, they got to Benin City, Carroll said they found "Bishop Kelly was not interested so we returned to Ondo". Dr Kelly chose the village of Oye-Ekiti, situated on four cross roads in a pleasant environment, to be the centre of a scheme and left Carroll among the Yoruba farmers to get it off the ground. The scheme, "a work of the Society" under the Irish Provincial, began with clearing ground, making roads and securing water. At this initial stage it employed no less than 185 men and 100 women. Workshops were erected and, before long, a great variety of indigenous artefacts were being produced. Carroll took charge of weaving, arts and crafts, and ceramic work, while Séan O'Mahony took charge of brick and tile making. The tiles, made from fine clay found around Oye, were the first to be made in Nigeria. Dr Kelly's plan was, not to remain in one village but, to spread the schemes to all seventeen villages of the district. Over the next two years, two more men were appointed to the scheme, John Mooney as Superior and John McElgunn to direct another scheme at Owo. In 1951, Michael Walsh replaced Mooney. Carroll reported that in the early Fifties, his Yoruba carvers and their apprentices were producing, and he was selling, at least a hundred pieces of carving annually, not to mention the weaving, beadwork and leatherwork.

Progress was made, but not without a lot of difficulties and high expenses. Even Bishop Hughes, began to suffer from "scheme fatigue". Writing to Stephen Harrington in December '48 he said, "I've had enough talk about Schemes to last the rest of my life. Things did not work out so well ... Dr Kelly did a tremendous amount of travelling backwards and forwards but he couldn't pin authorities down to anything definite and so we are left carrying the baby, or babies, for there are two of them [Oye and Owo]. Sickly little brats they are too and there's a lot of work to be done for them if they are to be kept alive".

Stephen Harrington by 1951 was also becoming sceptical, "After four years, it seems to me that little of the original scheme is taking shape. The actual achievement in Oye is excellent: tiles, church art in cane and beadwork, and weaving [but] these are worthwhile adjuncts rather than essential features". He felt the essence of the scheme, promoting self-reliance in the villages, had not been achieved and wondered, after all the time and money that had been spent, if it ever would, "Only Dr Kelly can decide if his idea is taking shape and if the problems of finance and personnel can be met and solved. It seems to me that it will scarcely be possible without government aid".

After 1947, "schemes" did not figure again in Benin-Cork

correspondence until 1950, the year the Vicariate of Asaba-Benin became the **"Diocese of Benin City"**. In 1950, Ned Coleman wrote to Dr Kelly about the scheme he was attempting to establish in Asaba district. Indicating that schemes had fallen out of favour with the missionaries, Ned said he felt, "strong opposition from some of the wiseacres in the Diocese", but he remained positive himself about them:

> The Government is now paying, at Divisional level, grants for the provision of social and educational amenities. The ideas behind the Village Development plan are exactly what you formulated in 1942-43. Of course some wise D.O. will get the kudos. I have a mild version in operation at Issele-Azagba where the people will build a school and the Government will refund one-third of the cost. This will, in turn, go into a maternity clinic and so on until they have a complete community centre, including playing fields, post office and reading room. The only proviso is that all the work and outlay must be borne by the people. In other words, they must be self-sufficient. Unless I am very much mistaken, that is the essence of what you envisaged.

Ned was also planning an electricity generating plant and had bought wiring and equipment at bargain prices, all he needed was another £500 or so to light up! He hoped the Provincial would provide the money and "help confound the critics". Meanwhile, on the pastoral front, he was busy making "Harvest". The church at Okpanam had come up with £33 and "they are building a new school as well". "Here in Asaba, I am encouraging people to present pews to the church and I have got six this month. Most surprising, the Asaba Council, which is predominantly CMS, presented one". Nevertheless, Ned needed a lot more finance, "I wish to goodness I could raise about £3000, then I could finish the Church in a year or two".

The first secondary schools

Though claiming he was not an opponent of development schemes Pat, definitely, was more interested in schools. In the Forties, his great ambition was to open a Catholic secondary school in Benin City, but the Government had already set up Edo College which, even though it went only as far as Class IV, was the only secondary school in Benin and Delta Provinces. As it was still struggling to get established, the Ministry, not wanting a rival school in its vicinity, offered £26,000 to the Catholic Mission to open a secondary school anywhere *except* Benin City. Tom Duffy in Asaba, whose parishioners for long had been pleading for higher education, applied for permission to start a college. This was quickly granted, along with a guarantee that his school would be grant-aided. Pat applied about the same time as Tom for a secondary school in Benin City, but got no reply. After three months of waiting, he went ahead, opening "Immaculate Conception College" (ICC). The Ministry, rather meanly, classified it as a Private School which could not go beyond Class III without formal inspection and approval (which it wasn't likely to give). Pat, however, out-manoeuvred them and, in time, ICC became one of the country's great colleges.

Duffy's Asaba college, at first called "St Augustine's", opened in 1944, using the converted premises of the Catholic Bookshop. After a short time it was re-located in a maternity centre. Tony McDonagh, Mayo, appointed the first Principal, at the time was completing studies in London University and did not take up his new office until January '45. In '46 the college, with three classes, was severely handicapped for space. A benefactor, Mr Ogbolumani of Umuagu, made 35 acres of land available and the construction of a proper college began under Bill Fegan. At this time the name was changed to "St Patrick's". Rapid progress was made until Pat, claiming there was no more money for cement and concrete blocks, told Bill, much to the annoyance of Tom Duffy, to continue building with mud blocks, "Tell the Asaba people", Pat added, that "if they want a college they'll have to pay for it". Such was his customary instruction to people who were begging for schools or churches. Often they did come up with the money. One of Pat's secretaries recalled being awakened in the middle of the night by an apologetic Bishop because a delegation from a far off village had just arrived with no less than £2,000 in pennies, three-penny bits, and sixpences, and he wanted help to count it.

When Pat received a Government grant for a school, he usually stretched it to build two or three schools. The Ministry did not complain, and neither did the people, all were getting good value for money. The Bishop's pride and joy, St Patrick's, Asaba, regarded as the first Catholic secondary school in the Vicariate, was the second one in the whole country – St Gregory's (founded by Leo Taylor) in Lagos being the first. Like Gregory's, St Patrick's became one of the outstanding colleges in Nigeria, where many future leaders and professional men were educated. (St Thomas Aquinas, Teacher Training College, opened by Bishop Broderick in Ibusa in 1928, also claims to be the first secondary school – allowing St Patrick's the credit of being the first *Grammar* school.)

Home again

Making his excuses, Pat did not attend the Superior General's meeting with the SMA Ordinaries in Cape Coast in April '47. Never keen on attending meetings outside Nigeria, he was busy tidying up affairs in the Vicariate as he wanted to depart for home leave in June. He was glad that John Mahon, his trusty Pro-Vicar, who had resigned his Provincial Council post in January '45, was back in Asaba-Benin. After handing over to him, Pat departed for Lagos and embarked for home.

The family at Tristaun hadn't seen their 'Africa man' for six years. Though looking a bit tired he hadn't changed much they thought. He walked, as usual, to the stream at the end of the farm and, finding it clogged with weeds, he spent the next few days raking them out. He was in time to help with hay making and, as he was good at 'heading the cocks' his brothers, Jack and Bill, left it to him. Later, they left him the hard work of opening the headlands with a scythe; he took pride in making a good job of it, wasting nothing. Sharing a room with Bill upstairs, a blanket hung between them for privacy, he had the side with a view of the front avenue, bordered by the fir trees which he had planted many years before. Eating everything, except chicken, enjoying the new potatoes with salt and 'country' butter, he felt good to be at home. His mother Kate, dead nearly three years, was sadly missed. Both his brothers were bachelors, though Jack, nearly fifty, had an interest in Ellen Feeney from Ballygar, a nurse who had been working in England for seven years. In November '47, Jack bade farewell to his bachelor days and married Ellen.

As planned, Pat went to the States and remained there from December to March '48, staying with his brothers and visiting the many Galway immigrants. In many places including Boston, Brooklyn, and Hartford he preached about the needs in Nigeria. People were especially interested in helping lepers, and the

New York. Mary (sister-in-law), Gerald (brother), Bishop Kelly, Michael (brother), Mary (sister-in-law), Malachy (brother).

Americans donated generously. Former neighbours of his like Paddy Larkin, the Kellys, Quinns, Curleys, Feeneys and others set up "The Bishop Kelly Club of New York", from which over the years a lot of aid, including big American motor cars, found its way to Nigeria. In Ireland he had already started a Leper Fund, to which people in Ireland and England donated throughout the Forties.

While at home, he heard of two exceptional young confreres, **Laurence Carr** and **John Creaven**, ordained in 1942 and 1944 respectively. He was particularly interested in Carr, generally called 'Larry', who was just then completing his doctoral dissertation in canon law. Since Pat had lost Doctors Glynn and PM Kelly from the mission, he was ever on the lookout for replacements. He wanted a canon lawyer not only to teach in the seminary which, despite the Ordinaries' plans, had not yet moved from Benin City, but to help him with the many complicated marriage cases he had to handle and the indults and decrees from Rome which seemed to worry him far more than they worried other bishops. Carr was teaching in Dromantine while finishing his dissertation, "Jurisdiction in Common Error". A first class sportsman, he had won two Leinster senior football medals playing for his county, Louth. A popular man who could combine sport and serious study, he was noted for a strong desire to win – both on and off the field. Pat, arguing that such young men should be given a chance on the missions before receiving home appointments, said Benin City seminary would be the ideal place for him, James Flanagan, in Ondo since 1945, could easily take his place in Dromantine. When Pat heard that the Provincial, who was then in Nigeria, was thinking of appointing Carr to the new University in Ibadan, he hastened to suggest that John Creaven would be better for that post. Creaven, then teaching philosophy in the Society's college in Cloughballymore, had gained a first class MA in philosophy in University College Galway before ordination. Pat wrote in haste to his classmate and fellow-missionary, John Cadogan, the Vice Provincial, in charge while Dr Kelly was away and, before long, Carr was appointed to Benin where he arrived in '49.

Towards the end of his leave in Ireland, June 1948, Pat wrote to the Provincial who was still in Nigeria, to remind him that though Asaba-Benin had lost five men in the previous year, only two men had been appointed to it. After the annual retreat in Blackrock Road, Pat, this time not forgetting a heavy box of altar stones, made his way to Liverpool, where he embarked on the 24th in the company of Bishop Taylor and John Lynott who were also returning to Nigeria after leave.

Bishop Kelly and Bishop Thomas Hughes of Ondo with priest-students of University College Cork, photographed at Doughcloyne.
Seated: Joseph Erameh, Benin; Pedro Martins, Lagos (future chief RC army chaplain). *Standing:* Francis Buah, Ghana; Bernard Elaho, Benin; Anthony Sanusi, Lagos (future bishop of Ijebu-Ode); Stephen Umurie, Benin; and Joseph Essuah (future bishop of Sekondi-Takoradi, Ghana).

Chapter 10

UNEVEN PROGRESS

The late Forties

After leave, in July 1948, Pat was welcomed back by John Mahon at the 'palace'. In his absence, John had painted the house and, risking the Bishop's ire, had thrown out the old yellowing kerosene fridge and bought a bright new white one.

"I see you did a bit of painting", observed Pat.

"Yes, my Lord, it was badly needed and didn't cost much".

Pretending he didn't realize that the fridge was new, Pat continued, "I see you painted the fridge too!"

Back 'on seat', his first major task was to compile the Vicariate's annual statistical report for Propaganda Fide. When completed he sent it to the Cardinal Prefect with an introductory note:

> Your Eminence,
> I forward herewith the Prospectus for the Vicariate for the year ending June 30, 1948. The Catholic population continues to increase, chiefly through the elementary schools. Apart from school children, few adults attend the catechumen classes. The personnel of the Vicariate is expending most of its energy at present on Higher Education and on the supervision of the elementary schools, but this is necessary owing to the rapid expansion of secular instruction in recent years. All the school children get a regular instruction in Christian Doctrine though many of them never come forward for Baptism.

This is chiefly due to the influence of their pagan parents, but gradually this prejudice against Christianity will break down.

We have only four Seminarians for this Vicariate in the Major Seminary but there are more than twenty in the Minor Seminary, and four or five of these are ready to come to the Major Seminary in the near future. One of our Nigerian priests [Fr Paul Emecete] died during the year. He was the first native priest in British West Africa. One other is studying at the University of Cork where he will receive academic qualifications in the midst of Catholic surroundings with a view to being a professor afterwards in our Secondary College.

The Vicariate has a good credit balance at present. Part of this money is given by Government to erect our secondary schools and to enlarge our normal colleges, and part of it is for the building of churches and the erection of a Mission Hospital. Building operations are delayed owing to the scarcity of material and the lack of skilled labour.

Our maternity centres are doing well under the supervision of the Sisters, and through them many babies are sent to Heaven each year. The Apostolic Delegate, during his visit in 1947, recommended maternity work as a great means of breaking down pagan prejudice and introducing missionary activity into the social life of the people...

+ P.J. Kelly, Vicar Apostolic.

A few figures from this 1948 report along with those of 1942-1943 (the closest available to the time he began as Vicar Apostolic), give an indication of the current state of the Vicariate and developments under Pat in his first five years as Bishop:

Personnel: 43 SMA missionaries and 3 Nigerian priests; not a big increase since 1943, when there were 39 missionaries and 4

Nigerian priests.

Parishes: 11 parishes with priests in residence, 5 stations with a priest in residence, and 398 non-residential outstations. In '43: 11 parishes, 7 residential stations and 320 outstations.

Churches: 36 capable of holding more than 400 people and 368 smaller ones. In '43: 37 large and 304 small churches.

Catholics: 47,627 – a fair increase on the 33,441 of 1943, the number of catechumens had nearly doubled – from 9,910 to 16,622. Though substantial, the number of Catholics was only a fraction of the whole population of 810,000 animists, 167,000 Moslems and 43,000 Protestants.

OLA Sisters numbered 16 in both reports, but there had been a huge increase in the number of 'consultations' in their medical centres – from 17,000 to 74,000 – and the number of centres had increased from 10 to 17.

Schools: elementary schools had increased from 202 to 285 with male pupils increasing in number from 16,584 to 30,523 and female from 2,324 to 4,988. 'Middle' schools had increased from 37 to 60 with a proportionate increase in numbers of pupils; 'higher' schools from 0 to 2 with 215 male pupils; and 'normal' schools from 2 to 3 with 290 pupils, 30 of whom were girls. Teachers had increased in number from 829 to 1,558.

Catechists had increased from 278 to 379 and 'baptizers' from 836 to 1,063.

The financial figures showed remarkable increases: the income over the year was £131,478, whereas in '42-'43 it had been £29,622; correspondingly expenditure had increased from £22,122 in '43 to £96,718 in '48! Money in Vicariate accounts had risen from £8,500 to £34,760.

After receiving a copy of the report, the Superior General, Stephen Harrington, wrote to Pat, "I must heartily congratulate you on the very successful position it reveals, both spiritually and financially".

In terms of finance and school work, the Vicariate had been very successful, but close examination of the statistics shows that pastoral progress was not so great. The increase in the number of Catholics was due as much to natural family increase as to conversions. The number of parishes, 11, was the same in both reports, while the residential stations had actually decreased from 7 to 5. This was mainly due to the shortage of priests whose number had increased by only 3 since 1943, also to the deployment of more men in schools, and to the closing of stations to favour living in community. The number of marriages – one of the more reliable gauges of genuine growth in Catholic life – was only marginally greater in '48 (308) than in '43 (299). The number of teachers (Nigerians) had greatly increased, even doubled, but the numbers of catechists and baptizers had not nearly increased in the same proportion. While the number of schools had increased, even doubled in some categories, the number of church buildings had not (though, of course, many school buildings were used as churches on Sundays); the number of large church buildings had actually decreased (by one).

Pat was aware of the uneven progress, but considered the emphasis on education worthwhile, not only as a value in itself, but in terms of religion – he believed that spiritual fruit would be gained in time and, on the other hand, that the church would lose opportunities of evangelization and seriously diminish its prestige and attractiveness in the eyes of the people if it did not go all out for schools at this time.

The remarkable increase in income was due to grants, mainly for schools, which began with the Government's 1946 Ten Year Plan. Grants to the Vicariate in '47–'48 amounted to **£90,246**. Grants in this era dominated Vicariate finances, and gaining or losing one made a huge difference to the balance sheet. Pat used grant money thriftily, stretching it to the limit, building "two or three for the price of one". His thriftiness in other spheres, combined with John Mahon's initiatives and support, paid off too. For instance in 1943 *Offerings of the indigenous faithful* amounted to £3,711, but in 1948 it was £8,701 – a substantial sum when compared with the SMA grants of the same year – £1,500, and the Propagation of the Faith – £2,423.

Motor cars and 'Regional Superiors'

After returning in '48, Pat noticed a lot of missionaries driving new cars, he couldn't complain too loudly as he had a new American Chevrolet himself! He noted with pleasure that Willie Keenan, the Visitor, still used a bicycle. However, Willie was trying to make up his mind whether to buy a new Ford Kit Car or a saloon like the Bishop's. Kit Cars' were popular: the Education Supervisor, Phil Mahon, had a new one, so had Tom Bartley the administrator of Holy Cross, and the nursing sister had one. Tommy Greene and Joe Styles, pooling their funds, had bought a Dodge Kit Car. Willie decided on a Kit Car. Even if he was replaced soon as Visitor, and he hoped he would be, the car would be there for the new man. Pat was very pleased with his own new Chev, except for its flashy chrome adornments on the outside and the fancy gadgets inside. He pulled out whatever wasn't necessary, like ashtrays and the radio (which passengers turned on when he wanted to say the Rosary), but he left the cigarette lighter in so that smokers wouldn't be wasting his matches.

With the on-going division of mission jurisdictions by Rome, it was no longer viable to have a Society Visitor in every jurisdiction. Already Kaduna, Jos, and Ondo-Ilorin areas had been separated from the larger jurisdictions of the Bight of Benin (Lagos) and Western Nigeria (Benin City). In 1948, the Society finally replaced the office of Visitor with that of a "Regional Superior" who would have authority over a number of jurisdictions. Asaba-Benin was joined with Lagos and Ondo under one "RS" residing at Owo in Ondo district. In November, Willie Keenan instructed the confreres in Asaba-Benin, not forgetting the Bishop, to send their consultative vote for the new

RS direct to the Vice Provincial (Dr Kelly was still in Nigeria completing his visitation of Etsako, Okene and Kabba). In May 1949, **Patrick Hughes**, was appointed the first "Regional Superior". In an outburst of fellow-feeling, Bishop Kelly asked the Provincial to let the out-going Visitor keep the new Kit Car, "After seven years faithful service as Visitor he deserves that much at least". Keeping a good car in the Vicariate might also have influenced Pat.

Appealing for school men

With the increasing numbers of schools, the Bishop intensified his badgering of Cork for qualified men, "I would like to know who are the new men we may expect in a couple of months", 1 August '48; "Kindly let me have a list of the Fathers coming here as soon as possible", 18 August '48. When Fr Cadogan informed him, "There are only five new men with Degrees available for the missions this year, you are getting two, Frank McCabe and Tony Jennings", Pat wasn't happy, "Luckily, your unwelcome letter arrived when the Provincial was here and seeing things for himself, he said he would write you immediately to release another man from Dromantine ... In this Vicariate there were nearly as many men in the care of souls when there were 10,000 Catholics as there are now with 48,000".

On 3 January 1949, **J.J. Healy**, sixty-two, died after a fall down the stairs in Warri mission. The Bishop, informing the Provincial, emphasised the loss in terms of personnel and demanded, "two extra men immediately", one to replace the deceased and the other to replace John Rafferty who was in America and apparently "not keen on coming back". He continued, "The Training College in Ibusa wants a fourth man, there are upwards of 300 students as against 60 in the old days. I have to remind you also that the only science man here is Fr Donnelly". Concerned for his former mission area in the Delta, he said, "Warri Province is quite neglected. A Catholic secondary school is necessary there, else all our boys will go to the pagan secondary schools that have been newly opened". Playing on congregational pride he added, "If the CSSp or the Kiltegan Fathers had Warri Province there would have been a secondary school there long ago". Previously he had already warned, "If Warri Province is taken away from the SMA, there would be good reason for it".

Such fears and warnings were not idle ones. The Apostolic Delegate had already asked Pat if he would be willing to give part of **Kabba Province** in the north of his territory to the Holy Ghost Fathers. Pat was willing, though he had some reservations. Endeavouring to enlist Stephen Harrington in his campaign for more men he wrote, "if you are opposed to the SMA parting with Kabba you must urge the Provincial to give this Vicariate special consideration when appointing new missionaries". Admitting that, apart from two or three centres, the Vicariate had made poor progress in Kabba, he argued that it was due to shortage of personnel and, "to the restrictions Government have put on the opening of Catholic schools". The Administration in this district favoured Community schools with "an agreed syllabus", which was unacceptable to the Catholic church. Despite Pat's appeal, Harrington, who estimated that upwards of twenty men would be required to build up Kabba, was of the opinion that the SMA should let it go. At this time John Duffy, working in one of Kabba's successful mission areas, completed the building of New St Mary's Catholic School and opened it on 8 September 1949.

The Bishop was also 'short' of personnel because many were on home leave and some were late in returning. He instructed the new, rule-conscious bursar in Cork, Phillip Corish, to book return tickets for Benin men "six months in advance" to avoid excuses and delays on the return voyage, and pointedly said, "Kindly speed up Fr Rafferty when you get this". Though the Bishop might have chosen air travel as a means of "speeding up" missionaries he was put off by the extra cost, "I would prefer to see the Fathers coming by boat, as £9 or £10 a man is something to save, especially when so many are coming and going".

Actually, John Rafferty was not in good health, and when he did return, he had to be invalided home again within two years. He took up work in America, but died there four years later.

In 1949, after receiving a stiff bill from Phil Corish for Benin missionaries on leave, Pat campaigned that the Province should pay half his missionaries' home expenses and half their holiday allowance (which was reckoned at the rate of £10 for each year on mission and £5 for the year at home). Pat said he would be prepared to pay up to £30 per man, and the Province should pay the rest. He pointed out that ocean fares were expensive and the cost of clothing and other expenses very high, "By the time the Father is back here after his year's leave there is not much left out of £400. So I think this request is reasonable enough". As the bursar didn't agree, Pat turned to the Provincial, "Fr Corish sends me a big bill. No balance of Mass stipends or donation from the Province to go against it ... besides the Province used to pay half the Fathers' holiday allowances". Adding salt to the wound, Pat thought, the Province had actually doubled the holiday allowance "without consulting those whom it wants to pay the bill"! "I shall defer payment of a portion of the Provincial Procurator's bill until I hear from you". He didn't make much headway on this and grumbled, " 'Head I win and harp you lose', says the Society to the Ordinary".

Pat also rooted for money everywhere he could within the Vicariate. Pat Braniff, from Co Down, a builder like his first

cousin Bill Fegan, sent a photo of Musa, his driver, and his Bedford lorry, to Cork and was only possibly joking when he wrote on the back, "The Bishop

Pat Braniff with Musa and his Bedford truck.

199

wants a rake off the grant given for the College. One thousand in every ten".

Pat didn't speak of the arrival of men as much as the departures but, new, qualified men were appointed to him such as, Tony Jennings and Frank McCabe in '48, and Paddy Gantly the following year. Ironically, McCabe's appointment was changed as soon as he arrived in Nigeria and he was posted to Ife Teacher Training College in Taylor's Vicariate. Worried about a replacement for Joe Donnelly, the Vicariate's only science graduate, who was due leave, Pat asked for a lay graduate, mentioning that the salary would be £550, "or £600, if he cannot be got for the former". In August '49 the Provincial sent a list of men destined for Asaba-Benin with no less than seven names on it, including four new men. Surprisingly, Pat refused one of them who was on transfer from Liberia. Pat was biased against Liberian missionaries since the time he got one who found the conditions in Asaba-Benin too tough, didn't learn the vernacular language and continued hearing confessions through an interpreter. Similarly, Pat was biased against confreres from the Gold Coast because, he thought conditions for expatriates there were too good and spoiled men. After further coaxing from the Provincial about the 'Liberian', he relented, "Let him come, but he should not be expecting an easy time", and so Tony Murphy arrived late in '49 along with newcomers Michael Scully, Mick O'Regan and Con O'Driscoll. Among those on the Provincial's list of seven, were Larry Carr (transferred from Dromantine), Dick Beausang (a new man), and John Rafferty and Joe Barrett who were returning after leave. Rather than showing elation at getting so many, Pat pointed out that five men were waiting to get the boat home.

"Not worthy to be a Bishop"
In April 1950, with the creation of the Nigerian hierarchy, the Vicariate of Asaba-Benin became the diocese of **"Benin City"**. There was jubilation in Benin, but not in Asaba. In fact, the

previous year the people of Asaba had formally requested Pius XII, to separate Asaba from Benin and appoint a new Bishop with headquarters at Asaba, "The Catholic Christians and people of Asaba have lost confidence in Bishop Kelly and in his grouping of Asaba and Benin Vicariates" – a reference to the transfer of headquarters to Benin and the naming of the Vicariate "Asaba-Benin", which was not Pat's doing, but he was often blamed for it. On one occasion, an angry member of the Asaba community told him, "You are not worthy to be a Bishop"! Pat absolutely agreed with him. Nevertheless, he went to Rome in May 1950 along with the other bishops for the Nigerian hierarchy's first official visit to the Pope. The visit over, he took a short holiday at home, which included three days of prayer and penance at Ireland's toughest place of pilgrimage, Lough Derg, before returning to Nigeria in August.

On 8 February 1951, **Charles Burr,** Issele-Uku, the last of the Alsatian missionaries in the Diocese, was struck and killed by a lorry as he cycled home after officiating at a funeral at Onicha-Ugbo. Sixty-nine years of age when he died, he was a legend in the mission and greatly loved by the people. Totally dedicated to his work in Nigeria, he went on home leave only twice in forty-five years, the last time being in 1925. At the people's request he was buried, not in the missionary cemetery in Asaba, but at the entrance of their parish church, St Paul's, which he had built. In an atmosphere of deep public mourning, Pat officiated at the solemn requiem mass; nineteen priests sang the office of the dead.

Informing the Provincial of Fr Burr's death, Pat said, "We are now short of priests again". Before the tragic accident John Rafferty and another missionary, John Moran, who had only arrived in '46, had been invalided home. At this time, four men were still overdue from Leave, but Pat admitted, "three of them I understand are recovering from operations". In a postscript he added that he was holding back two men, though they "badly need to go home", until replacements arrived. Desperate for a science graduate he requested the Provincial to exchange one of the BA men appointed to him for a BSc graduate.

In November '51, Stephen Harrington announced that Propaganda Fide had given permission for the date of the General Assembly to be advanced by one year, General and Provincial Assemblies would then both be held in 1952. He requested all to join him in a novena of prayer before the opening of the General Assembly on 26 June, and he asked the six Irish bishops of West Africa to vote for two delegates. Tom Hughes of Ondo was elected, but did not wish to attend. Next in line was Pat, who also refused. Regarding the third elected – Mgr Lumley of Jos – the General, greatly discomfited and hoping Pat might change his mind, said that he had no response from Lumley up to 21 May. Lumley, however, did travel and arrived in time for the opening session. Evidently there was little love lost between the mission Ordinaries and the Generalate at the time. The previous General Assembly, in 1947, had been called "the Visitors' Assembly" as sixteen Visitors had attended but only one Bishop (Hughes). After it, efforts were made to ensure that more Ordinaries took part; in 1952 five did. The Ordinaries, in general, were inclined to view their own role as 'work on the missions' and the home front's role as providing men and means to enable them to do it. Rapport between mission and home front leaders continued to be rather tense in the Fifties, but prior to the 1952 Assemblies, the Irish Province was occupied with serious home-front matters.

Chapter 11

A NEW BROOM ON THE HOME FRONT

The Provincial Superior, Dr PM Kelly, spent most of 1948 in Nigeria, engaged in promoting his development schemes but, a year or two after their inauguration, in spite of some success, he realized that his main aims were not being achieved. Disappointed, he said, "Provincials have so many masters and so many pulling at them that it often seems impossible to really get anything going fully and efficiently, and they must be content to keep the wheels just turning". At the Extraordinary General Council meeting of 1951 he said, "Society works on the missions had not got the attention they should have got". At the meeting he reported on the state of discipline in the Irish Province and, having looked into some cases, said he had tried to instil greater prudence in the confreres involved. However the Holy See was not satisfied and informed the Superior General that it had appointed an Apostolic Visitator to conduct an investigation into the Irish Province. In January 1952, Dr Kelly was asked to resign.

In February, **John Creaven** was appointed Irish Provincial Superior. A Galway man, he was born in Caherlean in the parish of Cummer, 20 October 1917. Cummer parish was exceptional for the number of men it gave to the SMA. Among notables who preceded Creaven were: Martin Bane, who began his mission work with Pat in Warri in 1930; and Larry Dolan who first went to Nigeria in 1935. From an early age, John Creaven's academic prowess and leanings towards priesthood were recognized. At Cummer National School, the Principal and one of the teachers (whose sister was a member of the OLA), encouraged him to enter the SMA Junior college at Ballinafad, Co. Mayo. Passing from there to St Joseph's, Wilton, he sat for the Intermediate Certificate in 1935 gaining the highest possible number of honours, including full marks in Latin. Matriculating the following year, he went to University College Cork, where he got first class honours in four subjects in First Arts, two first places in the University and two second places. Awarded a scholarship by UCC, he was unable to pursue it, as he had already entered the 'noviciate' in Cloughballymore. Continuing his studies at University College Galway, he completed his BA in 1939, gaining first class honours and a post-graduate scholarship. Availing of this scholarship, he obtained a first-class honours MA in Philosophy in UCG in 1941. His thesis, "The Philosophy of Personalism", was judged to be the best of seven presented to the National University of Ireland. In 1942, while studying theology in Dromantine, he was awarded the National University's "Travelling Studentship in Philosophy".

A tall, well-built man, he was a good athlete and footballer and had played for the Galway minor team. After ordination in 1944, he was appointed to teach philosophy in Cloughballymore. Later, he gained a doctorate from Cambridge and, subsequently, was called "Doctor Creaven".

Dr John Creaven

In February 1952, Bishop Kelly, congratulating the new Provincial, asked him to speed up one of the Benin missionary's return, "if he is well enough to come out, as we need him very badly". Pat needed a replacement for John Sheehan at Okpara Inland, who would have to be invalided home as soon as he was fit to travel.

In March, after Dr Kelly's provincial councillors had tendered their resignations as required by the Apostolic Visitator, Dr Creaven announced the name of his new Vice Provincial – John Reddington of Ibadan, and his new councillors: John Mahon (Benin City); Michael Mahony (Doughcloyne – a house for African students attending UCC); and Maurice Kelly (Cloughballymore). Pat, upset over the loss of John Mahon for the second time, hastened to point out to the Provincial that he had no one to replace him as Vicar General, "unless you send some one from home". He added that he had recently lost John Rafferty, John Moran, Michael Maughan and John Sheehan all of whom had to be sent home for health reasons. Understandably angry, he concluded his letter, "Don't forget to tell the Procurator to credit the account of this Diocese with Mahon's passage and expenses out to Nigeria".

John Mahon's younger brother, Philip, whom Pat had appointed Supervisor of Schools in '47, had become ill in February '52 and had to be invalided home. In Cork, in June, he underwent a gall bladder operation, but did not survive. Only forty-four when he died, he had been twenty years in the mission serving in St Paul's Major Seminary; working in Ozoro with Michael Foley; and on his own in remote Ashaka. An indefatigable visitor of outstations and schools, the people called him "Father all-weather". Describing him as an "ideal missionary", Pat told the Provincial, "We have suffered a great loss in the death of Fr Phil Mahon RIP ... he never spared himself, I hope he is now receiving the reward of all his labours".

The month Phil died, Pat received notice from the Provincial that he was recalling Larry Carr from the Seminary in Benin in order to take up his new appointment as Superior of Dromantine, and he should be released immediately. Pat protested, "It seems a mistake to me to take a young man home after a bare half tour ... he would make a good superior of the seminary at home had he a bit more experience out here. He is the third important man taken away from this Diocese by the Society in the last few months and, with Fr Philip Mahon's death, leaves us very short-handed".

Also in June, Paddy Gantly, who had replaced Phil Mahon as Supervisor of Schools, was called home to be Director of Aspirants of the Province's new "Spiritual Year" which was to be inaugurated in September in Cloughballymore. The Provincial wrote, "I am recalling him immediately as he requires a short holiday before assuming office". Exasperated, Pat replied, "Yours just received re Fr Gantly. I am appealing to the Superior General against his recall. He is in a key position here with the Education Department and there is no one of any experience whom I can put in his place at this critical juncture for Catholic schools. I shall release him if the Superior General says so". Nevertheless, obedient as always, he booked Gantly on the next boat home (boat rather than 'plane as that was Gantly's wish). However, the General also acted swiftly and informed Pat, "The Provincial has agreed to leave Gantly to you and will make other arrangements for home. Your mission has certainly lost the most of all in the recent changes".

Dr Creaven's letter recalling Gantly, contained good news as well: seven men had been appointed to Benin – four of whom had degrees, including John Flanagan DCL who was to replace Larry Carr, and three newly ordained men for pastoral work. Ever shy of over-doing gratitude, Pat nodded approvingly in the direction of the Provincial, "Some of us out here think the Spiritual Year is a move in the right direction".

Two strong characters were now in charge, one of the Irish Province and the other of Benin Diocese, but they were of very different personalities, experience, and approach. The first, with academic qualifications second to none, was new to high office and only thirty-four years of age – twenty-three years younger than Pat and much younger than most of the Ordinaries and Major Superiors of the Society at the time. He had been appointed to restore order, develop the Province at home, and steer its mission safely into the winds of change in Africa. The Bishop, with nearly three decades of experience in Africa, at fifty-seven was still very vigorous, highly effective and totally focused on his diocese and its needs. Dr Creaven, appointed to office rather than elected, and not a member of any particular mission in Africa, might well be independent of pressure groups and special interests, but the same factors, coupled with his age, might also diminish his standing in the eyes of the missionaries, especially the sun-dried bishops.

Bishop Kelly's tight-fistedness, asceticism, and somewhat fanatical urgency 'to save souls' (especially in his own Diocese), inevitably led him into confrontation with Society superiors. Initial clashes with Dr Creaven were mild enough. The Provincial Assembly of '52 agreed to raise the confreres' personal allocation, paid by the Province, from 30 shillings to £4 and the holiday allowance, paid by the Ordinary, from £10 to £15. Pat, unhappy with the latter, asked the Province to pay the extra £5, pointing out that the Province gave no subsidy to Benin, and no longer credited the diocese with any balance remaining in the Regional's account, as it used to do with the Visitor's account. Because of lack of money, he claimed, "The Catholic Mission must stand idly by, while rival groups, like the Baptists, build fine schools and buy up existing ones with American dollars". Dr Creaven replied that the Province was not in a position to pay part of the holiday allowance; apart from other considerations, it was burdened with an overdraft of £50,000 which was likely to increase due to growing formation needs at home. The new Provincial, as well as setting himself to reducing the Province's debts, aimed at promoting recruitment of students, whose numbers had diminished, and he wished to enlarge and improve the Province's colleges and seminaries.

As always, there was tension between mission and home administration over missionary appointments, withdrawals and delays. The Bishop didn't think that Bill Power's studying for two years for a diploma in Social Science in Dublin after his first leave in '52, was a good idea. The Provincial accepted that but, Bill wasn't ready to return to the diocese anyway for health reasons. He returned after gaining his diploma in June '54. After leave in '52, Ned Coleman received a home appointment in connection with the *African Missionary*, which delayed his return until December '53. Mattie Walsh fell seriously ill during his home leave in '52 and, though wishing to return, the superiors in Cork thought he should remain in Ireland and appointed him to 'promotion work' until he fully recovered. He returned in January '55. John Flanagan, entertaining ideas about joining the French Province, went to La Croix (and subsequently did not go to Nigeria). In these cases the maxim "mission before man" was inverted – men were put, or put themselves, before mission; this was not an inversion that sat easily with Bishop Kelly.

Some tension arose over efforts to engage Religious Orders to take over schools in Benin. Pat's aim was not to diminish the Diocese's involvement in schools, but to extend it. If a congregation of Brothers took over a school, his plan was to open another one with the personnel released. The efforts of the administration in Cork to get Brothers did not meet with success. Orders like De la Salle and the Irish Christian Brothers, had received many such requests, but were heavily committed at home. The Vice Provincial, John Reddington, having discussed with Dr Creaven, Bishop Kelly's "offer" to hand over (the undeveloped and non grant-aided) Aghalokpe College near Sapele, informed him, through the Acting Regional Superior, Tom

Murray, that the Council needed a better bargaining piece, "We believe no community of Brothers would seriously consider taking up such an offer". Furthermore, Reddington indicated that the Provincial's and his Council's motivation was not the same as the Bishop's, "Aghalokpe would not release many Fathers for *pastoral work* which is our immediate object!" The Vice Provincial suggested that the Bishop should reconsider the whole question of Brothers. Perhaps Tom Murray, when passing on the Administration's message to Pat, mentioned something about handing over *St Patrick's College*, Asaba. Whoever mentioned it, it caused Pat to lose his customary sang-froid, "I have no intention of handing over St Patrick's to anyone. If not for St Patrick's and Ibusa College we would be on the rocks long ago. Fr Reddington is thinking we have big fat Harvests [Church collections] here like they have in Yoruba country". He defended his offer of Aghalokpe College, "It is to be grant-aided this year" and, continuing in classic Kelly style, he declaimed, "If there is no Order in the Catholic Church, cleric or lay, prepared to rough it a little in the beginning for the good of souls, then truly the children of this generation are wiser than the children of light". He stuck to his conviction that the school apostolate was the best way forward, "I think men should be released to open more colleges". And, he didn't think "roughing it" was a bad way to start, "I am just back from a visit to Isoko country. It is predominantly Protestant because CMS parsons from England roughed it in the past, making their habitation in the swamps and opening schools all round them". He warned that the Catholic mission was about to lose another opportunity, "The Isoko people have about £8,000 collected to open a secondary school ... if the CMS get this college, the Catholic Mission will get nowhere in Isoko in the future. If Education is the door by which these people will enter the Church why should Fathers be released for pastoral work?"

Provincial visitation

Dr Creaven planned a prolonged visit to West Africa, September '53 to May '54. Shortly after arrival in Lagos he met the Nigerian Ordinaries and arranged his itinerary with them. Escorted by the Regional Superior, Paddy Hughes, he began with Lagos and afterwards, from November to January, toured Benin City diocese. Calling first at the Bishop's humble abode, he observed how sparsely furnished it was, "except for the Oratory which was decently appointed". His visit to Sapele coincided with the blessing of the new church on the feast of the Immaculate Conception, 8 December. Begun by Pat Shine, the building of the new church was continued by many different confreres and finally completed by Dan O'Connell. The Provincial witnessed how Bishop Kelly turned such an occasion into a parish 'mission'. Many Fathers were invited – mainly to help with the instruction of catechumens and to hear confessions. Even Dr Creaven was granted 'instant faculties', given a chair, a stole, and a position under a tree where he was left for hours, absolving a never-ending queue of penitents. It was a long, hot, tiring day, during which the Bishop ensured that everyone confined their celebration to the spiritual and sacramental.

The Provincial's visit to Asaba was timed for Christmas. The highlight of the feast was the coming of the Bishop to celebrate Midnight Mass – an event motivated by hopes of placating the Asaba Christians who were still disgruntled over the transfer of episcopal headquarters to Benin. Dr Creaven recalled the event, "It was hot in the lovely, if European, St Joseph's Church. The crowded congregation was shown no mercy by the Bishop as he preached at great length, using several interpreters, not just about the Feast but on other fundamental matters as well. Some people had taken to the window seats to get 'breeze' and I had a distraction, wondering if we had an accident, such as befell St Paul when he too preached far into the night, and a listener who had fallen asleep in a window fell down and was killed, would the Bishop be able to resuscitate him? It was well towards 3 a.m.

when we got back to St Patrick's College and a welcome shower".

The Provincial's knowledge of the Diocese was greatly enhanced by seeing things for himself and talking to the missionaries. Despite great progress in many areas, especially in education, there were problems which needed to be addressed. Dr Creaven also wished to promote the Society's rule of life in accordance with the latest edition of the *Constitutions* and *Directory*. His first set of special "Instructions" was addressed to Andy O'Rourke, Principal of the prestigious St Patrick's College, Asaba. The Provincial said, "Now that full facilities, a proper Staff house, Oratory et cetera, are provided I feel that it is time to organize a proper House Rule, with a more definite horarium". He recommended spiritual exercises in common, morning prayer and mental prayer before Mass, Rosary and Evening Prayers at a definite time, Spiritual Reading, and Pre-lunch Visit to the Blessed Sacrament. Finally, he commended "the fine spirit" which pervaded the House and gave thanks for the hospitality accorded him during his stay at the College.

After his visitation of the Diocese, the Provincial wrote to Bishop Kelly from the Regional headquarters at Owo, "As promised, I list some points calling for rectification or adjustment:

1. You will have gathered that I am dissatisfied with the facilities afforded the Regional Superior for the proper exercise of his duties. I now request your kind cooperation to ensure that the relevant prescriptions of our new *Constitutions* may be more strictly observed in future...
(a) That you adopt a method of consulting the RS which will fully implement the requirements of the *Constitutions*.
(b) Such consultations to be strictly formal and legal must be in writing with copies for the respective files and, in due time, allowing for consultations with the Regional Superior's councillors if necessary".

Turning to missionary accommodation, he said, "The housing position must be improved, new houses should be erected at Uzairue (urgent), Agbor, and the ETC Ubiaja. In these, and in any residences to be built in the future, a domestic oratory must be provided for. Oratories should be installed in the existing houses at Benin, Asaba, Ashaka, Onitsha-Olona and Ozoro. Better facilities and more space are required in the Benin Mission house".

He found that too many confreres were living on their own, "Besides being contrary to Papal law, it is in itself an undesirable and risky practice ... Before exceptions can be tolerated, *circumstantiae extraordinariae* must be shown to exist..."

He went on to mention some particular cases. "Fr Cavanagh [in the Niger delta since 1946] should not remain at Ozoro unless he is provided with a refrigerator, motor transport, a properly furnished house and stable financial support. Appointments to Ossiomo leper settlement should be on a voluntary basis, and those involved should have motor transport and an increased allowance. The Bishop's secretary should have better living conditions".

The Provincial was concerned over the number of institutions established in the diocese without the consultations required by the *Constitutions*, "In the circumstances I cannot accept responsibility, on behalf of the Society, for staffing such institutions".

In general he found too high a proportion of confreres in teaching posts and insufficient efforts being made to replace them with lay staff, African or European, or with Brothers, such as the Holy Ghost congregation had done in eastern Nigeria. While not referring to Benin alone, the Provincial said, "If the revenue from salaried posts is to be made the final consideration [in diocesan planning], then the responsibility for lost opportunities in other directions cannot be shelved. For the moment, in the assignment of qualified personnel, full priority will be given to those Ordinaries who are still building up their institutions". Ending his 'Instructions', he said he believed that their implementation would make for smoother organization and better results in the Diocese.

After reading and reflecting on the Instructions, the Bishop was not pleased. The 'rectifications' were more numerous than he had anticipated and would prove very costly to carry out. He felt a wind of change beginning to blow rather too warmly across his bows, demanding a new way of doing things – 'consultatively' and 'officially', with carbon copies and filing systems, and demanding that they be done 'according to the *Constitutions*' (as others interpreted them). Worrying questions assailed him: should he change? Should he become more liberal with the diocesan purse strings? Should he ease up on the school apostolate? On the other hand, he had led the Diocese for over a decade, had overcome many obstacles, and – with the grace of God – had seen the Mission grow and bear fruit by doing things 'his way'. His 1952 Prospectus for Propaganda, like his 1948 one, had won accolades from the authorities, including the Superior General who had congratulated him on his "mounting success all along the line". What would 'change' achieve?

Pat's 'conversion'
The process of change, never smooth, did not come easily to Bishop Kelly. At this time, the early Fifties, he and Archbishop Taylor ('archbishop' since 1950), the two senior SMA Ordinaries in Nigeria, were not satisfied with the way the Province was treating the missions, in particular, the Intervicarial Major Seminary, St Paul's, which was still in Benin City. They felt the Seminary was being denied qualified staff. Before the Provincial's visitation, the Regional Superior had informed Dr Creaven that Archbishop Taylor and Bishop Kelly were considering lodging a complaint in Rome against the Society. The Provincial objected to such "ex-

parte representations" and, in Nigeria, when endeavouring to clarify that responsibility for staffing the seminary was not the Province's responsibility but the Bishops', did not endear himself to the latter.

Most priests complain about their bishops. Were there complaints about Pat, and how serious were they? In February '54, the Diocesan Education Supervisor sent a copy of his Annual Report for the Ministry of Education to the Provincial. His complaints, in an accompanying letter (for the Provincial and not for the Ministry), at first were not about the Bishop, but about the job, "After correcting and adding up the marks of 1,300 candidates, each doing eight papers, and getting it all down in quadruplicate, a directive came from the Government in Ibadan to say that the marks had to be reviewed and the pass aggregate reduced to 40%". After this the Supervisor went on to share "a little personal grouse" about the Bishop and the £24 a month he received from him. Out of the £24, the Supervisor spent £13 on the cook's salary, 'chop' (food), clothes, and house. The remaining £11 was supposed to cover office expenses, driver, maintenance and fuel for his Kit Car (which did 15 miles to the gallon and he travelled an average of 1,200 miles per month, visiting and attending meetings from Kabba to Warri), "It simply cannot be done", he said. What really scalded him was that, "the Bishop drew nearly £500 in Government grants to cover his own and my office expenses only! For travelling expenses alone, he collects £200 a year on my behalf; and then there's my salary, furlough allowance and responsibility allowance on top". The Supervisor admitted losing his temper with the Bishop a few times, but it didn't do any good. The Bishop called him an "expensive Supervisor" and reminded him that he, the Bishop, had bought a new car for him (without admitting that he had sold the old one for £500). The Supervisor's *coup de grace* was, "Our Bishop, an excellent and most understanding man in many ways, would let his men exist on a diet of grass if they would agree to do so".

Writing from Lagos, before leaving Nigeria in April '54, the Provincial enquired of the Regional Superior about progress on the "rectifications" he had called for in Benin diocese. The reply was, **"In most cases nothing has been done"**. Believing sterner measures were required the Provincial attached sanctions to his previous instructions and requested the Regional to report again before the 1st of June. At the same time, he informed the Bishop, "Should the Regional's report again prove unsatisfactory, I shall, with regret, VETO any further appointments or re-appointments to Benin Diocese as from that date. Further, I shall have to consider recalling from your Diocese any confrere whom I judge to be placed in conditions of continuing unnecessary hardship".

The Bishop's stalled 'conversion process' came to life rather dramatically and he began to relate to Society authorities in a new way. His next letter to the Provincial was a model of humility, "I asked Fr Hughes (the Regional) for the opening of an Elementary Training College in Ozoro ... Also I asked him for permission to open another station for resident Fathers at Ughelli ... I also request two new priests and if possible one graduate priest, as a good few graduates are going on leave next year ... I am trying to comply with all your requirements although it is a very bad year for building with the big rush now on to build primary schools". The Provincial, receiving the letter in the Gold Coast, maintained caution in face of the new Kelly mode, and told him to refrain from initiating new projects like the ones mentioned for Ozoro and Ughelli until he, the Provincial, had first made a review of needs and resources of all the mission territories, only then would he be in a position to make an equitable distribution of available personnel.

In subsequent letters to the Provincial, Pat persevered in his conciliatory manner, "I am doing all that is possible to carry out the instructions you gave when you were here, even though there are very heavy commitments on the Fathers to build new schools due to the introduction of free compulsory education at the beginning of next year (1955)". Enclosed in his letter, were copies of instructions giving evidence of his good intentions: To Michael Grace, at the Teacher Training College, Uzairue, "Start building a Father's house immediately, 200 bags of cement are on their way"; to Michael Drew, at the Training College, Ubiaja, "Get cement at Uromi and send the bill here ... begin immediately, a block maker is on the way". Another letter went to the Regional, humbly requesting "renewal of permission" for Hugh Conlon to do another tour at Ossiomo leper settlement, and delicately requesting that Bill Fegan begin building a Fathers' house at Agbor on 1 September. The Provincial, accepting the sincerity of the Bishop's latest efforts, also mellowed, "I realise that you have many commitments, especially in school building and I am satisfied with what you have been able to accomplish so far" (Cork, August '54).

Dr Creaven's long visitation had not been easy. It was his first time in Africa, he had discussed with many confreres their individual and community problems, faced superiors and bishops on their home ground, tried to update all, and move men to see wider issues than their own. Having had no time for "acclimatisation" or relaxation and, being no more immune from fevers than anyone else, he became ill in March and had to adjourn his meeting with the Ordinaries in Ibadan on its second day; he was ill again in Cape Coast in May. Fifty years later, it was not the problems or the illnesses he recalled but, among other things, that "Bishop Kelly was one of the most constructive and practical of the mission superiors in matters relating to cooperation between the Society and the local church ... His contributions in general meetings of the Ordinaries with me and the Regionals were interesting – he was a man of few words, but very incisive, a man of faith and conviction with an integral personality".

For some time, relations between the Bishop and the Province proceeded relatively smoothly, Pat's conversion seemed to be holding. When sending the Provincial the views of the Principals of colleges regarding length of holidays, he thanked him for his conciliatory letter of 14 August, and regarding length of holidays, refrained from imposing any views of his own. After discussion with the Regional, he agreed to take a man whom he had refused earlier, adding "any instructions you give concerning him will be carefully carried out". In July, the RS, Paddy Hughes, residing at Owo outside Bishop Kelly's diocese, was co-opted on to the Provincial Council in place of John Reddington who had been nominated Bishop of Jos. The assistant regional, Tom Murray, rector of the seminary in Benin City, then became Acting Regional. This time, rather than complaining about the loss of a man, Pat humbly asked if Murray could continue to reside at the seminary, rather than at Owo, until a new Regional was appointed.

At his meeting with the Ordinaries at Ibadan, the Provincial had pointed out that staffing colleges in Nigeria with SMA graduates put a great strain on Provincial resources. He put it squarely to them that they lagged behind the Holy Ghost, Mill Hill, and the French SMA Ordinaries in finding teaching Orders to take over colleges and in recruiting lay graduates. In response to this, Taylor and Kelly promised to give a lead by taking two lay graduates each. By then, Pat had reviewed his intention of holding on to St Patrick's, Asaba, at all costs; he would let it go if a teaching Order could be found.

Other matters discussed at the Ibadan meeting were: the duties and competency of the Regional Superior; shorter tours and shorter leave. It was thought that a four year tour for pastoral men followed by nine months leave and, two years for teachers followed by three months leave, would be an improvement. There was general agreement on promoting SMA Rule in accordance with the new Directory; specifically that 'domestic' Oratories be installed in residences; that community life be endorsed; and that Ordinaries and Regional Superiors should determine "a reasonable sum for the 'Viaticum' (living allocation) of the confreres". Furthermore the Ordinaries agreed that two Regional Superiors were required for the southern jurisdictions of Lagos, Benin City, Ondo and Ibadan, and also two for the northern jurisdictions of Kaduna and Jos. It was further agreed to introduce an "ante-prandial" law – no alcohol before lunch; also to promote Catholic reading material for the laity; and to appoint one man in each jurisdiction to supply Mission news to the Provincial from time to time.

Despite grumblings about Pat, usually related to money, the confreres elected him to represent them at the Provincial Assembly of 1952. True to form, he did not want to attend, saying that he had work to do, and that it was only two years since he had been home. Tommy Greene, second in the poll, gladly agreed to go instead. Pat, however, sent some observations and suggestions:

1. Confreres from the missions are not edified by the confreres at home. These latter should be made keep the Rule, especially as regards getting up for the morning meditation.
2. Under the present system of grants, in places where there is good attendance, there can be a big profit from schools which is supposed to be spent on equipment, repairs and new buildings and not on the confrere himself, least of all on liquor.
3. Some things are neglected, regular visitation of outstations, of people in their homes, and supervision of catechism classes. Confreres must be prepared for plenty of self-sacrifice.
4. When a confrere applies for another diocese his request should not be easily granted.
5. The five-year tour with one-year holiday should be continued. A confrere in need of an earlier holiday, for health reasons, will always obtain it.

6. The balance of stipends, after the Regional's expenses and personal allocations, should go to the jurisdictions where the Masses were discharged as was the custom before...

7. If sponsors are giving money for catechists, none of it comes this way.

Demise of the Oye-Ekiti scheme

After his resignation, Dr PM Kelly was appointed to Nigeria as director of the development schemes. The arts and crafts centres in Oye-Ekiti and Owo were successfully producing top-quality African art work. Kevin Carroll felt that he and Seán O'Mahony were self-supporting. Weaving, vestment making, carving, beadwork, leatherwork and church furnishings were doing quite well and finding markets; brick and tile making, however, were not so remunerative. In October 1949, Carroll had sent a consignment of sacred art to Rome for the 1950 Missionary Exhibition. Composed of fine Yoruba carvings, such as the Three Kings, Mary, Joseph, Stations of the Cross, crucifixes and candlesticks, and valued by him at about £60, he gave the whole consignment as a free gift. Following the Exhibition, orders for liturgical ware and church furnishings increased. Bishop Taylor, highly impressed with the work, ordered vestments for Lagos, and others followed suit.

One of those not happy with the sacred artefacts was Bishop Kelly, and he banned their use in Benin. Writing to Kevin Carroll in October '53, he explained:

> I have not seen the Stations of the Cross myself, except one, but from what the Fathers report to me, I have judged that they are not according to approved usage in the Church, and so according to Canon 1279.2 I cannot allow them to be used in public by the Faithful. Apart from this, the wood used in them is not likely to last, as some kind of borer destroys soft wood – at least in certain districts in this part

of the country. Also they are too dear and none of the parishes here can afford to pay so much.

I don't know what the bead work crucifix is going to be like, but if it is like the one I saw in St Augustine's chapel in Gold Coast, I don't think I could approve of it for a public place in the church ... If it is more like what has been in use already there is no objection to your going ahead with it.

In March '52, Dr Creaven, keenly aware of the financial burden "Society works on the missions" imposed on the Province, requested the Fathers involved in the schemes, Walsh, Carroll, O'Mahony, and McElgunn, to report individually on their activities and prospects. Early in his Nigerian visitation, the Provincial had visited Oye-Ekiti, and discussed the value of the schemes with all the missionaries and Ordinaries. The latter, in general, were opposed to "Society works" (such as the schemes), and did not want to be responsible for them. At the end of '53, the Provincial decided to terminate Dr Kelly's schemes and, in January '54, the men involved were appointed to more conventional works: Dr Kelly and Seán O'Mahony to remain in the diocese of Ondo, while Kevin Carroll was transferred to Lagos and John McElgunn to Ibadan. They were encouraged to continue with the sacred art experiment as best they could but, without funding and a common workshop, the project declined.

One episcopal voice had been raised in favour of the scheme at Oye-Ekiti. Writing to the Provincial in August '52, Bishop Taylor said:

I understand that the continuation of the experiment at Oye is being discussed. I hope I am not too late to let you know that the closing of the work would be regretted by the Education and other Government departments. That no money grants have been made is due to the fact (of which we should be proud) that none has been asked. But the whole effort is of value to the rest of us indirectly. My own opinion, for what it is worth, is that the 'scheme' should be continued and encouraged.

By the time Pat received Kevin Carroll's response to his banning of Oye-Ekiti art work in Benin, the scheme had been closed. Nevertheless, Pat's reply to Carroll showed he could change his views on art but, evidently, would rather not:

> Thanks very much for your kind letter with the extracts from Propaganda [favouring the promotion of African sacred art]. I was afraid of the novelty, but I suppose there is no reason why such type of mission art as shown in your Stations of the Cross cannot safely be admitted in the light of these extracts. However Oye is closed now. Also I was not in favour of Agbor making an order for expensive Stations of the Cross until a church was built there first.

And so, succumbing to practicality and the persuasive force of conventional methods and attitudes, the experimental implementation of Dr Kelly's vision came to a rather sad end.

'The Three Kings', oil painting by K.Carroll of a Yoruba carving.

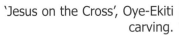

'Jesus on the Cross', Oye-Ekiti carving.

Chapter 12

THE FIFTIES, 1954-1959

In December 1954 to mark the end of the Marian Year, Archbishop Taylor hosted a National Marian Congress in Lagos. With pageants, torchlight processions, an exhibition of African arts and crafts and magnificent liturgies, it attracted huge crowds from all over Nigeria. The Papal Legate, Cardinal McIntyre of Los Angeles, chatting with Bishop Taylor and Dr Creaven at one of the ceremonies, congratulated Taylor, saying how amazed he was that a mission territory would attempt an event of such magnitude, "one which I would hesitate to undertake even in of Los Angeles". Creaven relished Taylor's lightning response, "Lagos rushed in where 'The Angels' (Los Angeles) feared to tread".

Bishop Kelly, always devoted to Mary and the rosary, attended and was happy with the Congress's success. The following year, he noted a great increase in the number of conversions in his own diocese. In Warri district, where the increase was remarkable, the priests attributed it to Mary and Marian devotion. Fr Jim Byrne, a friend of Frank Duff, the founder of the Legion of Mary, had begun to organize the Legion in Warri and from his legionaries came a request for a diocesan director. Pat appointed Jim to the job. Accepting it, Jim continued to promote the movement and earned from the people the name "son of Mary".

Following Pope Pius XII's emphasis on Catholic Action, the Bishops of West Africa chose the Legion as their primary means of promoting Catholic social activity. In total agreement, Pat requested all his priests to establish the Legion in their parishes and to encourage members to take a particular interest in seeking out, instructing, and baptizing dying pagans.

The Marian Congress in Lagos highlighted a much felt need of the confreres in Nigeria – suitable accommodation in the capital. Men travelling long distances to Lagos for business, medical attention, or arriving from or going on home leave, often had to put up at *The Services Inn*, or at *The Ambassador* or other hotels or guest houses. The existing mission houses had little or no accommodation for visitors and, understandably, Archbishop Taylor was reluctant to build and staff a hospice for all.

Meanwhile a lot of building was going on in Benin. The new Holy Cross cathedral was nearing completion, and great efforts were being made to bring missionary accommodation up to the standard required in Dr Creaven's 'Instructions' of 1954. New houses were being built and old ones renovated. A fine extension to the Benin City mission house was completed in '55. It now contained an additional upstairs bedroom and a domestic oratory where the Blessed Sacrament was reserved. Downstairs, there was a spacious office with a verandah-cum-waiting room. The days of the nightsoil bucket were numbered; provision was being made in all new houses for running water and proper toilet facilities. In the Bishop's compound, a bungalow had been completed, in which the Principal of Immaculate Conception College took up residence. His former bedroom, an annex near the Bishop's house, became his office, and he shared community life and meals with Pat. The new Regional Superior, Mattie Walsh, reported that living conditions in the 'palace' had improved (Pat had even installed an Electrolux refrigerator), and Bishop and Principal "are happy together". Before Easter '56, a telephone, running water, a septic tank and a flush lavatory had also been installed. 'Food', however, continued to be a problem; the abstemious and economising Bishop still insisted on doing most of the shopping himself. His secretary, Joe Stephens, had once tried to take the chore from him but, Pat, not happy with

Joe's 'extravagance', took it back again. The Provincial, concerned for men's sustenance, tried to command the Regional to ban the Bishop from shopping, but Pat was not easily deterred.

New residences at Uzairue, Ubiaja and Agbor were completed in '56, and new ones at Ughelli and Igarra were under way. At Warri mission, the old verandah, which was in a precarious state, was pulled down and alterations, including the fitting of a new bathroom with flush-lavatory, were planned. The biggest building project in the diocese, the construction of the cathedral, supervised by Tom Bartley, was completed and solemnly blessed by Pat on the 1st of May 1955. "On all fronts", the Regional reported, "there has never been more activity than at present".

While all this was going on, a part of Bishop Kelly's territory in the Kabba-Lokoja area was separated from Benin and established as the new Prefecture of Lokoja under Mgr Delisle and the Canadian Spiritans. Rome made the division at Christmas 1954, after long negotiations which stretched back into the Forties when Pat had pleaded in vain for more men to administer the district properly.

After the opening of the new Holy Cross cathedral, Tom Bartley went home on well-deserved leave. From Hollymount in Co Mayo, he first arrived in Nigeria in 1926 and over the years worked as a pastor, builder and teacher. In 1935 Bishop Taylor made him Supervisor of Schools and, after John Mahon was called home in '52, Pat made him Vicar General. Apart from running one of the busiest parishes in the diocese, Holy Cross, and building the cathedral, he was looking after sixty outstations (travelling about 1,500 miles a month in an old two-seater Morris), and administering over one hundred schools with some 10,000 pupils and 500 teachers. On leave, he spent much of his time trying to find doctors, nurses, lay teachers and Orders of teaching Brothers or Sisters for Benin. Having made contact with no less than forty-eight congregations, at one stage he informed

Pat that the Patrician Brothers seemed interested, but in the end they, like all the others, regretfully turned him down. Though he had booked his return trip to Nigeria for May '56, and was apparently in good health, he died unexpectedly one evening after returning to his family home, 23 January 1956. He was fifty-seven. Dr Creaven, informing Pat of the death, said that Tom "sat down to light his pipe and died". Shocked and saddened, Pat thanked the Provincial saying, "God's holy will be done, he worked very hard building the cathedral, building schools and in the management of schools". [In Hollymount church there is a memento of Tom – some Sapele hardwood, which he sent from Nigeria.]

Tom Bartley sets off from Benin City mission house.

On the day Tom Bartley died, the renowned Bishop Joseph Shanahan CSSp of 'Southern Nigeria' was given a second burial in Onitsha. He had been buried in Nairobi, where he died on Christmas Day, 1943. The SMA Bishops: Taylor of Lagos, Reddington of Jos, McCarthy of Kaduna, and the Prefect

Apostolic, Mgr Finn of Ibadan, as well as the Regional Superior and many confreres attended the second burial. Unfortunately, Pat, whose diocese was nearest Onitsha, was ill and did not attend. The bishops and other mourners crossed the Niger on the large Government motor launch called *The Shanahan* in honour of the one who had done so much to bring the Gospel and education to the Eastern Region.

One aspect of Dr Creaven's 'Instructions' of 1954 that seemed to be neglected by Bishop Kelly was, surprisingly, the building or installing of Domestic Oratories (suitably equipped rooms in the mission houses, for private or community prayer and the celebration of the Eucharist). By '55 the houses in Asaba, Ozoro, and St Columba's college Agbor had oratories, but most of the others had not. In '56, the Regional reported to Dr Creaven, "Although I am convinced of the necessity of Oratories and totally unconvinced by the arguments against, I regret to say my efforts to enforce your suggestion have proved a failure. Bishop Kelly told me he never agreed to this suggestion at the Conference in Ibadan, and said that he had power only to grant a Domestic Oratory in places where the church was at some distance from the residence". When a new regional house was opened in Uromi the following year, he refused to give permission to allow daily Mass to be said in it, or the Blessed Sacrament to be reserved in it, until he had assurance from a Canon Lawyer that it would be legitimate. Canon law required priests to celebrate Mass in a public church if there was one in the vicinity. Pat admitted that the distance to Uromi parish church, "over nine-tenths of a mile" (carefully measured *twice* by the Regional), justified saying Mass in the domestic oratory but, the fact that the Regional had a car, Pat thought, put the matter in doubt! At the beginning, he allowed Mattie Walsh to say Mass in the oratory once a week. Apart from 'Oratories', Mattie confirmed that he and the Bishop were enjoying "cordial relations", and the Bishop was doing his best to consult him on everything according to the letter of the *Directory*.

In 1955, Pat had wanted to go home, he was overdue leave but, a more serious reason was that he was very ill. He hung on, waiting for Tom Bartley, his Vicar General to return. Towards the end of that year, a worried Mattie Walsh requested the Provincial to persuade him to go home. Dr Creaven did so, urging him to book into the Tropical Institute at either Liverpool or London for a proper check-up on his way to Ireland. Informed by Stephen Harrington of the gravity of Bishop Kelly's condition, the Cardinal Prefect of Propaganda granted Pat permission to depart, temporarily, from his diocese. No doubt Pat would have gone then, had he not received the shocking news of Tom Bartley's death. Consequently, he delayed his departure, "until after Easter when the weather would be better". In April, he appointed Willie Keenan to replace Bartley as the new Vicar General. After Willie took up residence in the Bishop's house, Pat departed, and embarked on the *Aureol*, sailing from Lagos on the 10th of April '56.

On board he wrote letters on Elder Dempster notepaper and posted them when the ship called at Takoradi, Gold Coast. Normally on the voyages, he paced the decks of the big ships, saying the rosary – eight times up and down was about one mile and ten decades, but on this voyage he sat on a chair or kept to his cabin. Arriving in Liverpool on 23 April, he was met by an ambulance and taken directly to the Tropical Institute. There he was plied with numerous tests, "I am detained here", he said, "with my arm in a sling". Though the sling made writing difficult, he managed to write a letter to the Provincial about lay graduates who were interested in teaching in Benin. Before the end of May, after treatment for amoebic dysentery and other ailments, he was discharged and travelling on to Cork, arrived there in time to join in the Province's annual June retreat. After seeing him Dr Creaven wrote to Willie Keenan, "The Bishop has been through a very hard time but he still hopes to return to Nigeria". From Pat's retreat Resolutions we know that, at this time, he prayed for a spirit of detachment "from all things, including self". He resolved to nourish his personal love for Christ crucified and to bear his own crosses and humiliations in resignation to the divine will.

Society centenary, 1956

Summer in Tristaun was a good time to recuperate. Pat's brother Jack and sister-in-law Ellen proudly introduced the growing family. He had seen Mary Teresa, their first born, as a small baby when he was home in 1950, she was "six and a half now" she told him. Next was a sturdy five-year-old, Anthony Francis Malachy, who had run to open the gate on his arrival; then Patrick Joseph Mary, called after himself with 'Mary' added on as he was born in the Marian Year; and the newborn baby "Malachy John" who was just a month old. Home in the midst of the affectionate family, and aided by the prayers of many Nigerians, Pat quickly began to recover his health and strength. After Patrick's Day, 17 March, he received 'a spiritual bouquet' from the convent pupils of the OLA school in Sapele. The bouquet comprised of 1,859 aspirations, 245 Holy Masses, and 272 Rosaries, all offered for his speedy recovery to health. Touched and grateful, he kept the card among his few personal mementos until his dying day.

Bill holds the mare at Tristaun

From Tristaun, he wrote to the Provincial, accepting his invitation to attend the SMA centenary celebrations in Cork on Sunday 30 September – celebrating one hundred years since the Society's foundation in Lyons in 1856. Pat had hoped to go to America but, as he hadn't succeeded in securing a tourist passage, he said he would go later. He also accepted the Provincial's request that he preside over the three days of prayer preceding the celebration on the 30th.

At the time of the centenary, the Society was nearing its peak of over 1,600 members. Irish Province membership had increased to 455, nearly catching up with the Lyons Province, which had suffered a decline in vocations during the post-War years. Lyons had 474 members, but only sixty-two students 'with Society oath', while the Irish had ninety-three.

The Irish Province's Centenary activities were organized by a committee set up by the Assembly of 1952. Some literary works were proposed: a biography of the Founder, a history of the Province and the missions. Also programmed were: religious ceremonies, radio talks, press releases, and a missionary exhibition in the City Hall, Cork. A fine Centenary Booklet was published, which was much sought after, not only in Ireland, but on the missions where the confreres admitted that they knew little or nothing about the Founder and the early history of the Society.

The climax of the centenary celebrations in Ireland was the Solemn High Mass and dinner in Wilton on 30 September, to which many leaders of Church and State were invited. The Apostolic Nuncio, Archbishop Alberto Levame, arrived in Cork the day before and was treated to a civic reception in the City Hall by the Lord Mayor, Alderman Casey TD. Before it, a liturgical reception was given by the Bishop of Cork, Cornelius Lucey, at St Mary's cathedral. There the Butter Exchange Band played sacred music and the Catholic Boy Scouts of Ireland mounted a guard of honour, proudly saluting as the Bishops, including Pat, processed into the church. Bishop Lucey welcomed the Nuncio and, before Solemn Benedicton began, impressed on him how faithful Cork families were to the Church, to the Mass, to supporting the Foreign Missions and to the Diocesan Building Programme.

On the 30th, before noon, the dignitaries assembled in St Joseph's church, Wilton, for Solemn High Mass. Included were, Mr Seán T. O'Kelly, President of Ireland, John A. Costello, Taoiseach, Eamon de Valera, Cardinal D'Alton the Primate of all Ireland, the Papal Nuncio, Bishop O'Doherty of Dromore, and Dr Michael Browne, the Bishop of Galway, who preached at the Mass. After the ceremonies the distinguished guests posed for a photograph for *The Cork Examiner*. Bishop Kelly, lean and serious, stood in the second row between Stephen Harrington and the Vicar General, Joseph Guerin. Eighty-five special guests were invited for a sherry reception, followed by a magnificent dinner, cooked and served by the staff of the Imperial Hotel, which also supplied cutlery, ware, wine glasses and even eighty-five 'upholstered chairs'. "Thank God", said Pat, when he saw that 'Roast Stuffed Turkey and Ham' was on the menu and not 'Chicken Supreme'.

Later in the evening the deeply symbolic, solemn, and always poignant, Departure Ceremony took place in St Joseph's church, Blackrock Road. The class of '56, thirteen newly ordained young men, bade a formal *Adieu* to relatives, friends and well-wishers. After it, Pat met the group and asked "Who are my men?" meaning, who were those appointed to his diocese. Dick Wall, Cork, and Mick McGlinchey, Tyrone, stepped forward. "Only two", muttered Pat as he shook their hands. Noticing how big and gnarled his hands were and his lean and keen look, the two young men weren't sure whether it was a good thing, or not, to be appointed to Benin. Bishop Kelly had quite a reputation. Not delaying, he wished them a safe passage and hoped to meet them soon in the mission.

1956 Centenary of the Society of African Missions. Irish Province celebration at Wilton, Cork.
Seated (from left), Eamon de Valera TD; Bp Browne; Ab Levame, Papal Nuncio; Seán T. O'Kelly, President of Ireland; Cardinal D'Alton, Primate of Ireland; John A. Costello, Taoiseach; Bp Lucey; Bp O'Doherty; Seán Casey, Lord Mayor. *Middle row,* Prof. Atkins, President UCC; John Creaven, Provincial; Celsus O'Connell, abbot of Mount Melleray; Maurice Slattery; Stephen Harrington, Superior General; Bp Kelly; Joseph Guerin; Mgr Richard Finn; Mgr Kissane, president Maynooth; Joe Barrett. *Back row from left,* Paddy Gantly; Larry Carr; Anthony Glynn; ADC to Taoiseach; Paddy Glynn; Col. Heffernan, ADC to President; Dr James OFM Cap.; a Patrician Brother.

Well might Pat have a reputation. Though one of the quietest of the SMA Bishops, the statistics of his diocese spoke volumes, and placed it in the ranks of the longer-established dioceses of the whole West Coast. The West Coast of Africa had been the scene of early SMA missionary endeavour and many of its jurisdictions by the Fifties had attained the status of archdiocese – Abidjan, Cape Coast, Cotonou, Lagos, Lome. Nevertheless, statistically, Benin surpassed them in some respects. For instance, of all the twenty-two SMA jurisdictions in Africa at this time, only Kumasi in Ghana had more catechumens than Benin. Comparisons may be odious, but they are definitely interesting. Statistics record that Kumasi had 37,794 catechumens and Benin 30,567, but Benin would surely close the gap before long as it had 296 catechists in the field, whereas Kumasi had only 42. In educational matters, Benin's statistics excelled. It had 660 primary schools, while the nearest, Kumasi, had 343. Though Benin did not lead in numbers of 'Modern or Middle' schools, it was slightly ahead in numbers of 'Secondary schools'. In employing 2,840 teachers, Benin was well ahead of all the others, the nearest being Kumasi with 1,323 teachers.

In numbers of Africans ordained to the priesthood, the big West Coast archdioceses with large urban populations led the way. Cotonou had 21 African priests, Cape Coast 14, Abidjan and Lagos 12 each. Benin had 6, but was second only to Cotonou in numbers of Major Seminarians. Cotonou had 23 while Benin had 18. Despite having had the first ordination in British West Africa, the pace of indigenisation of the clergy in 'Western Nigeria' had slowed in comparison to other jurisdictions, but under Pat it was picking up again. Though Pat's personal reputation had a lot to do with prayer and asceticism, his diocese's statistics for services to the needy showed how much he cared for people. Benin's medical apostolate statistics surpassed all the other jurisdictions. For this he was hugely indebted to the OLA Sisters, lay doctors, nurses and helpers. Benin had 67 medical centres, Lagos 57, Abidjan 15, Kumasi 9 and Cotonou 6. In the numbers of marriages blessed in Church, the densely populated West Coast cities shone. Highest was Cotonou with 435, then Lome 428, Abidjan 406, Lagos 290, Kumasi 280; but Benin was not far behind, sharing third place with Abidjan. No matter what way one viewed the statistics, Pat's diocese had a record of which he and all his personnel could be justly proud.

For the centenary celebrations, the American Province chartered a Pan American World Airways, Super-Clipper. Pat's brothers in America, Gerald, Michael and Malachy, didn't travel but, instead, bought a ticket for Pat on the Cunard liner *Franconia* so that he could visit them. The liner, sailing from Liverpool to New York, called at Cobh, the port of Cork, on the 8th of October. Pat, and his breviary, caused a flurry of excitement before he boarded ship. *The Irish Independent* published the story with the title, "Cork launch dash with Bishop's breviary". On boarding the tender, *Killarney*, which brought passengers to the large ships lying outside the harbour, Pat realized that he had left his breviary in Blackrock Road. Fr Phil O'Shea, who had driven him to Cobh, sped back the twelve miles to Cork to fetch it, and returned to find the tender had just left the dock. All was not lost however, as the Cunard officers had arranged that a speedy launch would await the arrival of the breviary. With breviary on board, the launch raced after the tender and, before long, the crew proudly presented it to the Bishop. Along with the breviary, the *Franconia* took on 335 passengers, 481 sacks of mail, and five tons of Irish whiskey.

Well received in America, Pat stayed with his brother Malachy and family in the Bronx. Sadly, Peter Harrington, Superior of the American Province of the SMA and brother of Stephen, the Superior General, died in New Jersey on 2 December. Pat attended the funeral. Finding life very different in America from Ireland or Nigeria, Pat felt ill-at-ease in many places except in his brother's parish church, where he spent hours kneeling in prayer. His sister-in-law, sitting some distance behind him with the women's confraternity, was mortified to see cavernous holes in the Bishop's socks! After preaching, questing, and enjoying Christmas and New Year with his relatives, he returned to Ireland in February.

From Ireland he hurried to Rome where Joseph Guerin, an experienced hand in dealing with Vatican offices, looked over his Quinquennial Report, before Pat presented it to Propaganda. Guerin also made appointments for him with Superiors of international teaching Orders who might help in the schools in Benin, but he was disappointed. More pleasant was his re-union with two men from his diocese, Fr Patrick Ugboko, Asaba, whom he had ordained in 1951, and was studying at St Peter's College, and a seminarian, Anthony Gbuji, from Benin City, who was studying at the Collegio Urbano. Both were adapting well to life in Rome, doing their best to cope with the low temperatures and the high cost of living. The Bishop, Patrick, and Anthony were accorded a private audience with Pius XII, who posed with them for a memorable photograph. Anthony had been much impressed by the Pope's message to the SMA on the occasion of the Society's Centenary and quoted part of it at his episcopal ordination seventeen years later – "Let the gratitude felt by thousands of Christians who owe the inestimable gift of the faith to these missionaries, be the best recompense for your Society".

Rome, 1957, seminarian Anthony Gbuji, Pope Pius XII, Bishop Kelly, Fr Patrick Ugboko.

After leaving some of his American dollars with the Procurator in Rome, Pat returned to Ireland. At Tristaun, he gathered his few pieces of personal luggage and quite a lot of items collected 'for the missions' and made his way to Dublin. There, before taking the boat for Liverpool, he made a final attempt to persuade the Irish Christian Brothers to take over a school in Benin, but again he was disappointed. On 21 February '57, he sailed from Liverpool on the *Aureol;* also travelling was Bill Fegan.

To his great surprise, the Regional, Mattie Walsh, and his first councillor, Jim Healy, had driven all the way from Benin City to · meet him at Lagos. Mattie, accompanying Pat back to Benin City in the Bishop's new American Ford, which had also travelled on the *Aureol*, found the journey very long. The Bishop, driving and praying, insisted on travelling under 35 miles an hour! "It must be run-in", he explained, nodding at the New Owner's Manual. Sixteen miles from Benin, a cavalcade of cars awaited and escorted the Bishop in a triumphal procession to the city. At the Cathedral, he was given a tumultuous welcome. After speeches and prayers, he spoke a few words of thanks and concluded the ceremony with Solemn Benediction.

He was scarcely back in office when welcome news arrived from Rome, the Marianist Congregation was interested in taking over a school in Benin! His efforts had not been in vain after all. Stephen Harrington wrote, saying that he'd seen the Marianist Superior General several times and their Procurator had called to the Generalate requesting more information, especially about St Patrick's College, Asaba. Harrington, hopeful that the Marianist interest would not wane, worried that Pat's thriftiness might put them off. "For goodness sake", he advised, "don't let money discourage them now". In April, more good news came: the Superior of the American Province of the Marianists in Ohio was going to visit Benin in May, "We have assured the General", Harrington told Pat, "that from Benin City to Asaba there will be a car at the Provincial's disposal. Give him one of those fine ones you got in America and he will feel at home!! Do try to give him an excellent first impression ... I am hoping they will take over more than one college". He reminded Pat, "Man power is much more precious these days than money".

St Patrick's was then one of the best secondary schools in Nigeria. In 1954, for instance, in the Senior Cambridge Examination, fifty students passed out of fifty-four, twenty-one gaining Grade I and ten gaining Grade II. Wherever the Bishop went on confirmation tours, delegations of local people beseeched him to set up a college for them "like St Patrick's". While he couldn't always provide another St Patrick's, he did, in the long run, provide the people with nearly eighty new secondary schools, but first he tested the genuine-ness of their desire by requesting them to make a large financial contribution towards it, "Bring £1,000 (or more) in ten bags, then I'll build a school". Many of them did.

The Provincial from Ohio duly arrived and Pat, laying on the VIP treatment, drove him in his new Ford to see St Patrick's. Everything went well, the Provincial departed with an excellent impression and, in January 1958, the Brothers arrived to stay. Pat and the SMA, though nostalgic on relinquishing St Patrick's, were happy to have gained the help of the great teaching Order, and they readily agreed to leave Jim Flanagan with them until June to help them get started.

The Marianists arrive at St Patrick's College, Asaba, 1958. Welcoming them are Bishop Kelly, SMA Fathers, OLA Sisters (Enda Barrett and Aidan O'Sullivan), staff and local dignitaries. 1. Brother Roman Wicinski, the College Principal who lost his life in the aftermath of the Civil War. 2. Tony McDonagh, the first Principal. 3. Johnny Lyons, 4. Mick Harnedy, 5. Harry Jones, 6. Jim Flanagan, 7. Ned Rice, 8. Tom Murray, 9. Mattie Walsh, 10. Joe Hilliard.

Schools and strain

With the number of mission-managed primary schools climbing towards seven hundred, and secondary schools rising from one in 1943, to seven in 1954, and eleven in '59, not to mention Training Colleges, hospitals, clinics and other institutions, the lives of the missionaries were becoming more and more complicated, over-busy and stressful. In previous decades, fevers were the main cause of ill health, often requiring treatment abroad and sometimes resulting in death. In the Fifties, confreres, in quite high numbers, were being invalided home, but not because of fevers. The Provincial, becoming alarmed, queried the Regional as to possible causes. The Regional affirmed that the high incidence of illness was not due to inadequate nourishment, poor accommodation, isolation, or other living conditions. Provincial and Regional agreed that the stress and strain of building and managing so many schools was probably a factor. Amongst those who went home ill in this period, apart from the Bishop himself, were Ben Nolan, Tony Murphy, Michael Scully, Andy O'Rourke, Tommy Greene, Dan O'Connell, Bill Fegan, Joe Stephens and John Lynott. Ironically, Tom Bartley, who died during his leave, had not gone home for health reasons. Michael Scully, the founder and first Principal of St Peter Claver's college, Aghalokpe, went home ill in '57 and died two years later.

While all the confreres were involved in schools, some were under more pressure than others. Ben Nolan, the Education Secretary, even though he had two African secretaries and eleven assistant supervisors, became very run down. After treatment in the London Tropical Institute in October '56, specialists hinted that he might not be fit again for Africa. He did return but, two years later, had to go back to London to undergo an operation for stomach ulcers. Tony Murphy, superior of Bishop Kelly's minor Seminary in Benin City, suffering from hookworms and possibly tuberculosis was ordered home by the Doctors. Andy O'Rourke, Principal of St Patrick's Asaba until 1955, was appointed Education Adviser for the Western Region with residence at

Ibadan. In the summer of '58, he was invalided home and, not recovering his health sufficiently to return to Nigeria, was appointed to Dromantine.

Were people being pushed too hard and under too much of a strain? The Provincial and the Regional seemed to think so. If Pat thought so, he didn't change or relax anything. He continued to demand much of everyone and, in '58, agreeing with the Provincial, who had remarked that "Fr G's case hardly called for treatment in Europe", said, "in future Fr G and others will have to be content with medical treatment here, unless return to Europe is plainly necessary".

Lay teachers and medical personnel

Many lay men and women complemented the work of the Fathers and Sisters in schools and hospitals. At first, lay people willing to go to Africa were hard to get, until word got round that life could be quite good on the missions. Teachers' salaries of about £700 to £800 per annum, plus increments and inducement grants, passage paid both ways, and free accommodation were not bad incentives at a time when economic difficulties, unemployment, or the prospect of emigration faced many Irish at home. Between 1956 and 1961, eighty-six graduates entered into contracts with the Irish SMA Ordinaries in Nigeria. Fifty-four of these were Irish (women outnumbering the men: twenty-nine to twenty-five). The pioneers among them had to overcome fear of the 'unknown', and face a battery of inoculations against Small Pox, Yellow Fever, Typhoid and Para-Typhoid. Many of the graduates preferred to postpone signing contracts until they arrived in Nigeria and saw things for themselves. The contract, normally of twenty-four months duration, was easily renewable if both parties were satisfied. As the decade wore on, conditions in the mission schools improved and, with greater numbers of expatriate teachers present, more socialising was possible. Between October '59 and October '65, in Benin diocese alone, Bishop Kelly contracted about ninety graduates. At this time, his diocese had far more than any other Irish SMA jurisdiction, Lagos being the closest with about sixty graduates, then Kaduna with forty-eight, and Ondo with forty-six. Most of the graduates had BA degrees; Science graduates – the hardest to get – were in much demand at home as well as in Nigeria.

One of the valuable aspects of the Nigerian experience for young teachers was the high level of responsibility given them almost as soon as they arrived. In March '56, for example, the Bishop informed the Provincial secretary, "I will take that graduate and his wife. He can go to Ibusa Training College and his wife can open a girls' secondary school in Ibusa, or he can go to Ubiaja Training College and his wife open a girls' secondary school at Uromi seven miles away".

He also contracted many medical personnel. Among those who made significant contributions were the lay women, Nurse Maureen O'Sullivan (Kerry), Dr Joan Clathworthy (England), Dr Louba Lengauer (Russia), and Mary Cunnane (Galway).

When **Nurse Mary Cunnane**, the Bishop's niece, first volunteered for work in Benin, he turned her down as, at the time, he was looking for *Nigerian* nurses, especially for Ossiomo leper settlement. She worked in England for a while but, asked him again in 1962 and he agreed. She arrived in June, and the Bishop sent her, first, to St Camillus hospital in Uromi and, the following January, to Sapele to help Nurse Maureen O'Sullivan in the Catholic Maternity Hospital and out-lying clinics. She worked with Maureen until Maureen had to go home to Kerry to look after her mother who had become critically ill.

In Sapele, Mary was called "the White Doctor" by the people and "Mary Bishop" by the confreres who, at first, were careful of what they said in her presence, lest stories got back to her uncle. When they got to know her better, they relaxed. The Bishop had no favourites and listened to no one in particular. Only three days in

Sapele, a tanned stranger with a Mayo accent and a bad shin ulcer arrived at the clinic. She gave him a double dose of penicillin which cured him in no time, but also a heartache which he never got over. Ambrose Lavin, BA, H.dip., was teaching in the Sapele bush since his arrival in 1960. Mary went to see the Bishop, but there was hardly any need to tell him why, "He knew what was in your mind before ever you said a word". After giving the couple a strict talk *in loco parentis,* he married them in Sapele. They enjoyed a brief honeymoon across the river in Onitsha and then returned to Sapele, where Ambrose joined the staff of St Malachy's secondary school.

Sapele: the marriage of Bishop's niece, Mary Cunnane, to Ambrose Lavin. *From left,* Bernie Cunningham, Paul Gariaga - - - Con O'Driscoll, Bernard Elaho, Jerry Cadogan.

Needing a car for visitation and trips to Benin City for drugs and supplies, Mary bought Paddy Gantly's old Volkswagen, a bargain which had no third gear and no 'floor' on the passenger side. In it she travelled the hinterland, but baulked at crossing the Ethiope river on the Sapele ferry. At the ferry dock, she would give a local man five shillings and only take the wheel again when they were safely on the other side. When in Benin City, she used to call on the Bishop, who would reminisce about home, and treat her to whatever food was going – usually not much. One morning, en route to Onitsha with Maureen O'Sullivan and four other women, she arrived very early at her uncle's house. His Lordship, about to have breakfast, ordered boiled eggs for all. When the episcopal egg arrived, accompanied by six more for the visitors, the ladies declined; the Bishop, who hated waste, consumed all seven eggs.

Mary followed Maureen O'Sullivan's example in baptising babies and adults in danger of death. One morning after helping deliver a healthy baby, she informed the anxious father that God had blessed him with a beautiful baby girl. To her surprise, he became very angry and threatened to sue her. Hearing the commotion the parish priest, Con O'Driscoll, dropped in and, *as gaeilge*, explained to her that the man had wanted a *son*. Somewhat the wiser, she mollified the irate father, got him to hold the baby and drop the law case. Mary and Ambrose remained in Nigeria until 1966, when the outbreak of Civil War compelled lay volunteers to leave the country.

Another marriage between volunteers was that of Mary Rose Kelly, a teacher from Derry and an Italian, Dr Bruno Breschi, working in Okpara Inland. A teacher from Cork, Martha Scannell, founder and first Principal of St Mary Magdalene Grammar School, Ashaka, was pursued by a chief in the Delta, keen on having a white wife. She was appointed to another school 'out of range'. As with all the missionary personnel, the volunteers suffered from illnesses and some died. Sheila and Tim O'Brien, both teachers, were just over a year married when Sheila died at Agbor in April '64. A well-known Kerry footballer, Frank Sheehy, a teacher in St Thomas's, Ibusa, suffered a heart attack and died while on a visit to Fr Tom Kennedy in Bomadi. Among many other generous and able expatriate teachers were: Rita Nolan, Kay Lynch; Liam Standen, Pat O'Brien, and Mr and Mrs D'arcy (daughter of Seán Moylan, then Irish Minister of

Education).

Maureen O'Sullivan, "my best missionary" said the Bishop. A nurse from Cahirciveen in Kerry, she first arrived in Nigeria in 1949, and worked in Benin until 1964 when she returned to Ireland to look after her mother. Later, she returned to Nigeria for six months to re-establish St Camillus hospital, Uromi, which was about to be closed down by the Government because of poor standards. With the conviction that "Only Maureen can save it", the Bishop, on home leave, went to Caherciveen to make his plea. Protesting that she couldn't leave her mother, Pat promised that nothing would happen her while Maureen was away. She took him at his word and returned to Uromi. Before six months were up, she had the hospital up and running and approved by the Government. The Irish Sisters of Charity then took it over. Maureen opened many maternity centres and clinics, trained midwives, and promoted child welfare and community development. The Bishop liked her because she was a worker, a baptiser and an initiator who didn't waste money. In her early twenties when she first arrived, she quickly came to love Nigeria and its people. After returning to Ireland, she continued to support Bishop Kelly and other missionaries too. She described him as, "a tall strong man, with deep penetrating eyes and an open honest face. Straight as a die in character, he was a man of deep faith in God and in His goodness. He was kind to people in trouble and had a remarkable ability to locate sick and dying people ... Even so, we had many a row – which I always won!"

After leave in 1959, she travelled back to Nigeria on the same ship as Con O'Driscoll. At Lagos, Con collected a new Land Rover for Mick Higgins of Benin City. Phil Corish, the procurator at Lagos, handed over the papers for the new vehicle and then boarded the same ship to go on leave himself. Next day he died on board of heart disease and was buried at Takoradi, Ghana, unfortunately in an unmarked grave. Unaware of the death until later, Con and Maureen drove on to Benin City, where they paid their respects to the Bishop. While he entertained them on the verandah, a troublesome wasp got entangled in Maureen's hair. Pat beat Con to the rescue and, after an adroit display of daring and dexterity, extricated the wasp. Enjoying the drama, Con only regretted that he did not have a camera to record "The Bishop and the Nurse's hair affair". Maybe the grin on Con's face stung Pat into giving him a new appointment just then – to Boji Boji parish, Agbor, where the confreres were complaining of insomnia due to the twenty-four hours a day activity in the busy maternity centre nearby.

Maureen O'Sullivan with mothers and babies, Sapele

Dr Joan Clathworthy, a highly trained English doctor, began her medical career in South Africa. After becoming a member of an Anglican community of nuns in Liberia, she converted to Catholicism and joined Mother Mary Martin's 'Medical Missionaries' as a postulant in Dublin. Of an independent turn of mind, she disagreed with the Foundress and left the Order. Keen to work in Nigeria, she was welcomed by Bishop Kelly. Founder and first doctor of St Camillus Hospital, Uromi, she worked there from 1948 to '58 and then served elsewhere in the diocese especially in Ozoro. After a life of diligent service, she died of cancer in the midst of the Sisters whom she had nearly joined, the MMMs in Anua, Eastern Nigeria, 28 March 1966. Following her wish, her body was taken back to Uromi, where she was buried beside the church; a small headstone marks her grave.

Truly devout, Dr Clathworthy was a kindred spirit to Pat in some ways. She lived an extremely simple life style and spent her earnings on the needy (including animals, for she had a Franciscan affection and compassion for all suffering creatures). Skilled in diagnosing the causes of childlessness, she lightened many a barren woman's heart with her remedies. She could be out-spoken, challenging what she thought to be wrong and reprimanding the negligent, including priests. A frequent visitor to the SMA houses, she regularly dined at Jack Casey's house in Ozoro.

Dr Louba Lengauer, mentioned already in connection with the beginnings of Ossiomo leper settlement, was a Russian by birth, who had been obliged to leave her homeland after the 1918 Revolution. Having worked for three years in Eastern Nigeria, she arrived in Ossiomo in 1934, where, with six Belgian nurses, she built up the leprosarium. In the early decades, conditions in the settlement were spartan and remuneration meagre, but she was not put off by such things. Before long, the number of patients rose to about 2,000, with many more in out-lying colonies. Bishop Kelly thought highly of her work and, in 1955, when she was thinking of retiring, applied for a *Bene Merenti* papal medal for her. Few people knew her first name, always referring to her as "Dr Lengauer", or "the Russian doctor". Pat's application was returned to him with the request "Fill in the lady's *Christian name*". Pat extemporized with *"Mary Magdalene"* and sent it back. In 1964, he also sought a Papal award for Marie Delpierre, one of her Belgian assistants. Among many other medical personnel were Dr Courtney from Tipperary who worked in Benin City and Dr Enright from Kerry, who was the first doctor of St Mary's hospital Ogwashi-Uku in 1954.

Nigerian students overseas

In his desire to increase the number of graduate teachers, Pat sent some twenty-five Nigerian students to study for degrees in universities abroad. His counterpart in Eastern Nigeria, Archbishop Heerey CSSp, sent students, mainly to Dublin, where they were facilitated by Archbishop John Charles McQuaid who, like Heerey, was a member of the Holy Ghost congregation. In the national university of Dublin the students were assured of a Catholic environment. While agreeing with this, Pat also saw a value in sending students to English universities, or universities of English or Anglican mission origin, anticipating that in independent Nigeria, such graduates would get the highest Government posts. By this means he hoped to enhance the chances of maintaining a Catholic influence in the country. In 1956, as well as having two Nigerian students in Galway University, he had one in Hull, one in Edinburgh, one in Fourah Bay (the Anglican University in Freetown, Sierra Leone), and two in the University of Ibadan. Previously, he had students attending University College Cork, during which time they were accommodated in the SMA hostel in Doughcloyne. Some of the students found the regime in the hostel too restrictive and, as Pat found it expensive, he ceased using it. Nevertheless, he thought that Irish universities would provide a safer moral and religious environment than English ones and, in 1958, he had four male students in Galway and one female in Dublin. Nigerian women whom he had sponsored were particularly grateful to him, "He gave us a standing we never had before", they said. He made agreements with the Nigerian students that they would teach in his mission schools after graduation, usually two years teaching for every year of sponsorship. The majority honoured their agreements, though some disappointed him. He was also disappointed by some of his European teachers. Somewhat overstating the case he said, "Lay graduates are hard to get and very unstable. We have just got one from England who has decided to return home after a month in Ibusa Training College".

Though Society authorities at home had often expressed concern about the 'mushrooming' school apostolate in Benin, Pat was not deterred and, in the mission, he had support. In '57, the Regional, Mattie Walsh, wrote to Dr Creaven, "With regard to the opening of new secondary schools, I think it is a very wise policy to accept *every* offer that is made to us to open a Catholic college ... I fully realize that it looks foolish on account of the grave predicament of finding staff and accepting responsibility ... but if we hadn't taken risks in educational matters in the past we would not be as far advanced as we are today. I would advise therefore that you give the Province's agreement to Bishop Kelly for whatever Catholic Education project he has in mind... At present the Protestants are going around baptizing everyone they can so as to be able to claim children for registration in their schools. If we don't open secondary schools where we have a predominant Catholic influence they will quickly come to the people's 'rescue'." In a Postscript, he informed the Provincial that for some time two applications for secondary schools had been lodged with the Proprietor (the Bishop), one at Otua, Igarra parish, for which £2000 had already been handed in as a first instalment, and another at Uzairue. Mattie recommended the acceptance of both.

Mattie Walsh

Some schools were administered under the 'Joint Proprietorship' of different agencies or churches, an arrangement not favoured by the Catholic Church. Sharing contemporary attitudes, Pat clearly expressed his own non-ecumenical views in one of the articles he had written for the *African Missionary*, "Rivals in the Field", in

1934. Upholding the superiority of the "one true Church" and its right to teach he, nevertheless, admired the faith and dedication of Protestant missionaries and, drawing on the image of the Apostles sleeping while Judas was active, he pointed out that Protestant missionaries, pastors, teachers and their followers were often more zealous than Catholics. He envied the Protestants, their well-built churches, self-supporting missions, and the generosity of their members. Resenting the favour they enjoyed with the Government, he saw that they too realized the importance of schools, "The fight for souls in Nigeria is going on in the schools".

Mattie Walsh viewed 'Joint Proprietorship' as "risky, troublesome and fraught with many dangers". In 1956, a new 'Joint' secondary school at Ozoro in Isoko country, where the Church Mission Society was very strong, was soon to be opened. The Bishop wanted it to be a Catholic school, "Lose this school and we lose influence in Isoko country", he said. Before departing overseas that year, he promised the local Chief, a supporter of the Catholic claim, that he would provide a Principal. In '57, before Pat returned, with pressure mounting to open the school and the District Council supporting the CMS, the Vicar General, Willie Keenan, nominated Mick Drew, as Catholic Principal (Mick was already working in Ozoro as Principal of the Teacher Training College). Willie believed that if they provided a Principal, the school would be left entirely in Catholic hands within two years. Mattie, however, refused to allow Drew to accept the post, or any other confrere to teach in the school, unless permission was given by the Provincial. Dr Creaven endorsed his decision. When the correct procedure had been clearly demonstrated to all, Mattie changed his decision and approved of Drew's appointment. Informed of the change, the Provincial gave permission for confreres to work in the Joint School venture *for one year,* adding "It is up to Bishop Kelly to get control of it immediately if he wants the Society to supply staff". Pat, who had returned to Nigeria by then, demanded Catholic Proprietorship at the next meeting of the Board of Governors and, eventually, got it.

Most of the missionaries supported the Bishop in his desire to establish more secondary schools. Mattie, the Regional, speaking for them, urged him on, in a style quite reminiscent of Pat's own. In July '57, he wrote to the Bishop, "The Ijaw tribe of Western Ijaw country are very anxious to establish a secondary school. One of their spokesmen assured me that the Native Authority has £5,000 ready to help the Mission to start and an assurance of £10,000 from the Government ... I consider it a matter of urgent need and importance to send a priest to reside at Bomadi [a town on the Niger, 60 miles from Warri, remote and up to this time difficult of access] to minister to a tribe of nearly 90,000 people who have had no resident Father since 1908. I just wonder what the Holy Father would think of us if he realized the position in Ijaw. So whether you wish to accede or not to their request for a secondary school I see no way in which Your Lordship or the Society can defer any longer the locating of a priest in Western Ijaw ... I have discussed this matter with my council and they fully approve my recommendation ... If we don't seize this golden opportunity to establish a secondary school *we may have cause to regret it before long*. I have done all I can, it now rests with Your Lordship and the Provincial".

Finding it difficult to please everyone, Pat prayed and, on retreat in August resolved, "To be humble and mortified and detached from all things [including] my missionary problems in imitation of my crucified Saviour ... and to ask grace to bear trials patiently in resignation to the Divine Will when the trial is heavy".

His patient waiting was not in vain. Two years later, Dr Creaven gave permission to open a college and a residential station at Bomadi, attaching strict conditions to safeguard the health and well-being of the personnel who, at the beginning, he said, should be volunteers.

Irish missionaries were less than enthusiastic about the Royal visit to Nigeria made by **Queen Elizabeth and Prince Philip** in 1956. Mattie Walsh felt constrained, "for the sake of record-keeping", to report that "Her Majesty has conferred the award of MBE on Fr John Rafferty-Augustine-Duffy of this diocese for outstanding work in the field of education in the Northern Provinces". John, normally called 'John Duffy', hailed from Greenock in Scotland. He first arrived in Western Nigeria in 1938 and worked mainly in Kabba and Okene districts. When the Queen visited Benin City, Pat was one of those who were introduced to her. Among other 'Niger missionaries' honoured by the Crown at different times were: Sr Isidore Frey OLA (OBE), Sr Celerine OLA (OBE) (the sister of Stephen and Peter Harrington), Sr Enda Barrett OLA (OBE), Archbishop Taylor (CBE), and Dr Lengauer (OBE).

Like the 'Crown', the Church also honoured outstanding people. Mentioned already were some women for whom Pat sought papal honours. He also sought awards for outstanding catechists, teachers and Nigerian priests, but not for his missionaries whom, he hoped, God would reward. On applying to Propaganda Fide for awards he had to submit biographical sketches, some of which have survived and reveal the kind of character and virtues he admired. Of **Francis Bekewuru Ogu** of Western Ijaw he wrote, "A model Catholic in every sense of the word, Francis was baptised by Fr Piotin in 1917. He became a catechist in 1925 and taught by example as well as precept. In 1934 on the death of his father he was elected *"Père"* (Father) by the people. Owing to his opposition to bribery in his court, to the murder of twin children and to his refusal to worship the ancestors, the people turned against him and sued him in the Magistrate's court, Warri, in 1939 ... Today (1953), His Highness Francis B.O. Kalanama VI, having conquered his enemies, is ruling in peace".

In 1957, he sought a papal decoration for **Fr Joseph Erameh**. Son of the Chief of Alagbetta, Agenebode, Joseph was ordained a priest in 1936 and ministered in Asaba, Warri, Sapele, and Aragba. Describing him as "a humble and obedient priest" the Bishop said, "His twenty-one years in the priesthood have been characterised by zeal for souls and devotion to duty. He is one who knows and has experienced the value of sacrifice on the Mission and is ever ready to help the poor and afflicted ... In fourteen years in Aragba he increased the number of schools in the parish from seven to thirty-four including four Secondary Modern schools, the number of teachers from 20 to 250, and the number of pupils from 300 to 6,910. The number of baptisms increased proportionately".

Seminaries and seminarians

In 1957, St Paul's Inter-jurisdictional Major Seminary in Benin City, was finally transferred to Ibadan, in the Prefecture of Mgr Richard Finn. While the seminary was in Benin City the majority of the students were from Bishop Kelly's diocese. In 1954, for instance, seventeen of the total of twenty-three students were his. Of the other seminarians, two were from Lagos, two from Ondo, one from Kaduna and one from Liberia. Despite Pat's obvious zeal for the school apostolate, he regarded the training of indigenous clergy as more important. At Ibadan, there was also an inter-diocesan minor seminary, St Theresa's, Oke Are, where, in '57, he had forty seminarians. And, already in 1954, without the Provincial's knowledge, he had established a minor seminary in Benin. Also called St Paul's, it was near his own house and, in '57, it had fifty-eight students.

Pat was not happy with the fees Mgr Finn was charging in Oke Are – no less than £8 per student, "notwithstanding that he (Mgr Finn), gets £40 per student as an annual subsidy from Rome". Pat wished to upgrade his own minor seminary, but lacked staff. Dr Creaven in a memorandum in May 1957, exhorted the Ordinaries to give priority to seminaries over all other institutions, but reminded them that it was their own responsibility to provide the staff. However, the Provincial came to the aid of Oke Are seminary that year as it was in dire straits. He appointed three men to it: Tony Jennings, a teacher in the SMA apostolic college, Ballinafad, Co Mayo, whom he recommended to be Superior; Paddy Jennings, his own private secretary; and Donal O'Connor, who had just-completed a Diploma in Education at Cambridge. Bishop Kelly, aggrieved, pointed out that Tony Jennings had been one of his personnel and therefore should be returned to Benin. If he could not be released, then Pat wanted one of the other two men. Benin City Minor Seminary, he stressed, was also in dire straits. Its superior, Tony Murphy, had been invalided home, leaving Fr Chukwumah, just ordained, in charge with only two senior seminarians to help him. The only consolation the Provincial could offer was that Fr Murphy, after tests in London, had been declared free of tuberculosis and should be returning to Benin after normal leave.

To avoid further delay, the Major Seminary had been transferred to Ibadan without waiting for the appointment of new staff members. An emergency meeting composed of the Provincial, the Superior General, Bishop Kelly (on leave) and Mgr Finn was held in Cork, at which they agreed to appoint Mossy Maguire, as Superior of the seminary, and Jim Tobin and Jim Conlon as staff members. Two of the three were from Benin diocese, Maguire had already served for twenty-four years as seminary superior in Benin City, and Conlon, since his arrival in '53, had worked in Benin City parish and in the seminary. Needless to say, Pat was dissatisfied. The Regional Superior shared the Bishop's sense of deprivation and believed, with Benin personnel in general, that their diocese was unfairly treated when it came to the allocation of men. Arguing on the basis of numbers of Catholics (nearly 100,000 in the diocese), and of school children (13,000 in Benin City parish alone), he felt that Benin should be allocated more priests. The idea that Benin was being less than fairly treated evoked a sharp response from the Provincial who, in September '57, drew attention to the allocations for that year:

Ibadan	1
Jos	1 (against one withdrawal)
Monrovia	1
Lagos	3 (against one withdrawal)
Ondo	3
Kaduna	3 (against two withdrawals)
Benin City	7 (against one withdrawal)

He further pointed out that Propaganda Fide was not so much concerned about numbers of Catholics to be ministered to as numbers of *people* to be converted. Benin, with a population of 1.7 million people, had fifty-six SMA Fathers; Ibadan, population 1.2 million, had only eighteen (two of whom were in Oke Are Minor Seminary, and a third was an invalid); Ondo, with a population of 1.5 million had only thirty-three Fathers. In addition Benin had seven Nigerian Fathers, while Ibadan had none. Ibadan's need, said the Provincial, is far greater than Benin's, "we have never been able to assign sufficient personnel to it". He closed the argument, "Does the lusty Benin baby want all other jurisdictions to close down so that it may get all the milk?"

Chastened for the time being, further transfers caused Pat to complain even more bitterly. In '58 one of his new men, Dan Looney, was appointed to St Paul's, Ibadan, and Mick Drew was seconded to Jos. Pat asked for a graduate to fill the vacancy left by Drew and also one for Michael Scully, the former Principal of Aghalokpe College who, by then, had been invalided home.

The sign board outside the College with the name, *St Peter Claver's College"*, gave rise to one of Pat's Solomonic judgements. Being the first Secondary Grammar School in Urhoboland and the third to be established in the diocese, after St Patrick's and Immaculate Conception College, it was of no small importance. When Joe Donnelly was Vice Principal the local people, feeling slighted that "*Aghalokpe"* was not included on the name board, sent a vociferous delegation in two trucks to the Bishop in Benin.

Having a carefully concealed soft spot for the Urhobos, his first parishioners, Pat welcomed them warmly and listened intently to their complaint. When all had had their say, Pat pronounced solemnly: "You see the board no reach!". [Meaning, the board wasn't long enough to include the village name.] He continued, "Make you give more plank to Fr Donnelly". The people were satisfied, more plank was found and, on the addition of *"Aghalokpe"*, the village gained its rightful place among great centres of learning.

Pat realized that he could not moan too much about the loss of Dan Looney who, in the first place, had been appointed to him "for one year" only, but he feared he would lose another, temporarily-appointed newcomer, John Thornton, who was teaching in Uzairue TTC. But Bishop Kelly's staffing fortunes were about to change: Jim Conlon returned to assist Tony Murphy in the Minor Seminary; and, after two years in Ibadan, Mossy Maguire also came back; likewise Dick Beausang, who had been appointed to Cloughballymore after his first tour in Benin. Even Dan Looney was restored to him in '62 and, the same year, Mick Drew returned. Most of the 'invalids' also came back after various periods of recuperation. John Thornton, who had been given a home appointment for health reasons, returned in '66. In other ways Pat's fortunes improved too. The diocese, once considered by some as 'the poor relation' of the Province, or even as 'a dumping ground' for missionaries, began to exercise a growing attracting force – not only for older men, but for the newly ordained. Benin was becoming the place where young men wanted to be.

Some of Kelly's personnel, however, would not 'return'. Michael Scully aged fifty-nine died in Ireland in May '59. Two months later Willie Keenan, the Vicar General, after celebrating Mass and visiting schools in Asaba, complained of feeling unwell and, returning to his house, died within half an hour. Nearly thirty years in Western Nigeria, he had served especially in Asaba and

Okene, and had been Society Visitor. He died, 16 July, aged sixty-one and was buried in Asaba cemetery.

An important visitor whom Pat 'attracted' to Benin was Bishop Michael Browne of Galway. In Nigeria for the episcopal ordination of his friend, Richard Finn in 1959, Browne accepted Pat's invitation to visit Benin City. After seeing the wonders of the 'palace', Pat took him on a grand tour of the diocese and drove a little faster than usual to cover more ground. In the danger seat, Browne blanched more than once and feared he would never again see his own diocese. By the grace of God he survived, but ever afterwards whenever he met Dr Creaven or a Benin missionary, he would always ask, "Is Bishop Kelly alive and is he still driving?"

Regional house, Uromi

With fifty-six confreres in the diocese, the men in Benin felt that they should have a Regional Superior of their own, resident in the diocese and not in Owo or elsewhere. There were different views as to where his house should be located. Bishop Kelly, at first, wanted it in Benin City but others, fearing he would overburden the Regional with pastoral work, were against this location. The Acting Regional in 1954, Tommy Murray, favoured Agbor. It was half-way between Benin City and Asaba, was fairly central, and positioned near major roads. The Bishop after sometime, concurred and the Provincial Council approved. But, when Mattie Walsh became Regional he disagreed, stating his preference for the Ishan plateau which, according to medical authorities, like Dr Clathworthy who lived and worked there, was one of the healthiest places in Western Nigeria. Senior men, like Greene and Bartley, lent their support, pointing out that the Ishan plateau had a telephone line and quite good roads. Pat agreed and also stated that he would not oblige the personnel of the new house to do pastoral work. Following a request from the Provincial he further agreed that Uromi parish would be attached to the Regional House and be under the Regional's authority.

Mattie Walsh commenced building a two-storey house on an elevated site at Uromi. Called "St Philomena's", it was planned to accommodate, not only the Regional and an assistant, but newly-arrived Fathers who would spend six months doing their 'tyrocinium' there – Stephen Harrington's idea for the initial training of missionaries was finally being given a chance. The new house was opened on 5 July 1957 in the presence of the Bishop, twenty-five confreres, Sisters from nearby Ubiaja, Dr Clathworthy and many other well-wishers. The first 'tyros' Seán Flynn, John Dunne, Dan Looney, Mattie O'Connell and Frank Burke arrived in October.

When the new house was being roofed, the Regional requested £1,000 from the Province to help complete the work. The Provincial could only give a loan, as the Province was in debt, due to the extensive building programme in Ireland, necessitated by the greatly increasing numbers of students. All the formation houses had been extended or improved; accommodation in Dromantine had actually been doubled. By '59, the number of students in Dromantine had risen to eighty and over one hundred were expected the following year. Ireland was experiencing a 'vocation boom' and the Society of African Missions was not lagging behind in reaping the harvest. To help with rising costs the Provincial appealed to the mission Ordinaries for financial assistance. Pat, after consultation with his councillors, was one of the first to oblige, sending a cheque for £2,000, asking only that it be repaid, should the Diocese be in need and the Province able to afford it! The gift was paid back a few years later in the form of grants for the training of catechists.

General and Provincial Assemblies were held in 1958. Henri Monde was elected Superior General by a majority of only one vote over Stephen Harrington; Joseph Guerin was again Vicar General, while Harrington became one of the councillors. At the Provincial Assembly in Cork, John Creaven was re-elected and Phil O'Shea was elected as Vice Provincial. Pat did not have many points for the agenda of either Assembly but, expressed displeasure at the idea of a twenty-one month tour for priest teachers which, he said, would be inconvenient for Ordinaries and expensive in travel costs. The '58 Provincial Assembly fixed the normal length of tour at three years with six months holiday, and left decisions on arrangements for confreres in teaching posts to the Provincial administration.

In 1956 the Colonial Government's policy on schools began to change. Independence was in the air and the Government, probably reasoning that education was hastening its advent too quickly, reduced grants for secondary schools from £15,000 to £10,000. Sensing that time was running out, Bishop Kelly became more determined than ever to open as many schools as possible in the time available. Understating his plans, he told the Provincial in '57, "We are expanding a bit with secondary schools now because there may be difficulty in getting permission to establish them in the future".

The 1959 report of the Catholic Education Secretary of Benin and Delta Provinces, **Fr Johnny Lyons,** gives a clear picture of just how successful the Bishop's plans proved to be:

Secondary Grammar Schools:

9 Secondary Grammar Schools for boys, with about 1,200 enrolled
2 .... girls .... 185..............

Teaching in these schools were 37 graduate teachers, 14 of whom were lay, including 5 Africans. The Catholic mission planned to open 6 more Grammar Schools in 1960, 4 for boys and 2 for girls, for which the Ministry had already given approval. 'Grammar' schools gave a complete secondary education and were either fully, or partially, boarding schools.

Secondary Modern Schools:

Delta Province 29 Schools ...... 3,899 boys ...... 508 girls
Benin Province 28 .... 3,119.............. 706.......

('Modern' schools offered the first three years of secondary education and were not boarding schools. The diocese opened 17 in 1959 and had permission from the Ministry to open 27 more in 1960.)

Primary Schools:

Delta .... 205 schools.... 28,212 boys.................14,954 girls
Benin.............. 378 .... 45,459 .... 31,655........

4,183 teachers were employed in these three categories of schools.

In sum, in 1959 the Diocese had 11 Secondary Grammar Schools, 57 Secondary Modern Schools, 583 Primary Schools; nearly 10,000 secondary school pupils and over 120,000 primary pupils.

In addition to these, the diocese was running 8 Teacher Training Colleges, 5 for men and 3 for women.

The Education Secretary's final remark was *If we have any cause for worry it will concern our ability to meet the growing demands for expansion in every sphere of education.*

Pat had great confidence in Johnny Lyons, leaving him to be his spokesman in many higher educational affairs. Having arrived in Western Nigeria in 1937, he taught in secondary schools and in the Teacher Training Colleges of Ibusa and Ubiaja. He also served in parish work, especially in Onicha-Olona. In 1956 he was appointed Education Secretary. Extremely competent, he had a remarkable ability to listen patiently to people – after which he usually got what he wanted!   Driving back to St Columba's College, Agbor, late one night after a Gaelic football match, which he had arranged between the confreres and lay graduates of Benin and Warri, he was killed when his car struck a fallen tree. He was buried the following day in Asaba, 29 April 1964. He was only fifty-one years of age.

Johnny Lyons

Chapter 13

THE SIXTIES, 1960-1966

In the Sixties the 'winds of change' blew stronger than ever. Seventeen African countries, including Nigeria, gained independence in the first year of the decade alone. In the same year the Catholic Church began its preparations for the biggest General Council ever. Nearly a century had elapsed since the First Council of the Vatican which, maintaining a critical view of the secular World, proclaimed Papal Infallibility. The Second Vatican Council, 1962-1965, opened the windows of the Church to the modern world.

Pius XII died in October 1958. Within three weeks, Cardinal Roncalli, the Patriarch of Venice, was elected Pope and took the surprising name "John XXIII" – the name of a former impious 'antipope'. Jovial, pastorally-minded, and almost seventy-seven years of age, Roncalli was considered to be 'a stop-gap' Pope but, he astounded everyone, even himself he said, by announcing that he was going to call an Ecumenical Council. The first "John XXIII" had convoked the Ecumenical Council of Constance, which in 1417 put an end to the Great Western Schism. The new Pope, ardently desiring unification of the separated Churches – Catholic, Orthodox, and Protestant – worked zealously towards that end. In March 1960, the Pontifical Preparatory Commission circularised the Catholic bishops of the world, inviting them to send in their suggestions for the agenda of the future Council.

The Patrician Year
The commemoration of the 1,500th anniversary of the death of St Patrick took place in Ireland in 1961. Archbishop Heerey CSSp of

Onitsha, on behalf of the Nigerian hierarchy, asked Pat to represent the Nigerian bishops at the celebrations. As he was going on home leave anyway, he agreed to go a bit early to be in time for the inaugural ceremonies at Armagh on the Saint's feast day, the 17th of March. Sailing from Lagos in February, he arrived in Liverpool on the 6th of March and continued his journey on the ferry to Dublin.

Armagh, the Primatial See of Ireland, was thronged on the feast. Looking around him, after taking his place for the main celebration, Pat recognized a number of the dignitaries present: Cardinals McIntyre of Los Angeles, D'Alton of Armagh, and Cushing of Boston; the fourth, he was told, was the Primate of Armenia, Cardinal Agajanian. Archbishop Riberi, the current Apostolic Nuncio to Ireland, was there, as was Archbishop McQuaid of Dublin and Dr Browne of Galway. Eamon De Valera, on his first cross-border visit to the North as President of Ireland, also attended and, among many other dignitaries, were forty-three archbishops and bishops and thirty-five heads of religious orders.

Pontifical High Mass, in the hilltop cathedral overlooking the town, was celebrated by Cardinal McIntyre, the Papal Legate. Cardinal Cushing, in his sermon, said that in the past decade nearly 4,000 Irish had left home, as Patrick himself had done, to preach the Gospel in foreign lands, "The missionary vocation is the very heart of the vocation of Ireland". At the end of the Mass, Cardinal D'Alton made special mention of the missionary bishops present – Dr Moynagh SPS of Calabar and Dr Kelly SMA of Benin City. Cardinal McIntyre read a message from the Pope congratulating the Irish people, mentioning specifically its missionaries, male and female, saying "In missionary work Ireland is second to no other nation".

Pat arrived in Armagh without his mitre. A helpful aide rushed to buy him one in an elite clerical outfitters shop. It was expensive, but the occasion demanded it. Pat wore it, but the following day brought it to the shop and asked for his money back, as he had another one in Africa.

After Armagh, he went to the Medical Missionaries' Hospital in Drogheda, where an old friend of the SMA, Dr Forbes-Browne of the Tropical Unit, examined him. The Doctor, who had worked many years in Africa, declared that Pat had no symptoms of amoeba and that filaria, an old complaint, was no longer active; all in all, the Doctor said, he was "in quite good shape considering his age".

Pat required a mitre again on 21 May for the consecration of the Vicar Apostolic of Monrovia, Francis Carroll SMA, in St Peter's, Rome. Becoming quite a 'plane-hopper' by now, he returned to Cork by air to participate in the annual SMA retreat in June and, after it, he continued his holiday in Tristaun. Concerned not to overstay his six-month leave, and agreeing to share a cabin with two confreres, he managed to get a berth on a heavily booked ship, sailing from Liverpool on 31 August. One of his last public acts in Ireland on this leave was to preach on the feast of the Assumption, 15 August, in St Mary's Cathedral Cork where, according to himself, he preached "a *short* sermon on Our Lady".

The Second Vatican Council
Long before the great Council began, Preparatory Commissions were established to write position papers, make agendas and discern what the bishops throughout the world were thinking on specific church and religious matters. When Pat received a Commission's request for suggestions, he put a few thoughts on paper and worked on them. Though excellent in local Nigerian languages, his Latin was rusty – it was over thirty years since he had taught Moral Theology in Dromantine using Latin text books. He worked on the Latin expression of his ideas, changing the grammar a few times before he was satisfied. Then, with two

fingers, he typed out a final draft and sent it off.

Basically he had three requests. First, that the canon law restricting the baptism of pagans in polygamous marriages be made less prohibitive. Second, that the Faithful be allowed to recite the prayers of the Mass in local languages while the celebrant was saying them in Latin, from the beginning of the Mass to the Preface and from the Our Father to the end. Third, that the regulations for the setting up of marriage tribunals in mission territories be liberalised and that a temporary concession, already given, be made permanent. Brief as his requests were, they indicated his compassion for well-disposed people desiring baptism, his conviction of the value of vernacular languages, and his fidelity to 'law and order' which, however, should be modified to cater for particular situations.

Various committees were established by the bishops in Nigeria to help them in making their suggestions. One Committee met at Enugu in April 1960 under the chairmanship of Bishop John Anyogu. Among the participants was Larry Carr SMA, rector of the Major Seminary, Ibadan. The Committee proposed that the bishops ask for nine indults (concessions) and make seven suggestions. Pat's request for the use of the Vernacular at Mass was more radical, the Committee merely suggesting that permission be given, "To sing a hymn or recite prayers between the Consecration and the Pater in a Low Mass" and "To sing vernacular hymns during High Mass especially during the distribution of Holy Communion".

The Council was scheduled to open on **11 October 1962.** At this time, the SMA Generalate occupied temporary quarters on via Gregorio Settimo, as the former via dei Gracchi residence, near the Vatican, had been sold. The 'Gracchi' house had been the administrative headquarters since Maurice Slattery had moved the Generalate there from Lyons the year after his election as Superior General in 1937. Now, the Dutch Superior General,

Henri Monde, and his councillors were awaiting the completion of the spacious new house being built on the via della Nocetta in the suburbs. In these circumstances, the Generalate was not in a position to accommodate any of the twenty-four SMA Ordinaries attending the Council. Stephen Harrington, Vicar General, advised Pat to make his arrangements for Rome in good time, "with thousands of bishops around, everything will be scarce". For daily Mass in St Peter's, he told Pat, the bishops are required to wear a red soutane, red sash, pectoral cross, rings, zucchetto, white alb, red cincture and a white mitre.

Pat was relieved when he heard that Propaganda Fide would arrange the missionary bishops' accommodation in Rome. Allocated to the *Hotel Nova Domus* on via Savonarola, he recalled that Savonarola was a Dominican friar who was burned at the stake for heresy! On the 11th of October, properly attired and armed with his black-covered Vatican Council passbook and special pen for signing documents, he left the hotel and walked to St Peter's. By 8 a.m. some 2,540 bishops had gathered in the great piazza. For the first time in modern history indigenous African and Asian bishops attended. Counting expatriate and indigenous, there were 276 bishops from Africa present, including eighteen from Nigeria (five of whom were indigenous). Presenting a colourful spectacle, the red-garbed prelates filed into the Basilica. When they were seated, the smiling eighty-year-old Pontiff was carried in on the Gestatorial Chair. Alighting, he walked slowly to the high altar saluting the bishops as he went. Cardinal Tisserant, the Dean of the College of Cardinals, began the first Mass of the Council. After it, the Pope, speaking in clear and simple Latin, pronounced the Council open. Continuing, he said he wanted a Pastoral Council with more emphasis on the flock than on the shepherds; a Council giving a new presentation of the Faith set in Biblical terms, free of anathemas, tempered by compassion, striving for Christian unity. The bishops, sensing a breath of the Spirit blowing through St Peter's, heard a new, oft-repeated word, *aggiornamento*, renewal or up-dating – it was what the Pope wanted for the Church in the modern world.

Each day began with Mass at 8 a.m. The morning session, called a 'congregation' then continued until 1 or 2 p.m. Everything was conducted in Latin without translations – leaving many of the bishops feeling lost. The American bishops organised a translation service and, by 4 p.m. every day, anyone who wanted an unofficial translation of the morning's business could have one. A welcome break was taken at 10.30 a.m. in "John's kitchen", a cafeteria at the back of St Peter's. Afternoons and evenings were free and gave the bishops a chance to meet some of the theologians present, listen to lectures and get to know the subject matter of the following day's discussions. In addition to bishops, some 800 theologians, lay observers, including women and some non-Catholics were present. Queried about the presence of women, the Pope responded, "I don't see why not, they compose half the population of the world".

Pope John XXIII and Bishop Kelly, 1962

The Council was held in four Sessions between September and December of the four years '62 to '65. The bishops went back to their dioceses each December and returned in time for the beginning of the next Session. Before the Sessions, missionaries like Pat, took the opportunity of spending some weeks at home. Sadly, Pope John was not there to welcome them at the opening of the Second Session; he had died on the 3rd of June 1963. Much lamented by Catholics and non-Catholics, he was succeeded by Cardinal Montini of Milan who took the name, Paul VI.

Apart from Pat, six other SMA Ordinaries from Nigeria were among the Council Fathers. Archbishop Taylor attended the First and Second Sessions, but was too ill to attend the Third. He died in Lagos, during the Fourth Session, on 27 October 1965. The others were: Archbishop John McCarthy, Kaduna, Bishops Richard Finn, Ibadan, William Field, Ondo, John Reddington, Jos, and Mgr William Mahony, the Prefect Apostolic of Ilorin.

The Irish SMA Ordinaries at Vatican II: Mgr William Mahony, PA Ilorin; Bp Richard Finn, Ibadan; Bp Kelly; Bp William Field, Ondo; Bp John Reddington, Jos; Ab John McCarthy, Kaduna. (Ab Leo Taylor, Lagos, attended the first and second sessions; he died in Lagos, 27 October 1965.)

With Pope Paul VI, 1965

Pat didn't talk much about the Council and didn't record any serious reflections on it. From a few passing references of his, one can only conclude that, overall, it didn't greatly please him. Some of its new orientations disturbed theological ideas and spiritual ways that he cherished. Twenty years after the Council, on being asked about it, he said little more than express regret that after it private prayer declined in favour of reciting the Psalms in common, "I couldn't see what renewal there was in that, as we always had the Divine Office".

Somewhat impressed by the spectacular opening of the Council, Pat did not comment on the content of its debates. On the fourth day of the First Session, writing about mission business to the Vice Provincial in Cork, he made a brief reference, "The opening of the Vatican Council was a great display – the greatest ever even in St Peter's". The Provincial Superior, Dr Creaven, met the SMA bishops after every Session and chatted with them about the proceedings but, he "never gleaned any inkling of what Bishop Kelly thought". One suspects that during the long morning discussions, Pat's thoughts were often far away. Occasionally he wrote to Benin, reminding a missionary to visit the sick or to baptise the dying. During the afternoons, he did business in Rome on behalf of the diocese. One day, dropping in to the office of the Pontifical Work for the Propagation of the Faith, he requested $9,000 to build churches at Isheagu, Igueben, and Auchi. In these three places, Sunday Masses had to be celebrated in school rooms, even though the first two had congregations of nearly 1,000 and the third over 600. The local people, Pat said, would do their part too, contributing money and giving their labour free.

He visited various teaching and medical Congregations, trying to interest them in schools or hospitals in Benin. Walking the streets of Rome, he browsed in bookshops and souvenir stalls, looking for holy pictures and medals to bring back to Nigeria; one picture he particularly liked was that of Jesus the Good Shepherd with a lamb on his shoulders.

In many things, Pat wasn't one for change but, deeper than his conservatism, was his obedience. When the Council decreed change, he conformed. After the Decree on Liturgy was promulgated, he would not say Mass unless the altar, or a temporary table, was facing the people. Even the table that served as an altar for his Masses at home had to be pulled out from the wall, though it reduced space in the overcrowded kitchen. Committed to the liturgical changes, it was hard to draw him out on other matters. A young missionary in Nigeria, Willie Cusack asked him, "What does 'ecumenism' mean?" "It means we don't fight the Protestants as much as before", he replied. And when Jehovah Witnesses called to the home in Tristaun, Pat told the family, "We must be nice to them, it's what the Council wants". When preaching in Nigeria, he said, "Not the least of the decrees of Vatican II was that of Religious Liberty. According to it freedom in matters of religion is based on the dignity of the human person. A person may be invited to membership of the Church, but there must be no coercion. Faith in God must be free. Hence, Catholics are strongly opposed to herding all boarders in a boarding institution into Sunday service irrespective of the religious belief of the individual".

Though conservative by nature, he was ahead of the times in some respects. In his diocese, before the Council ever began, he had already put in place a number of practices which were later promoted by the Council – use of the vernacular for instance. He had always believed in using it as much as possible. On Sundays and feast days, he had the Epistles and Gospels read in the vernacular, while the priest was reading them in Latin. The Council desired greater lay participation in Church affairs; Pat had always encouraged it, placing catechists, head Christians, and teachers in leading roles in their parishes and he had always paid heed to what they had to say. Vatican II re-emphasised the use of Scriptures. Pat, while not promoting Bible study as such, did promote the 'ministry of the word', always insisting that his priests preach long sermons.

His own preaching, being long-winded and pedantic, was not as inspiring as his practice; young mothers were known to pinch their babies in the hope that their cries would make him stop! Though he could have preached in the vernacular, the custom, in tribally mixed areas, was to preach in English and use an interpreter, or even two or three, to translate into Ibo and into one or two other local languages. This made the ceremonies very long. Nevertheless, he reprimanded those of his priests who preached for less than thirty minutes on a Sunday.
"You're sermons are too short", he told one priest.
"The people fall asleep", protested the accused.
"Well, if you'd go on for another fifteen minutes maybe they'd

wake up again".

While he didn't found any new religious congregations, he did encourage groups of lay people, male and female who, without formal vows, were committed to the church and to apostolic work. The women, called "Ma's", were present in small groups in Benin, Asaba and Warri. Some, being elderly, needed care themselves, but most of them were involved in social work, such as looking after orphans, going on village visitation, helping the Sisters in the clinics, and in the Shelters for the aged and needy. The group in Asaba, took particular interest in caring for young girls 'in danger' and had a great influence on them. Some well known ones, like Ma Elizabeth, Ma Helen, Ma Mary John, and Ma Teresa stayed near the OLA Sisters' convents and, as well as helping them in their work, sometimes took part in liturgy and prayer with them; others prayed within their own communities. The men were called "Brothers", wore a black cassock and looked after Catholic bookshops, taught catechism and generally helped where they were needed.

Ma Teresa, Ma Helen, Ma Elizabeth with OLA Sisters, Celine, Norbert, and three Asaba women.

Pat was to the fore among the bishops in entrusting to lay people the management of, and later, the founding of schools. He also encouraged their involvement in medical work and had lay doctors, nurses and assistants in his hospitals and clinics. Not so well known was his founding of "a weak house" at Ossiomo where homeless lepers, on being discharged from the settlement, could reside if they were not suffering from contagious disease. This was looked after by an expatriate lay woman. Once a month he would visit Ossiomo, offer Mass for the patients and spend some time with them.

The Vatican Council stressed the importance of prayer and union with Christ as the means of promoting Christian social action. Both in his personal practice and in his preaching, Pat was doing the same. An illustration of this is seen in his reply to Mother Rosarii, the Provincial Superior of the Irish OLA Sisters, who had asked him for suggestions for their Provincial Chapter of 1970. He responded, "I wish and pray for God's blessing on your Chapter. I have no suggestions to make ... Renewal in accordance with the decrees of the Council will occupy you. More activity and self-giving in the apostolate is the post-Conciliar trend, but prayer and mental prayer at that will always be necessary to keep up one's union with Christ. Social work and maternities in outstations are to be highly commended, as also is visiting the people in their homes as far as possible. It is a pity so much of the Sisters' time is taken up with education, but even so, they might be able to visit some quarter of the town one or two evenings a week. I remember the good old days in Asaba seeing the Sister with one or two girls going out visiting every evening".

~ ~ ~

Meanwhile in Benin

The election for the Regional Superior to succeed Mattie Walsh in 1959 resulted in favour of Johnny Browne, a Kerry man, who at the time was working in Igarra in the north of the diocese. The choice was confirmed by the Provincial. Mattie replaced Johnny for a short time in Igarra, before taking up his own new appointment, fund-raising in Ireland and in America. At this time, due to the cost of building student accommodation and fees for the increasing numbers of university students, finance was as badly needed at home as on the missions, and it was less difficult to raise funds for Leper settlements and "Black Babies" in Nigeria than for buildings and college fees in Ireland. While agreeing with the Provincial that graduate teachers in mission schools were receiving substantial Government salaries (which were not personal emoluments but, were normally paid to the bishop), Pat pointed out that now, 1960, the Government did not come to the aid of mission schools *until they were three years in existence* and, far from receiving big grants, the diocese was paying the full amount of many teachers' salaries, averaging about £1,000 a year for each one. He agreed that the Province's difficulties had to be considered too and, more than some other Ordinaries, wished to defuse tension between 'home-front' and 'missions'.

Johnny Browne

While ill-health was a perennial problem on the missions, there was at this time, a very high rate of serious illness at home. Three of the Ballinafad staff were ill, two in Wilton, one in Dromantine, and several in Blackrock Road, "We are having a most calamitous time in this matter" said the Provincial, who feared that some of the patients might become permanent casualties. Illness at home meant that fewer men were available for Africa. Thus John Thornton, whom Pat wanted to make Principal of Aghalokpe College, was detained to teach in Ballinafad. The 'home' needs were as pressing to the Provincial, as the mission ones were to the Ordinaries, but some bishops, so long accustomed to the idea that "home supplied mission", were slow to accept that their jurisdictions were no longer fledgling missions but substantial dioceses capable of seeing to many of their own needs.

The major event of 1960 in Nigeria was the gaining of **Independence on 1 October.** Pat, with his Irish background of foreign domination and desire for political and religious freedom, had quietly looked forward to it and, more than most missionaries, was not surprised at how quickly it came in the end. In a real sense he had contributed to it. For centuries, the Irish had struggled for education in their own country seeing in it, not only the acquisition of knowledge, but of advance in other spheres, including national independence. In Africa, Pat and many others were well-aware that providing young Nigerians with education would prepare them for more than mere colonial employment. Thankfully, the hand-over of power from Britain was peaceful, "Never before were white and black in such beautiful harmony, the one in surrendering power, the other in receiving it", said Michael Foley, parish priest of Warri. However, it was only a matter of time, the missionaries felt, before the new Government would begin to take over mission schools. Such an eventuality might not be totally negative from the missionary point of view. PM Kelly when he was Provincial, and Stephen Harrington when Superior General, had expressed concern over Benin's heavy involvement in education. Dr Creaven, while commending Bishop Kelly on the Statistics of 1959 said, "It is quite a worrying prospect that so many of our young Fathers seem destined to spend the rest of their lives in classrooms, getting no real acquaintance with the people or the country and no real experience of missionary life".

John Mahon, Vicar General since his return in 1957, had much the same attitude to schools as Pat. In 1933, he wrote an article for the *African Missionary* entitled "Schools in Nigeria" in which, praising the early missionaries for their non-assisted 'bush' schools and, hoping to stimulate Irish readers to help financially, said, "All through the dark epoch of Ireland's passion, the education of children was a work dear to the heart of Ireland's people". But, in 1961, Mahon, in charge of the diocese while Pat was on leave, saw that perhaps too much had been sacrificed for the sake of schools and colleges. Agreeing with the Provincial that the Seminary in Benin had been neglected, he indicated that an adjustment of the pastoral-educational balance might actually be forced upon the diocese, "The future status of our Training Colleges is uncertain. Principals have been told to make no arrangements for the 1962 intake, pending Government decision on change of policy. It is generally felt that the Government is feeling the strain of paying for Education. We have been told not to apply for more Grammar or Secondary Modern Schools until applications are invited by the Ministry".

The Provincial visited Benin diocese in January 1962. Though he found the confreres' conditions much improved since his first visit, some of his observations re-echoed those of 1954. Some Fathers' houses were so small that he could not spend the night with them because there was no spare room. Too many confreres were living alone and too many were engaged in school work. Though he agreed that confreres should live frugally, he thought the 'viaticum', or monthly allocation for upkeep, should be standardised. Confreres at Ossiomo leper settlement and at Bomadi mission, might receive a little more. No special 'Instructions' followed his 1962 visit and, thanking the Bishop and the Fathers for their hospitality, he acknowledged, "There seems to be a good spirit of work in the Diocese".

Good news arrived in June. Paddy Gantly, after nine years as *Magister* in Cloughballymore, requested, and was granted, re-appointment to Benin. However, Pat would have to forfeit Jim Byrne who would take Gantly's place in the noviciate. Likewise, Mick Drew was returning and two newly ordained men, Colm

McKeogh BA and Tom Hasset, had been appointed to Benin. Four men at the cost of one wasn't a bad exchange, Pat thought, but he wasn't happy at getting only one graduate out of a class of nine. The Vice Provincial asked him if he would accept another confrere, a former missionary in Nigeria, who was currently doing a retreat in Mount Melleray. Though deferring the decision, until after hearing the Regional's views, Pat did take the 'Melleray' man. Adding weight to his request for more graduates, was the fact that in 1960, he had officially requested Rome to divide the Benin jurisdiction and erect the Warri-Delta area as a separate diocese. Hence, he argued that his diocese should really be treated as if it were two. Though the education tide, as far as the Catholic mission was concerned, was beginning to ebb, Kelly rowed on, urging the Vice Provincial to find more lay graduates for him saying, "We will take all we get", and "Events in Nigeria show that this is the last opportunity we will have for opening schools".

In August 1962, **Cardinal Montini** visited Nigeria. He received a huge welcome – as if the people knew he was going to be the next Pope (which he was within a year). Benin City did him proud. Pat white-washed his palace, doing most of it himself, togged out in tatty shorts and singlet and advising his assistant not to waste 'paint' on the 'backside' of the pillars, which the Cardinal wouldn't see anyway. Not feeling competent to entertain the Cardinal either conversationally or gastronomically, he sent for Tommy Greene to see to the first and Mother Raymond OLA for the second.

Mother Raymond, resident in St Philomena's hospital Benin, though short in stature was stout in heart and knew her way around kitchens and bishops. Not for nothing was she the Sisters' Regional Superior. Wisely, she went to investigate Pat's culinary arrangements a few days before the Cardinal arrived. On checking the Electrolux fridge, she found it contained nothing but a bottle of water labelled "I belong to Kelly". She called Pat out of the oratory where he had taken refuge and interrogated him as to what exactly he was going to give the Cardinal. Defensively he stammered, "We have a turkey in the yard that someone dashed me". "Indeed, but we'll have to have duck, lamb, rice, yam and spaghetti as well", said Raymond. On the eve of the Cardinal's visit, the turkey, suspecting the worst, went missing. After a hectic search led by the Bishop, the bird was run to ground and sent to the pot in St Philomena's where all the cooking was done. Mother Raymond, aided by a strong team, including Srs Eileen Wall and Henrietta Power from Maria Goretti School, gave Pat's palace a thorough cleaning before the big day. Kitchen ware, plates, cups and cutlery had to be borrowed; more food was bought and the Bishop received some more 'dashes'. In the end the Cardinal, who didn't eat much and had some difficulties with English (even Tommy Greene's) was treated to a very fine lunch. When Pat's niece, Mary Cunnane, visited later, she received a very fine repast of leftovers of turkey, duck and spaghetti.

The Cardinal was impressed by the enthusiasm of the people and the 'simplicity' of the Bishop's house. After lunch, Pat escorted him to Asaba, where again a huge crowd had gathered. School boys from St Patrick's and girls from St Brigid's OLA Grammar School lined the route, musicians, dancers, welcoming committees, priests and politicians jostled for positions where they could see and be seen. After the welcome speeches and entertainments, Pat handed the Cardinal over to Archbishop Heerey, who led him to the river, where a brightly painted blue and red barge awaited to take him to Onitsha. An escort of seventeen large canoes, paddled by warriors in traditional garb flanked the barge; seven on one side were from Asaba, while ten on the other side were from Onitsha. Powerful singing, accompanied by drums, tambourines and elephant horns rose from the flotilla as it headed towards the eastern bank.

When it was all over, Pat had time to read a letter, which had just arrived from his brother Malachy in New York. Malachy wrote twice a year, as he was treasurer of the *African Missions Club* in the Bronx. Also known as "The Bishop Kelly Club" founded by Paddy Larkin and other Galway friends and neighbours, they collected at least $30 every six months for Pat's projects in Africa. Along with the cheque which, on this occasion, was $36, Malachy sent some news: the New York Galway Group were flying home at the end of July '63 and hoped to meet Pat in Ireland, if he were home. They were also meeting Bishop Browne and attending the Galway Races! Malachy's son, Stephen, had qualified for Dunwoodie diocesan seminary and would be starting his studies in September. Another nephew, Pat Cunnane, had already joined the African Missions and was studying in Dromantine.

Interludes in Tristaun

Pat was home more often than usual in the Sixties. Home for the Patrician Year in 1961, he also managed a short holiday before each Session of the Vatican Council. In 1961, he was invited to attend the opening of the local hurling and football club's new pitch at Kiltormer and, as guest of honour, threw in the ball at its inaugural football tournament. His daily Masses in the family home were attended by many neighbours as well as the Kelly family which had increased by one – Carmel, born in June '59. As a small child, she had difficulties pronouncing 'Bishop' so she called him "the B". At first she had been named 'Philomena', but her parents changed the name when Pat told them that St Philomena had been taken off the calendar of saints and, following his suggestion, they re-named her 'Carmel'. Though only a toddler, she took over the job of opening the gate for him. Regularly at his Masses were the Quinns, Kellys, Larkins, Jennings, Hanrahans, Murphys, Hurneys, Clarkes, Dermodys and other neighbours. Sarah and Dotty Quinn were always there and Sarah, keeping an eye on the altar candles, would bring a new 65% beeswax one when necessary, carefully transporting it in her stocking. School children came on Saturdays as they had no school that day. The boys sat on the stairs and wondered how the Bishop always knew which one of them was talking during

Mass. Though he had his back to them, he could see their reflection in the glass of the large picture of the Sacred Heart which hung on the wall behind the altar. To serve at the Mass was an honour and no easy task, as it was all in Latin. Frank Jennings, a seminarian, had been Pat's main altar server in the Fifties. Later, Frank became a priest and worked in England. In the Sixties, it was the turn of the Curley brothers, Ollie and Frank. Problems arose when they were away helping their father on fair days, then 'subs' like Mike Cormican, and Frankie or Mike Shiel were called in. Following changes after the Vatican Council, the Bishop, with some reluctance, allowed girls approach the altar, arrange the flowers, read the lessons, and even serve Mass. Among them were Josephine and Maureen Murphy. Josephine became a missionary sister and went to Africa. Others were Annie and Breda of the "Wren Kellys" who lived next door. Being good at Latin, they taught the Bishop's nephew, Anthony, how to serve Mass and give the Latin responses. After him, his younger brothers, Pádraic and Seán, served. When the boys were so engaged, the headmaster allowed them to come half an hour late for school. Seán, the youngest, had the special task of running up to Larkins to fetch water for the Mass – the best water in the neighbourhood was to be found in Larkins' well. As the Bishop's holiday progressed, the congregation increased and, for his farewell Mass, as many as sixty or seventy people squeezed into the kitchen or stood by the door or the window.

Confirmations in Clontuskert with Bishop Ryan, Clonfert, John Kelly PP. Among the recipients is the Bishop's nephew, Seán Kelly, *second from right*.

On one of these home holidays, Pat took his young nephews to Clonmacnoise monastery on the feast of St Kieran. They left home early and, praying the rosary all the way, arrived before 11 a.m., the time at which Pat thought the devotions would begin, but they didn't begin 'till 4 p.m. Pat decided that the best way to occupy the youngsters was to continue saying rosaries. "We said rosaries all the way home too!" Pádraic recalled.

Ellen, Pat's sister-in-law, with whom he got on very well, served him his meals in the parlour. He relished her brown bread, boiled bacon, and apple tarts. Sometimes, when she was making tea, he'd check, as he was wont to do in Africa, "Have you boiled that water well well?" He always joined the family for the rosary and the angelus, but spent long periods praying on his own, going daily to Clontuskert for a Holy Hour, and attending as many Masses as he could there and at Aughrim or, occasionally, in Ballinasloe. He also said Mass at his sister Kathleen Cunnane's home in Pearse Park and at the Feeney's home in Ballygar and, for special occasions at other neighbours' or relatives' houses. Once a week, he used to send one of his nephews ahead of him to Fr Bruen, the parish priest in Aughrim, to ask if he would hear the Bishop's Confession.

~~~

In Rome, after the closure of the Council in December 1965, Pat made his way to see Sr Loretta Julie, the Mother General of the Sisters of Notre Dame. Mgr Mahony of Ilorin, who had three Notre Dame Sisters working in his Prefecture, had brought Pat to see her when she was on visitation in Ilorin the previous January. On that occasion Pat brought her to Benin in the hope that the SND might work there too. At the Generalate, he was well received by Sr Loretta but, even before a cup of tea could be brought, he asked her whether she had Sisters for Benin or not. She explained that she had requested the British Province to consider the matter and was awaiting their reply. Thanking her,

Pat asked to be allowed to pray for a while in the chapel. She showed him where it was and returned to her office. After some hours, she realized that he still hadn't emerged. Beginning to worry a little, she decided to telephone the British Provincial about his request. "Yes", was the reply, "we will send some Sisters to Benin". She hurried to tell the Bishop. Delighted with the news, he rose and made to depart, refusing her second offer of refreshments, "Thank you, Mother, but I must get to the Airport, I'm on my way back to Benin!

Indigenisation and Warri diocese

Before Bishop Kelly's time, only two Nigerians had been ordained to the priesthood in Western Nigeria, Paul Emecete by Bishop Broderick in 1920 and Joseph Erameh by Bishop Taylor in 1936. During Pat's reign the numbers greatly increased. Among the early ones were: Anselm Ojefua and Stephen Umurie (the first Urhobo priest), both ordained in 1942; following them: Augustine Emordi 1949; Patrick Ugboko 1951; Bernard Elaho (the first Bini priest) 1954; Christopher Chukwumah 1957; Peter Onogwe, Anthony Gbuji and Lucas Nwaezeapu 1958; Vincent Obudu 1959. In 1960 Stephen Ogbeide was ordained and from then on the pace accelerated – twenty-nine being ordained in the Sixties. In December 1970, Pat ordained John Umunnah, Michael Guobadia and Theophilus Uwaifo. These were the last he ordained for Benin City diocese. The following year his coadjutor, Bishop Ekpu, became the ordaining prelate. Some of the above priests, though Pat's students, were not ordained by him, for example Bernard Elaho who was ordained by the Nuncio in Lagos during the Marian Year celebrations, and Anthony Gbuji who was ordained in Rome. By 1973, when Pat retired, there were no less than *forty-seven* indigenous priests in what had been his jurisdiction.

In September 1960, Bishop Kelly formally requested Propaganda Fide to establish Warri as a separate diocese. Warri, where he had disembarked in 1921, held fond memories for Pat, especially of

Eku, his first mission. Later he worked in Sapele and in Warri itself. Over the years, mutual respect and affection had grown between him and the Urhobos, the major tribe in this ethnically mixed area. Even when he was quite a distance from them in Benin City, many came annually to 'make their Easter duties' to him.

After becoming bishop, he felt that Warri district was neglected by the Society and he would have done more for it if he had more personnel. In particular, he had wanted to establish a Catholic Secondary school in the Delta, as the youth had nowhere to go except to the "pagan" Government schools or "heretical" Protestant ones, "If the Holy Ghost congregation or the Kiltegan Fathers had Delta Province, there would have been a Catholic secondary school there long ago", he grumbled to the Provincial in 1949. That year the Superior General, Stephen Harrington, advised him to start thinking about dividing the Vicariate, suggesting an East-West line south of Agenebode, making a Northern and Southern Vicariate. But, Harrington admitted, the division might not be effected for many years. Despite Pat's charge of Society 'neglect', the Catholic population of Warri had increased from a few hundred in 1921 to over 43,000 in 1959, with another 23,000 catechumens awaiting baptism.

The booming oil industry of the Niger delta in the Sixties attracted thousands of immigrant workers and provided much revenue for development in Nigeria. Warri, one of the main towns of the area, was thirty miles from the sea and sixty from Benin City. The boundaries of the new diocese would correspond to the civil boundaries of Delta Province. Its population was about 630,000. Emphasising that the chief means of conversion were the schools, Pat said that the only place in the district where church progress was slow was in the Ijaw territory where state schools predominated.

Already parts of his territory had been separated in the making of new jurisdictions: Ondo-Ilorin Vicariate, erected in 1943, had taken parts of the north and west, and the Prefecture of Lokoja, erected in 1955, had taken much of the north eastern part. Ondo-Ilorin remained in Irish SMA 'hands', while Lokoja had been taken over by Canadian Holy Ghost Fathers. But, the day of indigenisation in Nigeria had dawned and Propaganda Fide wanted a Nigerian bishop for Warri. In 1963, nine Nigerian priests worked in Warri district along with fifteen European missionaries, but only two or three of the Nigerians were actually from the area; a few more Delta priests worked elsewhere.

Finding the task of proposing to Rome the right man for the episcopal office very difficult, Pat was not at all at ease in writing his *terna* (the names of three men he thought suitable). Following its formal way of doing things, Propaganda Fide consulted others about the appointment and paid special attention to the advice of the Apostolic Delegate. The diocese was officially erected on 10 March 1964 and **Lucas Olu Nwaezeapu** was nominated as its first Nigerian Bishop. From Ibusa in Western Iboland, he was thirty-eight years of age, six years in the priesthood, quiet, unassuming, a good preacher, and modest in speech and manner.

Lucas, born in 1925, had four sisters but no brothers. Being the only son, his parents and relatives wanted him to become a traditional (pagan) priest. But, after receiving his primary education at the local Catholic primary school, he requested and received baptism. Becoming a primary school teacher, after one year he entered Thomas Aquinas Teacher Training College, Ibusa, where a warm friendship developed between him and the Principal, Johnny Lyons. On completion of training, he was posted to the Delta. Feeling called to the Catholic priesthood, he postponed doing anything about it until after his father's death in 1947, then he entered the Seminary in Benin. Neighbours performed a 'mock burial' and sympathised with his mother on the loss of her son. In an effort to get him back, she went to see Bishop Kelly but, on speaking at length to "the strange man", she found that she got nowhere. Lucas was ordained priest on 2 February 1958. One of the first to receive Communion from him at his ordination Mass was his mother who, in the meantime, had become a Catholic.

As a priest, Lucas had been a curate in Ashaka, a member of staff in the Minor Seminary, and Principal of Ubiaja Teacher Training College. Taking *"Infirma mundi elegit Deus"* (God chose the weak of the World) as his episcopal motto, he was consecrated by Archbishop Pignedoli, on 24 May 1964 in Warri. A congregation of three thousand gathered in the large, but unfinished, cathedral of the Sacred Heart. Sadly, one who was not present was Johnny Lyons. A bare three weeks had elapsed since his fatal car accident. Presiding at the consecration, Pat was pleased that everything went so well. Determined to help the new Bishop in what ever way he could, he hoped that he wouldn't lose too many of his own priests, already a number of Urhobo priests in Benin had informed him that they wished to transfer to their own diocese and the Apostolic Delegate had recommended that Lucas be given a good Vicar General. The new Bishop requested Con O'Driscoll to be his Vicar and, after some persuasion, Con accepted.

Bishop Lucas, Ab Pignedoli, Bp Kelly

1965, Episcopal Silver Jubilee

On 2 June 1965, with Solemn High Mass in Holy Cross cathedral, Bishop Kelly celebrated the Silver Jubilee of his episcopal consecration. The Apostolic Delegate, Archbishop Belotti, some bishops, Sisters, civilian VIPs, a multitude of the faithful and practically all the priests of the diocese attended. Joe Donnelly preached and, after the Mass, a Jubilee dinner was held in Pat's honour. To present him with a fitting gift, every mission and college in the Region had been levied with a sum ranging from £25 to £100. On the day of the Jubilee, John Mahon the Vicar General, proudly presented him with the key of a new Peugeot 404. The Peugeot became Pat's favourite kind of car.

The Jubilee was a gala day but, as with his consecration in 1940, he felt uncomfortable to be at the centre of attention and was glad when it was all over. Before the celebration, he had received the good wishes and a gift of money from the Provincial. Thanking him Pat said, "The amount was far more than I expected, in fact I wasn't thinking of anything at all". Continuing, he more or less tried out the gist of his Jubilee speech on the Provincial, "I have to thank God and his Blessed Mother for having given me twenty-five years in the episcopacy and I hope He will pardon all my offences and make up for my mistakes. The priests were all very kind and good and obedient and I kept the advice I got from the old Parish Priest of Aughrim long ago, 'never suspend anyone'."

Bishop Nwaezeapu gave a delightful speech at the reception. Following him, John Mahon spoke movingly of Pat's twenty-five years as Bishop. Though a tough man by any standards, John became choked with emotion during the speech and had to stop. Many more spoke, all wanting to praise and thank the Bishop, which only served to make him more uncomfortable. Though endowed with ample wit *tête-à-tête*, he was not an accomplished after-dinner speaker. On occasions such as this, he unwittingly failed to give credit to his co-workers, by over-labouring his own weaknesses, and by attributing to God all the good done.

However his hearers were not offended, they knew "Pajo" only too well, and didn't expect praise from him; on the contrary, it was almost a mark of missionary maturity to be worthy of rousing his ire. The more severe the scolding one got from him the better, as it ensured the recipient a place in the growing annals of Kelly lore. Concluding his speech, Pat thanked everyone for their prayers, gifts, and for coming to the celebration, especially the priests who had travelled long distances but, as one confrere remarked, he would probably have been far happier if it had been all his old *catechists* who could have attended.

The 1940 class, ordained by Pat, celebrated their Silver Jubilee, on 22 December '65. Most of the seven who were appointed to Western Nigeria, celebrated their jubilees in Holy Cross cathedral with Pat presiding and Fr Anselm Ojefua, at the Bishop's request, preaching. Joe Donnelly was one of them. From Roscommon, he had arrived in the mission in 1945. By then he had a BA from Galway University and a BSc from Cork. Pat first appointed him to help Tom Bartley in Holy Cross parish and teach in Immaculate Conception College. When "ICC" moved from the Bishop's compound to the other side of town, Joe supervised the building work and eventually became the Principal. He also taught in St Patrick's, Asaba, and in Aghalokpe College where he was Vice Principal. As Bishop's secretary in 1952, he asked Pat, "How is it that men are always content to go where you send them?" Pat replied, "I talk to them first, find out where they want to go and then I send them there".

Another of the seven, Ben Nolan, having overcome the health problems he had while Education Supervisor, had returned to the mission and, among other works, opened St Joseph's College, Otua, in 1959. Another educationalist, Joe Stephens, secretary to the Bishop in 1946, had opened St Malachy's college, Sapele, in 1959 and, after the erection of Warri diocese, became a member of the personnel there. Maurice Maguire was the rector of St Paul's Minor Seminary. Michael McFadden was working in Ibadan where he had been transferred in 1953, and Andy O'Rourke, in poor health, was on the point of retiring from his post on the staff of Dromantine College. Jim Byrne, having completed his appointment in Clough, was preparing to take up a new appointment in Liberia.

Continuing the school apostolate

When requesting a place for Fr Andrew Nwesi in Cork University in 1963, Pat revealed his fears about the future of mission schools, "If we are to have any hold on our Grammar Schools in the future, it is necessary that as many of our African priests as possible obtain a University degree". Meanwhile, he did not reduce pressure to establish new schools; his perseverance proved efficacious. Between 1960 and 1970, no less than twenty-four new Catholic Grammar Schools were founded, bringing the total number to forty-one. Frs Anselm Ojefua and Bernard Elaho were founders and first Principals of two of them, Mater Dei, Ashaka, 1960 and St Martin de Porres, Onicha-Olona, 1966. Two lay men, Michael Ojo and Joseph Ebhore, were the founding Principals of St Peter's, Agenebode, 1961, and St Dominic's, Iruekpen, 1970. Four Irish lay women, Mary Kelly, Martha Scannell, Mrs P. Enright, Kay O'Callaghan, and one Scot, J. McKay, were the founding Principals of five schools for girls. Srs Teresa Nolan OLA and Annette Sullivan SND opened two more. The remaining thirteen schools were opened by SMA Fathers. Though the numbers of Nigerian graduates were increasing, expatriate teachers were still needed. In 1965, Pat requested the Vice Provincial to find ten more male and four female teachers, four of the men should have science degrees and one or two of the ladies. They were to come as soon as possible by *plane* "as it is now cheaper than the boat".

New congregations of Sisters

When in Ireland in 1965, Pat had requested the **Irish Sisters of Charity** to take over a school for girls in Benin. Since 1961, the Charity Sisters had been running Archbishop Taylor's school for visually impaired children in Lagos and, by 1965, had become interested in starting a second school elsewhere. Sr Carmel McAteer, principal of the school in Lagos, was delegated by the Mother General to visit Bishop Kelly in Benin. Keen to make a good impression, she put on her new white dress, her best white shoes and carried her new white handbag. On entering Pat's mud walled palace "so unpretentious and simple", she realized she might have made a mistake. In the presence of the quiet man in his simple cassock, she felt 'overdressed'. But he put her at ease immediately. "He was gentle and kind", she said. While Pat may have appeared shy before women, he never failed to make an excellent impression on most of them! However Carmel had bad news! Just before she set off for Benin, she had received a telegram from the Mother General, which said briefly, "School unacceptable". The congregation just did not have Sisters to spare. She decided to travel to Benin anyway, if only to say "Sorry". After introducing herself to Pat, and trying to make her bad news sound less disagreeable, she tailed off with, "Now, if it were a *hospital*, we might have some Sisters". Pat, grasping the opportunity, interrupted, "But that's just what I want" and began to outline the medical needs and possibilities. Nurse Maureen O'Sullivan had finished renovating St Camillus' Hospital in Uromi and had returned to Kerry. The Bishop desperately needed new personnel to run the hospital. As Sr Carmel remained silent, the Bishop's enthusiastic flow of words dried up and, looking out the window for inspiration, he saw Nurse Marie Delpierre parking her car. Thanking Heaven, he asked her to take Carmel to Uromi. After being shown around the hospital, Carmel wrote a favourable report and, before long, a positive response came back.

From the beginning, relations between the Charity Sisters and the

Bishop were so good that they wanted to do more for him. In 1967, Our Lady of Lourdes Grammar School, Uromi, run by the OLA Sisters, faced a crisis when, due to the outbreak of Civil War, the expatriate teachers departed. The OLA, already overburdened, could not continue on their own. Pat asked the Charity Sisters to help and they agreed. Pat got Mick McGlinchey, by now one of the noted builders in the diocese, to build a convent for them and they moved in as soon as it was ready. The school, popularly known as Uromi Girls Grammar School, re-opened under the Charity Sisters in January 1968. The Bishop came to open it and said Mass in the library. The school girls sang the *Missa de Angelis* which was his favourite piece of Gregorian chant. Whenever he came subsequently they sang it. It became so popular in the neighbourhood that townspeople could be heard singing, or whistling, choice pieces from it as they went about their business.

Among the pioneer Sisters in the Hospital and School were Srs Margaret Cecilia (Superior), Mary Raphael (School Principal), Muriel Larkin and Nuala O'Brien. Sr Raphael in 1967 had been on leave in Ireland from her mission in Zambia when she was

Staff of Our Lady of Lourdes College, Uromi, 1968.
Srs Mary Gabriel, Margaret Cecelia, Mr Okuduwa *(back on right)*.

288

suddenly asked to transfer to Nigeria. She and Margaret on their visits to Bishop Kelly in Benin always found him a wise and understanding guide, a good listener, one who understood and was able to lighten their anxieties and burdens. The Sisters, especially those in the school, had arrived in Nigeria when the country was in the throes of the most difficult period in its modern history – the Civil War. Above all, the Bishop impressed them as a man who was "in touch with God".

When the Charity Sisters 'went International', they dropped the word 'Irish' from their title, and became the Religious Sisters of Charity, RSC.

Sisters of Notre Dame

Mentioned already were Pat's encounters in Nigeria and in Rome with Sr Loretta Julie, the Superior General of the Sisters of Notre Dame. After Pat drove her to Benin from Ilorin, she said to some of her Sisters, "I had been told that the Bishop was a very holy man and the nearer he got to God, the faster he drove. Well, he must have been very close to God on our journey to Benin". Nevertheless, she was favourably impressed by him and his diocese and promised to send Sisters. Mick McGlinchey, at Pat's request, began building a convent in Uzairue. Pat wanted it big enough to accommodate at least six Sisters, as the Congregation was going to start a hospital and take over St Angela's Girls Grammar School which, up to then, had been run by a lay

Two SND Sisters
with Mick McGlinchey

woman, Mrs Enright. The convent was just finished when the first SND Sister, Margaret Howse, arrived in August 1966. Despite teething problems, the school term began. While teaching one morning Sr Margaret, noticed a car passing outside. She told one of the pupils to see who it was and, if the visitor was important, to call her. The young girl went to the parlour and told the visitor, "If you're important, Sister says she will come, if you're not, you'll have to wait". Pat said, "I'm the bishop"; someone else added, "He's important".

Sr Mary Dolores, from the SND Convent in Oro, Ilorin, helped in the school at the beginning and, in December '66, Sr Marie Nugent, arrived from South Africa. In January '67, another Sister, Bernadette Gannon, arrived from Zimbabwe. Bernadette's task in Uzairue was the founding of a maternity hospital. Building work began under the supervision of Mr Rondi an Italian, with finance provided by the British Province of the SND who pledged to double whatever the Bishop would give. Pat laid the foundation stone in the presence of many local people including the Moslem ruler. In fact it was His Higness the Ogieneni of Uzairue who had been the first to request him to provide Reverend Sisters for a school and a hospital. The stone-laying ceremony took place during the month of Ramadan. The VIP Moslems present, though fasting, took their places at table, but abstained from eating, while the Bishop ("like a cat with cream", said Mick McGlinchey), and the rest indulged themselves. McGlinchey, sitting next to the Moslem Otaru of Auchi, teased him, "Are you not tempted to taste something?" "No", said Otaru, "we are showing Bishop that we are strong in our religion". With a chuckle, he confided, "Sister will give us our own in the evening". In this hospital venture there was great cooperation between Catholics and Moslems. The latter also contributed to the cost of the building.

Later, Pat had a personal reason for appreciating the hospital. After developing nasty boils on his lower regions during a

Confirmation tour, he called at the hospital looking for Sister Gannon. Sensitive to his modesty, she gave him a tin of Johnson's Baby Powder and instructed him to apply the powder at home. His secretary, on discovering the baby powder in the palace bathroom, subjected him to an unholy teasing. For once, Pat was caught for words, only managing a feeble, "I am obeying the Reverend Sister".

The rapport between the Sisters and Bishop was well summed up by Margaret Howse when she described him as, "A very holy man, always courteous, kind and available, ever ready with a cup of tea. He gave a great deal of joy to many people in Benin and he was always easy to talk to".

~ ~ ~

Benin City: Bishop Kelly with the Oba of Benin, Akenzua II, Apostolic Delegate Ab Belotti, and OLA Sisters: Regis Harris, Arcade Harding, Norbert O'Keeffe, Veronica O'Keeffe, Fidelma Caffrey.

In June 1966, Dr Creaven, informing Pat of the appointment to Benin of three new confreres, John Quinlan, Sexton Cahill and Brian O'Kane, once more stated his disapproval of over-investment in education and advised him to transfer men from colleges to pastoral positions as soon as possible, "It is dangerous to leave a Father too long in college life, especially if he has no taste for it. He should spend the whole of his first tour in a parish". The Provincial felt that if this practice had been adopted earlier it might have prevented some casualties in the ranks, such as departures from the mission and from the priesthood. Aware of growing internecine strife in Nigeria, he concluded his letter on an anxious note, "I hope there is peace in your area, elsewhere the situation is very disturbing".

Chapter 14

THE CIVIL WAR YEARS

1967 - 1970

On 16 January 1966, Bishop Kelly and confreres had just finished their annual retreat at Annunciation College, Irrua, when they heard startling news: The previous day the Government had been overthrown by a military coup, Prime Minister Sir Abubakar Tafawa Balewa had been kidnapped; the Northern Premier, Sir Ahmadu Bello and the Western Premier, Chief Samuel Akintola had been assassinated and six senior army officers were among those killed.

The body of the Prime Minister, a northerner, was later found riddled with bullets. Bello, as well as being Northern Premier was an important Moslem religious leader; the six officers were all northerners. The leaders of the coup claimed they wished to liberate Nigeria from tribalistic policies but the majority of the victims were northern Hausas and their Yoruba allies, while the majority of the assassins were eastern Ibos. Major General Aguiyi Ironsi, an Ibo, who had not been involved in the coup, became head of the new Military Government. Ibo military Governors were appointed in the Federal Regions; Lieutenant Colonel Ojukwu in the Eastern Region.

Since Independance, the country had been beset with political and economic problems, civil unrest, strikes and ethnic tensions. People of the Islamic north, never really in harmony with southerners or easterners, were becoming extremely agitated at the thought of domination by Ibos; tension between indigenous northerners and Ibos living in the north rose to dangerous levels. Religious affiliation also divided them; the Hausas were Moslem while the Ibos were Christian. After the January coup, the north seethed with resentment against Ibos, but this did not erupt into violence until after the 23rd of May when Ironsi dissolved the Federation and announced other measures, seemingly inimical to northern autonomy, such as the banning of political parties and the unification of the Civil Service. Trouble began with student demonstrations in Zaria and Kano, which spread to all the big towns. Mobs ran riot, destroying Ibo property and slaying hundreds. Ibos began to flee back to Eastern Nigeria in great numbers.

In July '66, Bishop Kelly, on a confirmation tour in an outstation of the large parish of Ubiaja, noted with satisfaction the large number of candidates the parish had for examination – over 1,200. He didn't tell the parish priest, Bill Kennedy, or his curate Sexton Doran, but he was very pleased. Though suffering from dysentery, he began the exhausting task of examining so many candidates. A nursing Sister, seeing how poorly he was, gave him some medicine and a new blanket; Ubiaja, on the Ishan plateau, was a lot cooler at night than Benin. Over supper, when Sexton asked him how he was feeling, Pat said, "Well, I got a new blanket out of it!" After a few days in the outstation, an urgent message for the Bishop arrived from Benin City – "Return immediately, General Ironsi is coming". Ironsi, a Catholic, was making his first official visit to the city and 'the top man in the Church in Benin' would be expected to lead a prayer of welcome. "I'd better go", said Pat, "otherwise the Anglican bishop will do it". Next morning he drove the eighty miles back to Benin, prayed, welcomed the General and returned to the outstation that evening.

When the confirmation ceremony was over, the Bishop and Sexton returned to Ubiaja mission. There they were told that another military coup had taken place! General Ironsi had been assassinated in Ibadan together with the Western Governor, Lieutenant Colonel Fajuyi, with whom he had been staying. In Ibadan and elsewhere many Ibo army officers and men had been killed by fellow soldiers.

This coup, called the "Second Military Coup", aimed at removing the Ibo officers, who had gained power in the January coup. The July coup brought to power Lieutenant Colonel Yakubu Gowon, a northern officer of a minority tribe and an Anglican.   A reasonable man with a charming personality, he revived the Federation and raised hopes that good governance might prevail. He sought peace, but chances of achieving it just then were remote.   Acts of violence against Ibos continued, including a particularly nasty act of vengeance which took place in Benin City in August when northern troops lynched detainees of the January coup.   The Eastern Government estimated that forty-three officers and 170 men had been put to death.   In September, violence in the North against Ibo civilians broke out on an unprecedented scale.   Thousands were killed and hundreds of thousands fled to the East. In the Eastern Region more and more voices were encouraging Colonel Ojukwu to secede from the Federation.

Archbishop John McCarthy of Kaduna was the senior SMA Ordinary in northern Nigeria. A missionary there since 1929, he was appreciated for his good work and sound judgement. He knew Colonel Ojukwu, an Ibo Catholic, who had been commanding officer of the army in Kano.   With continuing violence in the north, it seemed likely that Ojukwu would lead the Eastern Region into secession.   Aghast at the thought, a number of high-ranking military men approached McCarthy with the request that he try to turn Ojukwu from this path which, they said, would lead to a terrible civil war. Though approving of peace initiatives, the archbishop felt that he was not the one to parley with the Colonel. Instead he asked two of his personnel,

Frs Liam Burke and David Hughes, to go, instructing them to seek Bishop Kelly's advice as they passed through Benin. Benin diocese lay between Western and Eastern Nigeria and was connected to the East by the new Niger Bridge, opened in 1965, which spanned the river between Asaba and Onitsha.

The emissaries found Pat at Ekpoma. After hearing their story, he encouraged them saying, "It would be a great blessing from God if they could do anything to avert war". Next morning they drove to the mile-long bridge where, to their surprise, they found no police or military checkpoints. More disconcerting was the fact that the place was deserted and they were the only ones preparing to cross. They drove slowly, hoping their white cassocks were more visible than their car's northern registration plate. Reaching the other side without mishap, they continued to Enugu, where the Governor resided. Lodging at the Government Rest House, the two men sought an interview with Colonel Ojukwu. One of his close aides spoke with them and passed on their message. The Governor, however, was not be swayed from his planned course of action. Assuring the missionaries of a safe passage back to Asaba, the aide urged them not to delay.

Ibos inhabiting the west bank of the Niger and farther west, as far as Agbor (half way between Asaba and Benin City), were called "Western Ibos". Like their eastern cousins, they were an ambitious, entrepreneurial people. Most of the Ibos were Christian and they composed the vast majority of the Catholic members in the parishes of Benin and Warri. In 1963 Western Nigeria region had been divided into "Western" and "Mid-West", Benin and Warri lay in the latter. In 1967, twelve states were created, one of them was the "Mid-West State". As yet there had been no violence against Ibos in the Mid-West, but the Provincial Superior in Cork, wrote to Bishop Kelly in August '66, recommending that he visit his missionaries in case any of them needed reassuring. Though aware of tension, Pat continued with his normal pastoral schedule.

Following the September massacres in the North, Catholic bishops, and non-Catholic church leaders of the Eastern Region, met in Benin City on 7 October 1966 to discuss how best they could help the Ibo refugees. In December, the Catholic bishops of Nigeria issued a joint pastoral letter calling for prayers, peace and unity. The ecumenical group of church leaders met again in Benin in March '67. From it a delegation, led by Archbishop Aggey of Lagos, went to General Gowon to plead with him to persevere with efforts to maintain peace and to avoid the use of force. However, by New Year 1967 it had become increasingly clear that the country was heading towards war. A final effort to pull back from the brink was made in January when the Nigerian leaders met at Aburi, Ghana, but it was not successful.

On 30 May 1967 Colonel Ojukwu declared the independence of Eastern Nigeria, calling it the "Republic of Biafra". The Military Government in Lagos, unwilling to countenance dismemberment of the Federation, or to allow an oil-rich, and probably hostile, independent state to exist on its borders, blockaded the ports of the East and closed the Niger Bridge.

6 July, the Federal army invaded northern Biafra; heavy fighting took place at Nsukka. The 'Nigerians', expecting to crush the rebels in a matter of days, were surprised at the determined resistance they encountered and, as fighting dragged on, both sides claimed victories. Biafra's airforce, consisting of a few helicopters, an antiquated B-26 and, later, a B-25, mainly piloted by a Czech mercenary, 'Kamikaze' Braun, dropped some bombs on Lagos and on other towns. A few people were killed, more were wounded, and buildings damaged. The loss of life and destruction of property was not great, but the psychological effect of attack from the air was considerable. Ironically, one of the Biafran planes crashed into the Czech Embassy in Lagos.

9 August, at dawn, a long column of mammy wagons and assorted vehicles, carrying about 1000 Biafran soldiers led by Brigadier Victor Banjo in a Peugeot 404 crossed the Niger Bridge and took control of Asaba without a shot being fired against them. Ojukwu, hoping Banjo, a Yoruba man, would attract the support of Yorubas and other tribes, had appointed him army commander only the previous day. At Asaba the invaders were hailed as conquering heroes and liberators.

11 August, the Federal Government declared all-out war on Biafra, closed colleges and schools and imposed a dusk to dawn curfew. The same day, the evacuation of lay expatriates began. On the eve of the 'expats' departure from Benin City, an Irish couple, who wished to be married by Bishop Kelly before they left, arrived at his house. Pat's secretary, Sexton Cahill (a nephew of the former Society Visitor of the same name), hurriedly completed the marriage dispensation papers for them and tried to hasten the Bishop through his preparations for Mass. Little time remained before the hour of curfew. Pat, as always, took an agonisingly long time before Mass "to form his intention according to the mind of the Church". But, once started, he kept going and, validly, if a little hurriedly, married the happy couple in the Minor Seminary church.

12 August, some 300 expatriate teachers, nurses, Peace Corps volunteers and others gathered at the port of Sapele where they took ship for Lagos and then for home and safety. With mixed feelings, the missionary Fathers and Sisters bade them farewell.

Having taken Asaba without resistance, the Biafrans continued their 'liberating' westward sweep. In the Mid-West towns, the majority of the army officers were pro-Biafra Ibos who, even if they wanted to resist, were ill-equipped to do so. The secessionists, apparently intent on sealing off the oil-rich delta area and establishing control over the whole Mid-West, established bases and divisional headquarters as they went, often in school compounds in towns like Ibusa, Ogwashi-Uku, Issele-Uku, and Agbor. At Agbor, where Western Ibo territory ended, the army split up – one division going south to Warri, another north to Auchi, while the main body continued towards Benin City, forty miles to the west.

Much to the chagrin of the Binis, Benin City was taken overnight. The Governor of the Mid-West, Lieutenant Colonel David Ejoor, an Urhobo Catholic was, like Victor Banjo, a Sandhurst-trained officer. A moderate in politics, Ejoor favoured peace and Nigerian unity. After a brief meeting with Banjo, he departed, and the Biafrans took control of the city.

At the time of the invasion, Bishop Kelly was away, somewhere to the west of his own diocese. Missionaries in Benin City at the time were: Jim Healy and Paddy Rooney in Holy Cross parish; Joe Donnelly and Peter Thompson in Immaculate Conception College; Tony Murphy, and two senior seminarians, Patrick Usenbor and Charles Imokhai, in the Minor Seminary; and Sexton Cahill in the Bishop's house. Among the OLA Sisters, who worked at the hospital and school near the cathedral were Cora Healy, Eugenius Colebert, Arcade Harding and Norbert O'Keeffe; outside the city, at Maria Goretti Grammar School, were Henrietta Power and Philippine Buckley.

By August 16, the Biafrans had penetrated the whole of the Mid-West. The following day they crossed the Ofusu river into Western State, heading in the direction of Lagos. Seventeen miles inside the state border at Ore, they were forced to stop. Here the Federal troops were massing and had destroyed two bridges to stop the Biafran advance. Fighting began and 'the battle of Ore', which lasted about two weeks, resulted in heavy casualties on both sides.

Bishop Kelly, trying to get back to Benin City, was held up by troop movements and many check-points on the roads. He got back to his house shortly before the 4th of September on which day he wrote to the Provincial, "Just a line to let you know that we are all well here – priests and Sisters alike. We are all able to carry out our missionary work without being disturbed. Biafra has taken over the Mid-West, though it is opposed by the Federalites, we hope they will come to some sort of a settlement soon. At present there is no contact between here and Lagos. We trust in the Sacred Heart and His Blessed Mother that a lasting peace will come soon and that we will all come safely through". This was the last letter from him that would get through to Cork for the next five months.

Reinforced with British light arms, ferret armoured cars and Russian jet planes, the Federal army began to gain the upper hand, forcing the Biafrans to retreat along the way they had come. The Biafran army was poorly equipped. When they dug in at Ore, it was reported that they had only one rifle between five men. The assistance that Colonel Ojukwu had hoped to receive from other African countries and foreign powers had not materialized. Following the Biafran army's retreat, mobs took to the streets killing Ibos and looting their property. The Biafrans made a stand at Benin City but were routed. After six weeks of occupation, the city was 're-liberated'. Ibos were hunted down and slaughtered. In some cases neighbours hid them or helped them to escape but hundreds died and corpses lay unburied for days.

Bishop Kelly, distraught, went out on the streets anointing the dying, until he was confronted by an angry soldier who asked him if the man he was tending was dead, clearly intending to kill him if the Bishop said he wasn't. Further on, Pat, stopping his car to anoint another man, was accosted by an angry soldier who threatened to shoot him if he helped the enemy. Some allege a soldier fired a shot over Pat's head. After such incidents, he told his priests to stay in their cars and to give absolution from the window. A macabre story circulated, that corpses anointed by Bishop Kelly, were being shot again, lest they rose from the dead. Greatly disturbed by the bloodshed, Pat went indoors and spent more and more time in prayer. But even in the house the ageing bishop was not left in peace. A group of Federal soldiers burst in and, when he attempted to use the telephone, one of them knocked it from his hand. John Mahon, who had returned from leave during the Biafran retreat, complained to the soldiers' commanding officer and received an apology.

On 30 August, Benin airport, less than a kilometre from the Bishop's house, was bombed by the Biafrans but the damage was slight. Sr Norbert heard five air raids one night, but no one seemed to know to which side the planes belonged. By now the bulk of the Biafran army had gone from the city, but snipers and guerrilla units remained. One evening after helping with confessions at the cathedral, the Bishop asked Peter Thompson to drive him home. On the way they were caught in cross-fire and were fortunate to escape with their lives.

The Bishop's house was surrounded by high grass. Fearing that soldiers or looters might lurk in it, Pat took out his well-worn cutlass and began to clear the surroundings. He slashed grass regularly, especially in Lent and Holy Week, saying "Jesus suffered, so must I". But in 1967 he was seventy-three years of age and the years were beginning to tell. Earlier in the year he had fallen at Uromi mission, hurting his hip so badly that he couldn't get out of bed the next morning and, for some time afterwards, he walked with the aid of a stick. This time he tripped on a hidden root, which caused him to fall heavily but, making light of it, he told his secretary, "I cracked my ribs, and the Sisters strapped me up".

One day, armed men burst into his house, shouting that if he didn't give them money they would kill him "like we killed the white man next door". Believing that the robbers had killed Tony Murphy, Pat thought they would kill him too. Never keeping much money in the house, he gave them what he had and they departed. Great was his relief when he discovered that Tony had not been harmed. Fearing other thieves might come and demand that he open the office safe, he telephoned Sexton Cahill, who was at the parish house in town, and asked him in Irish where the key was. Sexton, whose Irish was not as good as Pat's, returned to find out what was wrong. The day before, Sexton himself had been called down from the upper storey of the parish house by soldiers who suspected the mission was harbouring Ibos. On descending the steps, he was aware of the weapons levelled menacingly at him. After the house was checked, he was let go.

Asked to plead with the Oba (King) of Benin to intercede with the army to stop the killing of Ibos, Pat prayed, then asked Joe Donnelly to drive him to the royal palace. Oba Akenzua, one of the oldest and most respected of Nigerian leaders, though a non-Catholic, was on good terms with the Catholic church and most of his

The Bishop and Joe Donnelly

children had been educated in Catholic schools. On the way, Joe drove and Pat prayed. The Bishop was ill-at-ease. Conscious that he was bishop of the Bini people, he did not wish to appear biased in favour of the Ibos and perhaps jeopardize the Church's position in Benin in the future. As the car entered the roundabout near the Oba's palace he instructed Joe, "Go round again". They went around three times, before he finally told Joe, "Drive home". Joe later went himself to see Colonel Mohammed Murtala, who had replaced Banjo as army commander. Murtala heard him out but whether his plea to stop the killings had any effect is difficult to gauge.

Bishop Kelly's 'roundabout decision' may seem odd to an outsider but most of his missionaries would have endorsed it. They were acquainted with his surprising decisions and knew that none of them were made without serious prayer and reflection. His decisions, surprising or not, seemed to turn out right in the long run. Advised to send a message to the priests in the mission stations east of Benin City telling them to move with the people when the Federal army approached, Pat agreed but, after prayer, decided to tell them to remain where they were! As these stations were cut off, his message didn't get through. Most of the missionaries had decided to remain anyway.

One such place was **Agbor**, a small town with a large number of Ibo businessmen. It had two first rate grammar schools, Marymount for girls, and St Columba's for boys, which were usually packed to capacity with pupils. Both had many vacancies now as the Ibo pupils had fled. Mick Drew, the Education Secretary, resided at St Columba's. Seán ('Mitter') Flynn, the parish priest and Willie Cusack, his assistant, lived at the mission overlooking the town. John Dunleavy, who had opened a new parish at Igueben twenty-five miles to the north in Ishan country, where he was alone, joined the Agbor parish men after the Biafrans set up camp near him. Johnny Browne, the Regional, went to Igueben to visit Dunleavy, not knowing he had already departed. There he was arrested by the soldiers who accused him of being a spy for 'the Nigerians'. He was forced to drive some of them to Agbor where, fortunately, he was able to prove his identity. In Agbor, he was in a Biafran enclave and wasn't allowed to leave, so he stayed for two weeks with Mick Drew at St Columba's. Shortly after Johnny's arrival in Agbor, soldiers apprehended Eugene Casey in the Bini bush and, accusing him of being a 'mercenary', brought him to the Agbor parish house. The words 'mercenary' and 'missionary' were often confused and soldiers of both armies were keen to lay hands on anyone who might be in the pay of the other's army.

For two weeks Agbor, on the fringe of Western Iboland, was cut off, while the Federal troops gathered strength a few miles to the west. On 1 October the army moved closer and bombarded the town. The Biafrans retreated, blowing up bridges as they went, leaving the town cut off, at least to motor traffic, on the eastern side. After the withdrawal, in contrast to what had happened in towns to the west, no killing of Ibos took place, as if the Nigerians accepted that the Ibos had a right to be in these parts.

Before the attack on Agbor, a number of confreres, mainly school Principals of Benin and Warri, gathered at Joe Donnelly's house at Immaculate Conception College to discuss school matters. The Bishop was not present. All of them, young and old were badly shaken at the bloodshed and wondered if they could do anything to stop it. They decided to send a message to the Apostolic Delegate, or to the Irish Ambassador, in the hope that they might be able to do something. However, before any message was sent, Johnny Browne and Willie Cusack arrived from Agbor with news that the town had been re-taken and that there had been no killing of Ibos.

Likewise in towns east of Agbor no massacres had taken place, until the Federal army reached Asaba. Here the Biafrans put up a fierce last-ditch fight, but were forced to retreat, blowing up the

Niger Bridge as they went. The Federals entered the town 'red-eyed' and began rounding up prisoners. While thus engaged, one of their officers was shot dead. In fury the soldiers lined up about 800 men and boys and machine-gunned them to death. Killing continued in and round Asaba for days, as if the army were intent on punishing the Asabans for their pro-Biafran stance and for allowing the Biafran army through in the first place.

Something of the background and tension of the Civil War in the Mid-West, from the missionary point of view, is perhaps best illustrated by a few incidents. Not involving Bishop Kelly in person, the incidents are ones in which his personnel came into close contact with the combatants or the fighting:

Ogwashi-Uku
Dick Wall, parish priest, and his assistant Brian O'Kane, in their mission station in Biafran-occupied Ogwashi-Uku, were becoming more and more apprehensive as the fortunes of the Biafran army fell. On Saturday night 19 September, Brian, a first-tour man from Tyrone, just five months in the mission, woke abruptly to find a Biafran soldier in his room. The soldier, after searching through books and letters on Brian's desk, left without comment. Outside, heavily-armed soldiers surrounded the house.

The following day was All-Ireland football final Sunday, Meath were playing Cork. Radio Brazzaville carried the game to Africa, as it had done two weeks previously for the Hurling Final in which Kilkenny beat Tipperary by 3-8 to 2-7. Dick Wall, a keen hurler from Cork, tuned in but was disappointed to hear his native County beaten by Meath, 0-9 to 1-9. After the game Brian, putting on his cassock, went to the church to prepare for evening Benediction. Called out of the church, he thought someone wanted Confession. Outside, he was confronted by a soldier with a gun who ordered him to "Dance" while he sprayed the ground around his feet with bullets. Soldiers then put Brian in the back of an army truck, which drove off eastwards to Asaba. From Asaba the truck took him to Issele-Uku, from where, after a sleepless night, he was driven to the Biafran headquarters at Ika Grammar School, Agbor. After four hours of waiting, a senior officer, Colonel Ochei, in command of a company of soldiers in trucks, took Brian eastwards again in a London type taxi. At Ibusa they stopped and, while the Colonel was haranguing soldiers over a breach of discipline, Brian saw a green Volkswagen beetle approach. Recognizing it as Mick Harnedy's, he desperately flagged it down. In the car were Mick, from the Ibusa Teacher Training College, and John Quinlan. Parking in front of the 'London taxi', Mick was told by the Colonel that the prisoner was being taken to Asaba where he would be tried for collaborating with the enemy. The two confreres stayed with the convoy and, when they reached Asaba, accompanied Brian into the Government Rest House. There, an accusation that he was drawing maps for the Federal army was quickly dismissed for lack of evidence. After being lectured on keeping out of the war, the Fathers were told to go.

Back in the mission, Dick and Brian, cut off from the other missionaries, waited with growing anxiety for the Federal attack on the town. It began at 11 a.m. on the 3rd of October with the customary shelling by heavy artillery. Fearing their house would come down on top of them, Dick and Brian went outside and sheltered behind the pillars of the verandah. A shell exploded forty yards in front, making a deep crater in the football field. Believing their end was near, they gave one another absolution and moved back inside the house. After five hours of shelling, a deathly silence descended. Looking out, they saw Nigerian soldiers, the first they had seen in this war, going from house to house 'mopping up', but the townspeople had long fled and the Biafrans had retreated. The onslaught over, the Fathers realized that they hadn't eaten all day. Before they had a chance to touch anything, army trucks drove into the compound and all hell broke loose again. A company of Biafrans, unaware that the town

306

had been re-taken by the Federals, had driven right in to the mission compound. The newcomers took shelter behind the church; the Federals were on the other side of the compound. Caught in the cross-fire, Dick and Brian lay on the floor of the mission house. The battle raged for another few hours until darkness fell.

Talking in whispers and keeping away from the windows, the two Fathers finally broke their fast, and decided to risk dashing upstairs to bed. Unfortunately, the stairway was outside the house in full view of the combatants. Brian, the younger, after removing his white cassock, went first. On opening the door, a burst of gunfire drove him back. Five minutes later he tried again, with the same result. On the third attempt, taking the stairs three steps at a time, he made it to the top, closely followed by Dick.

Dawn found the battered town eerily quiet. Not a soul was about, no dog barked nor cock crew. The Fathers seemed to be the only ones left. The retreating Biafrans had blown up the bridge at Ibusa, cutting off Ogwashi-Uku. However, Mick Harnedy, using a small motor cycle and a canoe, managed to visit Dick and Brian.

The leper settlement in Ossiomo had about 1,200 residents before the war. Divided in two by the Ossiomo river, the Ibos lived on the east bank and Binis, Yorubas, and others on the west bank. When the Biafrans invaded in August, they swept through the Ibo side and, crossing the river to the west side, killed all the Binis and Yorubas they could find. Six weeks later the Federals came from the other direction, set up their artillery on the Bini side and shelled the Ibo side, after which they crossed the river and killed any Ibos remaining. Ned Coleman, the chaplain, whose house was on the east bank survived the bombardment and the attack but, suffering from severe shock, he had to be withdrawn from the settlement. Most of the residents fled and the place remained a shambles.

Tommy Greene, now in his mid-sixties, with thoughts of the hereafter in his head, and claiming he had always got appointments he liked, asked the Bishop to give him one he didn't like – Ossiomo – so that he could do penance for his sins before he died! The Bishop obliged and appointed him to replace Ned. His first task was to coax back the lepers, only about 150 remained in the camp. While numbers were slowly increasing, the Federal Army sent to the settlement twelve Hausa soldiers who had mild leprosy. They were troublesome, every now and then going on a rampage and molesting women. Tommy went to army headquarters in Benin and complained to a Hausa Lieutenant. The officer came and gave the soldiers a proper 'bawling-out'. Next morning when Tommy entered the sacristy to prepare for Mass, he found one of them inside, pointing a gun at him.

"You want something?" asked Tommy.

"Yes, I want to shoot you for bringing the Lieutenant".

"Let me say Mass first, you can shoot me afterwards. There's no hurry".

"No, I'm going to shoot you now", the soldier said, raising his rifle.

Just then, another soldier burst into the room and knocked the gunman to the ground.

Tommy went again to the army headquarters, complaining this time to the Commandant, a Yoruba man, who swiftly removed the offenders.

Ekpoma

John Mahon, the parish priest of Ekpoma, returned from leave in August '67, but was prevented from going to his station by the Biafran occupation. Sexton Doran was substituting for him in the parish. In early September, Mahon, hoping to get back, followed the Federal Army as it 're-liberated' the towns of the Mid-West. On 5 September the Federals took Agenebode on the Niger, then

Igarra and Auchi. On the 17th, they closed the road to Irrua and Ekpoma. On the 18th, shelling and rifle fire was heard in the vicinity of the mission. Sexton Doran's cook and catechist were the only ones with him in the house when the Federal soldiers approached but, believing the mission was harbouring Biafrans, the soldiers laid down heavy fire on it. Encountering no resistance, the soldiers eventually moved on. Sexton and staff, who had lain on the floor, had not been injured. When Mahon arrived, he was glad to see them alive and exclaimed, "Your uncle (Fr Sexton Cahill, the former Society Visitor) must have been praying for you".

Sexton should have gone on leave himself then but, lacking news of his sister, a Missionary Sister of the Assumption working in the war-torn Eastern Region, he preferred to remain. Hoping to gain another man, Bishop Kelly complained to the Provincial that "Fr Doran can't go home because there is no one to replace him". Sexton went the following year.

Bomadi

Dan Looney and Con Murphy in Bomadi, Warri diocese, lived near the Niger, which formed the border with Biafra. Near them was a Federal army camp from which soldiers constantly patrolled the river. Days and nights for the Fathers were often disturbed by the sound of battle. Sleeping fitfully, Con had a recurring dream that he was safe at home in Cork, only to be awakened by the sound of gunfire and explosions. One day two Federal soldiers came to borrow the mission boat. When the Fathers refused to give it, the soldiers ordered them to march to the river. Con and Dan obeyed, but feared they were going to be shot and their bodies thrown into the river. When they reached the river, one of the soldiers got down on one knee, rummaged in his kit bag and produced a bottle of beer for Dan and a Guinness for Con!

On another occasion, Con and Dan, driving to Warri on school business, were stopped by Biafran soldiers who accused them of being mercenaries and took them to their headquarters at Our Lady's High School, Efferun. After they were held for some hours, Con O'Driscoll, the Vicar General, arrived and negotiated their release with the Commanding officer. The Vicar General, refusing to allow Con Murphy to return to Bomadi, sent him to Dan Cashman at Aghalokpe College, where he remained for three months. During his stay there, a group of Biafrans arrived in a station wagon, commandeered the mission car and forced the two Fathers to accompany them 'as hostages' on a looting expedition. On completion of the exercise, the Fathers were brought back to the college where they, and their car, were released.

All the missionaries in the Mid-West suffered in one way or another during the war, whether in close encounters such as the ones described, or from the inescapable tension and privations that war and military occupation always impose. The Bishop, though concerned for his personnel and for his flock, did not go about reassuring or encouraging them. It was not his style. Neither did he call meetings to discuss what to do, or formulate an evacuation policy should things became critical. Maintaining a low profile, he left things to Providence and prayed that the war would end soon. At heart, a non-gregarious type of man, he didn't go about, even in peace time, socialising or joining in general camaraderie. He rarely travelled without a specific sacramental or educational purpose. His mode of operating was in keeping with contemporary western culture which promoted the principle that individuals should "do their duty and stick to their posts", and with the current missionary thinking which promoted self-sacrifice and put 'mission' before 'man'.

There were, however, other factors which inhibited Pat from playing a more dynamic role during the Biafran war: the suddenness of the Easterners invasion, coupled with the fact that he was out of Benin when it began. Subsequently, communications, tenuous enough at the best of times, broke down, telephones were non-existent in most places, and roads were particularly bad during the heavy rains of the war years. A number of mission stations were cut off and many of them remained difficult of access due to damaged roads and destroyed bridges. A personal factor, not to be forgotten, was that Pat was seventy-three years of age when the war began, one of the oldest of the confreres in the mission and one who, even in normal times, carried a heavy cross of indecisiveness and scrupulosity.

A few other church leaders did attempt a more out-going and supportive mode of leadership. The Anglican Archbishop of West Africa, for instance, Reverend Patterson, accompanied by Udoh Dek, President of the Red Cross, visited Asaba while the Federal Army was engaged in 'mopping up' operations. He was shocked at the carnage and wrote to General Gowon, "How you and your soldiers treat the people of Asaba and environs will prove to the whole world whether this war is against secession or genocide against the Ibos". His letter and visit, it seems, had some effect. Already aware of atrocities at Asaba, General Gowon changed the leadership of the Second Division of the army and issued a new code of conduct for the soldiers west of the Niger. Asaban Anglicans, who had lost many of their church members in the massacres, were grateful to the Archbishop for his visit and support, whereas the Catholics felt left down. Nevertheless, typical of the amazing loyalty that existed between Pat and his personnel, none of them complained of lack of support on his part. On the contrary, some felt that they should have been lending their youth and strength to help him, and many believed that it was his prayers that brought them safely through the war.

During the tense pre-war months, Dr Creaven visited Nigeria, January to April 1967 and, after the outbreak of hostilities, wrote reassuring letters to the families of confreres working in the 'war zones'. After his election in '68, the new Provincial, Larry Carr, visited and, in '68, Barth McCarthy, Provincial Councillor, went to Benin to see especially those men who had been, or still were, in difficult situations. He surprised at least one confrere, Brian

O'Kane, when he asked him if he would like to go home for Christmas. Brian and two others did go home for a break at that time (their tours were nearly completed anyway).

~ ~ ~

The retreating Biafran army crossed the Niger Bridge on 8 October '67, blowing up two spans on the Onitsha side. With the Federal army re-gaining the Mid-West, a semblance of normalcy began to return. Some of the more inaccessible areas were still occupied by groups of Biafran 'commandos' and renegade 'vandals', who continued to make raids on the hinterland. Occasionally, Asaba was shelled from the Onitsha side. Bitter fighting continued in Biafra, with thousands of federal soldiers from the north and west continually on the move to 'the Eastern front'. Early in December, Federal soldiers, crossing the Niger in canoes and small boats, made a frontal assault on Onitsha. Lured into thinking they had succeeded in driving out the Biafran army, they began to celebrate. Suddenly, the Biafrans fell on them, forcing them back into the river where many drowned or were mown down by rifle and machine gun fire. In this and in two further attempts to storm Onitsha, some 2,000 Federal soldiers lost their lives. Subsequently, the Nigerian army crossed the Niger further north at Agenebode.

Christmas '67 was a sad one for many in the Mid-West. Life had been disrupted, many were bereaved, many were wounded, and many feared for relatives in Biafra. No Christmas Midnight Masses were celebrated because of the curfew. On Christmas Day, Pat was surprised by the unexpected visit of Mgr Dominic Conway, rector of the Irish College in Rome, accompanied by the director of the Catholic relief agency, *Caritas*. Mgr Conway, who had already given several retreats to missionaries in Nigeria, had been sent by the Pope to visit the missions in the war zones. Caught off guard, Pat wasn't prepared for entertaining VIPs; he had only four or five cups in the house and the minimum of food in the larder. Peter Thompson, summoned in haste from ICC, had to go back to the college to forage for the wherewithal to entertain the Papal envoy. Meanwhile parish men and teachers, hearing of Mgr Conway's wish to see them, began to turn up at the 'palace'. Soon, even the ICC cups and saucers began to run out. When Sexton Cahill returned from a busy day helping with Christmas Masses, he found there was no cup left for him. Pat called him, "Father, go to my room and get the mug I keep my teeth in, you can use that".

That Christmas, Hugh Conlon, stationed at Asaba where he was ministering in the refugee centre located at St Patrick's College, was able to celebrate Mass for the soldiers in the town. A few weeks previously he had averted a massacre of Ibos in the college grounds by pleading with the officer in charge of the 'execution' squad. Emma Okocha, in *Blood on the Niger*, gave credit to Hugh for the brave intervention which saved his life. At the end of the year, Hugh went with Bishop Kelly to Agenebode for the ordination of Thomas Oleghe;

Johnny Browne and Hugh Conlon 1968

Hugh was given the privilege of preaching the homily.

1968: With most of the Federal 'mopping up' operations completed in the Mid-West, Bishop Kelly and the missionaries started getting back to their normal routines. A severe harmattan (a dust-laden wind from the Sahara), ushered in the New Year at Irrua where they had gathered for the annual retreat in Annunciation College. This time it was preached by Bob Molloy, the professor of dogmatic theology in Dromantine. After the retreat, Pat met with the priests to discuss diocesan business and, following their discussions, wrote to the Provincial on 19 January. This was the first letter that Dr Creaven received from him since September.

In correspondence Pat, like most of the missionaries, avoided speaking of the war but an occasional allusion to it can be perceived in a remark such as, "more Fathers will have to go home before the end of their tours". His letter of January '68, played down "the crisis", the term the Nigerians preferred to 'war', "Everything is practically back to normal here now", he wrote and continued, emphasising the great shortage of priests, at least eight confreres had departed and were not likely to return. Others on leave would not be able to return at the proper time. Though he had ordained many Nigerian priests, several of them were away, "four are studying overseas, another is at Ibadan University, one is missing since last September, and one has gone to join a religious Order" (Anselm Ojefua joined the Benedictine Fathers at Port Harcourt). "Several more Fathers are due home leave, but I have no one to replace them". In a postscript he added, "Another of my African priests is an army chaplain which leaves just *nine* to work in the diocese".

Bishop Lucas and Warri

On 3 March, there was a quiet farewell for Pat at Immaculate Conception College. The following day he left for Lagos, first to attend a Bishops' conference and then to take ship for home leave. Also attending the conference was Con O'Driscoll, the Vicar General of Warri. The bishops were most anxious that Bishop Lucas Nwaezeapu would return to his diocese, Warri, from which he had been absent since before the war. When the Biafrans invaded, Lucas was fund-raising in Germany, Ireland, and America. In Ireland he visited Dromantine and Wilton and made quite an impression on the students with his ready smile and friendliness. But, sadly, things had not worked out well in his diocese. While on good terms with the Ukwamis, Ijaws and

Itsekiris, he had not succeeded in endearing himself to some of the other ethnic groups, especially the Urhobos – the major tribe – whose language he did not speak. Tension, involving people, clergy and missionaries increased and was capped by the war which made it well nigh impossible for an Ibo to be the chief pastor of the area.

When the Biafran army was driven out of Warri, non-Ibos took advantage of the Federal presence to settle old scores. Massacres of Ibos took place in the big centres. Reports said that 5,000 had been killed in Warri and 6,000 in Sapele. At this time Lucas, not realizing the danger in the delta, had gone to Bouea in the Cameroons, in the hope of finding a way to Warri. At that time, the bishops instructed Con O'Driscoll to fly to Bouea to persuade him to remain there. Reluctantly, Lucas agreed and took up a teaching post in the local seminary. By the time of the Bishops' meeting in March '68, things had much improved and the Bishops now sent Con to bring Lucas back. He did return but, sadly, diocesan affairs did not settle down. In 1981, Rome appointed Bishop Edmund Fitzgibbon SPS as Apostolic Administrator of the diocese. Lucas departed from Warri and went to Eastern Nigeria, where he joined the staff of the Catholic Institute of West Africa, at Port Harcourt. He remained there until illness forced him to retire. Hospitalised in Issele-Uku, he died there in 1996. His body was brought to the Cathedral in Warri for burial.

Regarding Lucas's nomination and Bishop Kelly's part in it, the question has often been raised, especially *after* things began to go wrong, "How wise was it?" Lucas was an Ibo, and many indigenous people in Warri were, to put it mildly, not fond of Ibos. At the time of the nomination, Pat was far from being the only one who saw Lucas as a suitable candidate. It is easy to be wise with hindsight, but there were some who considered the nomination inappropriate even *before* things went wrong and thought it indicated a lack of awareness of ethnic tensions on the Bishop's part. Before the war, however, few expatriates appreciated the depth and the ferocity of the latent animosity towards Ibos.

Home leave 1968

After the bishops' meeting, Pat took ship for home. Again he spent most of his leave in Tristaun, taking part as usual in all the farm activities, just a little bit more gingerly than of yore. Now, post Vatican II, he celebrated Mass in the evenings, and instructed that the altar table would have to be pulled out from the wall, as he would stand behind it facing the people. The neighbours came for Mass as usual and, his reputation for holiness growing, many brought •candles, water, rosaries, prayer books and medals for him to bless. Mothers-to-be, childless couples, owners of new cars, and people with ailments of all sorts began coming in increasing numbers to seek his prayers and blessing. Some arranged their weddings so that he could be the celebrant.

Every time he was home he took the family to Our Lady's shrine at Knock, saying fifteen decades of the rosary on the way, another fifteen on the way back, and stopping for a visit at every wayside chapel en route. He 'did' Lough Derg again with his niece, Mary Teresa, and en route called on Benin missionaries who were "a little bit late" in returning to Nigeria. While the family loved having him at home, the young nephews were a bit irked by the lengthening of the family rosary, or the delayed start of an evening Mass, which kept them late for hurling practices at Kiltormer. And Ellen, his sister-in-law, on mornings when he tried to rouse the household early by rattling pots and pans in the kitchen, would remind him, "Its not a convent you know".

Towards the end of his leave, he attended the Provincial Assembly, which began in Cork on 18 July. Larry Carr, Secretary General *emeritus* of the Catholic bishops of Nigeria, was elected Provincial and Joe Donnelly, the delegate of the confreres of Benin, was elected Vice Provincial. At one of the

Assembly's sessions, Pat raised the question, "Has the SMA no ascetical aim?" and continued, "Formerly the first aim of a member of the Society was personal sanctification and the second, evangelization". The discussion that followed focused more on evangelization than on personal sanctification. At the Plenary Session on 10 August, he defended his emphasis on education:

> We Ordinaries always did what we thought best for the missions. If we had neglected education, we would have at present no standing in the country. If we have any standing, it is through those people who passed through our Secondary Schools and Teacher Training Colleges who now wield authority and are favourable to us. We do not admit we made a mistake here. Fifteen years ago I received a letter from Propaganda Fide requesting me to devote all my energies to schools as the most important field of evangelization.

After this, he left Cork to return to Nigeria.

~ ~ ~

Perhaps the confreres were right when they felt that Bishop Kelly's prayers got them safely through the war for, though some had narrow escapes, none lost their lives. While Pat was on leave, the only violent death among expatriate Church personnel occurred, that of **Brother Roman Wicinsky,** the Marianist Principal of St Patrick's, Asaba. The Brothers had left the College in October '67 because of the fighting, but returned, with Brother Roman as Principal, early in 1968. On 16 April, on his way to a meeting in Benin, he was stopped at Ogwashi-Uku by Biafran guerrillas who were raiding the town. Dragged from his car, he was taken behind the Post Office and, despite the protests of local people who pleaded for him, was shot as a mercenary. The

Marianists buried him at their Centre in Ekpoma; the Vicar General, John Mahon, said the Requiem Mass. The Brothers departed from the College until January '69. In the meantime the army billeted soldiers in the school buildings.

St Thomas Aquinas TTC, Ibusa, where Mick Harnedy had been Principal, was located near Asaba and it was also a dangerous place during the war. The Fathers' house had been burned down and several other buildings destroyed by rocket attacks. Forced to flee in '67, the staff and students transferred to Issele-Uku where the institution re-commenced as a Higher Elementary college with Fr Anthony Gbuji as Principal. The TTC campus at Ibusa became a refugee centre, and at times was catering for over 4,000 people.

~ ~ ~

OLA Sisters, Teresa Nolan and Lelia Dineen, remained at St Brigid's Grammar School, Asaba, during the Biafran occupation. On 7 October, when the Federal army mounted its final attack to drive the Biafrans out, fighting raged around the school. One of the convent primary school girls, while walking past St Brigid's was killed by a Biafran bomb. Sr Lelia, hoping the girl was still alive, braved cross-fire to bring her to hospital, but she was already dead. After the Biafran withdrawal, the Federal army ordered all whites to leave while they pacified the area but, anxious to give the impression that everything was getting back to normal, they requested Bishop Kelly to persuade the Sisters to return and keep the schools going. Teresa and Lelia returned, the only white women allowed to do so. An English lady, who ran the Anglican mission school, was refused entry. Teresa and Lelia looked after the remnant of her pupils, along with those of St. Patrick's College and their own. They set up school for all in an old church and mission house near their convent.

The OLA Superior General refused to allow the Sisters to reside in Asaba, so Teresa and Lelia took up residence in the OLA convent at Agbor, forty miles away, and commuted everyday over the war-damaged roads, passing through no less than twenty-eight check points between Agbor and Asaba. Negotiating check points could be a frightening experience, as some of the soldiers manning them were unruly and given to smoking hemp. Teresa recalled that most of the soldiers they encountered were huge men from Chad. Intimidating in size, they were also difficult to converse with as they didn't speak English. The Moslem soldiers, thinking the two European women were nurses, harassed them for medicine, especially for treating venereal complaints. The Sisters, coming from Agbor convent, where Sr Celestine ran a *maternity* clinic, didn't have access to appropriate medicine but, Celestine provided them with a quantity of *antenatal tablets* for "emergency use" at road blocks. The tablets did help the Sisters, but the men found them no use at all.

~ ~ ~

Pat didn't find it easy to pick up 'business as usual' after the war. Writing to the Provincial at the end of August '68, he again emphasised his need for priests, both pastoral and school men. Complaining that no graduates had been appointed to his diocese since Pat Byrne in 1965, he said many schools now had no priests and, in his opinion, schools without priests were no different from State schools. Since the war began he had not been sent any new men at all; the tyrocinium at Uromi was empty. In November, he went with Johnny Browne to Ibadan for the opening of the new Pastoral Institute, a project set up by the Lagos ecclesiastical province. Under the direction of Fr Dierks, a Dutch confrere, it proved a great success. After the opening, Pat and Johnny stayed on for the 'Study Week' at which SMA Fathers, Peter Brady and Peter Daffy, of the Major Seminary were among the lecturers.

1969: In January, Jackie Power, the new Vicar General of the Society, visited Benin and gave the annual retreat at Irrua. Known for his keen mind and sharp comments, Jackie was thought by some to be critical of the Bishop. But after the visit he wrote to Pat, "Thank you most sincerely for all the generosity I experienced from you during my stay in Benin. I have the happiest memories of that week and of the kindness of all the confreres". Jackie, erstwhile professor of Scripture at Dromantine and author of several books, never worked in Bishop Kelly's diocese. If any confreres were critical of Bishop Kelly or were considered to be so, invariably they were not from his diocese. By the Sixties an extraordinary affection for and loyalty to the Bishop had developed among his personnel. This did not mean they always agreed with him and they welcomed the setting up of a diocesan senate of priests in January '69. Fathers John Mahon, Mick Drew, John Thornton, Christopher Chukwumah, Willie Cusack, and John Osia were elected to it by the confreres and three more, Ben Nolan, Jack Casey, and Lawrence Balogun were appointed by the Bishop. The same month, he was notified by the Provincial that Mick Drew was confirmed as the new Regional Superior and Dick Wall as Vice Regional.

Bill Kennedy after returning from leave early in '69, stayed with the Bishop in Benin and waited to receive a new appointment. As time passed, he wondered why Pat didn't say anything about it, and asked:

"My Lord are you not going to give me an appointment?"

"Well, Fr Browne must come out of Asaba". (Johnny, having no Tyros during the war, spent quite a lot of time doing 'supply' in Asaba.)

"So you're going to appoint me to Asaba?"

"No. I can't appoint you to Asaba. The Provincial says nobody can be appointed to Asaba, unless he volunteers and he can remain there for only six months".

"So I have to volunteer?" Silence.

"Okay, I volunteer".

Ibusa, like Asaba was frequently the target of rebel attacks from the other side of the river. A bomb attack in June '69 forced the refugees at the Training College to flee to safer quarters but, on 28 August, some of them joined Fr John Osia and the members of his parish who were celebrating the feast of their patron saint, Augustine. Bishop Kelly travelled there to celebrate 'episcopal High Mass'. Smiling and chatting, he took part in the grand procession, which was accompanied by a smartly turned out military guard and by music and dancing. To get to Ibusa, he had had to pass through Asaba. There he met Bill Kennedy, and commiserated with him on his 'cook-palaver' (despite the war and poor communications, Pat had heard of this small domestic problem). Bill recalled the meeting, because Asabans often claimed that the Bishop *never* visited them during the war.

The same month, the Superior General, Henri Monde, accompanied by the Irish Provincial, Larry Carr, made a quick visit to Benin after attending the installation of Bishop Sanusi in the new diocese of Ijebu-Ode. In December, Larry visited the Mid-West again and spent Christmas at Uromi. He spoke to all the confreres, focusing especially on his plan to transfer the students from Dromantine to the national diocesan seminary at Maynooth, Co Kildare, where they would, henceforward, do all their post noviciate seminary studies. Larry, a persuasive man, won most of the confreres to his cause, though some expressed concern about 'missionary identity'. Bishop Kelly was one of the few who didn't agree with the move to Maynooth.

Taking into account factors like the horrendous civil war and its effects, the on-going indigenization of Church leadership, and Pat's age – seventy-five years – one is bound to think that by the end of the Sixties, thoughts of retiring must have entered his mind. Nevertheless, when another Bishop asked him, "Are you thinking of your retirement?" he replied "I'm not, but others are!" Despite the denial, however, he was at this time engaged in some activities that could be construed as 'tidying up' and 'winding down'. Writing to Fr Guerin, the Procurator in Rome, he said he wished to pay for a set of breviaries he got from Lyons "about 1938 or 1939"!   While he was on leave in Ireland in '68, he admitted to the Provincial that he would have requested the appointment of an Auxiliary Bishop earlier, if it were not that "the African clergy are split by this tribal warfare but I will apply and refer the difficulty to higher authority". Was it mellowing or 'tidying up' that prompted him, in a circular of February '69, to tell his priests that he had discovered that Benin was the only diocese in the West and Mid-West where people were turned away from Confession for non-payment of monthly contributions; in future whether they had paid or not, "they must not be turned away". Adding to this liberalizing mode he said, "there are only two days on which fast and abstinence must be observed during the year – Ash Wednesday and Good Friday, and it only obliges those over fourteen years of age".

Pat was close to the truth when he joked that others were thinking of his retirement. In May 1969 a 'Resolution' was addressed to the Holy Father, Paul VI, by "Eminent Catholics representing all the Major tribes in the Mid-West State" saying, "There are strong speculations, which can neither be affirmed nor denied, that His Lordship, Dr PJ Kelly will retire very shortly". The resolution went on to say that, contrary to what some people might think on account of the current 'crisis', the people of the diocese would warmly welcome the appointment of one of their own indigenous priests as Bishop Kelly's successor. Attached was a list of the names of forty-three diocesan clergy.

The end of the war, January 12, 1970

"The outbreak of peace" was how the SMA Mid-West Newsletter termed the cessation of hostilities between the Federal Government and Biafra. The Government proclaimed a general amnesty and, though the State of Emergency was not lifted for some time, tension diffused rapidly, business and the free movement of people re-commenced. Midwestern Ibos returned from the East, considerably disillusioned and somewhat down-at-heel but, otherwise, none the worse for wear. Credit must go to the Mid-West government and the Military Governor, Colonel Ogbemudia, for the tolerance shown to the returned fugitives and 'rebels', many of whom were accepted back into their former domiciles, schools, and places of employment – even in the higher ranks of the Civil Service. Though the cost of living had spiralled, the work of rehabilitation and reconstruction began energetically in all areas. It must be said too that, when the Ibos departed, church members of other ethnic groups took over parish leadership roles and did so satisfactorily. Many parish priests even noted, with some surprise, that the 'Harvest' income had actually increased.

The Bishop's office, through Sexton Cahill, became involved with aid for the war victims, initially in the form of food and clothing and, later, with funds from Oxfam, Misereor and other agencies for repairing war-damaged schools, hospitals, and clinics and for other humanitarian works. Sexton never found out what the Bishop thought of this apostolate as he gave no sign of approval or disapproval. Meanwhile stocks of rice, dried fish, baby food and other commodities, piled up on the Bishop's verandah, as they did on those of many other missionaries. Bill Kennedy in Asaba, also much involved in relief work, had come to the end of the six-month stint, mandated by the Provincial for 'volunteers' in Asaba, but the Bishop readily let him stay on "for another month or so" to help complete the work of repatriating refugees who had congregated there.

Supplementing the work of the Federal Government and the Nigerian Red Cross, overseas Catholic relief agencies sent much needed supplies to Lagos. From there the Catholic Secretariat of Nigeria (CSN) arranged transport of the goods to needy areas where it was distributed with the help of diocesan coordinators like Cahill. Others involved in this work were, Frs Dan Looney, Hugh Conlon, John Osia, Mick Higgins, and Sr Celestine

Sheridan OLA who was constantly on the road with her five-ton CSN lorry.

Sapele mission house burned to the ground in 1967.
The fire was caused by a domestic accident.

Repair work on damaged buildings such as St Mary's hospital Ogwashi-Uku, St Patrick's College, Asaba and the Training College at Ibusa began. The building of the new social centre at Benin, halted during the war, re-commenced. Colleges and schools re-opened, many of them with 'Kelly-sponsored' Nigerian graduates as the new Principals.

Pat, no doubt, exhausted and shocked after the horrors of the war, preached in a softer, more ecumenical manner than previously, insisting that the Christian Churches could do much to promote peace by prayer and by the example of their members' love for others and willingness to forgive. The remedy for humanity's ills, he said, "is the law of charity, the love of God and one's neighbour and the forgiveness of injuries. All men are brothers, children of the heavenly Father, brothers in Christ ... The Churches can do much by word and example to promote social justice, without which peace and concord and national progress will never be achieved". Reflecting on how the Church fared during the war years he said, "I would not say that Church membership has diminished; though many lapsed, many will return to the Father's house later, like the Prodigal son".

In the Retreat which he did that month, January 1970, he stressed "Closer union with Christ", and resolved, "To see Jesus in my neighbour and to do all I can to make Him known and loved". Writing to his sister, Kathleen Cunnane, in Ballinasloe on 21 January, he said, "The war is over Thank God. There is a lot of relief work and rehabilitation going on at present, but all are happy that there is no more fighting". Brief as ever, his relief was palpable and his hand shook a little as he signed himself, "Your Loving Brother, PJ".

Chapter 15

FINAL YEARS IN NIGERIA

1970-1973

Largely due to Bishop Kelly's efforts, the number of indigenous clergy in Benin continued to rise and, by 1970, there were over thirty but the number of missionaries had decreased. In June, there were thirty-five SMA priests attached to the diocese but ten of them were either on leave or just about to go. The civil war and its aftermath were major factors in reducing the number. After the war, there were difficulties in getting re-entry permits and, as time went on, it became impossible for new missionaries to enter the country. In 1970, five confreres, two new ones and three returning after leave, were held up for a long time waiting on visas. Eventually, this problem led the Irish Province to start new missions in other parts of Africa.

At this time, the era of indigenisation of church leadership in Nigeria began in earnest. In 1971 alone, seven Nigerian bishops were ordained. Bishop Kelly had already asked Rome to nominate a Coadjutor bishop for Benin, but he was not in a hurry to retire, preferring to wait until another division of the diocese was effected and a Nigerian nominated as its first bishop. This division lay in the east of the diocese around Asaba. The local clergy and people, though wishing Bishop Kelly a long life in Nigeria, also desired that a Nigerian would succeed him. Throughout Africa, Propaganda Fide was promoting the indigenous clergy but, mindful of the Warri case, was concerned to make the correct 'ethnic choices' in the cases of Benin and its new division.

326

While the civil war occupied minds in Nigeria, dramatic changes had taken place in European society and in the universal Church – basically a new emphasis on individual freedom and an intense desire for democratic government. In the wake of the Vatican Council there was a desire for collegiality, consultation and participation in administration at all levels in the Church. The new trends ushered in a type of leadership with which veterans like Pat were not at ease. Though believing in 'consultation' in his own way, he believed more strongly in obedience, in Church law, and in the authority of ecclesiastical leaders. In discussion and argument, he often chortled, "I'm the Bishop here" but, deep down, he wasn't joking. The confreres, while in no way rebellious or disloyal, wished to participate more in administrative decision-making. With this end in view, the Regional, Mick Drew, and seven confreres met with Pat at Immaculate Conception College in February 1970. At the beginning of their proceedings, the Fathers and the Bishop "shared a grouse" that all the SMA dioceses in Nigeria had received Society grants except Benin. No official reason was given, but it was hinted that Benin had sufficient money to look after itself. Next, after endeavouring to squeeze a little more out of the Bishop for allocations, the confreres raised their main concern – working towards a more democratic type of administration in the diocese or, at least, more consultation in decision-making. This did not sit easily with Pat and he argued strongly that he would only accept advice on the running of the diocese through the Senate of priests. On the ever-diminishing length of tour, the Fathers desired a twenty-one month tour, while the Bishop favoured a thirty-two month one but, he said, he would not prevent anyone going home after twenty-one months and, following a request from the Regional, he agreed that he would pay the fare. At the SMA Extraordinary Provincial Council meeting the same year, the first point in the Benin Regional's report was, "Relations between the confreres and the Bishop are good and healthy. While all may not agree with his methods, all respect him and have confidence in him as their Bishop, a holy man and an able leader". The report also stated that relations between missionaries and local clergy were very good.

Pat's view of Nigerianisation was simple enough, "In places where there are sufficient indigenous clergy the expatriates will hand over, in places where there are not, the expatriates will remain. Nigerianisation has to be slow in some places but, in a place like Benin, there will be no more expatriate bishops". At the time there was a number of Nigerian priests from among whom Pat's successor could have been chosen. One of them was the first Bini priest, Bernard Elaho. A year after Bernard's ordination by Cardinal McIntyre in Lagos, Pat sent him to University College Cork to do a BA. Afterwards he proved to be an excellent teacher, a good administrator and the founder of two new colleges, one at Ebu and the other at Eguaholor. Popular with the people and noted for fidelity to work, he was one of the Bishop's consultors and a member of the Mid-West Education Advisory Board. Some thought he was 'bishop material' but, tragically, in April 1970, at the age of forty-six, he died at his desk in St Kizito's Grammar School, Eguaholor, where he was Principal. Though he was suffering from fever at the time, his death was totally unexpected. *The Daily Times* said 10,000 people attended his funeral at Holy Cross cathedral. [1]

Though aware that his time as bishop of Benin was drawing to a close, Pat continued working as usual. In 1970, the Marianists, transferring from Ekpoma to Fugar, handed over to him their beautiful preparatory seminary at Ekpoma. Very pleased with the gift, he turned it into a diocesan junior seminary. In August he gave his Imprimatur to *The Angels Choirs' Hymnal*, compiled by Ambrose Ekhosuehi but, *before* giving it, he insisted that all

---

[1] Two other untimely deaths occurred in 1970. Fr Michael Walker SMA of St George's College, Obinomba, Warri, twenty-nine years of age, was killed in a road accident while on leave in Ireland after his first tour in Nigeria. Also from Warri, the newly ordained Fr Columbanus Uwarievwe was killed in another road accident.

choir members must be taught the answers to the 318 questions of the catechism before learning any hymns. And he prioritized fifty-five questions which he considered absolutely necessary for those seeking the sacrament of Confirmation. Ambrose attached a hymn to each of these questions to facilitate memorizing the answers. On 6 November at Abavo, Pat laid the foundation stone for the new church to be built there under the direction of John Thornton. Apart from these special events, the Bishop continued as usual working in his office, praying in his oratory, visiting the sick and dying, going on confirmation tours, and helping with Masses and confessions in the cathedral.

The Angels' Choral Society, Benin City, 1969:
Bishop with Chief Asemota and choir members.

In view of Pat's probable retirement, the Bishops of Nigeria desired that the Pope would grant him the personal title of 'Archbishop' in recognition of his many years of devoted service. Archbishop Aggey, Chairman of the Nigerian Episcopal Conference, confirmed the request in writing in May 1971.

Complementing the bishops' action, the diocesan senate of Benin petitioned the Apostolic Delegate with the same request. The Regional Superior, on behalf of all the confreres in Benin and Warri, added his voice, asking the Provincial Superior to request the Holy See to make Pat an honorary archbishop on the occasion of his Golden Jubilee of priesthood, 29 June 1971. Replying, on behalf of Larry Carr, who was in West Africa, the Vice Provincial, Joe Donnelly, said the same request had been made to Rome in 1965 on the occasion of Pat's Episcopal Silver Jubilee but nothing had come of it. Some confreres suggested that the Province should offer a trip to Nigeria to Pat's fellow Jubilarians, John Cadogan and Jerry Sheehan, so that the three classmates could celebrate together in Benin. Joe reminded them however that John had left the Society and was incardinated into a diocese in New York, and that Jerry, who was not in good health, would probably not want to travel. Disappointingly for the SMA and for Benin, Rome did not confer the personal title of Archbishop on Pat.

Meanwhile, with regard to the future leadership of the diocese, Propaganda Fide nominated another 'Patrick', **Patrick Ebosele Ekpu**, an Ishan man, as Pat's Coadjutor with right of succession. The Ishans were 'first cousins' of the Binis, hence from the ethnic point of view, the new Patrick would be acceptable in Benin. Born on 26 October 1931 in Uromi, after primary education he went to Catholic schools in Benin City, including Immaculate Conception College, and then to the Minor Seminary at Oke-Are, Ibadan. He did his philosophy and theology at St Paul's Major Seminary, first at Benin and at Ibadan when the seminary transferred there. He was ordained priest by Bishop Kelly in Uromi along with classmates Paul Emonyon, Paul Gariaga and Peter Oyemonlan in July 1963. Appointed to Iyekovia, he and Vincent Obudu opened a new mission there. The following year, Pat appointed him to St Augustine's parish, Ibusa, where he remained until November 1967 when he was transferred to Igueben. With the help of the Marianists, he went to Boston

College, Massachusetts, in 1968 where, after obtaining an MA in Sociology, he continued studying for a Ph.D. While engaged in summer pastoral work in New York, he received the news of his nomination. He returned to Benin in October and his episcopal consecration was set for 21 November 1971.

Bishop Ekpu

Bishop Ekpu was consecrated by the Apostolic Delegate, Archbishop Amelio Poggi, assisted by Pat and Bishop Finn of Ibadan. Speaking at the ceremony, the first Nigerian Bishop of Benin said he was bishop for all the people and not for any particular ethnic group. Assuring the missionaries that they were still needed, he said he would do all in his power to increase the number of indigenous vocations in the diocese. At the luncheon which followed in the Hotel Bendel, Pat led the opening prayers.

Bishop Kelly and confreres celebrated the Golden Jubilee of his priesthood in June, but the people preferred to postpone their celebration of it until the day after Bishop Ekpu's consecration. On that day, the *Nigerian Observer* carried an admirable tribute by Fred Konwea. Praising the seventy-seven year old Bishop with his "Do it yourself motto", the journalist described him as "strongly built, tall, handsome, spare and stately", and continued, "He still drives, teaches catechism and hears confessions. He is

331

hardly ever indisposed, wears no spectacles, lives in a humble house, is abstemious, neither smokes nor drinks, and lives on prayer. The last of the renowned pioneers, he is still approachable, young at heart, friendly and cheerful".

An important task for Pat in his last few years in Nigeria was the equitable division of diocesan funds between Benin and the new diocese-to-be. Dealing through the SMA bursar general, Gerard Scanlan, he added $50,000 to a fixed deposit he had in Rome. The bursar informed him that he had $6,664 in another account. Pat quickly wrote back saying the sum was $6,646. Always interested in getting the best possible deal for his assets, he asked the bursar whether he thought he could trust a certain gentleman in Belgium who was offering him a much better rate of exchange than the Bank. After consulting the Vatican Bank, Scanlan replied in Gaelic, telling him to have nothing to do with the man. By ' 73, Pat had over $77,000 in his fixed deposit. At this time he was also concerned with paying off diocesan debts and setting up bursaries for special situations – £2,500 in Cork for the training of Nigerian Sisters; $1,500 in Rome for the Benin Seminary. "All the rest" he said, "is to be invested for sick or old priests of the Diocese, not expatriate priests".

In January 1972, Pat took up his pen to write a short Preface for Chief Utomi's *History of St Thomas's Teacher Training College*, Ibusa. Praising it, he said, "I could not lay down the manuscript until I came to the end of the last page". Chief Utomi, former Mid-West Minister of Education, was one of the first class of the College, 1928-1930. When the book went to print, St Thomas's had no less than 2,782 names on its register of students. Among them were many prominent men, including Bishops Lucas and Gbuji (who was headmaster in 1972). Established as a training college for males, it began to accept females in the late Sixties.

A tragic death occurred in Warri diocese in February. Tommy Hassett was shot dead as he drove home one night to Ozoro mission. The thirty-four year old Dubliner, accompanied by Harry Jones, was on the road from Obiaruku when he was stopped at a road block. After he had turned off the engine, quenched the lights and opened the window as instructed by the unseen assailant or assailants, a single shot was fired, which hit him in the head and grazed Harry Jones' neck. The gunman fled into the bush, leaving no clues as to his identity or motive. Ironically, some years previously, Tommy had told a new Irish teacher never to stop at that place as it was bad juju country. Tommy's funeral, presided over by Bishops Lucas and Pat, took place on 4 February '72 and was attended by confreres from Benin, Warri and neighbouring dioceses, among them Tommy's brother, Fr Michael SMA, who was then ministering in Ibadan. Tommy was buried beside the church in Ozoro.

Government take over of schools

Since the late Sixties, more and more schools were coming under Government control. Nevertheless, in 1969 about two-fifths of the Grammar Schools in the Mid-West were still Catholic mission schools and a correspondingly large number of missionaries were still involved in them. However, this was fast changing. In 1970, for instance, most school Principals were Nigerians and, at this stage, most expatriate priests preferred the role of 'teacher-chaplain' to that of Principal. The priest in a school, no matter what position he held, always provided a pastoral service for the local people and, from his own point of view, enjoyed the considerable benefits of having a place in which to live, a work routine and a salary (which was not a personal emolument, but went to the bishop or the mission). After the take-over, the role of 'priest-manager' of schools remained unclear for a while but, soon enough, Nigerians took over all the managerial roles. Some priest-teachers found it difficult to adjust and, without a regular work routine, felt as if they were in a vacuum. Others rejoiced to be free of school responsibilities and devoted their time to pastoral work.

The Mid-West Government intended to take over all schools by 1 October 1972. In view of this, the diocesan senate appointed a committee of twenty-one Fathers, Sisters and a Brother to formulate guidelines for the bishops in their dealings with the Government. They met at Ekpoma in May and agreed that the church leaders should not ask for compensation, nor accept it should the Government offer it. Desiring that the dioceses should maintain ownership of buildings such as churches, presbyteries and convents located in school compounds, the committee suggested that the right of way to the buildings should be ensured and that Mass on Sundays and Feast days should be allowed to continue where that was already the practice. Stressing the principle of freedom of religion, they wished that all pupils should be free to follow the services of whatever church they belonged to. They felt that the teaching of religion might best be served by concentrating on producing good teachers in the Training Colleges. Hoping that the Catholic names of old and well-established colleges would be retained, they agreed that the bishops should cooperate with the government as far as possible.

By 1973, all the voluntary agents had relinquished control of their schools. The Catholic Church had not asked for, nor did it receive compensation. The Permanent Secretary for education in the Mid-West, a Catholic, tried to maintain something of the Catholic ethos when he appointed missionaries as Principals of three Teacher Training Colleges: Jim Higgins to St Joseph's, Ozoro; Harry Jones to St Thomas's, Ibusa; and Sr Loretta OLA to Sacred Heart, Ubiaja. However it wasn't long before this ethos trickled away. It was the end of an era of intense mission involvement in schools. When asked to comment, Pat replied resignedly, "We accept it, but we would like the names of the schools to be retained. We still need the protection of the patron saints".

Whatever might happen in the future, Bishop Kelly and the many Catholic teachers and managers, clerical and lay, male and female, expatriate and Nigerian, over the decades, had made an enormous contribution to education in Nigeria and through it to evangelization. Fr Jim Higgins, himself one of the foremost teachers and Principals of the era with the superb record of fifty-five years' work in the Mid-West (and he is still there) in his recent book *Kindling the Fire*, gave the number of Catholic schools and colleges at the end of the 'Kelly era' as follows – about 700 primary schools, forty-five Secondary Modern Schools, and forty-one Secondary Grammar Schools. The number of Teacher Training Colleges had been reduced to four as the Ministry of Education closed St Columba's, St John Bosco's and Assumption College. While many people collaborated in the Catholic mission school achievement, it would not have been as great without Bishop Kelly's vision, leadership and endurance.

On 26 October ' 72, the Regional informed all the clergy that "His Lordship, Bishop Kelly, has handed over the administration of the diocese of Benin City to his Coadjutor, Most Rev. Dr. P.E. Ekpu. As from the date of this letter, all business will therefore be directed to Bishop Ekpu". But even after that, Pat, still waiting for the diocese to be divided, did not tender his resignation to Propaganda. This could have resulted in an impasse, as Propaganda was waiting for him to resign before dividing the diocese. In December ' 72, at the end of a visit to Nigeria, the Provincial, Larry Carr, spoke with the Apostolic Delegate in Lagos who, hoping to expedite matters, suggested that Bishop Kelly offer his resignation with the proviso that it come into effect only *after* the diocese was divided and the new bishop named. But Pat still hung on and was even thinking of postponing his resignation for a year or two. Propaganda at this stage, requested the Superior General and the General Bursar to encourage him to hand over to his Coadjutor without further delay. Gerard Scanlan wrote to him saying, "Mgr Pignedoli spoke of the great work you have done, the Holy Father is quite aware of it too from his visit as Cardinal Montini ... You can retire with 'full marks' any time you wish". Pat, mindful of the adage, "Rome has spoken, the case is concluded", delayed no longer and informed Bishop Ekpu that he would hand over after Easter. Writing to the Provincial, he said he would remain in Benin until 6 June and then embark for home, "I don't intend to return" he added. The finality of the last remark surely welled up from a lot of personal pain and sadness at the thought of leaving but, not given to dwelling on himself or his feelings, he changed the subject, "I think the SMA Fathers and the Bishop will get on all right".

He met with his Diocesan Consultors and Bishop Ekpu on 24 March. They agreed that the capital funds of the diocese would be divided in proportion to the numbers of Catholics in the parent part of the diocese (Benin) and in the part to be divided ("Asaba" – many people thought). With 73,000 in the former and 64,000 in the latter, a ratio of seven to six was agreed. Twenty-one Nigerian priests were then working in Benin and seven were working in Asaba district. Ten more were studying, mainly overseas, or working elsewhere. Seventeen SMA missionaries were in Benin and eight in the diocese-to-be. After the division, it was agreed that the priests would remain where they were. The reduction in the number of missionaries was due to the re-allocation of men to new missions in East and South Africa, to retirement, and to departures from the mission or from the Society for personal reasons. Among the retirees were: John Mahon, Pat's Vicar General of long-standing, and the genial Tommy Greene who, after forty-five years, retired in 1972.

Church membership had greatly increased during Pat's episcopacy – from approximately **30,000** in 1940 to over **180,000** at the time of his departure. (The figure includes 43,000 Catholics of Warri, the number Pat gave when requesting that Warri be erected as a separate diocese).

On 26 March, Pat sent notification of his resignation to the Delegate, asking him to forward it to Cardinal Rossi, the Prefect of Propaganda. If the resignation was accepted, he requested the Delegate to be present at the installation of Bishop Ekpu on a convenient Sunday in April or May. The installation did not take place, however, until 23 September, by which time Pat had departed, though he didn't get away in June as he had first planned.

It was near the end of July before the Chargé d'Affaires at the Apostolic Delegation in Lagos informed Pat that his resignation had been accepted. He was also informed that the new division of Benin would be the diocese of **"Issele-Uku"** (not "Asaba"!), and that **Anthony Gbuji** had been nominated as its first bishop. All that remained for Pat to do was to publicise the Holy See's acceptance of his resignation and prepare for Bishop Ekpu's installation. The new diocese of Issele-Uku would remain under Bishop Ekpu's authority until Anthony Gbuji's consecration and installation.

Anthony Gbuji, mentioned a number of times already, was a Western Ibo who lived in Benin City. A doctor of Canon Law, he was an experienced teacher and college Principal, a consultor of the Bishop and an elected member of the diocesan Senate. Popular with the people, he was well-known to the missionaries, having worked with many of them, and having examined some of them for competency in the vernacular at the end of their tyrocinium.

Understandably the Asabans were not happy with the choice of Issele-Uku as the centre of the new diocese. Once more another town had been preferred to theirs. Sorely disappointed, when Bishop Taylor moved headquarters to Benin City in 1938, they were even more disappointed this time. Again Pat was 'blamed'. Years after the move, Mons. Patrick Ugboko wrote to him from Asaba, stating his deep dismay. In reply Pat said, "I was not pleased myself with the choice of the new diocese of Issele-Uku" but, he admitted that in his *first* application for the erection of the new jurisdiction, he *had* put down Issele-Uku as the centre, because it was generally believed that the Government was going to establish it as the headquarters of the area. Pat didn't say so, but the war-damaged town of Asaba was not in favour with the Federal Government because it had sided with Biafra. He continued:

> This application was refused and it was only after much persistence for over a year or more that the separate diocese was granted. I then made a new application putting down Asaba as the headquarters. When the final acceptance came announcing Issele-Uku I was very disappointed and even thought of phoning the Delegate, but he was away and there was no time to contact him and Propaganda. This is as much as I remember of the setting up of the new diocese now, but I never had any hatred for Asaba Christians or people.

> +P.J. Kelly, Cork, 30 November 1977.

Farewell

Agreeing with a suggestion that he should do a round of farewell visits to the Christians before departing, Pat began at Ubiaja and visited as many parishes and centres as he could throughout the diocese. Many of the people, especially the older ones, he knew by name and family history. Many of them presented him with gifts of chickens, eggs, and yams, which he received with humble gratitude. In his words of farewell in the various places, he focused on encouraging whatever activities were going on. In some centres, he combined the farewell with a confirmation tour. Okpanam in Asaba Division was his last confirmation tour, June '73. The people of his first station, Eku, were most anxious to see him and the feeling was mutual. The night before going there, he stayed with Fr Dan Cashman at Aghalokpe College in Okpara parish. At Eku, he was received as if Heaven-sent. With dancing, singing and speeches, the people made it very clear to him that he was greatly loved and would be remembered. He didn't normally say Mass on these farewell visits, but the Eku people had so ardently requested it that he agreed. The celebration turned out to be a memorable one for the Bishop and the people. Surrounded by the older men and women whom he had baptised as infants, by their children and grandchildren, by his old catechists and teachers, Pat felt extremely happy. Throughout the day's activities he laughed and smiled and enjoyed everything. Afterwards, he spent the night on his own in the house he had built half century before when he had been the first resident priest. On returning to Aghalokpe, he told Dan that the farewell at Eku "was the greatest uplift I've received for many a long day". Dan understood, however, that it had been a 'sad-happy' occasion for Pat, as it marked the end of his long mission in Nigeria, yet the Bishop did not become sentimental. Later he admitted, "Saying Goodbye to my friends and colleagues in Benin was one of the hardest things I have ever done". The people of St Joseph's parish, Benin City also did him proud, presenting him with a fine gift and a printed farewell in which, among other things, they said, "Your piety, humility, love of labour, your unpublicised help to orphans, the poor and the needy; your orderly and simple habits in food, drink, dress, socials and sermons, coupled with your parental care for those who come your way, are just a few of your outstanding qualities to be mentioned here". They also asked him to stay on in the diocese after his retirement, adding, "We need your powerful prayers for the growth and stability of the Church here".

Shortly after his round of farewell visits, he was interviewed by Mike Oputa of *The Sunday Observer* who asked, "What were your first impressions of Nigeria and Nigerians?" Pat replied simply, "Nigeria was undeveloped and the Nigerians were a peaceful and happy people".
"What do you intend to do now that you are retiring?"
"I will go back to my home in Ireland where I hope to secure a

light job in the ministry".

"What if you were offered a job here, would you remain?"
Softening his earlier statement about not returning, he said, "I will
go home first and then decide whether to come back or not".

"After your farewell visits, what were your feelings?"
Lowering his emotional guard a little, he admitted, "Sad! Parting
is a sad thing".

It was time for him to pack. This usually meant doing little more
than throwing a few clothes into an old battered suitcase but, this
time, with a little more luggage, Mother Brendan and Sr Kathleen
OLA, assisted him. Most of what he had was for the Society,
family and friends, not for himself. In a box of "unaccompanied
luggage", he had two brass heads, one brass effigy, one ebony
flower vase and one carved box. The whole lot, valued by the
Customs officer as 110 Naira (the new Nigerian currency
introduced in January), was worth £55 sterling – not a great
amount after half a century in the country. The priests and Sisters
organized a send-off for him in his own compound. Many words
of praise were spoken and many requests made that he return to
Nigeria. His farewell message was brief, and not very original,
"Work and Pray!" Clergy, missionaries and all the people of the
diocese contributed to a farewell gift – the price of a new car for
use in his retirement.

Mattie O'Connell, the administrator of Holy Cross cathedral,
accompanied him to Lagos. Pat prayed all the way. After staying
the night at Apapa he boarded ship and sailed from Nigeria 17
August 1973. Bishop Gbuji, at his own episcopal consecration the
following month, referred to him as "one of the greatest prelates
the Church in modern times has produced – the beloved father
and shepherd of the flock of God in the Mid-Western state of
Nigeria. He should have been here today, but he left the scene
very quietly, telling us, 'Not to us Lord, but to your name be the
glory'. When he left the shores of Nigeria, his face beamed with
a striking joy and satisfaction ... With St Paul he felt that he had
fought a good fight and had finished the race".

Presenting an effigy of Oba Eweka of Benin who reigned
when Pat arrived in 1921.

Mark Oyo and knights of St Murumba present a tusk.

Chapter 16

RETIREMENT, 1973-1991

Back in Ireland Pat spoke with the Provincial, Larry Carr, about taking on a light pastoral ministry, mentioning chaplaincy work for religious sisters. Leaving the matter in the Provincial's hands, he set about buying a car, his Nigerian retirement gift. At PJ O'Hea, Motor Dealers, he chose an Austin 1100 and as soon as they filled the tank he headed for Tristaun and an autumn holiday. Like the donkeys of old, "PZF 205" got to know the road home, for Pat spent his summer holidays there and visited at Christmas and Easter. The family enjoyed drives to Sunday Mass, pilgrimages to Knock and other excursions. Now resident in Ireland, Pat needed an Irish driving licence and found it wasn't so easy to get. Writing from Tristaun to the bursar in Cork about car tax and insurance, he admitted, "I failed the driving test twice in Loughrea" but, he explained, "The testers there are very strict". The nephews and nieces, Anthony (an SMA student in Maynooth College), Pádraic, Seán, Mary Teresa and Carmel, all keen GAA fans, took it in turns to use the two All-Ireland tickets a kind benefactor in Cork gave Pat every year. He used them only once himself when he brought a visiting African bishop to Croke Park.

In November, with the winter setting in, he left Tristaun to take up residence in Wilton, Cork. Fr Michael Collins, Pat's trusted confidant of longstanding, who had been living in retirement in the SMA House in Wilton, had died just a month before Pat's return to Ireland. Pat was given his room, a pleasant south-facing one with a view over the fields towards

Doughcloyne where the African undergraduates used to lodge. As yet, no 'light ministry' had materialised. On being requested by Larry Carr to look for a place for Pat, the Auxiliary Bishop of Liverpool found a vacant position in a convent of cloistered nuns engaged in Perpetual Adoration but, after reflection, Bishop Gray thought the accommodation too spartan for a man of Bishop Kelly's age and rank and reserved the post for a younger man. Benedictine Sisters in Oultan Abbey, Staffordshire, were also looking for a chaplain, but favoured a son of St Benedict. Finally, a community in Whitby, Middlesbrough, agreed to have Pat and he agreed to go there but, the old chaplain changed his mind and decided not to retire after all! A non-corroborated report said that Sisters in Montenotte, Cork, at first showed some interest in having an ex-missionary chaplain, but baulked at the idea of a resident octogenarian bishop. Having little to do was not easy for Pat and, still wondering about returning to Africa, he prayed "to know the Divine Will and to do it in all things". On 1 April 1975, the Provincial felt that it was time Bishop Kelly settled down to a quiet life in an SMA community. Pat accepted his decision and took up residence in St Joseph's, Wilton, where he had begun his missionary formation sixty years previously.

In 1969, St Joseph's had become the location of the Province's noviciate or "Spiritual Year", transferred there from Cloughballymore. The Wilton community was composed of priest 'formators' of the novices and a few retired men. The number of students varied, sometimes there were over twenty, all being inducted into the ways and spirituality of the SMA. Paddy Jennings, formerly of Oke Are Seminary in Ibadan was the Superior. Under his direction, the resident Fathers administered the public church of St Joseph's. In 1982 St Joseph's, Wilton, became a parish of the diocese of Cork.

Pat liked to say the early Mass in the public church but, as he was inclined to take time and wasn't very audible, he had to be weaned off it. From then on, he said Mass privately about 8 a.m., having first devoutly attended all the other priests' Masses. Insistent on correct performance of liturgy, he would cue in a priest who forgot the Gloria or Creed on a feast day, by calling out loudly, "Gloria – Gloria", or "Credo – Credo", or he would have a quiet word with the celebrant after Mass if he thought he was guilty of some other rubrical *faux pas*. Sometimes he was wrong, as when he called the Superior to order for a liturgical gesture which he, the Bishop, claimed should be performed earlier in the Mass. Fr Jennings pointed out that some things had changed in the new rite. Pat was disappointed as he had just bought a new missal and, now, it was already out of date.

After a Holy Hour or two in the morning, he used to cross the Bishopstown road to the "Regional Hospital" where there was Mass at noon. In the afternoons he walked down Wilton road and along College Road to the Convent of the Poor Clares for Benediction at 5 p.m. In churches or oratories, he chose a place where he had an unimpeded view of the tabernacle. This place became special to him and, if he found anyone else occupying it, even the Provincial, he would ask him to move. On one occasion, his view of the tabernacle in Wilton church was blocked by flowers arranged for a wedding. Pat asked the celebrant to move them. Never one to approve of short Masses, he didn't like it when some of the Sunday Mass congregation left before the last blessing. Hoping to dissuade them, he would stand near the door. On Holy Thursday, when the altars were stripped and the Blessed Sacrament removed, he would be quite uneasy until he found out where it was reserved. When he discovered that it was kept in the safe in the sacristy, he put a kneeler in front of it and stationed himself there, ignoring the detours that the disapproving sacristan, Fr Frank Doyle, had to make around him.

In Wilton, Pat continued to be rather conservative and scrupulous about sacramental and liturgical affairs. In the Lenten season, he was not happy with the way the Stations of the Cross were performed. According to him, the priest should process with the cross bearer from station to station, instead of remaining at the ambo. He offered to demonstrate, but his offer was not taken up. Reminiscent of his views on Oye-Ekiti sacred art, he took a dim view of the replacement of traditional church furnishings, pictures, statues and crucifixes, with symbolic artefacts such as bog oak carvings. Arguments about the venerability of the oak or "our ancient Celtic heritage" didn't really win him over. With his insatiable desire for the Eucharist, an innovation which suited him was the introduction of an evening Mass in Wilton and, though it clashed with Benediction in the Poor Clares convent, he chose to attend the Mass. He made up for the lack of the walk to the convent by doing a few extra rounds of the beautiful tree-lined avenues in Wilton, saying extra rosaries and reading his breviary. Sometimes, one of the Fathers, like Peter Thompson his former secretary in Benin who had become the Superior in Wilton, joined him 'round the walks' and they talked of Nigeria and mission affairs.

If somebody known to him was in hospital, or if he was asked to visit a patient, he would always go, walking to the Regional Hospital or "The Bons", as the Bon Secours hospital was called, and driving or being driven, to hospitals farther away. If anyone went to him with a problem, he listened carefully and, though he never said much and certainly wasn't intrusive, people felt he understood them and they believed that his prayers were efficacious. On bidding them farewell, he always asked for prayers for himself, not only because he strongly believed in 'a communion of prayer', but because he seemed to believe that they were closer to God than he was and that their prayers might well be answered before his own. At the end of his first Retreat while in Wilton, March 1974, he resolved, "To imitate Jesus Christ more closely and to live constantly in His Divine presence".

A good community man in the spirit of the Society's *Directory*, he joined the Fathers for liturgy, meals and the "Nine o'clock news". Before retiring for the night, he participated in the customary 'cup of tea' after the News, though for him it was cocoa. He was well aware of current affairs and joined in chat about the missions, politics (Fianna Fáil) and sport (Galway hurling and football). As one who had preached that "the art of conversation is to bring out the knowledge of others more than one's own", he rarely led in conversation and was not one for idle gossip. Nevertheless he did sometimes make a surprising 'revelation', as when he admitted that, as a young man, he used to smoke and even drink an odd bottle of stout!

"Seven-up" had been his favourite, if rare, recreational drink in Nigeria. In Wilton, after seeing a "7-up" television ad showing seven shapely female legs above the surface of a swimming pool, he changed to Coca Cola. He liked serious political programmes on television and, even lighter ones, like Gay Byrne's *Late Late Show*, until he judged that too much 'sex' had crept into it. He enjoyed the popular rural based serial *The Riordans* until Benjy, one of the leading characters, got married and part of the post wedding nuptials was screened. Viewing this episode in Tristaun, he fled from the room and never watched *The Riordans* again. When he thought he was in danger of being assailed by some titillating scene, he would cover his eyes with his hands. Frank Doyle claimed that he was peeping through his fingers. Hand-before-face technique was also employed for horse racing, attendance at which was forbidden to clergy by the Maynooth Statutes.

Though he wasn't officially involved in the training of the Wilton students, he donated a "Mission Cup", for the winners of a football league to be played between the SMA students and their counterparts in St Patrick's missionary Society, Douglas.

At times the student body included non-Irish students; in 1976 there were six English, one Italian, and eleven Irish students. One day the Italian, Antonio Porcelato, politely joined the Bishop on his walk. "I don't know what to call you" said Antonio, practising

346

his English. "Call me 'My Lord'," said Pat. Though taken aback by this, the young man was genuinely impressed by the Bishop's daily routine – which to him seemed like: eight hours private prayer, eight hours liturgical prayer and eight hours 'walking prayer'. Impressing all by the amount of praying he did, Pat inspired one student by the amount of oranges he ate! In the 1981 Wilton students' magazine, Peter Kerrigan wrote:

> Now some eating habits are strange,
> from caviar to boiled turnips they range,
> But, try as you wish,
> you can't beat our Bish
> for along with each meal has his orange.

On one of his walks in the Bishopstown area, Pat met Martha Scannell, a former lay teacher in Benin. She was surprised that he remembered her, even her name, but he didn't tarry, he was fingering his beads and going somewhere purposefully. Walking a lot, he wore down many pairs of boots and shoes but he extended their lifespan every now and then by hammering a few nails into the soles using a hammer and cobbler's last which he kept in his room.

Wilton 1979: Bishop with students and E. Hogan, P. Thompson, S. Nohilly, P. Kelly, J. Redmond.

Christmas at Tristaun

He loved Christmas and New Year in Tristaun. Sister-in-law Ellen cooked a wonderful dinner of turkey on the 25th and a goose, which he really liked, on New Year. He let himself go with desserts – trifle and pudding, with a drop of sherry in them that Ellen said wouldn't do him any harm. Indulgence in these required intense diversionary prayer. He also enjoyed card games and draughts with his nephews, nieces and neighbours. Roads at Christmas time were not always the best and, when he heard of Finance Minister Charles Haughey's 'Free Travel' benefit for pensioners, he applied for and received a Pass card. But, at the railway station on Christmas Eve, he discovered to his dismay that the Free Travel "wasn't free" at peak times.

In Summer, he spent long holidays in Tristaun, pottering in the fields and doing what he could to help. One thing he would never do was work on a Sunday even for the, sometimes, 'necessary' work of saving the hay. Believing in home-grown fruit, he purchased good blackcurrant and gooseberry bushes in Ballinasloe and planted them near the house. Before too long he was proudly picking the fruit of his labour and leaving bowls of it on the kitchen table for Ellen to make jam. Praying even more now, he liked to say his breviary walking the road as far as Pat Hurney's Forge, having the odd chat with a neighbour on the way. To give Ellen a spell during mid-holiday, he would drive to Banagher to spend some time with his married niece, Mary Tanner and go with her to Lough Derg. Before going on the island, the two pilgrims stayed at Fintona with Pat's brother, Gerald, and Gerald's wife, Mary. The couple had settled there after returning from New York. Lough Derg's ascetical Gaelic ambience, Celtic crosses, and barefooted prayerful rounds of the rocky beds of Ireland's ancient saints appealed to Pat. He didn't mind the endless Hail Marys, the diet of dry bread and black tea, but he found the night without sleep trying. He was in his eighties the last time he went to Lough Derg.

The *Cork Examiner* published an interesting interview entitled "Patrick Kelly, The Nigerian Irishman" in September '77. The interviewer, describing the Bishop as "one of the old school", found him, at first, "a hard man to get to talk, but he loosened up a bit on the subject of ecumenism". Admitting, that in his early days in Nigeria, he was no friend of the Protestant missionaries or their church members, in present times he said, he would be more accommodating but, he added, "While we are more charitable in unity, in essentials we are as far away as ever". Speaking on the contemporary debate on legislating for divorce in Ireland, he agreed with "some sort of separation, but the partners should not remarry". On the decline of female vocations in Ireland, he thought that Irish convents should be made more attractive for women. He remained optimistic about the Irish missionary spirit, "We will always have people willing to go abroad" and he was as convinced as ever of the absolute value of preaching Christianity in foreign lands. He said he did not regret one minute of his long missionary life in Nigeria.

Familiar with the spirit-filled church congregations in Nigeria, he was not upset by the liveliness of the new charismatic movement in Ireland, "but they shouldn't go too far with laying on of hands and the gift of tongues". A charismatic group met in Wilton and he attended at least one of their sessions. At its conclusion, a much younger confrere of the same name, Pat Kelly, led the recitation of the 'Our Father'. Quietly, from the back, the Bishop added a 'Hail Mary' and a 'Glory be'. Ever afterwards this became the group's 'official' way of concluding.

Though retired, he did not appear to be relaxed. In his Retreat of April 1979, he prayed "To realise that God is with me and is merciful" and he resolved, "To have confidence that He will get me through all my problems". He also prayed to be able to "leave my past to His mercy, my present to His love, and my future to His Providence". To distract himself a little he decided to go to the All-Ireland hurling final – Galway were playing Kilkenny. At the game Kilkenny looked unbeatable until, with only about fifteen minutes to full time, Noel Lane scored a goal for Galway. The supporters went wild, rising from their seats and throwing their hats in the air. Pat stood and cheered with the rest (but held on to his hat). Despite his encouragement, Galway lost. He had brought an African bishop, James Owusu, with him to see the game. Mgr Owusu was the bishop of Sunyani in Ghana, where Pat's nephew, Fr Anthony Kelly SMA, was working since he had been ordained by Pat in Clontuskert in 1977. The ordination of his nephew was one of Pat's "proudest moments" in Ireland. When Anthony was departing for Ghana, Pat pressed a small envelope into his hand. When he opened it, Anthony found, "Instructions on how to baptize a dying pagan".

Ordination of Anthony Kelly at Clontuskert 1977.
The Tristaun Kellys: Seán (nephew),   Ellen (sister-in-law), Anthony (nephew), Mary Teresa (niece), Carmel (niece), Pádraic (nephew).

Nigerian award

In June 1980, in appreciation of Bishop Kelly's long and dedicated service, the President of the Federal Republic of Nigeria conferred on him the honour of "Commander of the Order of the Federal Republic". Pat's reaction was not recorded but, in general, he preferred 'merit' to be stored up for him in Heaven. He feared that praise on earth would diminish the eternal reward and might even be a cause of sinful pride.

He had a bad fall in Wilton in January 1981 injuring his head. Surgery was required to remove a clot outside the brain. Happily, the operation was a success. After it, the surgeon remarked that he felt his hands were 'blessed'. The fall was the second one Pat had that Winter.

In 1981, a report circulated in Nigeria that Bishop Kelly had passed away on the 7th of March. The mistake arose out of a telephone call from a convent in Nigeria to one in Ireland. The caller, on requesting to speak to the Reverend Mother, was told that she had gone to the "Bishop's funeral in *Kilkenny*", the caller thought it was "Bishop *Kelly's* funeral". The deceased bishop was, not Kelly, but Peter Birch of Ossory, Kilkenny. News of 'the death' was passed on to the Nigerian hierarchy who happened to be concluding a Conference in Lagos at the time. On returning to their respective dioceses, the Bishops passed on the sad news. The fact that Bsihop Kelly, at eighty-eight years of age, had just undergone a serious operation lent credence to the report. An obituary was printed, Requiem Masses were offered for the repose of his soul, a concelebrated Memorial Mass was scheduled for Holy Cross cathedral and condolences were sent to Ireland. When Pat heard about his 'death', he grinned and asked, "Will I get the merit of those Masses offered for me?"

Far from dying, on 29 June he celebrated the Diamond Jubilee of his priestly ordination along with Jerry Sheehan, the only other surviving member of the class of 1921. This was the first Diamond

Jubilee the SMA celebrated in Ireland since its arrival in 1878. Pat was the chief celebrant at the Mass at which, the Provincial, Con Murphy, the retired SMA Bishops, John Reddington and William Field, and over thirty SMA priests took part. The homily was preached by Joe Donnelly. Jerry did not survive the celebration long. He died, unexpectedly, a few days later on 3 July at the age of eighty-seven. This year, Pat's Retreat resolution was, "To have the pure interest of pleasing God in all my actions and to live in the presence of Jesus Christ".

Bringing congratulations from Nigeria for Pat's Jubilee was a former student of his, Ambrose Alli, the Governor of Bendel State. (The Mid-West State was re-named "Bendel" in 1976.) Alli and his entourage were entertained in the parlour in Wilton where, along with conversation and refreshments, Pat presented a gift to the Governor, and the Governor presented Pat with £500. As a boy, Alli had been brought by his father, a Moslem policeman in northern Nigeria, to Bishop Kelly for schooling. Pat took him to Immaculate Conception College and, showing him the chapel, reminded him to pray morning and evening as a good Moslem should. Impressed by the sight of the Bishop himself praying there daily, Alli asked for a Catholic catechism. Studying it on his own and, with a little help from Joe Donnelly, he had all the questions and answers off by heart within six months. He asked for baptism, but Pat told him, "No chance Alli, you go do two years like everybody else". Nevertheless, as Alli knew the catechism inside out, the Bishop relented and, within a year, baptised him. Alli went on to become a lecturer in Zaria, then in Birmingham and in the University of Benin, which became "Ambrose Alli University" in his honour. When he became Governor of Bendel he was the only Catholic State Governor in Nigeria. The *Evening Echo* published a group photograph of the Governor and his aides on the steps of Wilton with the Bishop, Provincial Superior, Con Murphy, House superior Peter Thompson, and Fr Pat McGovern. After the Governor had gone, Pat was teased by one of the Wilton staff over his £500 windfall.

Counting out £100, Pat gave it to the bursar "for house expenses". The rest, he said, was for catechists in Benin.

State Governor, Ambrose Alli, visits Wilton: 1. Alli, 2. C. Murphy (Provincial), 3. P. Thompson, 4. P. McGovern.

Having worked with African catechists, training many of them himself, Pat continued supporting this apostolate during his retirement. In 1980, after reflecting on the information that the American Province had put $300,000 at the disposal of the Generalate for projects in Africa, Pat wrote to the Provincial recommending that the Province apply for a grant to help pay catechists' salaries in Nigeria and Ghana. Pat said that catechism, neglected in state primary schools, was not being taught outside the schools because missionaries could no longer afford to pay the salaries. The Provincial did not think it appropriate to seek such aid, so Pat took it on himself to do all he could, using all his resources, including his retirement pension of $4,800 per annum from the Vatican, to help pay catechists' salaries. Towards this end he sent substantial sums to Bishops and missionaries, not only those in Benin, Warri and Issele-Uku, but to Regional Superiors and missionaries in places like Jos, Kano and Kaduna in Northern Nigeria, and Ghana. Some missionaries had their first contact with Pat when he let them know that he was going to pay their catechists' salaries, Fionnbarra O'Cuilleanáin of Jos, for example, who received £2,100 between 1982 and '84. All the Bishop asked in return was that "the catechists pray for me".

Pat's successor, Bishop Patrick Ekpu, congratulating him on his Diamond Jubilee and sending him greetings for his eighty-seventh birthday, invited him to spend his last years in Benin, recommending that he come before the Irish Winter began. It is customary in many African cultures to be buried in one's home place. Many missionaries, including bishops, have been buried in their African 'homes'. Bishop Terrien of Lagos "died at sea" but, his successors, O'Rourke and Taylor were both buried in Lagos, and Bishop Shanahan of 'Southern Nigeria' had been 're-buried' in Onitsha. Charles Imokhai, secretary of the West African Bishops' Conference, whom Pat had ordained in 1968, wrote wishing him "Many Happy Returns" (of his Diamond Jubilee) and, on visiting him in Cork, asked him, "When you die My Lord will you be buried in Benin?" "Of course I will", Pat replied, "if I die there, but if they put me down here first, I'll stay here". Pat had never favoured the custom of 'second burials'.

His thoughts frequently returned to Benin and he did intimate to a few trusted missionaries that he had thought of returning and that he sometimes felt he had left too soon. However, as his former secretary, Dick Wall, said, "Bishop Kelly knew when it was time to go and didn't linger, though every fibre in him wanted to remain; the people and the clergy also wanted him to remain". Leaving Nigeria had been a sacrifice. He had departed to favour the growth of the indigenous church in accordance with the wishes of Rome. Meanwhile, he continued helping Nigeria with his prayers and donations.

Like most religious houses, Wilton had its quota of callers looking for help. Despite his reputed tight-fistedness, the Bishop sometimes helped people in a quiet way. He gave Sr Nathy, doyen of the Wilton domestic services, an old trousers to give to a regular caller. Nathy incinerated it, saying "the man wouldn't be seen dead in it, it was bent at the knees like a hurley from all the Bishop's praying". Later, Pat asked her if she had given the man the trousers, "You see, I put £10 in the pocket". Another version says it was a ten-shilling note and Pat wanted to retrieve it!

Often blessing others, Pat liked to receive blessings too. Before he retired, he went to see Fr Joe Hilliard, SMA missionary, army chaplain and historian of the mission in Benin, who was then nearing the end of his days in hospital in Dublin. Joe, being very weak and Pat, not being the liveliest of bedside companions, conversation quickly dried up. In a scene reminiscent of St Colmcille's last blessing of his followers in Iona, Pat knelt by the bed saying, "Father before I go, give me your blessing". Joe, raising a weary hand, blessed him. The dying man then said, "Now Bishop give me yours, where I'm going I'm likely to need one more than you". Pat, doubting the last part, gave his blessing with some awkwardness. Apart from his feelings of personal unworthiness, he was sorely aware of the large number of missionaries much younger than himself who had died before him. Joe was fifty-seven.

Probably reminded by his 1981 'death' of the inevitability of the real thing, Pat wrote his will in December that year. In it he was primarily concerned with the obligation of discharging Masses that he might have, unwittingly, omitted during his long life. Having bestowed gifts on family members, he requested Masses for the happy repose of his own soul, for relatives, donors, the most abandoned souls in Purgatory, the conversion of pagans, heretics, Mohammedans, dying sinners and all sinners, especially in Mid-Western Nigeria. The remainder of his estate was to be used for the support of catechists in Africa. In his next Retreat, 1982, the last recorded one; he resolved "To think of himself as being loved by Christ and to have great confidence in the Blessed Virgin Mary".

On 31 August 1984, he celebrated his 90th birthday. Congratulations flooded in from around the world. A special celebration was held in his honour at which more than twenty ex-Benin missionaries took part along with local well-wishers and a group from Galway. The *Evening Echo* commemorated the occasion with a short profile of the Bishop, referring to him as "one of Ireland's most popular and esteemed churchmen". Accompanying the article was a fine photograph of a quietly smiling Pat. The following day its sister paper, the *Cork Examiner*, published an interview with him, entitled "Lay down your arms bishop tells IRA", in which he spoke of the futility of violence and pleaded that it should not be allowed to disrupt the current peace talks between Foreign Minister, Peter Barry, and the Northern Ireland Secretary, Mr Prior. Pat said the violence in the North of Ireland saddened him and he prayed every day for a peaceful solution to its problems.

In 1985 he suffered a heart attack and was taken into intensive care in the Bon Secours. When the immediate crisis was over, the Provincial visited him. With a trace of his old puckish humour, Pat told him, "I'm not gone yet; I have to wait for the call". While recovering, he was confined to bed and not allowed to say Mass – a great deprivation for him. A considerate young priest one Sunday said Mass at his bedside. After following the Mass devoutly, Pat told the celebrant that it wasn't lawful to say Mass in a bedroom so he would have to say another one elsewhere! Proving Michael Foley of Warri correct when he said, "Bishops live to above the average age in every climate", Pat at ninety-one made a good recovery but, on being discharged from the Bons, was moved to Blackrock Road, where medical care was more readily available. In Wilton, Dr Owen O'Sullivan had gone out of his way attending to Pat, and he continued to do so at Blackrock along with Sr Rosalie OLA and her staff. In his new place of retirement he remained "his own man", maintaining his routine which centred more and more on the Blessed Sacrament, the Breviary and the Rosary.

He still drove, but found it increasingly difficult to get the annual licence required of elderly drivers. From Blackrock he managed to drive to Dromantine for a retreat, but requested Brother Jim Redmond of Wilton to drive him home, having ascertained first that Jim did have a valid licence. They began the journey with a rosary, then Jim concentrated on driving and Pat on praying. On arriving at Cork city's bus station, Pat took the wheel, driving on to Blackrock while Jim got the bus home to Wilton. Pat availed of Jim's services a few other times. On one occasion, they drove to Midleton to visit Pat's niece, stopping on the way at the Brothers of Charity's home for handicapped boys at Lota. Pat had been asked by one of the boys' mothers to visit and bless her son who was severely affected with Down's syndrome. Indoors or out of doors the Bishop always wore clerical attire but, by now, his old black suit was the worse for wear. At Midleton his niece Ann welcomed them. She was married to Pat Burns, a former maths and science teacher in Benin. Over tea and scones, she told Jim that the Bishop had actually done "baby-sitting" for her and was very good with the children. When she asked Pat why he didn't get a new suit? He replied in his old bantering style, "I keep a good one at home for special occasions!"

He celebrated the Golden Jubilee of his episcopal ordination[1] in June 1990, a truly remarkable achievement and he was the first to do so in the history of the Society. Unfortunately, he was again in the Bon Secours, but well enough to concelebrate Mass in the hospital chapel along with his successor, Bishop Ekpu, Bishop William Mahony of Ilorin, Fr John Quinlan the Irish Provincial, and Pat's nephew, Fr Anthony. Among the many who sent their congratulations was Dominic Conway, who had become the Bishop of Elphin in Sligo. With his felicitations, Bishop Conway recalled Pat's "inspiring sharing of his Christmas dinner" with him in Benin in 1967.

After celebrating the Feast of the Assumption on 15 August 1973, Pat departed from Benin. On the same Marian feast, eighteen years later, he was admitted to the Regional Hospital after a fall in Blackrock. As he was also suffering from blood pressure and heart complications, his family were informed of his critical state. Fr Peter Thompson, administering the Last Rites, was struck by his calmness in the face of death. Fr Anthony Kelly rushed to the hospital and, finding his uncle in repose with his eyes closed, decided to say the Rosary. Anthony began, counting the Aves on his fingers, as he had forgotten his beads. Nearing the end of the fifth decade, unsure whether he had said nine or ten Hail Marys,

---

[1] Up to the year 2006, only one other SMA confrere has celebrated an episcopal Golden Jubilee, Mgr Andre van den Bronk of the Dutch Province, who was ordained Coadjutor Bishop of Heliopolis, Nile Delta, in 1946. He ruled over three different jurisdictions in succession: Nile Delta, Kumasi in Ghana, and Parakou in the Republic of Benin. He died at the age of eighty-nine in the Netherlands in 1997. A French confrere, Msgr Pierre Rouanet, aged eighty-seven, in retirement in Montferrier will, Deo volente, celebrate his Golden Jubilee in November 2006.

he decided to say two more for safety. When he had said them and was about to begin the 'Glory be', a not-so-weak voice from the bed instructed, "*Four* more, *four* more"! On the following day, Anthony visited again, the Bishop seemed to be in a coma. Anthony said Mass in the room in the presence of Fr Dick Wall and some family members. Pat lay unmoving throughout the Eucharist, except at the consecration when he raised his hand and placed it on the pectoral cross on his chest. Sr Grace OLA, and others who had attended to him in his last days in Blackrock and in the Regional Hospital, where he survived for three days before breathing his last, found him prayerful and serene. He, who had often preached to others that it was a terrible thing to fall into the hands of the living God, at his own death seemed to manifest that it was the living, merciful, and loving Father that he believed in and was going to meet. Long ago in a retreat in June 1948, he had made the resolution, "To love God as much as I can, so that when death comes I may feel how sweet it is to be judged by Him". He slipped away quietly on Sunday morning, 18 August 1991. He would have been ninety-seven years of age on the 31st.

The funeral was delayed until the 22nd in order to give Bishops Ekpu and Gbuji a chance to be present but, though they stormed Heaven and British Airways, they could not get seats on the already overbooked summer flights. Pat was buried in the Society's cemetery at Wilton in the presence of a large congregation of relatives and friends, including three busloads of neighbours from Galway, Protestants as well as Catholics. Mgr William Mahony, former Bishop of Ilorin, was the chief celebrant at the Requiem Mass. He was assisted by the Provincial, John Quinlan; Superior General, Paddy Harrington; Anthony Kelly and Stephen Kelly (New York), nephews; and Dick Wall and Jim Higgins, who were both on leave from Benin. Bishops Michael Murphy and John Buckley of Cork presided and Gus O' Driscoll, Wilton, was the master of ceremonies. Ninety SMA priests concelebrated along with twenty-one non-SMA clergy. Eight more SMA priests and three SMA Brothers were among the congregation in the church. Many OLA Sisters and representatives of the Medical Missionaries of Mary, St Louis Sisters, Notre Dame Sisters, Sisters of Mercy, Sisters of Charity and Sisters from the Bon Secours attended. Alderman Jim Corr, a friend of the SMA and a former lay missionary in Nigeria, represented the city fathers. The choir of St Joseph's Church, Wilton, under Brother Jim Redmond, accompanied by organist Phil O'Donovan sang, and the Catholic Boy Scouts of Ireland mounted a Guard of Honour.

A Benin missionary, Mattie O'Connell, one of the first 'Tyros' at St Philomena's, Uromi in 1957, found it "the saddest funeral" he had ever attended. Recalling that in Benin, the funeral of one who had lived a full life is celebrated joyfully and the coffin is borne to the grave accompanied by singing and dancing, he found the atmosphere in Wilton very sombre and sad. Most of the people present did not know the Bishop as did the Nigerian catechists he had trained, the hundreds of teachers he had employed, the diocesan priests he had ordained, or the old people he had instructed in the faith, baptised, confirmed, counselled, haggled with and laughed with for almost half a century. They were his real flock and he was their good Shepherd.

After the burial, a couple spoke to one of the SMA priests at the graveside, telling him that they had a son in his thirties who had been suffering from terminal cancer. Not long before Pat's death, they brought their son to see him in Blackrock. The young man, diffident about 'miracles' and visits to holy men, went reluctantly. The three met Pat in the parlour, where he prayed with them and gave his blessing. "Our son made a complete recovery", they said.

Chapter 17

CONCLUSION

Bishop Patrick Joseph Kelly SMA deserves a special place in the history of Western Nigeria. His contribution is most clearly seen in his work for Church and schools.

When he was nominated Vicar Apostolic of Western Nigeria in 1939 there were some 30,000 Catholics in the area, when he retired in 1973 there were over 180,000. The increase in the numbers of schools was even more remarkable. In 1939 there were 157 elementary schools and 20 higher schools in the Vicariate. In 1973 the numbers had grown to about 700 elementary schools, 41 secondary grammar schools and 45 secondary modern schools. The numbers of pupils and teachers had increased in proportion. Already in 1959, Bishop Kelly employed no less than 4,183 teachers.

The mission schools were of a high standard, noted for discipline and good results. The secondary schools ranked among the most prestigious in the land and many of the alumni attained high positions in public life, becoming State Governors, ministers, commissioners, high court judges, lawyers and school principals. The schools and Kelly's seminaries prepared the way for the formation of an indigenous clergy and hierarchy. When Bishop Kelly retired he left behind a thriving local church led by Nigerian Bishops assisted by Nigerian priests as well as by a diminishing number of missionaries. The large vibrant congregations in the churches of the new dioceses of Benin, Warri, Issele-Uku, and Lokoja, all at one time in his jurisdiction, and the hundreds of students in the seminaries augured well for the future.

In the education of girls Bishop Kelly was greatly indebted to the Religious Sisters, OLA, RSC, and SND and to their many helpers. In this biography, not much has been said of the extensive medical apostolate in Benin, for which major credit must go to the Sisters and their staffs. But, apart from his wholehearted support for existing medical works, Bishop Kelly was also the inspiration behind many new ones.

Furthermore he deserves credit for helping to establish an indigenous sisterhood. Bishop Taylor of Lagos is usually mentioned alone as the one responsible for motivating the OLA Sisters to found a Nigerian congregation but, from the beginning, Kelly was with him in the venture. The 1942 Contract between the Sisters and the two bishops stated, "The Congregation of the Sisters of Our Lady of Apostles undertakes the formation of a Society of African Sisters according to the wishes of the Ordinaries of the Vicariates of the Bight of Benin [Lagos] and Western Nigeria [Benin]". Mother Enda Barrett OLA founded and began the training of the Sisters of the Eucharistic Heart of Jesus in Taylor's Vicariate. Known as "the Ibonwon Sisters", they began working in Taylor's jurisdiction. Later, Kelly appealed to the OLA Provincial in Cork, saying "Something has to be done about the establishment of the Native Sisterhood [in Benin]. I was thinking of making arrangements for them at Ughelli or Sapele. If you agree I can start building immediately" (25 November '55). The following year he asked for three African Sisters for Benin "to encourage other girls to join". The Ibonwon Sisters finally came to the diocese in the early Sixties. Shortly after the arrival of the missionary Sisters of Notre Dame in 1966, Bishop Kelly asked them to help in the foundation and training of another congregation of Nigerian Sisters and, hoping for a positive response, he began building a convent in Agenebode. The Sisters felt that it would be premature for them to undertake such work, but they kept his request in mind and, shortly after his retirement, with Bishop Ekpu's blessing, they began training Nigerian postulants, using Pat's unfinished convent at Agenebode.

A man of God, the spirituality of Bishop Kelly

Pat's unceasing labour to evangelize Benin was motivated by his missionary zeal, deep faith and unshakeable conviction that baptism was necessary for salvation. He believed he was an instrument of God's salvific will and that Christ was with him in his mission; he also believed that the force of evil, or the Devil, was working against him. He nourished his work with prayer and adoration, convinced that progress would not be made without continual communing with God, constant efforts towards personal sanctification and generous self-sacrifice. In keeping with the ascetical theology of the times he extolled highly 'love of the Cross', and preached and struggled against 'self-will'. Personality traits and early formation facilitated his espousing a severe type of spirituality. Reducing personal relaxation and recreation with others to a minimum, he cultivated 'friendship with God' rather than with individual men and women. In this he adhered to the letter of the SMA Directory which forbade "particular friendships" and cautioned missionaries against familiarity with lay expatriates and the ruling elite.

In Ireland and in Nigeria, Bishop Kelly has a reputation for being a 'saintly man', but whether he reached that state of "heroic virtue" required in the Roman process of beatification is another matter. Many consider him to be "the holiest man" they ever knew and quite a number consider him a saint. The majority of the Christians in Benin revered him and some are calling for his canonisation. A few, including high-ranking prelates in Nigeria, have aptly pointed out that the SMA are pursuing the cause of Melchior de Marion Brésillac, "whom we don't know, while it neglects to pursue the causes of some that we do know, like Bishop Kelly". Both in Ireland and in Nigeria there are people who pray to him and some people relate stories about him that we associate with 'Saints' – cures, bilocation, appearances in dreams and visions and other 'wonders'. None of these phenomena, or the oral reports of them, have been rigorously tested, but they are part of the 'cult of saints' and possibly the beginnings of something that may develop into a more serious consideration of his sanctity. In both countries there are 'cures' accredited to his prayers or to intercession through him. In Eku, his first mission, there is a strong desire that the house he built there in 1922 be preserved in his memory and used as a library, youth hall or some other useful parish institution. Incidentally, the church in Eku is called "St Patrick's" and the patron of the archdiocese of Benin is also St Patrick.

In order of precedence the Binis, convinced of Bishop Kelly's closeness to God, placed him second only to their traditional ruler, the Oba. In the streets of Benin City and in the villages, people were known to run after him, like the woman in the Gospel, "to touch the hem of his garment". The Nigerian view, or popular memory of him, is of special interest. Less reserved than the Irish, Nigerians readily affirm, "We loved him; everyone loved him and we knew he loved us and was praying for us". The faithful and non-Catholics too were very impressed by his concern for the sick, the poor, the homeless and the dying. His prayerfulness sowed seeds, the churches in Benin are noted for the numbers of individuals and groups who frequent them, not only for ceremonies, but at other times. It was one of Pat's great joys to find people, especially the young, in prayer before the Blessed Sacrament.

Nigerian priests, who knew him from the time they were altar servers and junior seminarians, were fond of him and regarded him not only as their Bishop but as a good uncle. They are, in fact, less likely than Irish confreres to highlight his 'tight-fistedness' and are more likely to defend him, even his driving! One said, "He didn't crash cars like many of his priests did"! A number of the African clergy even attested to his generosity! "When we were seminarians, he gave us pocket and travel money. He never turned anyone away and was very good to those in trouble". They recalled that he was difficult to deceive, "Your face be like 'water side'," he would say to someone who was trying to trick him ('water side' was a place where rubbish was dumped). He was able to talk to young seminarians in a way they understood, "God be no small boy, no give him half penny" or, "Go shave the grass" (cut the grass), to someone caught breaking rules. If altar servers indulged in tasting the Mass wine, he was quick to notice, "Go wash 'em", he'd say pointing at purple stained lips. And bidding farewell to a young priest, Fr Pedro Martins, about to begin teaching in the seminary he advised him solemnly, "When you teach, pray for your students", adding with poker face, "that they will understand your English"!

Priests and people found him very accessible, "He didn't wait for you to go to him, he visited everyone in every corner of the diocese and he knew how to talk to people. He treated you as an equal and didn't talk down to you". The Nigerians were impressed by his work for education and by his lifestyle, "He established schools where the Government couldn't and set up more schools than any Ministry of Education ever did. His way of doing things attracted many to the seminary and to the church – he was a kind priest and father".

Brother Jim Redmond SMA, who worked for the *Nigerian Independent* in Ibadan, recalled that one bishop never failed to send a cheque of £100 every Christmas for the support of the paper, which was then running on a shoe-string – Bishop Kelly! To Jim's knowledge, he was the only bishop, apart from Bishop Finn who founded the paper, to give support. His generous 'dash' paid the workers' salaries for a month. Another one surprised at Pat's 'generosity' was Mgr Delisle CSSp who took over the Kabba-Lokoja district from Pat in 1955. Despite what he had heard about Pat's tightness with money, he found him generous and prompt in handing over funds due to the new division. Pat was likewise unstinting in settling financial affairs with the new bishops of the other divisions of his diocese. His reputed 'tight-fistedness' was not meanness but thrift combined with a scrupulous desire to see that money was used in the most beneficial way possible. For him to waste anything was anathema, and he was firmly convinced that when people had to pay for something they appreciated it much more than if they got it for nothing.

Nigerian women remembered that he had time for them when they were children. They were not afraid to play and skip around him. A favourite question he used to ask them was, "What would you say to a dying pagan?" When it was time for prayers, he 'shoo-ed' them into church with a stick, but he never struck anyone. Finding little girls chattering in church he'd scold them mildly, telling them to "Say sorry to Jesus". He liked to speak to them of the Infant Jesus and, for confirmation, recommended that they take the name of 'Mary'. Men, who had been his altar servers, recalled marvels that occurred on journeys with him to out stations. For instance, on the way home one day, his car 'broke down'. After checking the engine and finding nothing wrong, he realized that the car was out of petrol. "Pray, boys" he said and, blessing the car, sat in, started the engine and drove home. On reaching his house the car stopped again – out of fuel!

Some people feared him, regarding him as a powerful "juju man". His righteous anger, or that of his God, was not to be provoked. His reading of Lamentations and other severe scriptural passages at a place where a Catholic girl had been abducted was not forgotten, nor was the fate of some men who had defied him bitterly on a church matter. Though sympathetic to the people and their culture, he was well aware that Benin had been, and still was in many respects, 'a pagan place'. He had opposed what he considered to be unacceptable customs, ranging from the wearing of amulets (charms against evil) to sacrifices to traditional gods or spirits. But, in retirement, he admitted that he had probably been too severe in his opposition to some customs, 'second burials', for example, "After all", he said "the Nigerian priests understood them better than we did".

On leave in Ireland and during his retirement, there was a growing demand for his prayers and blessings, and sometimes for healing. A healing, not mentioned already, was that of a child, Gabrielle Kelly, the daughter of the local postman. She suffered seriously from eczema which was very hard to cure in the Forties when doctors had no antibiotics. Having tried everything without good results, the parents asked Bishop Kelly to see her. He went to their home, prayed and blessed the child. Shortly afterwards the rash cleared. Gabrielle's parents, older sister, and Pat's sister-in-law Ellen, a nurse, believed that the healing came about as the result of his prayers. In another case, Sr Celestine OLA requested Pat to pray for a childless couple. Subsequently, the couple had three children.

After Pat's death, the Kelly family received a number of requests for fragments of his clothing or personal effects as 'keepsakes' or 'relics'. A number of people, both in Ireland and in Nigeria, include him in their panoply of saints and ask for favours through his intercession.

It is beyond the scope of this book to evaluate 'miraculous' phenomena or private convictions about him. The process of canonization is rigorous and the requirement of having critical documentary evidence brings many cases to a halt. Usually, reports of 'favours' or 'cures' are not lacking, but authoritative documentation about them is. Such difficulties are now being encountered in the beatification processes of both Marion Brésillac and Joseph Shanahan of Southern Nigeria. Without waiting for judgement in their cases, one might ask, "Does Bishop Kelly have 'the makings of a saint' and would it be worth introducing his cause?" The people who worked in his diocese have some interesting views.

The OLA Sisters, without overlooking some 'thorny' character traits, in general held him in very high esteem. "We liked Bishop Kelly; he was a saint in his own odd way. He was good to the poor. We understood him and he was great to us" – Dominica Geary. "We all admired him for his goodness. He had some 'charism' and enthusiasm for what he was doing. He usually didn't look like a bishop; he was more like a farmer with no pretensions. He came for my final vows in Warri and gave three of us our canonical examination, he was so nice, so gentle" – Maura Hayes. "He was a wonderful man, a saint, people idolised him. He was severe and tough but very genuine" – Teresa Nolan. "Bishop Kelly, our saintly SMA was a wonderful missionary, full of zeal and vision for the spread of the Kingdom. Every spare minute he had was spent in the oratory. We thank God for him" – Nora Culleton. "He was like Christ, especially in poverty. We had vows, but he kept them" – Stella Marie. "A great old man, a Saint" – Perpetua Hanbury.

The Sisters of Charity held similar views. "Bishop Kelly was unique, a man who walked with Christ" – Marie Gerard. "Our relations with him were so good regarding the hospital that we agreed to run a school for him. He was shy and quiet, but kind and gentle" – Carmel McAteer. "Every one of us thought he was a saint, a humble saintly man. That was the first impression and the last. He was a real missionary and a devoted follower of Christ" – Mary Raphael. Notre Dame Sister, Bernadette Gannon, who built the SND hospital in Uzairue said, "I have marvellous memories of Bishop Kelly, he was my inspiration even if he ran out the back door when he thought I had come to request money. I pray to the Holy Man".

Naturally, the SMA confreres often discussed 'Pajo'. As bishops went, he was different. Joe Donnelly, who lived with him, saw him as a man who was in close union with God and very open to the Holy Spirit but, also, as one who viewed God as a strict taskmaster. No doubt, his adherence to such a view increased his tendency to push his personnel to the limit. For instance, he expected school men, after a hard week teaching, to hear Confessions 'till late on Saturdays and say two long public

Masses in places far apart on Sundays. Joe, a school Principal, heard Confessions on Friday nights instead of Saturday because of inter-school games on Saturdays. Pat berated him over this and "In matters like that he could be very harsh". "But", Joe admitted, "no matter how angry you got with him, he heard you out and allowed you to make your point even if it was diametrically opposed to his own. Afterwards he would never hold anything against you. In fact, he was likely to make a cup of tea for you as if nothing had happened".

Pat never lowered the high expectations he had of his personnel. Fr Jim Tobin, as well as being a full-time staff member of a Teacher Training College near Ossiomo, was Welfare Officer of the leper settlement and, at the same time, was building a new church at Abudu. When the day for opening the new church came, the Bishop arrived early and blessed the church without waiting for the arrival of the local dignitaries or the inaugural Mass. He then departed without a word of explanation or commendation to the young priest. "Pat" got away with things like that. All his personnel could do was shrug their shoulders and add another story to their growing trove of Kelly lore and legend. It was useless to expect praise or appreciation, Pat didn't believe in it. As one confrere, not referring specifically to this case, said, "The actions of Saints don't always make good sense and Bishop Kelly was no exception to that rule".

If Pat saw God as a taskmaster, he also saw Him as an absolutely trustworthy one. This probably facilitated the great trust he placed in his own personnel and in his staunch support of them if they ever got into difficulties. Well might he quote Ecclesiasticus 6, 37, when directing young priests on retreat in Asaba in the Fifties, "Always think on God's commandments, and be constant in following His will; be sure he will give you perseverance, and all your desire for wisdom will be granted you". While he believed in appointing a man to a place that suited him and did his best to accommodate his talents and preferences, he also believed that if a priest didn't like his appointment he should persevere in it "for the good of souls". It wasn't academic brilliance or outstanding pastoral efficiency that Pat looked for, "The whole thing is to make the Fathers faithful to their spiritual exercises and put their own personal sanctification first as the chief means of winning souls for the love of Christ". This maxim almost paraphrased the SMA Directory which put personal sanctification as the first aim of the members of the Society. As Visitor and as Bishop, Pat believed that, "Whoever is ruling should aim at the personal holiness of his men before all other things".

His spirituality is rather well illustrated by his favourite prayer, the *En Ego,* a popular post communion reflection, said kneeling before an image of the crucified Christ:

> Behold, O good and most sweet Jesus, I cast myself upon my knees in Thy sight and, with the most fervent desire of my soul, I pray and beseech Thee to impress upon my heart lively sentiments of faith, hope and charity with true repentance for my sins and a firm purpose of amendment; while with deep affection and grief of soul I ponder within myself and mentally contemplate Thy five most precious wounds, having before my eyes that which David spoke in prophecy of Thee, O good Jesus: "They have pierced my hands and my feet, they have numbered all my bones".

Though a much loved prayer, the *En Ego* reflects a rather anxious type of spirituality, emphasising human sinfulness on the one hand and Christ's physical sufferings on the other. Like the SMA Directory, it tended to promote a striving for 'perfection' on an individual, interior basis, stressing the need of sorrow for sin and the performance of penance. Pat, acutely conscious of human sinfulness, was dominated more by a sense of God's Judgement than by His mercy and loving kindness. The grim theology and spirituality to which he subscribed is well described as the "Alone with the Alone" type or the "Agere contra" (go against oneself) type. This spirituality was acceptable to many, not least to 'foreign missionaries' who often found themselves alone in difficult situations, but few of Pat's contemporaries subscribed to it as much as he did. Neither did all his confreres agree with the Directory's formulation of the member's First Aim – "to seek one's personal sanctification". Joe Barrett, in Ubiaja for instance, thought "to seek the Glory of God" would have been a better way of putting it.

"To seek the Glory of God in all things" was the aim of the Jesuits who opposed a powerful, but insidious, movement in the Church in the seventeenth century. 'Jansenism', inspired by Bishop Cornelius Jansen's flawed interpretation of Augustinian anthropology, had spread widely in Europe. Augustine affirmed the basic goodness of human nature but Jansen emphasised concupiscence and the need to control the 'flesh'. His teaching developed into a severe, legalistic type of theology which, over-stressing God's justice, allowed little scope for His love and mercy. In the faithful it engendered an unholy 'fear of God' and doubts about the possibility of personal salvation. Introduced into Ireland by Irish priests trained in France, it affected especially serious-minded individuals inclined to scrupulosity. Pat Kelly did not escape.

Tommy Greene, Joe Barrett's near neighbour in Ubiaja, was another confrere who felt ill-at-ease with some aspects of contemporary spirituality. He recalled how his own father, a Galway man, would receive Communion only once a year and spend the whole of Lent 'mortifying' himself in preparation for it. It took time before Pope Pius X's encouragement of frequent communion became effective. In the early Fifties, African Missions superiors were engaged in reviewing the Society's Constitutions and Directory and in the revised edition of the Directory of 1954, the first aim was re-stated as personal sanctification "after the Glory of God". This came too late for some and because of fidelity to a grim type of spirituality Pat, and many others, suffered anxiety about the life to come and were uncomfortable about enjoyment in this life.

In 1939, Tommy Greene had wondered whether Bishop-Elect Pat Kelly would turn out to be "a bit of a Hitler". Half a century later he thought he had turned out to be a saint! In retirement in the Eighties, Tommy paid tribute to Pat, "We benefited from the great leadership of Bishop Kelly, a really holy man; like all holy men he could be very harsh and strict and if you didn't do your work he'd 'floor' you, but beneath it all he had a very loving heart; he was a saint".

A large number of confreres would concur with Tommy, while others, more reserved on the question of sainthood, had other (good) opinions about him. Michael Foley of Warri, saw him as a shrewd leader with a talent for putting men in the right place and leaving them to get on with the job. Jim Byrne described him as "one of our greatest and most outstanding personalities". Foley and Byrne knew Pat when he was a 'young' bishop and it was rather soon then to be commenting on his 'sanctity'. Nevertheless, even before he became a bishop, many saw sanctity beyond the ordinary in him. Georges Krauth referred to him as "a holy priest who would draw down God's blessings on his work". A large number of confreres, impressed by his 'godliness' more than his ability, thought he would be Bishop Broderick's successor in 1933. But it was Leo Taylor who was chosen. When Taylor was in office, Stephen Harrington, wrote to him saying, "In your absence Pat Kelly will maintain the Faith in the Vicariate". And when Pat succeeded Taylor, the missionaries agreed that whatever else might suffer, spiritual matters would not. The newly arrived Principal of Immaculate Conception College in 1943, Andy O'Rourke, told the Provincial, "You need have no worries about my spiritual life while I am in such close proximity to Bishop Kelly". But, never one to attribute virtue or holiness to himself, Pat became irritated if others did and, if he heard confreres praising another man, he told them to desist, "You will only make him proud". For Pat, everything was God's doing, "God can make up for the defects of the instruments He uses and if the missionary always keeps His Holy Will in view and relies on His Goodness, his career on the Missions will be a success".

His acceptance of contemporary theology's negative view of human nature and view of God as a strict Judge, is seen in his severity on himself and, occasionally, on others. It is also seen in his anxiety about laws and rules and in his extreme concern to baptise dying pagans as if God was more likely to damn them than to save. Though having much to do with personality, especially shyness, his avoidance of close human relationships also partly stemmed from this kind of theology. He didn't reciprocate the friendship offered by people like Pat Keohane, his old school master, class mates like Stephen Harrington and John Cadogan, or mission men like Georges Krauth. John Mahon, his loyal Vicar, was one he trusted and admired, but from whom he also kept a distance, even telling him on one occasion,"You can't stay with me in Benin City in case people think there are two bishops here". No doubt he said this in jest but, humour was one of his ways of imparting serious messages. Bishop Taylor esteemed Pat, but admitted they weren't 'friends'. The only 'close human relationships' Pat sought were those of the spiritual type – with confessors and spiritual directors. While he didn't go regularly to others for the sake of company, he went weekly for absolution. Careful how he addressed his personnel, he never, or hardly ever, used first names, but called everyone by an impersonal "Father" or "Sister", and avoided signing letters with anything more personal than "Oremus pro invicem" (Let us pray for one another). On one occasion he actually crossed out "Yours sincerely" in a letter to a man he knew well, considering it too familiar, and concluded instead with the usual Oremus...

More conscious of the righteous, punishing God than of the

forgiving, compassionate One, he often said, "I'd prefer to do penance in this life than in the next" and, thinking of Bishop Broderick's final sufferings, said, "I believe he has his Purgatory over him". Despite his constant communicating with God in prayer, there was a strong mixture of fear in his attitude to Him. Though he understood the Gospels and their practical import of charity better than most, his putting of 'soul' before body often gave the impression of excessive other-worldliness and extreme miserliness. At times it seemed as if he wanted people to suffer now so as to improve their chance of getting into Heaven. The kind of scriptural passages he most often used were of the Hell-fire type: "What does it profit a man if he gains the whole world and suffers the loss of his soul"; "It is a terrible thing to fall into the hands of the living God"; "Terrible to hear the words, 'depart from me into the eternal fires prepared for the Devil and his angels'." He emphasised sin and repentance in his sermons and told young priests "When you preach, never forget to mention Hell, you have to make people afraid sometimes". His major theme in retreat giving was "The four last things" – death, judgement, Heaven and Hell. He feared that the eternal lives of the non-baptised were in great danger and he asked readers of the *African Missionary* to "Implore God that our labour will benefit the souls of these poor people who are still under the power of Hell".

In Pastoral Letters to his flock he insisted, "The first thing God wants from you is your conversion and repentance, unless you do penance you will all perish". In his 1967 Pastoral he said, "If there are sinners who find it hard to repent, let them meditate on the Passion of Christ. Let them meet Jesus carrying His Cross and ask themselves who is the suffering one? For whom does He suffer and why? He suffers for love of you. It was your sins that brought Him to this miserable state. Shall you repent now or still continue to inflict more wounds on the Sacred Humanity of Jesus? 'Deny yourselves, take up your cross and follow me', seems a hard saying to many, but it will be much harder to hear the words, 'Depart from me ye cursed into everlasting fire'." He seemed to have accepted that it was extremely hard to get into Heaven. When informed of the death of his mother, his response was, "I hope she has gained the eternal reward", and after the death of a good man, noted for asceticism, he said, "I hope he is in Heaven, if he's not what chance have some of us". Perpetually begging for prayers, he seemed to be over-conscious of personal sin – a feature of the age, but one which many of the great saints manifested!

In his Lenten Pastoral of 1972 he picked on Christians who had slipped back into 'idol worship'. Fearing that they were "even more numerous than those who remain faithful", he quoted Jeremiah 11,12, "Be ye astonished, o ye Heavens, for my people have done two evils, they left the fountain of living water and made for themselves broken cisterns that can hold no water". He recommended that all in Lent do penance for sin and pray, not only for the conversion of pagans, but for "bad Catholics" adding, "Don't forget to pray for yourself that you may never become one of them". Much given to performing the Stations of the Cross, he was happy to be able to add a postscript saying, "ALL priests now have the faculty of erecting the Way of the Cross. They should be erected in every church".

Despite his grim spirituality Pat, when corresponding with members of his family, was warm and affectionate. In his letters to them he always concluded with something like, "Your fond brother" or "Your loving Uncle". His basic familial instincts were warmer than the theology he had imbibed but, never letting go of the latter, he maintained severe views to the end of his days. In retirement in Wilton when one of the staff defended the buying of new padded seats for the oratory, saying people might pray better if more comfortable, Pat retorted, "Did you never hear Jesus's words, 'Unless you do penance you will all perish'." In a community meeting about topics for a day of recollection he exclaimed, "I haven't heard a sermon on mortification since 1938" and, in a discussion about the decline of vocations he said, "What do you expect with soft seats in the oratory!"

Pat's personality and his strong spirit of obedience to church law and Society rules, combined with the grim theology of the times to make his life and ministry more anxious and demanding than they needed to be. But as each bout of anxieties and fears assailed him, he struggled, prayed, wrestled like Jacob with God and, at times, with the Devil, but he never allowed himself to be overcome. His way was a tough one but he persevered, carrying his cross on a road that bore exceptional fruit in service to others and brought him close to the God who is closer to the weak and suffering than to the strong.

While his preaching was forbidding, it would not be true to say that he was a dour or depressing person. Jim Higgins, one of the longest-serving missionaries in Benin said, "Despite the hardships and the ascetic life he lived, Bishop Kelly always gave the impression of being a happy, contented man, sociable, good-humoured and witty. He was relaxed and at ease in the company of confreres and Africans, especially catechists and head Christians". Indeed, Bishop Kelly was a man fully alive, in love with Jesus Christ, and overcome by His Spirit. As death approached he became calm and peaceful, as if the God he really believed in, the Triune God of healing, love, and mercy, broke through his fears and claimed the central place in his consciousness.

The severity of his spirituality was softened a little by his devotion to Mary, the Mother of God. On being asked to talk about missionary spirituality, the first thing he mentioned was the importance of the Rosary. Constantly saying the rosary himself, he was never without his beads, "the most useful tools he ever had" observed Mary Coughlan who helped nurse him in his final days. As a pastor he established Holy Rosary Societies in his parish centres. He recommended that girls take the name 'Mary' for Confirmation and, at least once, concluded a letter with "Pray to the Sacred Heart and His Blessed Mother for the Vicariate and us all". Rarely mentioning miracles, he entertained hopes that Bishop Broderick would be cured at Lourdes through the Divine Mother's intercession. The patron of Ossiomo Leper Settlement was "The Virgin Mary, mother of Orphans". For the feast day, 17 September 1955, Pat got special permission from Rome for Marian readings for the Mass, and he instructed Benin City and Asaba convents to celebrate the feast too. Many of the institutions in the diocese were named 'for' Mary, significantly his first secondary school in Benin City, "Immaculate Conception College". He was not pleased when, ironically, intending to honour him, the name was changed to "Bishop Kelly College". He was happy when the name was changed back to the original. A great number of the schools, hospitals and clinics in his diocese were named after Mary and, although the Sisters of Our Lady of Apostles, Notre Dame, and the Sisters of Charity were responsible for most of these, Pat gave his approval.

His retreat resolutions (see Appendix II) show how devoted he was to Mary, whom he regarded as Intercessor, Protector, Counsellor and "Mother of the Sacred Heart". To Our Lady of Good Counsel he turned in his doubts and to her, as Mother of Perpetual Succour, he turned in his difficulties. She was included in practically all of his sets of resolutions and he concluded many of them by entrusting their fulfilment into her hands. While trying to imitate her, especially in her humility, meekness and confidence in Jesus, he wished to love and serve her as Joseph did.

~~~

Pat's manner of organizing things or dealing with people might not always have been the best, yet the esteem of his flock and the loyalty of practically all his personnel were never in question.

Hard taskmaster and tight-fisted as he was, few Irish missionary bishops could claim as much love and loyalty as he did. A partial explanation for this was that he never asked anyone to do anything he hadn't done, or wasn't doing, himself. Probably more important, was his example of total fidelity to his missionary vocation and his self-sacrificing concern for people, especially the poor and needy. He did not cultivate particular friendships, but treated everyone equally and, as one confrere well said, "We had an affectionate joking relationship with him. We liked him, respected him and loved him". The gruff, awkward man who was too shy or fearful to let his love be seen, was greatly loved. People saw that he was a genuine man of God and, therefore, could truly point the way to loving companionship with Him and to Christ-like service of others. Applicable are the words of Zechariah (8, 23), "We want to go with you, since we have learnt that God is with you".

Bishop Kelly at 90, 31 August 1984

APPENDIX I

Nigerian priests ordained by Bishop Kelly

Anselm Ojefua	20/12/42	Sacred Heart, Warri
Stephen Umurie	–	–
Augustine Emordi	5/6/49	St Paul's, Issele-Uku
Patrick Ugboko	1/4/51	St Joseph's, Asaba
Lucas Olu Nwaezeapu	2/2/58	St Augustine's, Ibusa
Peter Onogwue	--	–
Vincent Obudu	18/1/59	Sacred Heart, Warri
Stephen Ogbeide	27/3/60	St Benedict's, Ubiaja
Peter Nyowheoma	1/1/61	Sacred Heart, Warri
Alphonsus Obine	–	–
Alexander Nzemeke	8/1/61	St John's, Illah
Andrew Nwesi	–	–
Joseph Efebe	7/1/62	Sacred Heart, Warri
Stephen Okotete	–	–
Patrick Ekpu	7/7/63	St Theresa's, Uromi
Paul Emonyon	–	–
Paul Gariaga	–	–
Peter Oyemonlan	–	–
Lawrence Balogun	5/7/64	St Mary's, Igarra
Raphael Nweke	19/6/66	St John's, Agbor
John Osia	–	–
Patrick Isichei	19/12/66	St Joseph's, Asaba
Thomas Oleghe	31/12/67	Sacred Heart, Agenebode

Thomas Areleme	21/12/68	St Peter's, Uzairue
Charles Imokhai	–	–
Joseph Okoh	–	–
Michael Onwueme	29/12/68	St Charles, Ubulu-Uku
Victor Emumwen	1/1/69	Holy Cross, Benin City
Francis Ogagbor	20/12/69	St John's, Illah
John Umunnah	20/12/70	St Joseph's, Asaba
Michael Guobadia	27/12/70	Holy Cross, Benin City
Theophilus Uwaifo	–	–

Benin seminarians ordained for Bishop Kelly by other prelates:

Bernard Elaho, ordained by Cardinal McIntyre, 1954, in Lagos

Christopher Chukwumah, ordained by Bishop Reddington, 1/1/57, St Joseph's, Asaba

Anthony Gbuji, ordained in Rome, 23/12/58

Lawrence Attah and Thomas Obozuwa, ordained by Bishop Nwaezeapu, 25 June 1966, Agenebode

The list is taken from Bishop Kelly's personal Register of Ordinations, but is not complete. Other men ordained during his reign include: Benjamin Bello 1964, Francis Atabouku 1966, and Patrick Usenbor 1968. About ten more men were ordained for Warri diocese before Bishop Kelly retired; most of these men had joined the seminary before Warri diocese was erected. From 1971, Bishop Ekpu, Pat's Coadjutor, ordained the priests for Benin diocese.

Senior seminarians, St Paul's, Benin City

At St Paul's, 1953: *in front* Julius Adeniyi, Joe Stephens, Dr Creaven,
Bp Kelly, Paddy Hughes, Bill Kennedy.

APPENDIX II

RETREAT RESOLUTIONS OF BISHOP KELLY

The Resolutions of Bishop Kelly were found recently in the parlour of the 'old house' at Tristaun. Made during retreats over the years, they were jotted on odd scraps of paper, single pages, and the backs of envelopes. Seán Kelly, the Bishop's nephew, kindly sent me copies. I have incorporated the 1940 resolutions in the main text (see Chapter 7), and the rest are here. Though normally of use to the retreatant only, Bishop Kelly's resolutions are of great interest to us because they reveal so much about him and because they give evidence of a life "hidden in God". His resolutions, unpolished as they are, may truly be viewed as stepping stones, marking the growth of a progressive love affair with Christ. Intended for personal use only, they were not written with an eye to grammar, punctuation, or style. Many sentences are incomplete and words are often abbreviated, hence a little editing was required and some repetitions have been omitted, otherwise the text here is a faithful copy of the Bishop's own.

Though he made reference to Resolutions written in 1937, those of his long retreat in Cloughballymore in 1940 were the earliest ones found. Added to these resolutions is his note that they were "not binding under pain of sin of any kind". This admonition is repeated in many subsequent Resolutions. Members of the SMA, following Society Rule, normally make a retreat of approximately a 'week's' duration every year. In Nigeria, two retreats were organized annually (usually in January and in July or August), so that priests could go to one or the other; Pat liked to take part in both. As well as an annual retreat, the Rule required confreres to do a "Monthly Recollection", consisting of a day or two of quiet personal reflection. After the 1940 Resolutions, the next ones of

Bishop Kelly to survive were those of:

July 1942
"To keep the rule of monthly retreat, spiritual reading, and quarter hour Visit before lunch and ten minutes before supper. To be charitable towards servants and not correct them in an angry way. To keep up to little rules forgoing [the next word is abbreviated as 'scs', most likely 'scruples']. To watch over angry words to people or confreres". He concluded, "Jesus, Mary and Joseph help me. My Good Angel guard me. All ye Holy Angels and Saints of God, especially those to whom I have any devotion, pray for me and obtain from God the graces to keep these resolutions through Jesus Christ Our Lord and through the intercession of His Blessed Mother and St Joseph".

June 1945
As in 1940, he began with the heading "AMDG" (for the greater glory of God) and continued: "Same as June 1944 plus – To cast my cares and wounded feelings onto the Sacred Heart [and to pray] 'Cease, the Sacred Heart of Jesus is with me'. To ask Our Lady of Good Counsel to help me in doubts and in examining my conscience and to trust in the Sacred Heart and His Blessed Mother for pardon for past [sins] and grace to lead a good life henceforth and die a happy death. Amen".

January 1946
"To ask for humility and avail of all occasions of humbling self, plus resolutions of January 1937 and those of July 1945, AMDG".

July 1946
Adding to those of January '46 he resolved: "To show charity to all by seeing Christ in neighbour. To have compassion for Jesus in His sufferings for me by accepting patiently my own and to give Jesus all He asks and always AMDG".

In January 1947, along with some of the foregoing points, he resolved: "To accept frustrations of desires for love of my crucified Saviour".

June 1948

Repeating earlier resolutions, he developed one or two points: "To have a great external charity and zeal for souls by seeing Jesus in my neighbour. To have unbounded confidence in the Sacred Heart, in the intercession of His Blessed Mother, in St Joseph, in St Teresa of the Infant Jesus and in all the Saints, especially those to whom I have devotion. And to love God as much as I can so that when death comes I may find how sweet it is to be judged by Him".

July 1952

"Confidence in Sacred Heart to direct me in scs [scruples], through Our Lady of Good Counsel to avail of prev[entions] of scruples. [To grow in] Fraternal Charity and zeal for souls. [To have] a great love of Christ, and desire to please Him and be united more and more closely to Him. These resolutions [I place] in keeping of the Sacred Heart and Our Blessed Lady".

January 1953

"To see Christ in neighbour. To accept with resignation frustration of desires and be more aware of [my] own misery and inability to do any good. [To ask for] humility. [To have] Confidence in the Sacred Heart and His Blessed Mother".

June 1956

"Same as January '54 and '55 plus – Detachment from all things and self. To foster a personal love of my crucified Saviour and to bear the cross of scs [scruples] for His sake and Crosses and Humiliations in resignation to the Divine Will. Keeping [these resolutions] in the hands of the Blessed Virgin Mary, St Joseph, St Teresa of the Infant Jesus and all the Saints, especially those to whom I have any devotion, including St Anthony and St Pius".

August 1957

"To be humble and mortified and detached from all things and [from] my missionary problems in imitation of my crucified Saviour, through the merits of His Passion and death and through the intercession of His Blessed Mother, St Joseph and all the Saints especially those to whom I have devotion. To keep the rule regarding spiritual reading and Examen of Conscience. To ask grace to bear trials patiently in resignation to the Divine Will when trials are heavy".

January 1958

"Same as January 1955 together with – abiding sorrow for sin and thinking on the Passion of Our Lord. To have humility and confidence in the Sacred Heart and peace in thoughts. [I] place all in keeping of the Blessed Mother, St Joseph, St Teresa of the Infant Jesus and all the Saints to whom I have devotion".

August 1958

"Detachment from earthly things. A greater desire to love, please and be united with Christ. Humility and self-denial. Confidence in the Sacred Heart. Pure in thoughts. Placing these resolutions in the keeping of the Blessed Mother, St Joseph, St Teresa of the Infant Jesus and all the Saints especially those to whom I have devotion".

January 1959

"Not to be too set on anything outside God. I desire to know, love, be resigned to, and do His Holy Will".

August 1959

"To accept humiliations and frustration of desires (which is what I really deserve) with resignation to the Divine Will and to have great confidence in the Sacred Heart and in the Protection of His Blessed Mother".

August 1960
"To be faithful to Particular Examen, monthly retreat and spiritual reading. [To have] Greater trust in the Sacred Heart and His Blessed Mother. Not to be too absorbed in earthly affairs. To be resigned to the Divine Will out of love for Jesus and Mary".

[Undated page; the first resolution appears to be influenced by Vatican II and its new emphasis on openness to the Spirit.]
"To be docile to the promptings and inspiration of the Holy Spirit. To practice little acts of self denial for love of Christ suffering for my sins. To have a joyful hope in the promises of Christ. To have a strong Faith and personal love of Christ".

January 1970
"To have closer union with Christ (in thinking and loving) and not to be too absorbed in external affairs [opposing] this Union. To have sincere and abiding sorrow for sins by thinking of the suffering of Christ on the Cross. To imitate the virtues of the Blessed Virgin Mary especially purity, humility, confidence and meekness. To see Jesus in my neighbour and to do all I can to make Him known and loved by others".

March 1974
"To have more confidence in the Sacred Heart through intercession of His Blessed Mother. To imitate Jesus Christ more closely and to live constantly in His Divine presence. To imitate the purity and humility of the Blessed Virgin Mary. To improve my Particular Examen. To pray always for a sincere desire to love Jesus perfectly and the Grace to do so. To do all I can to know and love Jesus better and to make Him known and loved by others".

March 1975
"[To have] great confidence and faith in my prayers to know the Divine Will and to be able to do it in all things. To have true sorrow for my sins and to do penance for them. To love and serve Jesus and Mary as St Joseph did".

March 1976

"To listen to Christ speaking to me and allow Him to sanctify me as He wants, not the way I want. To have a deep Faith in the presence of Christ everywhere and not only in the Holy Sacrament of the altar. To leave myself and all that concerns me in the hands of Christ's merciful Providence with humility and confidence and sorrow for my sins".

Lent 1977

"To have a closer union with Jesus Christ by thinking of Him and His great love for me. To make aspirations of love to Him in return and to be faithful in little things. Sometimes to make meaningful mortifications and to continue striving against selfishness. All these I place in the keeping of the Sacred Heart, the Blessed Virgin Mary and St Joseph".

1978

"To have joyful hope in the promises of Christ. To leave myself and all that concerns me in the hands of Christ's merciful providence. To be aware of my own sinfulness and nothingness. To strive against selfishness and to have sympathy for the needs of others. To have a strong Faith and confidence in the Sacred Heart and His Blessed Mother – in their care I place these resolutions".

April 1979

"To realise God is with me and is merciful. To have confidence that He will get me through all my problems. To leave my past to His mercy, my present to His love, and my future to His Providence. Sacred Heart I place all my trust in Thee, Mary Immaculate Mother pray for me".

1980

"[To strive for] gentleness and charity especially in my thoughts about others [and] forgetfulness of my selfish interests. To leave all my cares spiritual and temporal in the hands of Divine

Providence with resignation to His Holy Will, 'To those who love God all things work together unto good' and to give to Jesus all He asks of me, relying on God's grace to carry out my resolutions. Sacred Heart of Jesus I trust in Thee for all, Immaculate Heart of Mary pray for me".

1981
"To have the pure interest of pleasing God in all my actions and to live in the presence of Jesus Christ".

1982
"To think of self as being loved by Christ and to have great confidence in BVM".

A comment on his Resolutions

Throughout his life Bishop Kelly was concerned with rule keeping but, it is noticeable that, while his resolutions of 1940 were predominantly concerned with Rule and detachment from temporal things, later ones were mainly concerned with love of Christ and acceptance of the Divine Will. It is not reading too much into his resolutions to say that they give evidence of a progressive love affair with Jesus, an ascent to Love and growth in union with God.

Around the middle of the resolutions recorded above, we find a tendency towards mortification, a striving for virtue, especially humility, and a stress on personal sinfulness with a corresponding desire to focus on the sufferings of the crucified Lord. Later, more 'forgetfulness of self' and of 'the past' is discernible; he appears less anxious to engineer his own advance towards perfection, more is left to God and His grace. His later sets of resolutions are shorter than his early ones. In fact his first extant one, 1940, is the longest, and his last, 1982, is one of the shortest. In the last decade of his life, he didn't appear to write any at all, at least none have been found.

The influence of contemporary spirituality is apparent: devotion to the Sacred Heart and His Blessed Mother, to St Joseph, and to St Teresa of the Infant Jesus (and though he doesn't mention it, he would seem to be a follower of her "Little Way" and, like her, was much taken by the sufferings of Christ). Other favourite saints of his were, St Patrick, St Anthony, and St Pius X (who was canonised in 1954). Angels also figure in his devotions and prayers. His reference to the Holy Spirit, a 'latecomer' in western spirituality, was not repeated in his resolutions and, though seemingly impressed by "AMDG" in 1940, he did not repeat it after 1946.

APPENDIX III

BISHOP KELLY'S RETREAT NOTES

Shortly after receiving Bishop Kelly's personal Retreat Resolutions, I received five copy books of the notes he used for giving retreats. Two of these note books are quite substantial, one having 163 pages of notes and the other 143. The other three have less than 40 pages each. Dating back to the Thirties, the books have been much handled, sweat stained and termite bored. Some pages are missing and in a few places some extra notes on loose pages have been added. The retreats were preached to priests, sisters, catechists and student teachers.

The smallest notebook ("Warri" printed on the cover) contains 18 pages of notes for a retreat given to catechists and teachers in July 1931. In it the Bishop dwelt on concupiscence, mortal sin and punishment, but he also spoke of charity, obedience, the imitation of Christ, devotion to the Sacred Heart and to the Blessed Virgin Mary.

The second notebook ("Benin" on the cover) contains 26 pages of notes for a retreat to Sisters, in which he concentrated on the vows, rule, devotion to Jesus and Mary, and mortification. On the flyleaf he jotted some travel expenses including "petrol, Warri, £1-10" and the date "11 November 1939".

The third notebook ("Abas") contains 38 pages of notes for a retreat to missionary priests; no date appears, but it would appear to be of the Thirties or Forties. On the second page in pencil he wrote a rough outline of the Retreat, giving ten conference topics: death; passions (as in strong emotions), mortal sin, hell; judgement and eternity; the Incarnation; redemption; venial sin and tepidity; confidence and love of God; eucharist; charity;

prayer.

In the Exercise Book of 163 pages he penned his ideas for a retreat to student teachers. Beginning with the parable of the man born blind, he exhorted his hearers to take the retreat seriously, and then went on to speak of sin, death, eternity, and judgement. An indication of a relatively early date for this retreat is his complaint that large numbers of students were striving to enter the Teacher Training College but "no one at all was striving to enter the Seminary". After 56 pages, he began a new set of notes for a retreat to missionaries and paginated it 1 to 107. This retreat began with the Incarnation, and went on to speak of the missionary apostolate, the necessity of self-sacrifice, tepidity and venial sin, Mass, and community life.

In the note book of 143 pages, his main themes were: death, judgement, sin, Mass and devotion to the Eucharist, Incarnation, prayer and meditation, zeal, tepidity, temptations and perseverance. A few miscellaneous points were written on a page of notepaper headed, "Saint Charles College, Onitsha Town, S. Nigeria", where he gave a retreat to Holy Ghost missionaries in August 1937. On another loose leaf he referred to the Vatican Council's document on the Liturgy, pointing out that, by extolling the value of community prayer, the Council did not at all intend to diminish the value of private prayer. In a third insert he began writing on 'missiology' and the conciliar document *Ad Gentes*, but crossed it out and continued, speaking approvingly of traditional missionary methods such as village visitation, the catechumenate system, and the training of catechists.

At the beginning of this retreat, which was preached to missionaries, he referred to blindness, as he had done in his catechists and teachers' retreat, illustrating the point with the story of the Blind Man at Jericho. He hoped that the retreatants would be able to see their sins and take their retreat seriously. Treating again of themes such as judgement, death, detachment, mortification, and prayer, he evidently saw life on earth, especially the 'spiritual life', as warfare, and missionaries were "soldiers in the vanguard of Christ's army". After giving some 80 pages to this retreat, he followed it with notes for other conferences, beginning with "Obligation to holiness and love of God". The last conferences were addressed to confreres in Lagos. He stressed personal sanctification and the Rule (mentioning especially the rule about avoiding frequent socialising with Europeans).

Some quotations from Bishop Kelly's retreat notes

"Our sufferings are nothing like Christ's. This is the thought that will give us courage in our darkest hour".

"Remember God loves you and says to you, 'just do the best you can and I will do the rest'."

"Devotion to the Eucharist is the distinct characteristic of a priest. The Eucharist is his 'all'; take it away and he ceases to be".

"If we think we can be successful missionaries by leading soft and easy lives, with no worries and no boulders rolling into us, then we are far away from our Crucified Master".

[Regarding poverty] "The example of Christ who was poor should encourage us to attempt new spheres of mission enterprise even though we do not have all the means that Worldly men think necessary".

[Chastity] "He who does not guard his eyes is like a driver who does not look where he is going".

[Obedience] "Our lawful superior takes the place of God".

[Quoting St Margaret of Cortona] "Do not ask me to make any truce with my body, I cannot afford it. Between me and my body there must be a war unto death".

"Sacrifice of self is necessary for [missionary] success". "The missionary who is not prepared to sacrifice himself will achieve

little or nothing on the foreign mission".
"The privations that we endure are probably the means of obtaining God's grace for the people".

"Are we convinced that prayer is as necessary for us as food is for the body? It is the most important work of daily life".
"Even trekking in the bush we should always have time for Meditation, Rosary, and perhaps Spiritual Reading".
"We are so often hampered with creatures when we should be alone with God; 'detachment from self' should be our slogan, not only during days of retreat, but all through our lives".
[Quoting St Augustine] "He knows how to live rightly who knows how to pray rightly".
"Intimate and real conversation with God should occupy a considerable portion of the priest's daily life".
"Meditation is not an appropriate name for the half hour prayer to God every morning because it implies thinking. The essence of prayer consists in acts of the will by which the soul elevates itself to God".

"With fear and trembling work out thy salvation. The greatest danger is to be too immersed in external occupations".
"I know of a whole village that was converted from another Church because the [Catholic] missionary made regular visits to a sick man".

"The man who does not discipline his passions is like a driver with a damaged steering wheel".
"Do not speak when angry; count to twenty or say three Hail Marys".
"We spend too much time scolding the people ... If we went into the Church and said a few Hail Marys for them it would be better".

"Saints are the only people who live real lives".
"The more external cares the Saints had, the more they felt the

need of prayer".

"The sanctity of many great Saints was occasioned by meditating on Hell".

"Being too anxious about health is enough to make one sick".
"When we [missionaries] consider that every four years we have a whole year to get the old man overhauled, we should not begrudge doing our best while on the mission".

"In Africa I used to preach that the Devil was a fisherman fishing for souls".
"The Holy Ghost leads us safely along the narrow way to victory over self and detachment from creatures".
"Who can disturb the peace of mind of him whose sole desire is to be scoffed at and insulted".

Comment

This selection of quotations may give an over positive impression of the Bishop's spirituality; not many of his grimmer type of statements have been included. In keeping with the spirituality of the times he dwelt on the topics of sin, judgement and eternal punishment. Many of his conferences were given over to the battle against concupiscence and temptation and his talks on Christ were dominated by the Cross and suffering.

Every now and then gems of earthy wisdom are seen, especially when he speaks on the apostolate. But, overall, he emerges more like an Old Testament prophet trying to keep his people on the straight and narrow than a New Testament shepherd leading them forward to new pastures.

The Bible was his main source and reference book. He quoted from the Old Testament more than from the New and the verses he chose were often from the Law books of Leviticus, Numbers, and Deuteronomy. His biblical protagonists for emulation or reprobation were such as David, Saul, Aaron and Job. When quoting from the New Testament, he favoured the Apocalypse, John's Gospel, St Paul and Hebrews more than the Synoptic gospels.

After the Bible he was fond of quoting Church Fathers like Augustine, Jerome and Chrysostom, and spiritual writers like Francis de Sales and Alphonsus Rodriguez. Saints, especially Teresa of the Infant Jesus, were also quoted. His favourite reading included *The Imitation of Christ.* In one retreat he referred to a French book, *L'Ame de tout Apostolat* (The Soul of the Apostolate) and, in another, to a biography of Countess Ledóchowska [foundress of the Sodality of St Peter Claver for African Missions] but he did not use much material outside of the Scriptures, the Saints and well-approved spiritual writers.

ACKNOWLEDGEMENTS AND SOURCES

The principal sources for this biography have been documentation in the African Missions Archives, Cork, and interviews, or correspondence, with those who knew Bishop Kelly. I am indebted to Fr Edmund Hogan, the Irish Provincial archivist for facilitating me in my research and for other assistance; thanks also to Fr Oscar Welsh. To the large number of people who shared their knowledge of Bishop Kelly with me, I must express my sincere thanks, in particular to those who worked in Benin, among whom are the following:

Members of the SMA (Benin):
Jim Higgins,
Dick Wall,
Con O'Driscoll,
Con Murphy,
John Quinlan,
Peter Thompson,
Sexton Doran,
Willie Cusack,
Jack Casey,
Mattie O'Connell,
Jim Conlon,
Dan Cashman,
Bill Kennedy,
Michael Boyle,
Brian O'Kane,
Hugh Harkin,
Bob O'Regan
Seán Ryan,
Sexton Cahill,
Jim O'Brien,

Aidan Anglin,
Jim Tobin,
Jim O'Connell.

John Creaven, former Provincial, Cork,
Seamus Nohilly, Jos, Ibadan, Wilton,
Jim Redmond, Ibadan, Wilton,
Paddy Jennings, Ibadan, Wilton,
Liam Burke, Kaduna.

OLA Sisters (Benin):
Kathleen Sweeney,
Dominica Geary,
Nora Culleton,
Mary Maddock,
Teresa Nolan,
Henrietta Power,
Perpetua Hanbury,
Stella Marie O'Sullivan,
Eileen Wall,
Maura Hayes,
Norbert O'Keeffe,
Clare Fitzgerald.

Marciana O'Keeffe, OLA Provincial archivist, Cork,
Sr Grace Rowan, OLA, Cork.

SND Sisters (Benin):
Bernadette Gannon,
Margaret Howse.

RSC Sisters (Benin):
Mary Raphael,
Carmel McAteer,
Patricia McGraw.

Lay missionaries (Benin):
Nurse Maureen O'Sullivan,
Nurse Mary Cunnane (niece of Bp Kelly),
Martha Scannell.

I interviewed Mons. Joseph Omesa of Benin in Ireland and availed of the taped interviews Fr Anthony Kelly made when he visited Benin in 2004. I had intended travelling with him on this trip, but was prevented from doing so by an injury. Among those he interviewed were: Archbishop Patrick Ekpu, Bishop Edmund Fitzgibbon sps, Mons. Patrick Usenbor, Mons. Pedro Martins, Mons. Thomas Oleghe, Mons. Stephen Okotete, Fr Theophilus Owaifo, Mr Gregory Iamu, Mr Mark Ojo, Mr Ilo Okwudiafor, Ms Felicia Ugbugwu, and Ms Bridget Nwadilim.

Galway:
My thanks to the Kelly family of Tristaun, the Bishop's nieces and nephews, especially Mary Teresa, Fr Anthony, Pádraic, Seán, and Carmel; and to the Cunnanes of Ballinasloe. Thanks to neighbours, Joan Ward, Paddy Hurney, Paddy Quinn, and the staff of the Interpretive Centre, Aughrim. A special word of thanks is due to Colette Hanrahan, Ballinasloe Library, to Professor Joseph Kelly, genealogist of the Kelly clan, and to Seán Kelly for Bishop Kelly's Retreat notes and Resolutions.

I have made much use of Edmund Hogan's "Short biographies" of deceased members of the Irish Province and transcripts of the interviews he made with Bishop Kelly, Joe Donnelly, Tommy Greene and others. I interviewed Bishop Kelly and other missionaries myself in 1984. Jim Higgins' *Kindling the Fire, SMA missionaries in Mid-West Nigeria, 1884-2003*, was a mine of information, and, among other books consulted were: *My Life Story*, by Denis Slattery sma, and *The Nigerian Civil War*, by John de St. Jorre. Bishop Kelly, in his early years on mission, wrote a few articles and letters for the *African Missionary*, most of them in Irish; thanks to Fr Páraic Kelly for translating them. I am grateful to the authors of other articles on Benin in the magazine, especially John Thornton, and to Vincent Boyle for his three humorous articles in the bulletin of the Irish Province. I have also consulted the interesting, unpublished autobiographies of Michael Foley and Jim Byrne, the diaries of James Ward, and the fine "History of the Sisters of Our Lady of Apostles" by Sr Kathleen Sweeney.

For dipping into other archives or sources on my behalf, I am very grateful to Jean-Marie Guillaume, Strasbourg; Kieran O'Reilly and Martin Kavanagh, Rome; Jos Pijpers, Oosterbeek; Bernard Favier, Lyon, Bruno Semplicio, Rome, and Sr Angela Ruddy mshr, Dublin.

Most of the photographs came from the African Missions archives in Cork, my thanks to Fr Bennie Raymond. For other photographs, thanks to the Kelly family, especially, Seán, Anthony, and Mary Teresa; to Sr Marciana; to *"Examiner Newspapers"*, Cork, and to *The Frontier Sentinel*, Newry.

A number of people, over the past three years read all, or parts, of drafts of this book and offered much valuable advice and assistance, to them I am greatly indebted. Among the main ones were: Paddy Jennings, Owen Maginn, Páraic Kelly, Jim Higgins, and Dick Wall. Many others have helped in various ways but have not been named, my sincere thanks to all. Most of the writing of the book was done in St Augustine's Major Seminary, Kabwe, Zambia, where I am a member of staff, and most of the research and re-writing was done in St Joseph's, Blackrock Road, Cork. I am very grateful to the superiors and communities of both 'houses' for their hospitality and encouragement.

M.O'S.

INDEX

Iyekovia, 330

Jansenism, 371
Jennings, Paddy, 252, 343f
Jennings, Tony, 197, 252
Jones, Harry, 333f
Jos, 112, 196, 218, 253, 354

Kabba, 40, 81, 107, 114, 115, 155, 167, 198, 224
Kaduna, 140, 170, 196, 218, 251, 253, 295, 354
Kano, 294f, 354
Keary, Walter, 67, 81
Keenan, Willie, 126, 130, 158-173, 177, 196, 227, 248, 254
Kelly, Antonine, ofm, 128, 130f
Kelly, Gabrielle, 367
Kelly, Gene, 98
Kelly, Mary Rose, 242, 286
Kelly, Maurice, 205

Kelly, Bp Pat, VA of W. Nigeria,
Bp of Benin City:
iii, 3, 8, passim
grandparents, 2,
parents, Malachy (Lacky),
2ff, 8, 24f
Catherine (Kate), 2ff,
8, 98, 125, 127, 130, 140,
168, 189
Siblings:
Ellen (Ellie), 3ff, 98, 130
Mary, (May) 3, 98, 130
John (Jack), 3, 8, 9, 98, 130,
189, 228
Malachy, jr, 3, 8, 9, 98, 233,
276f
Kathleen (Mrs Cunnane),
4, 8, 98, 130, 279, 325

Michael (Mick), 4, 8, 98, 180, 233
Gerald, 4, 98, 233, 348
William (Bill), 6, 8, 98, 130, 189

Family background, 2ff
childhood, 56
school, 3, 4, 5
vocation, 6, 8, 9, 22, 69
priestly formation, 12ff
friendships, 29, 373, 378
personality, 8, 43, 56, 58,
60, 72, 80, 100, 111, 124,
207, 216, 331f, 363, 368,
373, 376, 378;
worrier, anxious 190, 370f,
372f, 376;
scrupulous, 79, 83, 86, 226,
322, 371, 383ff.
conservative, 175, 219-221,
267-269, 344f.

Irish speaker, 4, 37, 54, 69
Ordination, 29

First missionary journey, 32ff
Eku, 45, 46, 47, 49f, 58f, 72, 103,
364
Nigerian languages, 46f, 49f,
74, 136, 148f, 263, 269
catechists, 46f, 144, 146, 165,
167, 180, 219, 250, 285, 352f,
356, 376, 390f
community life, 47, 51, 99, 103,
106ff, 161, 345, 391, see general
index
rule ('a rule man'), 82, 106, 115,
123, 135f, 218, 263, 373, 383ff,
388

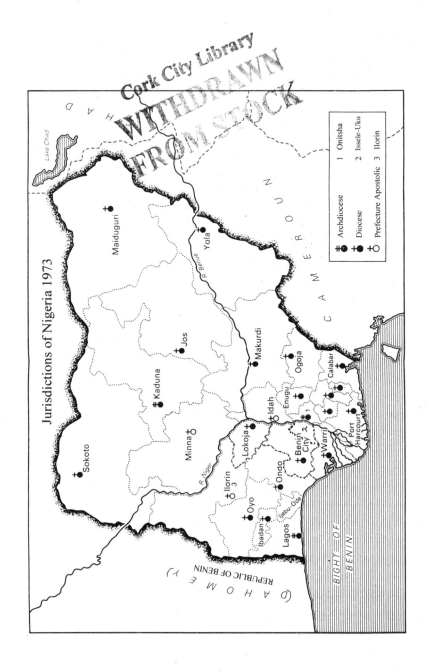

Jurisdictions of Nigeria 1973

	Archdiocese	1	Onitsha
	Diocese	2	Issele-Uku
	Prefecture Apostolic	3	Ilorin

Lake Chad

C H A D

Maiduguri

Yola

R. Benue

C A M E R O U N

Jos

Makurdi

Kaduna

Ogoja

Calabar

Enugu

Idah

1

Port Harcourt

Minna

Lokoja

Warri

Sokoto

Benin City 2

Ilorin 3

Ondo

R. Niger

Oyo

Ijebu-Ode

Ibadan

Lagos

BIGHT — OF BENIN

(D A H O M E Y)
REPUBLIC OF BENIN